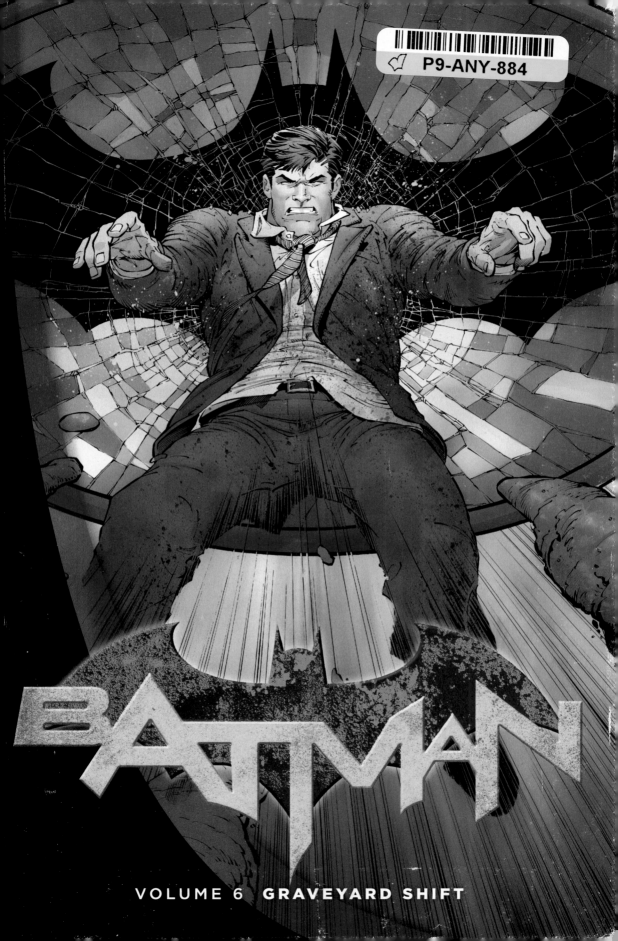

BATMAN

VOLUME 6 GRAVEYARD SHIFT

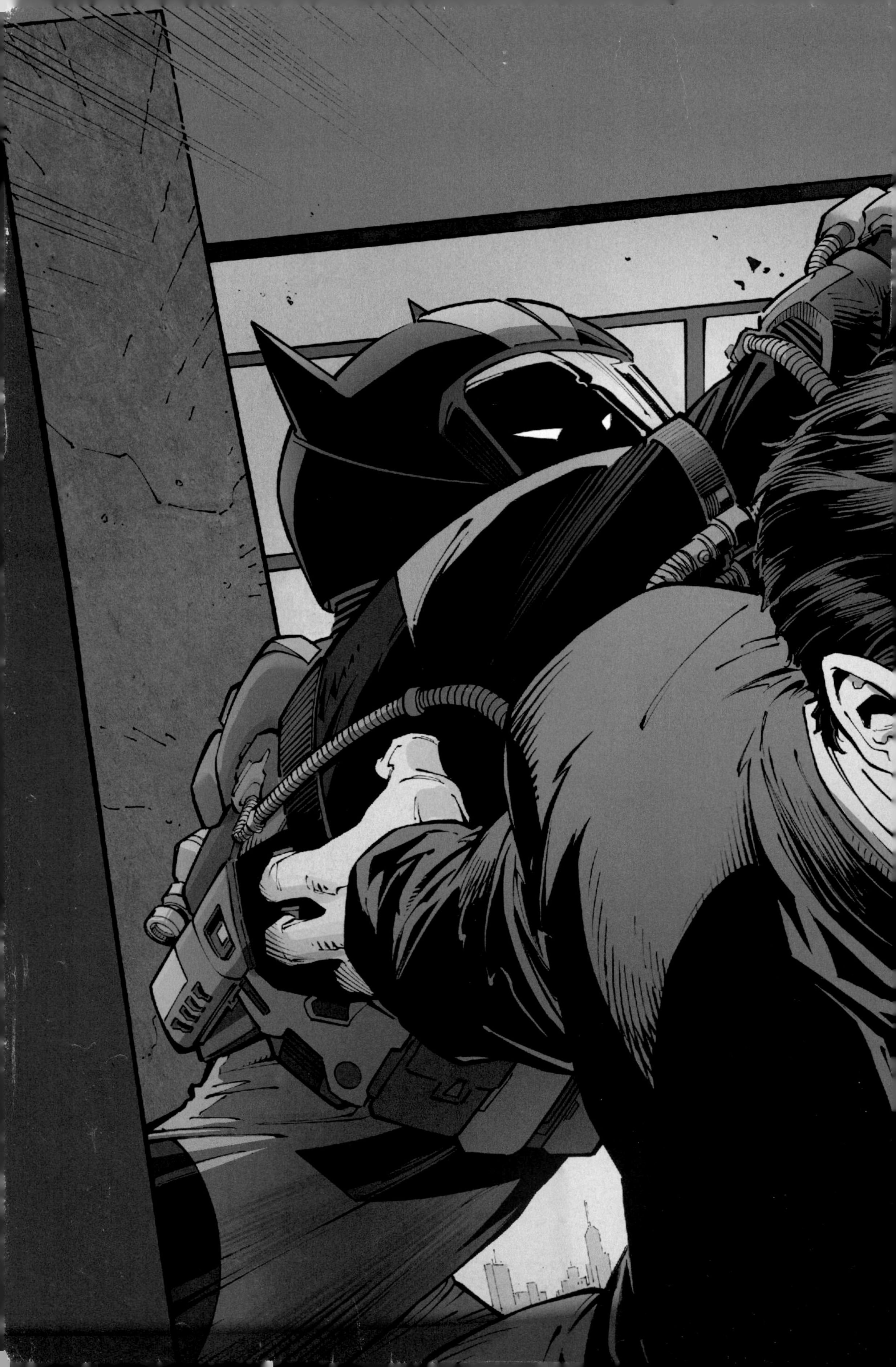

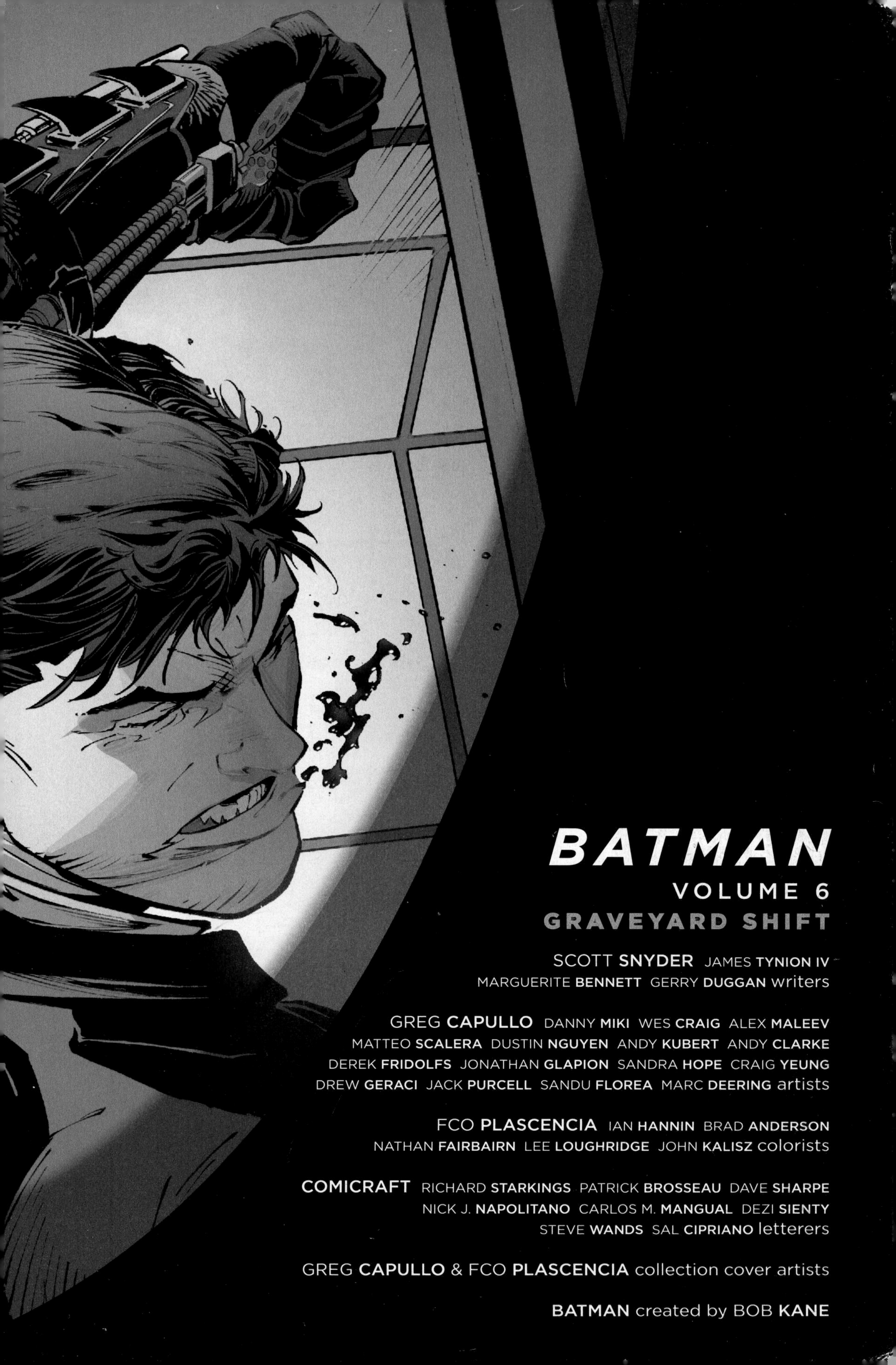

BATMAN

VOLUME 6

GRAVEYARD SHIFT

SCOTT **SNYDER** JAMES **TYNION IV**
MARGUERITE **BENNETT** GERRY **DUGGAN** writers

GREG **CAPULLO** DANNY **MIKI** WES **CRAIG** ALEX **MALEEV**
MATTEO **SCALERA** DUSTIN **NGUYEN** ANDY **KUBERT** ANDY **CLARKE**
DEREK **FRIDOLFS** JONATHAN **GLAPION** SANDRA **HOPE** CRAIG **YEUNG**
DREW **GERACI** JACK **PURCELL** SANDU **FLOREA** MARC **DEERING** artists

FCO **PLASCENCIA** IAN **HANNIN** BRAD **ANDERSON**
NATHAN **FAIRBAIRN** LEE **LOUGHRIDGE** JOHN **KALISZ** colorists

COMICRAFT RICHARD **STARKINGS** PATRICK **BROSSEAU** DAVE **SHARPE**
NICK J. **NAPOLITANO** CARLOS M. **MANGUAL** DEZI **SIENTY**
STEVE **WANDS** SAL **CIPRIANO** letterers

GREG **CAPULLO** & FCO **PLASCENCIA** collection cover artists

BATMAN created by BOB **KANE**

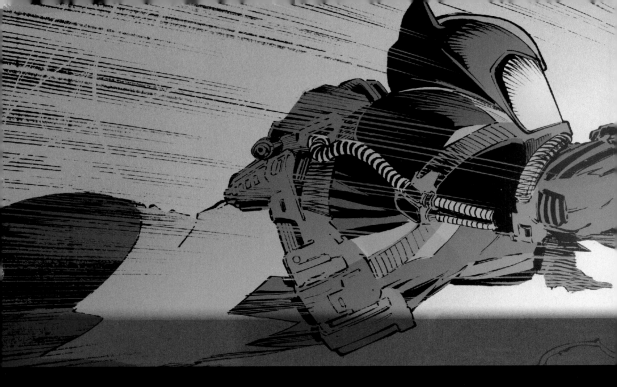

MIKE MARTS MARK DOYLE Editors – Original Series KATIE KUBERT Associate Editor – Original Series
MATT HUMPHREYS Assistant Editor – Original Series ROBIN WILDMAN Editor
JEB WOODARD Group Editor – Collected Editions ROBBIE BIEDERMAN Publication Design

BOB HARRAS Senior VP – Editor-in-Chief, DC Comics

DIANE NELSON President DAN DIDIO and JIM LEE Co-Publishers GEOFF JOHNS Chief Creative Officer
AMIT DESAI Senior VP – Marketing & Global Franchise Management NAIRI GARDINER Senior VP – Finance
SAM ADES VP – Digital Marketing BOBBIE CHASE VP – Talent Development
MARK CHIARELLO Senior VP – Art, Design & Collected Editions JOHN CUNNINGHAM VP – Content Strategy
ANNE DePIES VP – Strategy Planning & Reporting DON FALLETTI VP – Manufacturing Operations
LAWRENCE GANEM VP – Editorial Administration & Talent Relations ALISON GILL Senior VP – Manufacturing & Operations
HANK KANALZ Senior VP – Editorial Strategy & Administration JAY KOGAN VP – Legal Affairs
DEREK MADDALENA Senior VP – Sales & Business Development DAN MIRON VP – Sales Planning & Trade Development
NICK NAPOLITANO VP – Manufacturing Administration CAROL ROEDER VP – Marketing
EDDIE SCANNELL VP – Mass Account & Digital Sales SUSAN SHEPPARD VP – Business Affairs
COURTNEY SIMMONS Senior VP – Publicity & Communications JIM (SKI) SOKOLOWSKI VP – Comic Book Specialty & Newsstand Sales

BATMAN VOL. 6: GRAVEYARD SHIFT

Published by DC Comics. Compilation copyright © 2014 DC Comics. All Rights Reserved.

Originally published in single magazine form as BATMAN 0, 18-20, 28, 34, ANNUAL 2 © 2012, 2013, 2014 DC Comics. All Rights Reserved.
All characters, their distinctive likenesses and related elements featured in this publication are trademarks of DC Comics.
The stories, characters and incidents featured in this publication are entirely fictional.
DC Comics does not read or accept unsolicited ideas, stories or artwork.

DC Comics, 4000 Warner Blvd., Burbank, CA 91522
A Warner Bros. Entertainment Company.
Printed by RR Donnelley, Salem, VA, USA. 8/28/15. First Printing.

ISBN: 978-1-4012-5753-8

Library of Congress Cataloging-in-Publication Data

Snyder, Scott.
Batman. Volume 6, Graveyard shift / Scott Snyder ; illustrated by Greg Capullo.
pages cm
ISBN 978-1-4012-5753-8 (paperback)
1. Graphic novels. I. Capullo, Greg, illustrator. II. Title. III. Title: Graveyard shift.
PN6728.B36S687 2015
741.5'973—dc23
2015000603

In these pages are a selection of exceptional standalone stories from Scott Snyder and Greg Capullo's acclaimed BATMAN, following the Dark Knight through his past and future and tying into ZERO YEAR, BATMAN INCORPORATED, BATMAN ETERNAL and more.

In the first of these lost tales, "Bright New Yesterday," readers flash back six years to the time now known as the Zero Year, when the newly returned Bruce Wayne was not yet calling himself Batman, but was already at work fighting Gotham's underworld. Likewise, "Tomorrow" and "Ages" explore the long-lasting effects of Batman's actions during the pivotal Zero Year.

Back in the present in "Resolve" and "Ghost Lights," Batman must process the death of his son and crime-fighting partner, Damian Wayne (whose tragic end in BATMAN INCORPORATED rocked all of Gotham's crime-fighters), before getting back to his detective roots in the mysteries "Nowhere Man" and "The Meek."

Finally, flashing forward to the near future in "Gotham Eternal," the Dark Knight and his new partner explore the darker world of BATMAN ETERNAL...

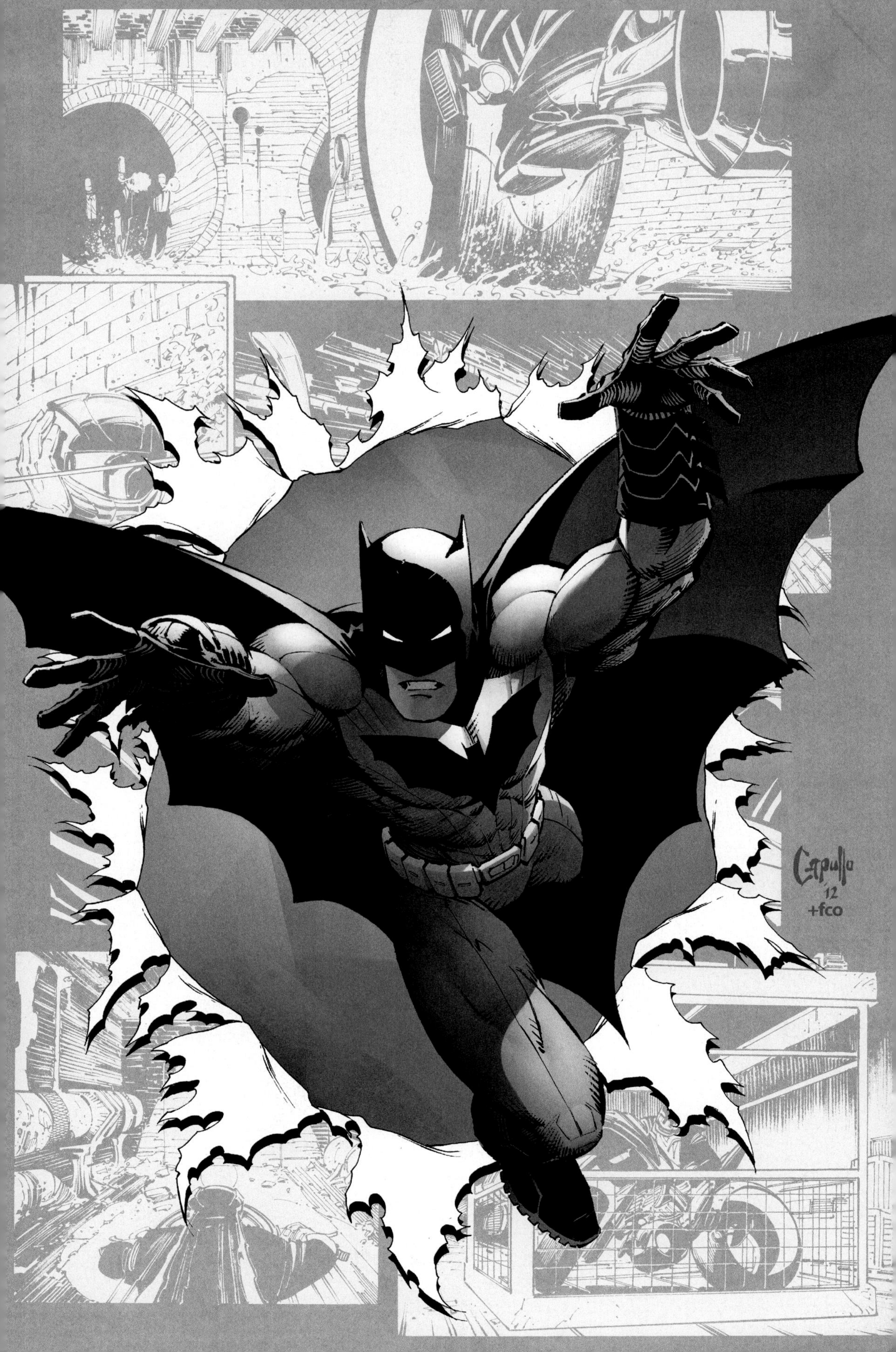

BRIGHT NEW YESTERDAY

SCOTT SNYDER writer **GREG CAPULLO** penciller **JONATHAN GLAPION** inker **FCO PLASCENCIA** colorist cover by **GREG CAPULLO** and **FCO PLASCENCIA**

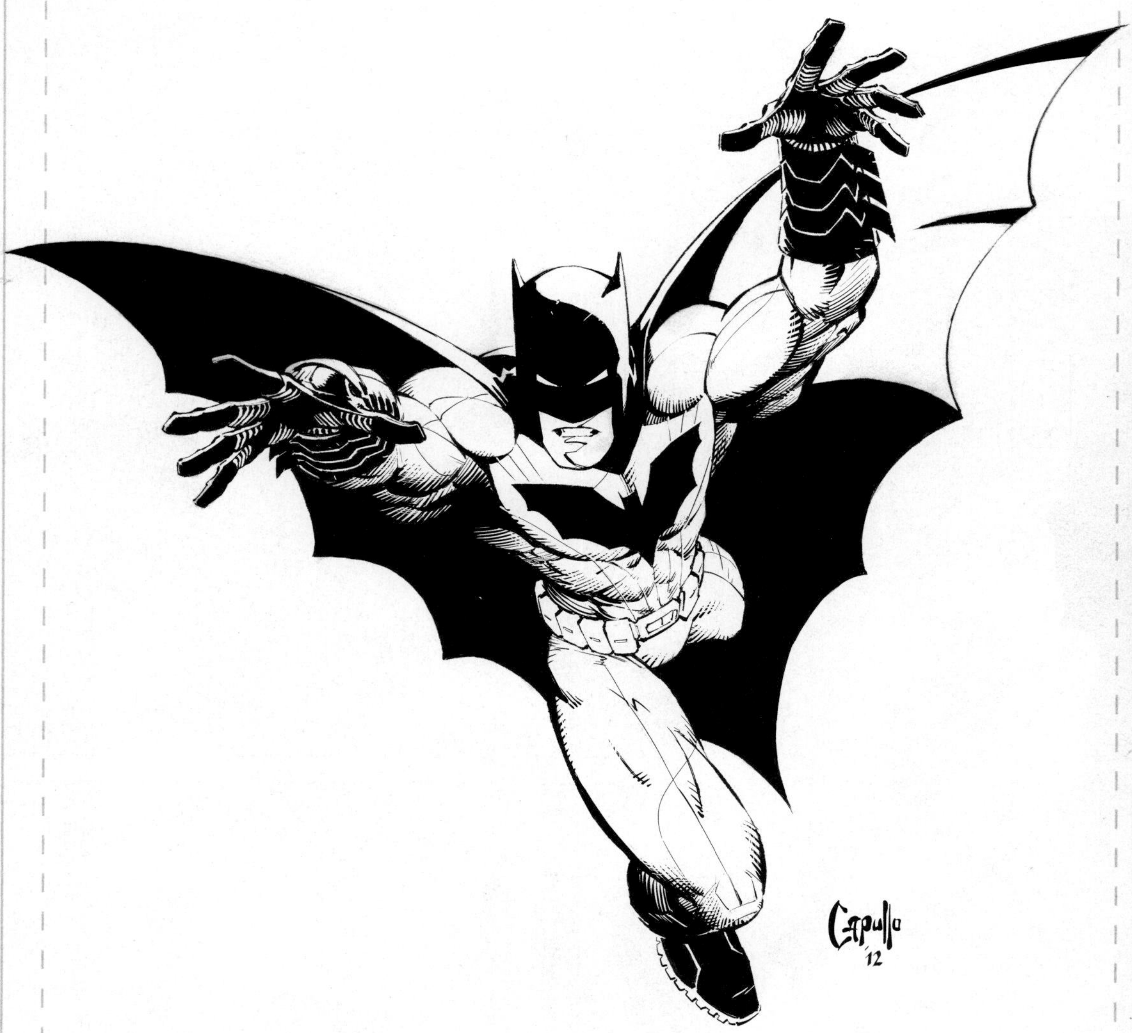

CAPULLO '12

MINIMUM BLEED 1/4 ALL AROUND

LIVE AREA

CROP

BLEED

PRINTED COVER SIZE: 6 5/8 X 10 3/16

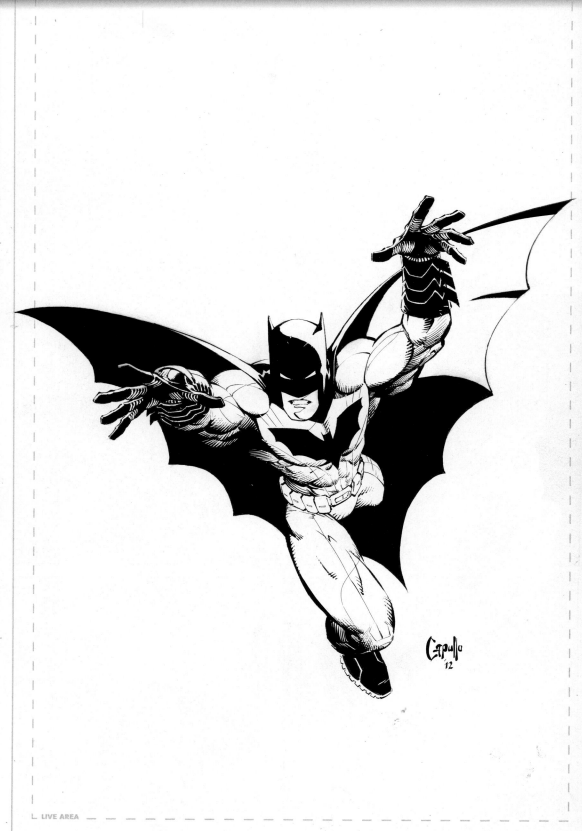

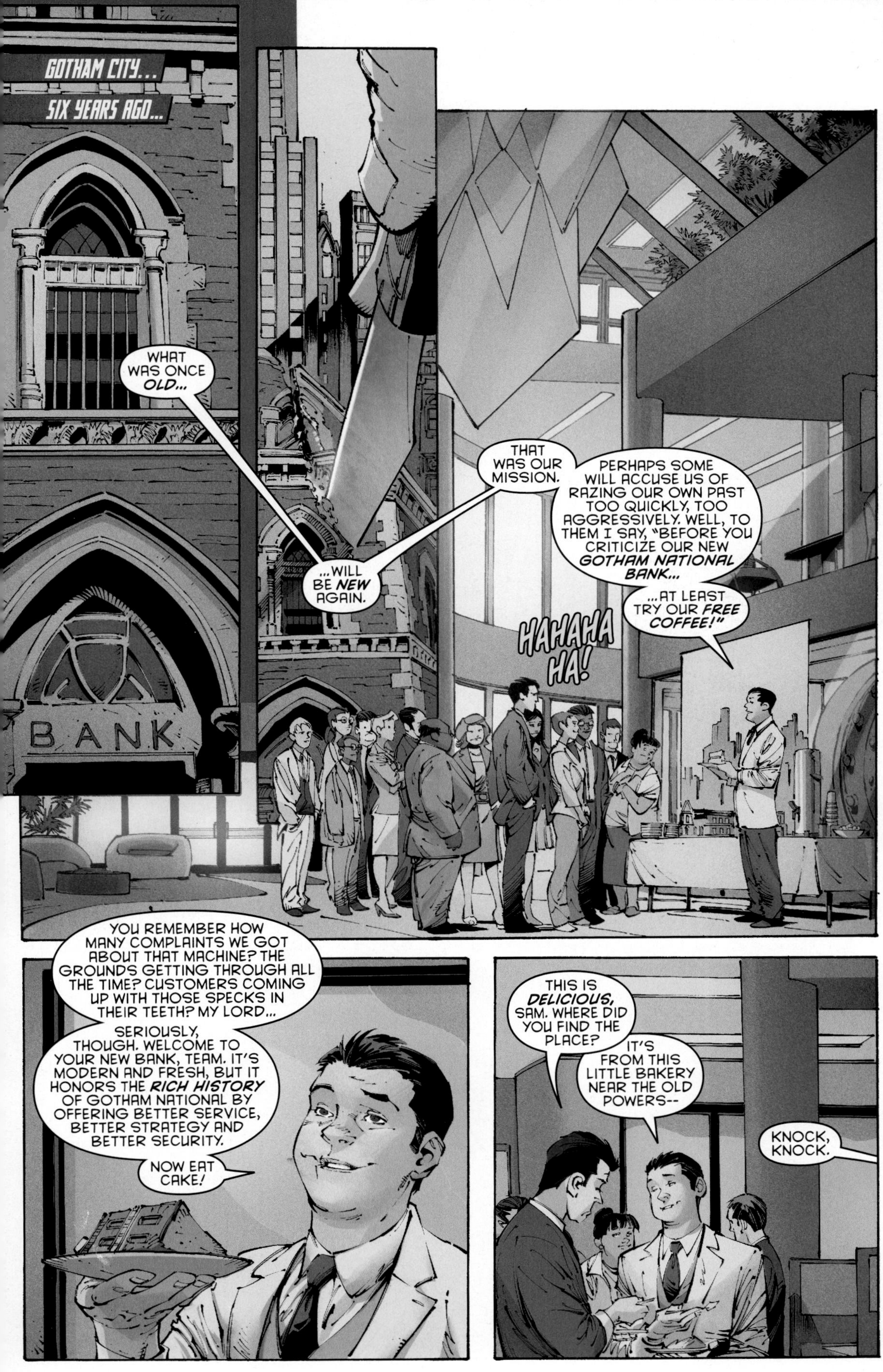

GOTHAM CITY...
SIX YEARS AGO...
WHAT WAS ONCE *OLD*...
...WILL BE *NEW* AGAIN.
THAT WAS OUR MISSION.
PERHAPS SOME WILL ACCUSE US OF RAZING OUR OWN PAST TOO QUICKLY, TOO AGGRESSIVELY. WELL, TO THEM I SAY, "BEFORE YOU CRITICIZE OUR NEW *GOTHAM NATIONAL BANK*...
...AT LEAST TRY OUR *FREE COFFEE!*"
HAHAHA HA!
BANK
YOU REMEMBER HOW MANY COMPLAINTS WE GOT ABOUT THAT MACHINE? THE GROUNDS GETTING THROUGH ALL THE TIME? CUSTOMERS COMING UP WITH THOSE SPECKS IN THEIR TEETH? MY LORD...
SERIOUSLY, THOUGH. WELCOME TO YOUR NEW BANK, TEAM. IT'S MODERN AND FRESH, BUT IT HONORS THE *RICH HISTORY* OF GOTHAM NATIONAL BY OFFERING BETTER SERVICE, BETTER STRATEGY AND BETTER SECURITY.
NOW EAT CAKE!
THIS IS *DELICIOUS,* SAM. WHERE DID YOU FIND THE PLACE?
IT'S FROM THIS LITTLE BAKERY NEAR THE OLD POWERS--
KNOCK, KNOCK.

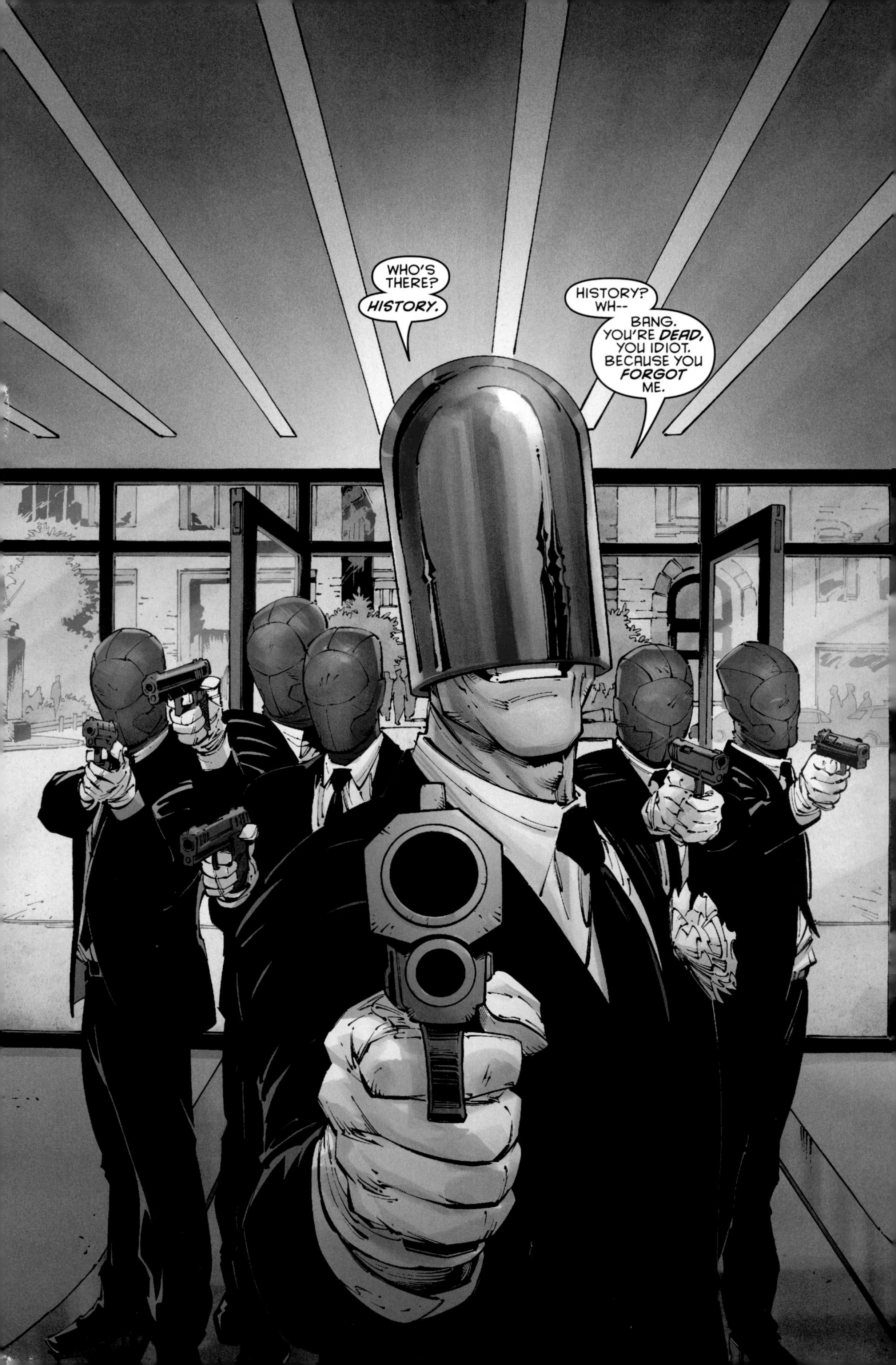
WHO'S THERE?
HISTORY.
HISTORY? WH--
BANG. YOU'RE DEAD, YOU IDIOT. BECAUSE YOU FORGOT ME.

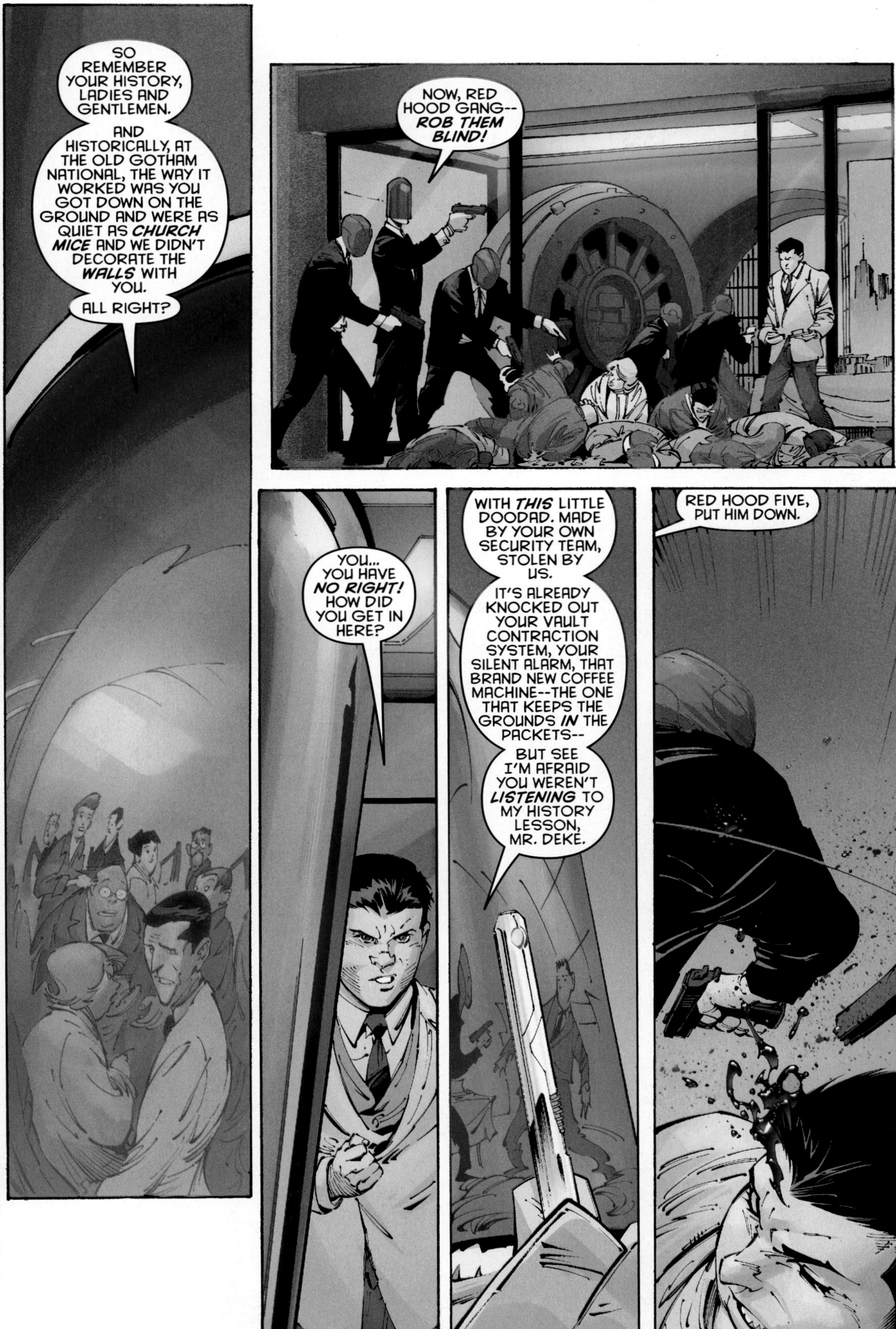
SO REMEMBER YOUR HISTORY, LADIES AND GENTLEMEN.
AND HISTORICALLY, AT THE OLD GOTHAM NATIONAL, THE WAY IT WORKED WAS YOU GOT DOWN ON THE GROUND AND WERE AS QUIET AS *CHURCH MICE* AND WE DIDN'T DECORATE THE *WALLS* WITH YOU.
ALL RIGHT?
NOW, RED HOOD GANG-- *ROB THEM BLIND!*
YOU... YOU HAVE *NO RIGHT!* HOW DID YOU GET IN HERE?
WITH *THIS* LITTLE DOODAD. MADE BY YOUR OWN SECURITY TEAM, STOLEN BY US.
IT'S ALREADY KNOCKED OUT YOUR VAULT CONTRACTION SYSTEM, YOUR SILENT ALARM, THAT BRAND NEW COFFEE MACHINE--THE ONE THAT KEEPS THE GROUNDS *IN* THE PACKETS--
BUT SEE I'M AFRAID YOU WEREN'T *LISTENING* TO MY HISTORY LESSON, MR. DEKE.
RED HOOD FIVE, PUT HIM DOWN.

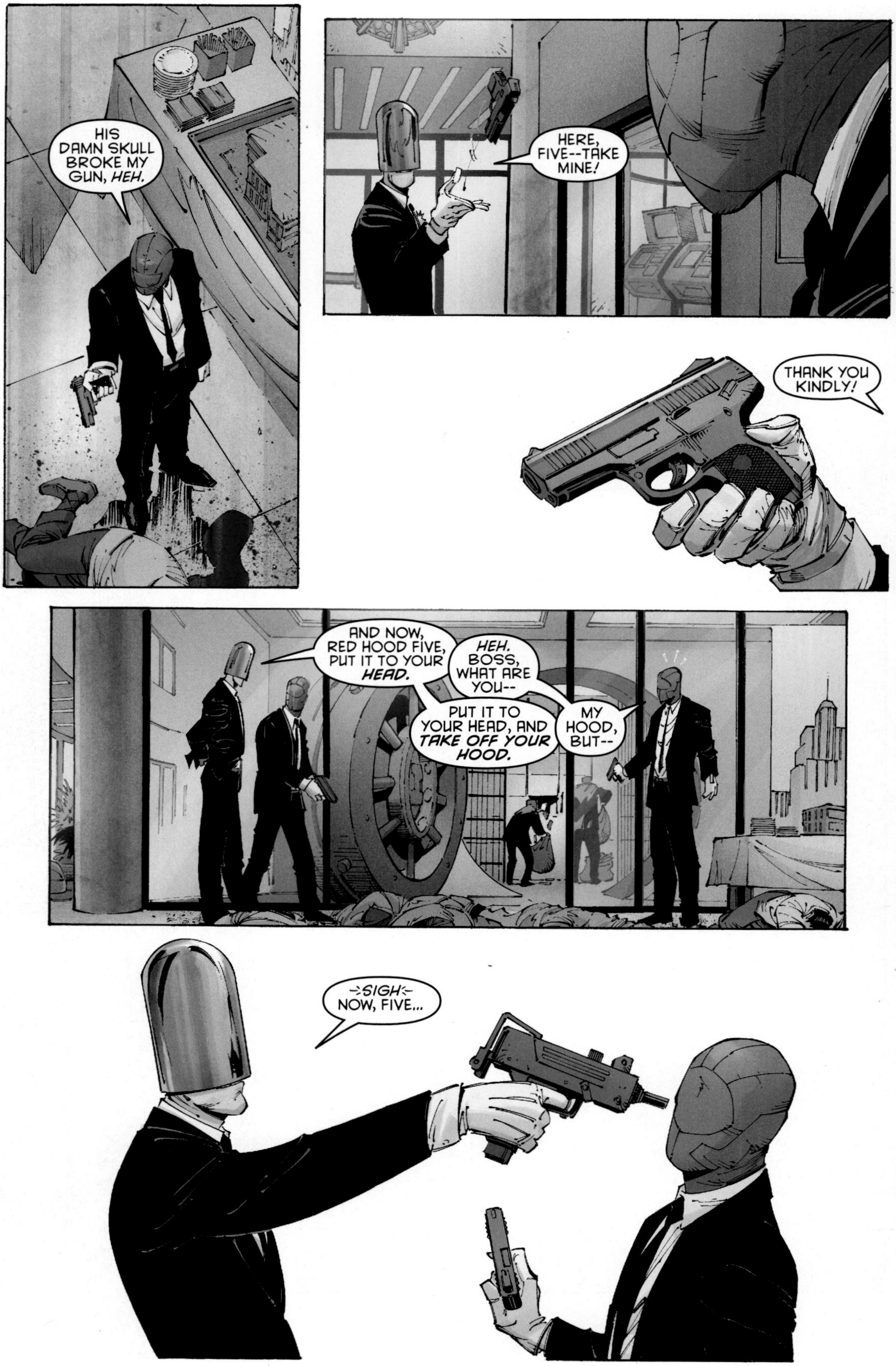
HIS DAMN SKULL BROKE MY GUN, *HEH.*
HERE, FIVE--TAKE MINE!
THANK YOU KINDLY!
AND NOW, RED HOOD FIVE, PUT IT TO YOUR *HEAD.*
HEH. BOSS, WHAT ARE YOU--
PUT IT TO YOUR HEAD, AND *TAKE OFF YOUR HOOD.*
MY HOOD, BUT--
-SIGH- NOW, FIVE...

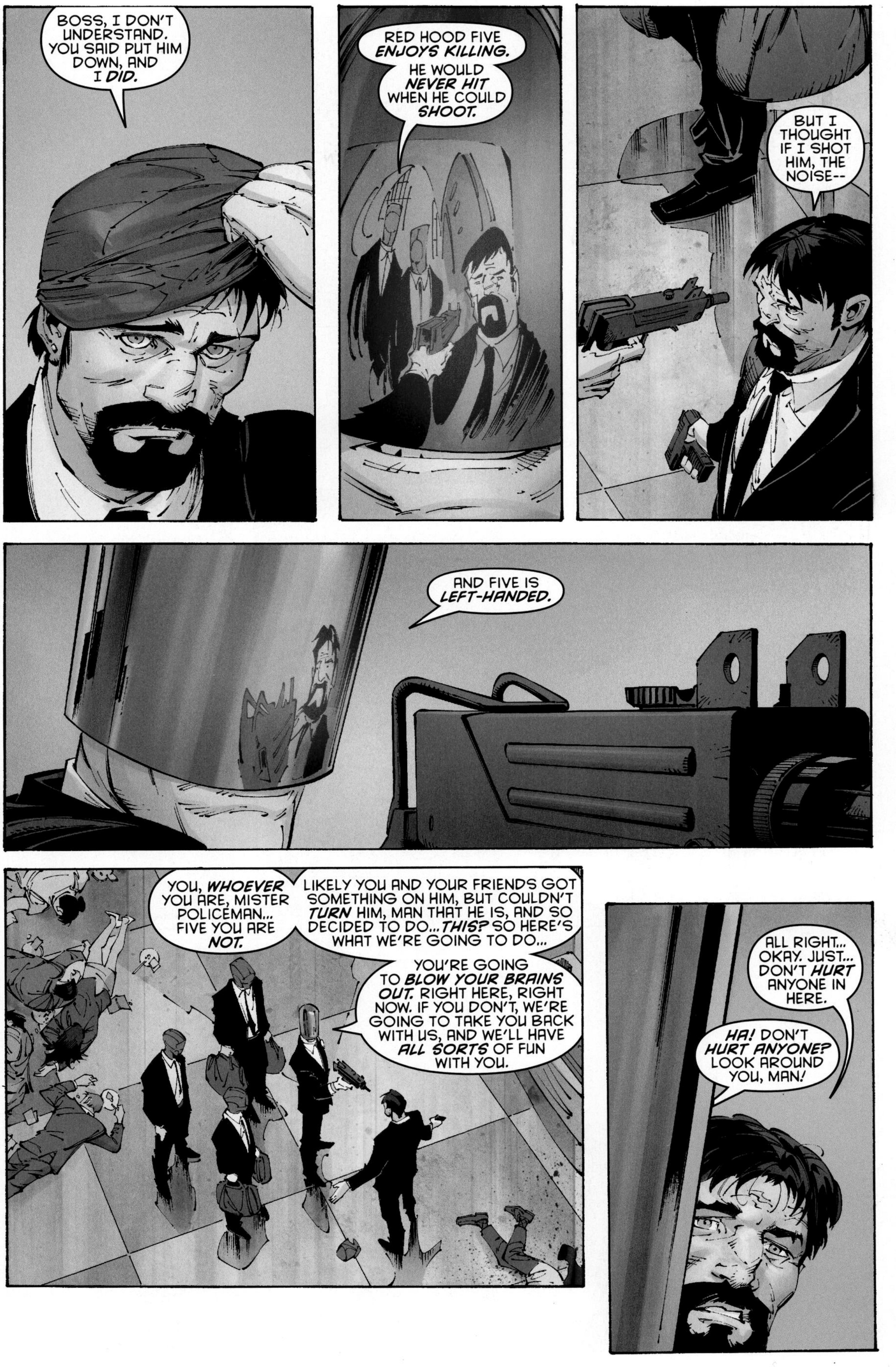

BOSS, I DON'T UNDERSTAND. YOU SAID PUT HIM DOWN, AND I *DID*.
RED HOOD FIVE *ENJOYS KILLING.*
HE WOULD *NEVER HIT* WHEN HE COULD *SHOOT.*
BUT I THOUGHT IF I SHOT HIM, THE NOISE--
AND FIVE IS *LEFT-HANDED.*
YOU, *WHOEVER* YOU ARE, MISTER POLICEMAN... FIVE YOU ARE *NOT.*
LIKELY YOU AND YOUR FRIENDS GOT SOMETHING ON HIM, BUT COULDN'T *TURN* HIM, MAN THAT HE IS, AND SO DECIDED TO DO...*THIS?* SO HERE'S WHAT WE'RE GOING TO DO...
YOU'RE GOING TO *BLOW YOUR BRAINS OUT.* RIGHT HERE, RIGHT NOW. IF YOU DON'T, WE'RE GOING TO TAKE YOU BACK WITH US, AND WE'LL HAVE *ALL SORTS* OF FUN WITH YOU.
ALL RIGHT... OKAY. JUST... DON'T *HURT* ANYONE IN HERE.
HA! DON'T *HURT ANYONE?* LOOK AROUND YOU, MAN!

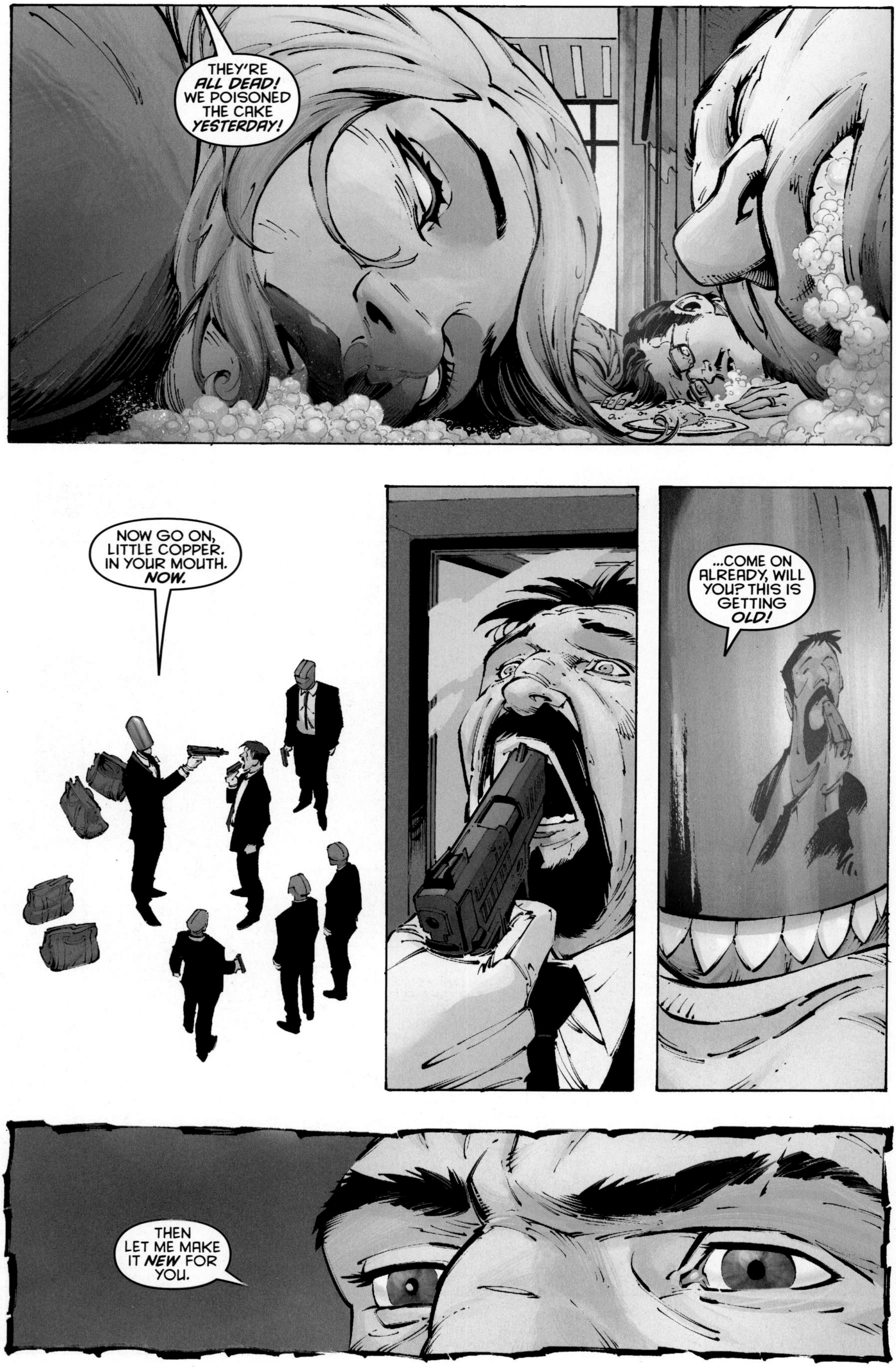
THEY'RE ALL DEAD! WE POISONED THE CAKE YESTERDAY!
NOW GO ON, LITTLE COPPER. IN YOUR MOUTH. NOW.
...COME ON ALREADY, WILL YOU? THIS IS GETTING OLD!
THEN LET ME MAKE IT NEW FOR YOU.

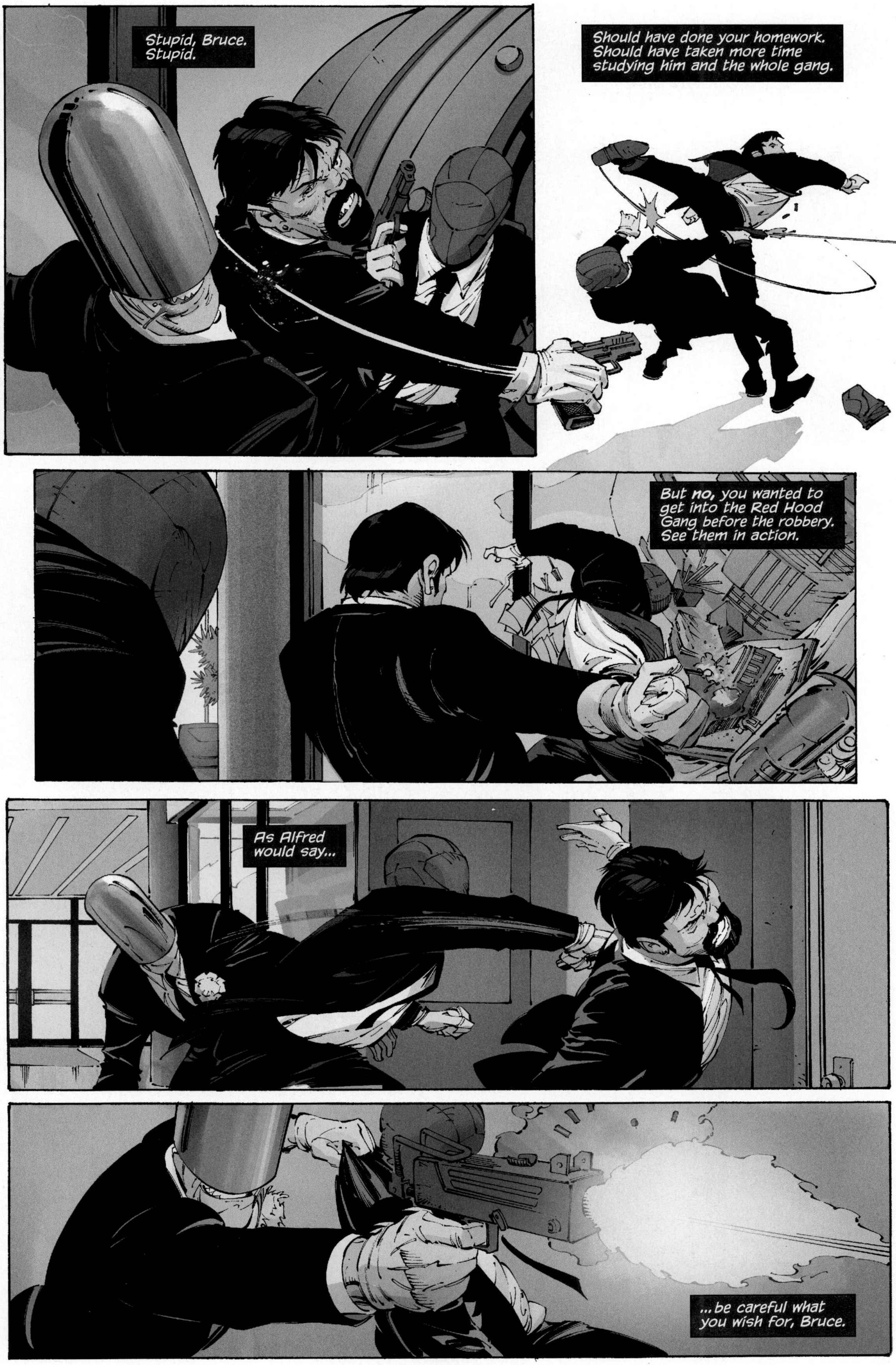
Stupid, Bruce.
Stupid.
Should have done your homework. Should have taken more time studying him and the whole gang.
But **no**, you wanted to get into the Red Hood Gang before the robbery. See them in action.
As Alfred would say...
...be careful what you wish for, Bruce.

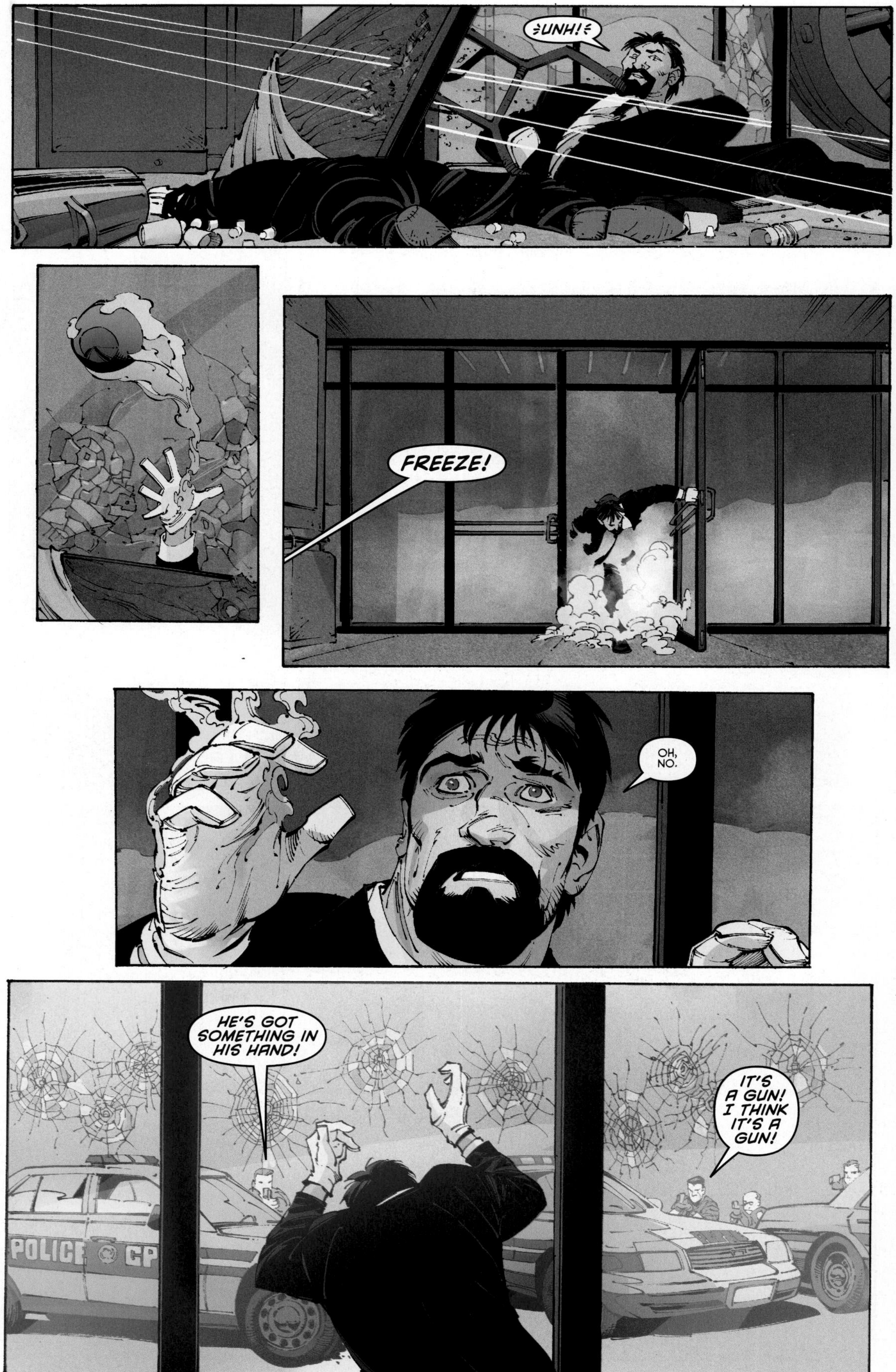
UNH!
FREEZE!
OH, NO.
HE'S GOT SOMETHING IN HIS HAND!
IT'S A GUN! I THINK IT'S A GUN!
POLICE

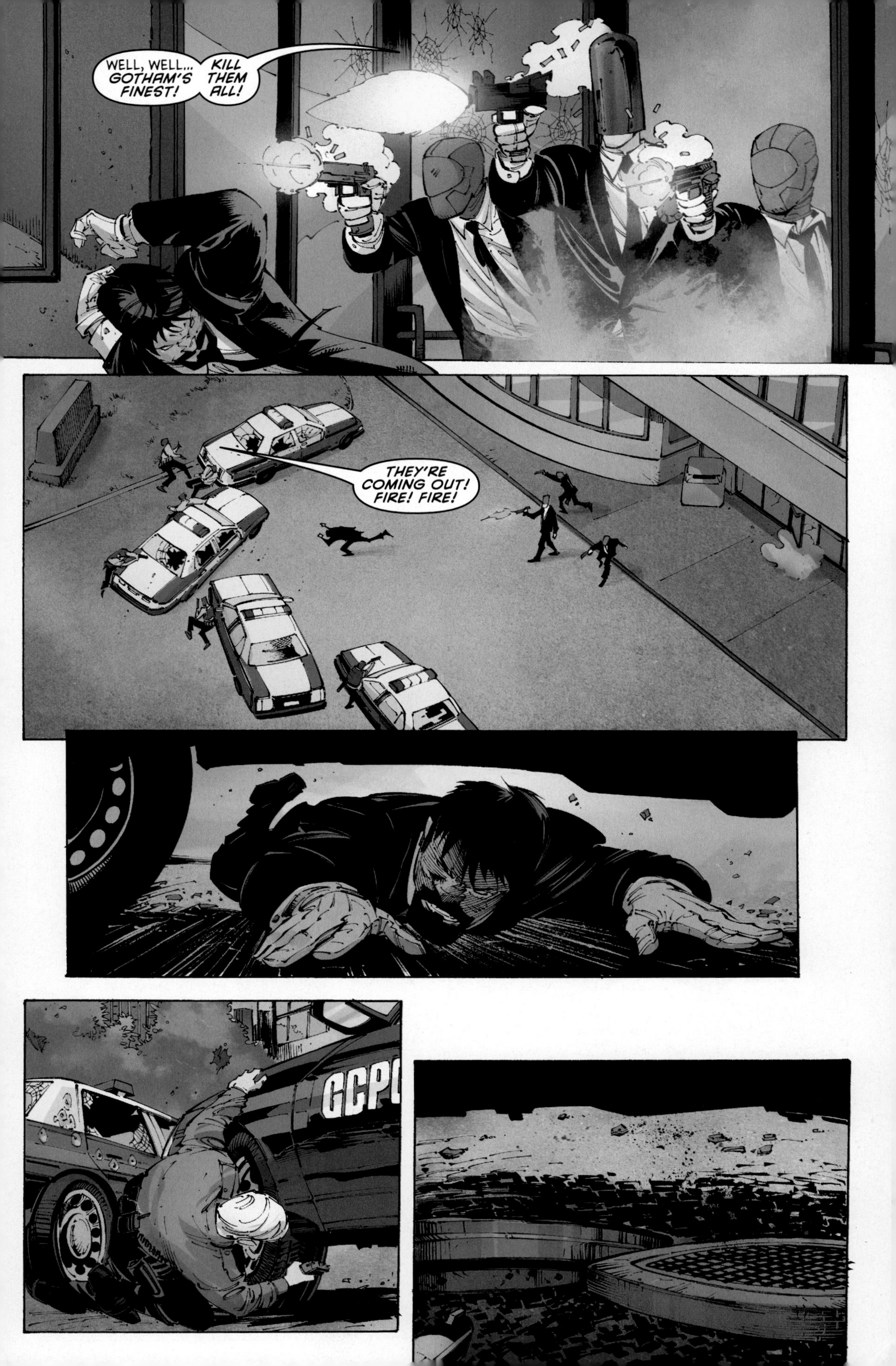
WELL, WELL... GOTHAM'S FINEST!
KILL THEM ALL!
THEY'RE COMING OUT! FIRE! FIRE!
GCPD

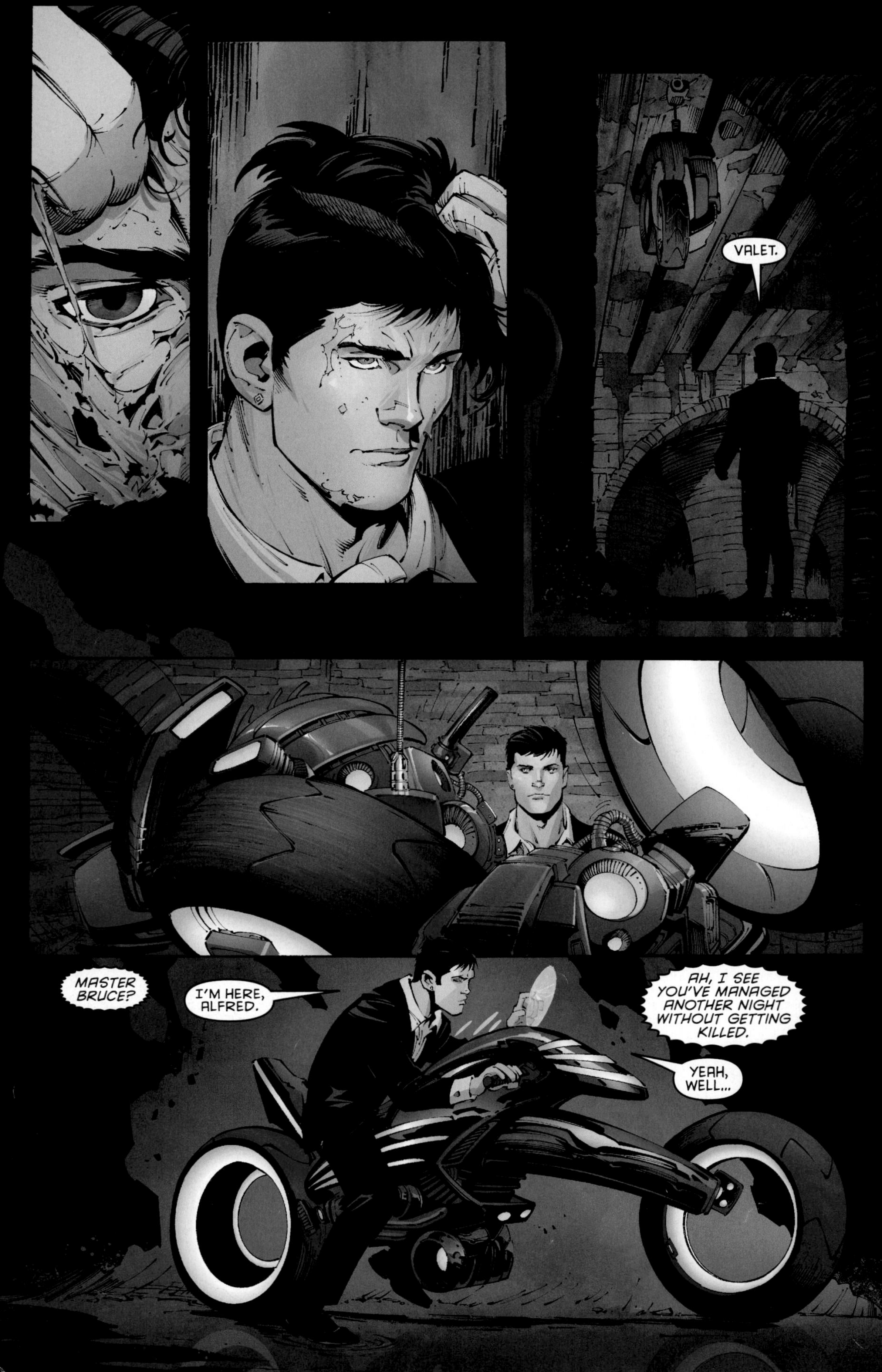
VALET.
MASTER BRUCE?
I'M HERE, ALFRED.
AH, I SEE YOU'VE MANAGED ANOTHER NIGHT WITHOUT GETTING KILLED.
YEAH, WELL...

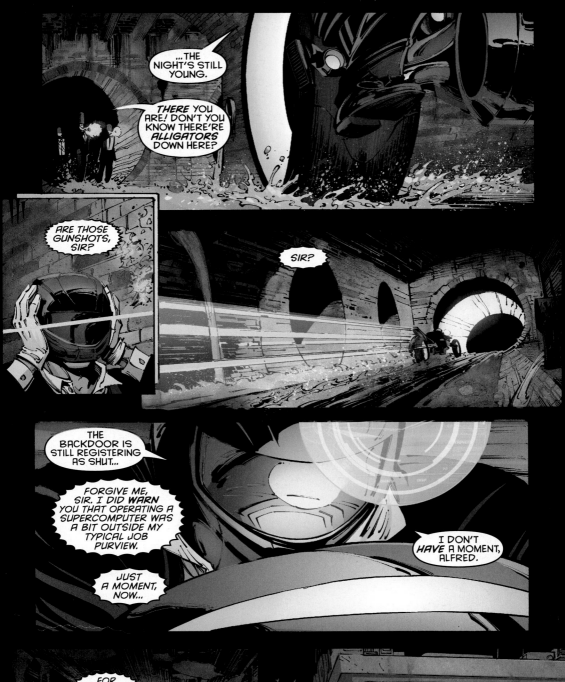

...THE NIGHT'S STILL YOUNG.

THERE YOU ARE! DON'T YOU KNOW THERE'RE *ALLIGATORS* DOWN HERE?

ARE THOSE GUNSHOTS, SIR?

SIR?

THE BACKDOOR IS STILL REGISTERING AS SHUT...

FORGIVE ME, SIR. I DID *WARN* YOU THAT OPERATING A SUPERCOMPUTER WAS A BIT OUTSIDE MY TYPICAL JOB PURVIEW.

I DON'T *HAVE* A MOMENT, ALFRED.

JUST A MOMENT, NOW...

FOR GOODNESS SAKE... THERE! DID *THAT* WORK?

PERFECTLY...

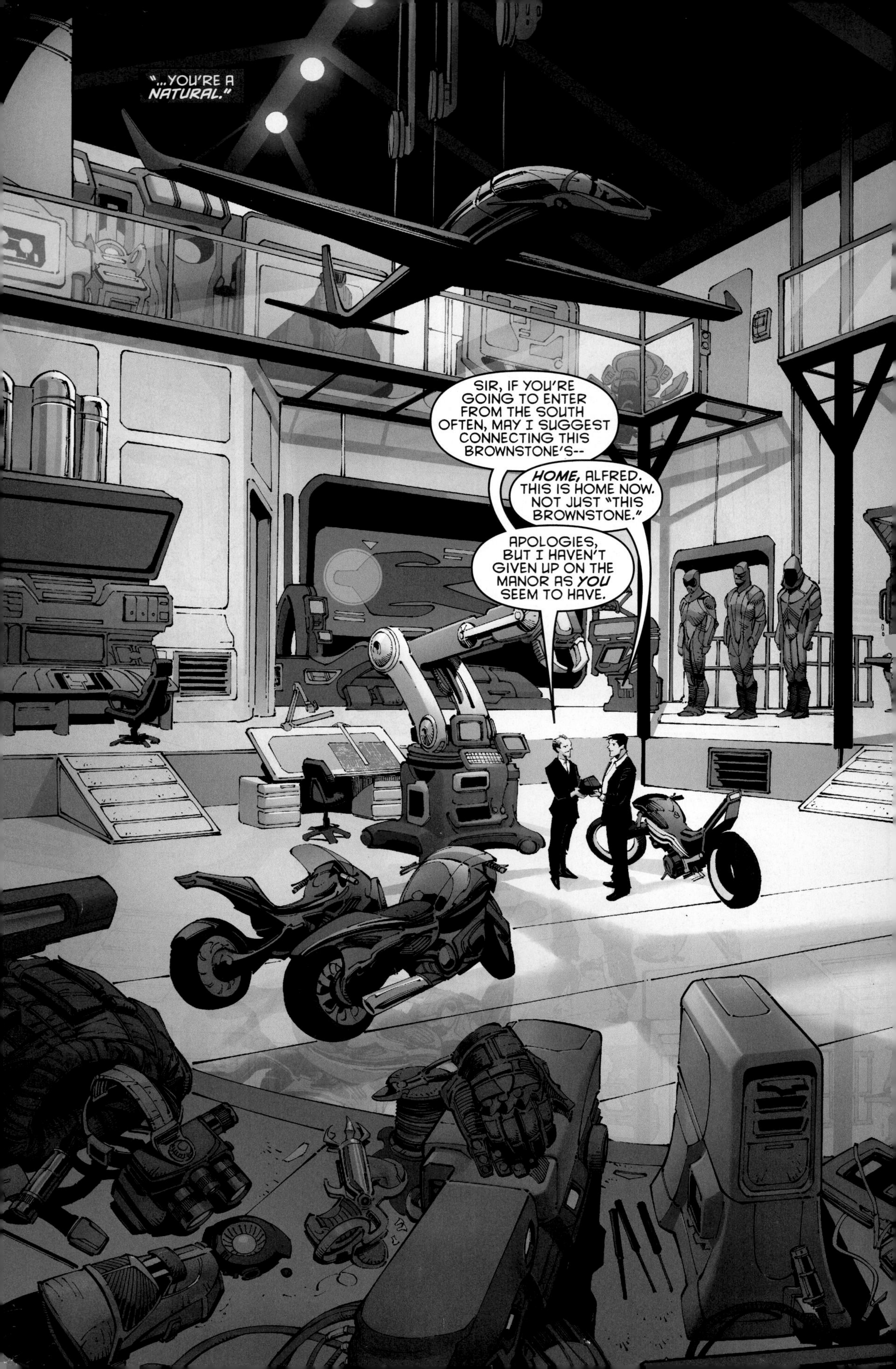
"...YOU'RE A NATURAL."
SIR, IF YOU'RE GOING TO ENTER FROM THE SOUTH OFTEN, MAY I SUGGEST CONNECTING THIS BROWNSTONE'S--
HOME, ALFRED. THIS IS HOME NOW. NOT JUST "THIS BROWNSTONE."
APOLOGIES, BUT I HAVEN'T GIVEN UP ON THE MANOR AS YOU SEEM TO HAVE.

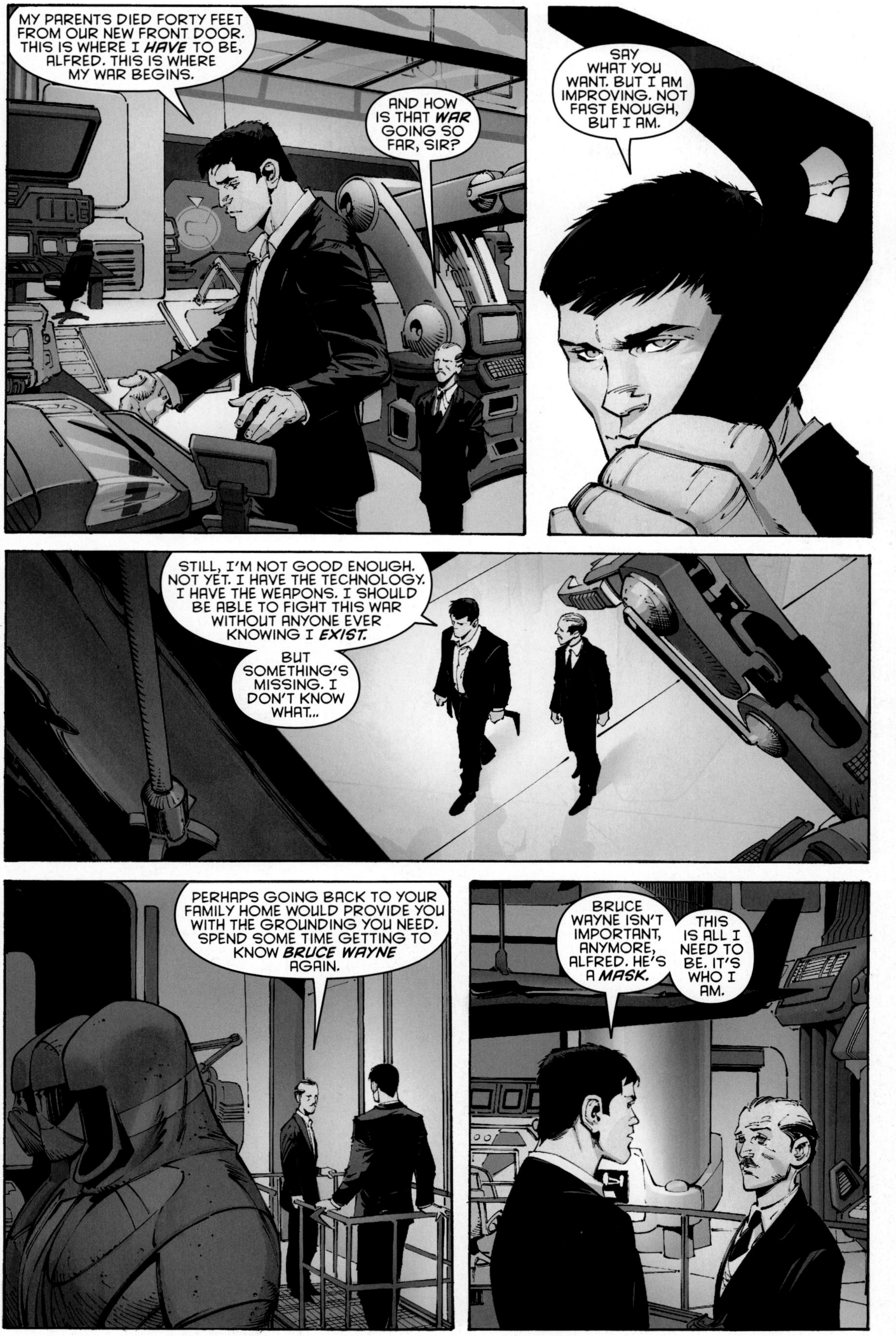
MY PARENTS DIED FORTY FEET FROM OUR NEW FRONT DOOR. THIS IS WHERE I *HAVE* TO BE, ALFRED. THIS IS WHERE MY WAR BEGINS.
AND HOW IS THAT *WAR* GOING SO FAR, SIR?
SAY WHAT YOU WANT. BUT I AM IMPROVING. NOT FAST ENOUGH, BUT I AM.
STILL, I'M NOT GOOD ENOUGH. NOT YET. I HAVE THE TECHNOLOGY. I HAVE THE WEAPONS. I SHOULD BE ABLE TO FIGHT THIS WAR WITHOUT ANYONE EVER KNOWING I *EXIST.*
BUT SOMETHING'S MISSING. I DON'T KNOW WHAT...
PERHAPS GOING BACK TO YOUR FAMILY HOME WOULD PROVIDE YOU WITH THE GROUNDING YOU NEED. SPEND SOME TIME GETTING TO KNOW *BRUCE WAYNE* AGAIN.
BRUCE WAYNE ISN'T IMPORTANT, ANYMORE, ALFRED. HE'S A *MASK.*
THIS IS ALL I NEED TO BE. IT'S WHO I AM.

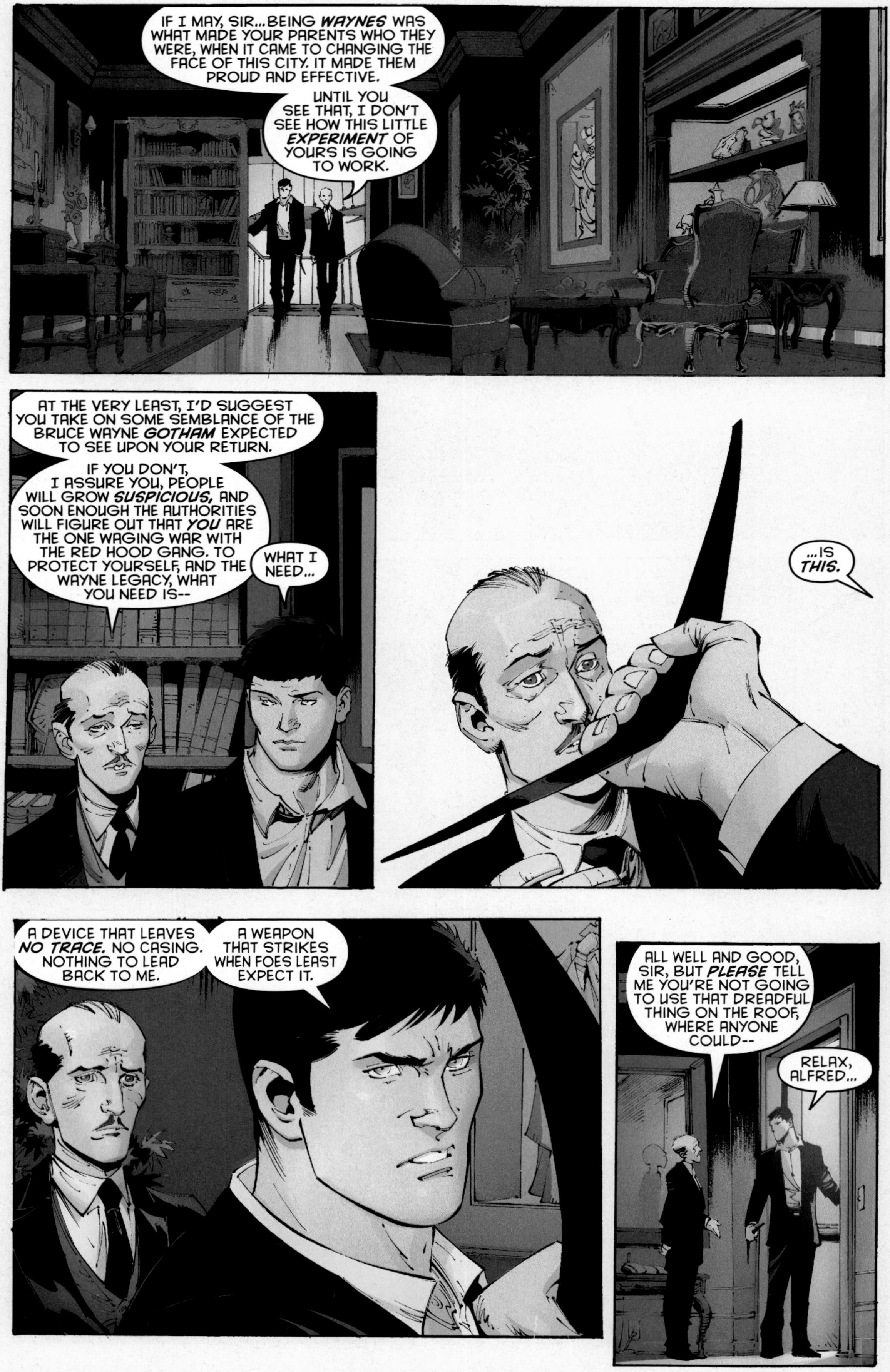
IF I MAY, SIR...BEING WAYNES WAS WHAT MADE YOUR PARENTS WHO THEY WERE, WHEN IT CAME TO CHANGING THE FACE OF THIS CITY. IT MADE THEM PROUD AND EFFECTIVE.
UNTIL YOU SEE THAT, I DON'T SEE HOW THIS LITTLE EXPERIMENT OF YOURS IS GOING TO WORK.
AT THE VERY LEAST, I'D SUGGEST YOU TAKE ON SOME SEMBLANCE OF THE BRUCE WAYNE GOTHAM EXPECTED TO SEE UPON YOUR RETURN.
IF YOU DON'T, I ASSURE YOU, PEOPLE WILL GROW SUSPICIOUS, AND SOON ENOUGH THE AUTHORITIES WILL FIGURE OUT THAT YOU ARE THE ONE WAGING WAR WITH THE RED HOOD GANG. TO PROTECT YOURSELF, AND THE WAYNE LEGACY, WHAT YOU NEED IS--
WHAT I NEED...
...IS THIS.
A DEVICE THAT LEAVES NO TRACE. NO CASING. NOTHING TO LEAD BACK TO ME.
A WEAPON THAT STRIKES WHEN FOES LEAST EXPECT IT.
ALL WELL AND GOOD, SIR, BUT PLEASE TELL ME YOU'RE NOT GOING TO USE THAT DREADFUL THING ON THE ROOF, WHERE ANYONE COULD--
RELAX, ALFRED...

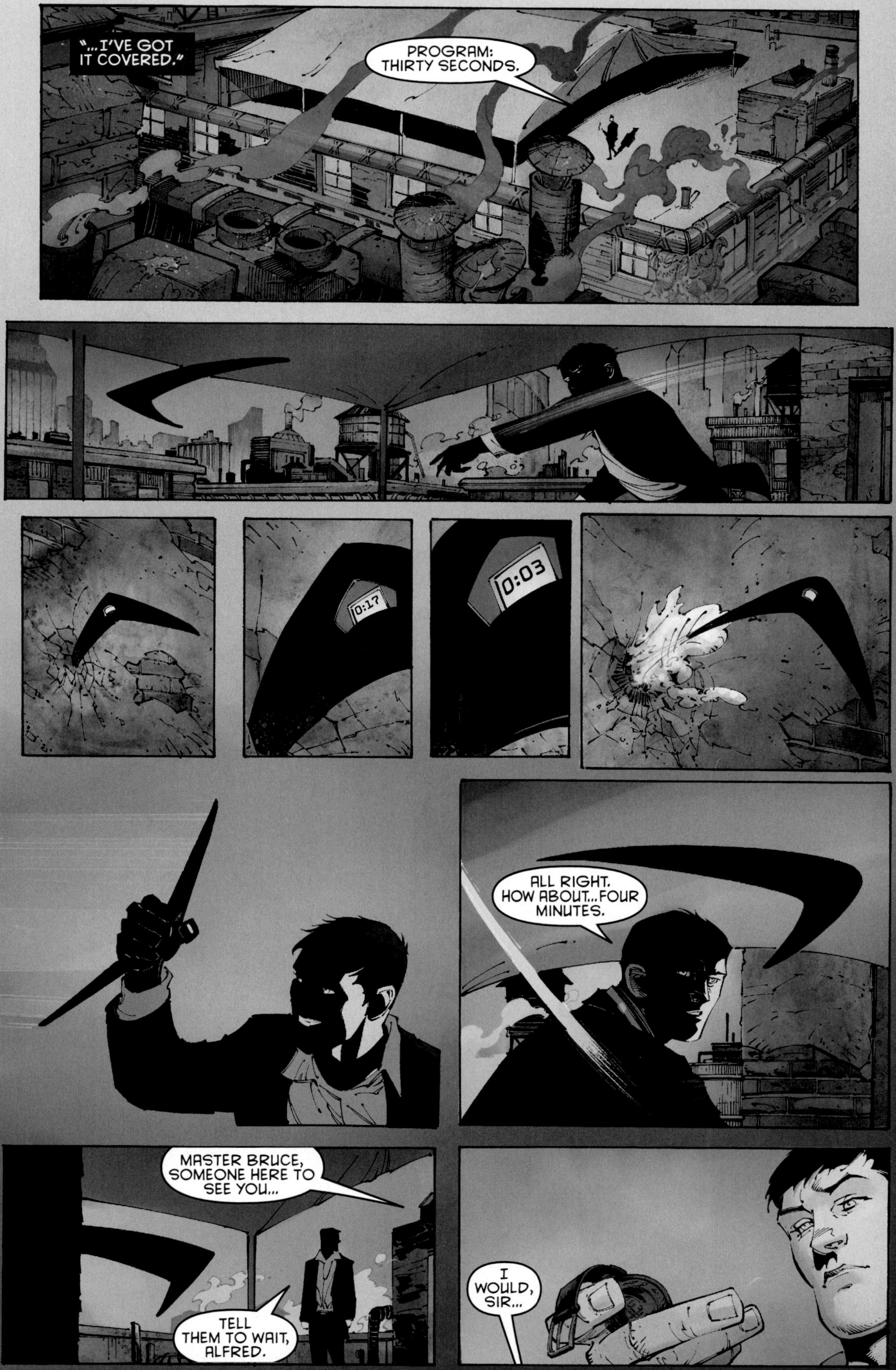
"...I'VE GOT IT COVERED."
PROGRAM: THIRTY SECONDS.
0:17
0:03
ALL RIGHT. HOW ABOUT...FOUR MINUTES.
MASTER BRUCE, SOMEONE HERE TO SEE YOU...
TELL THEM TO WAIT, ALFRED.
I WOULD, SIR...

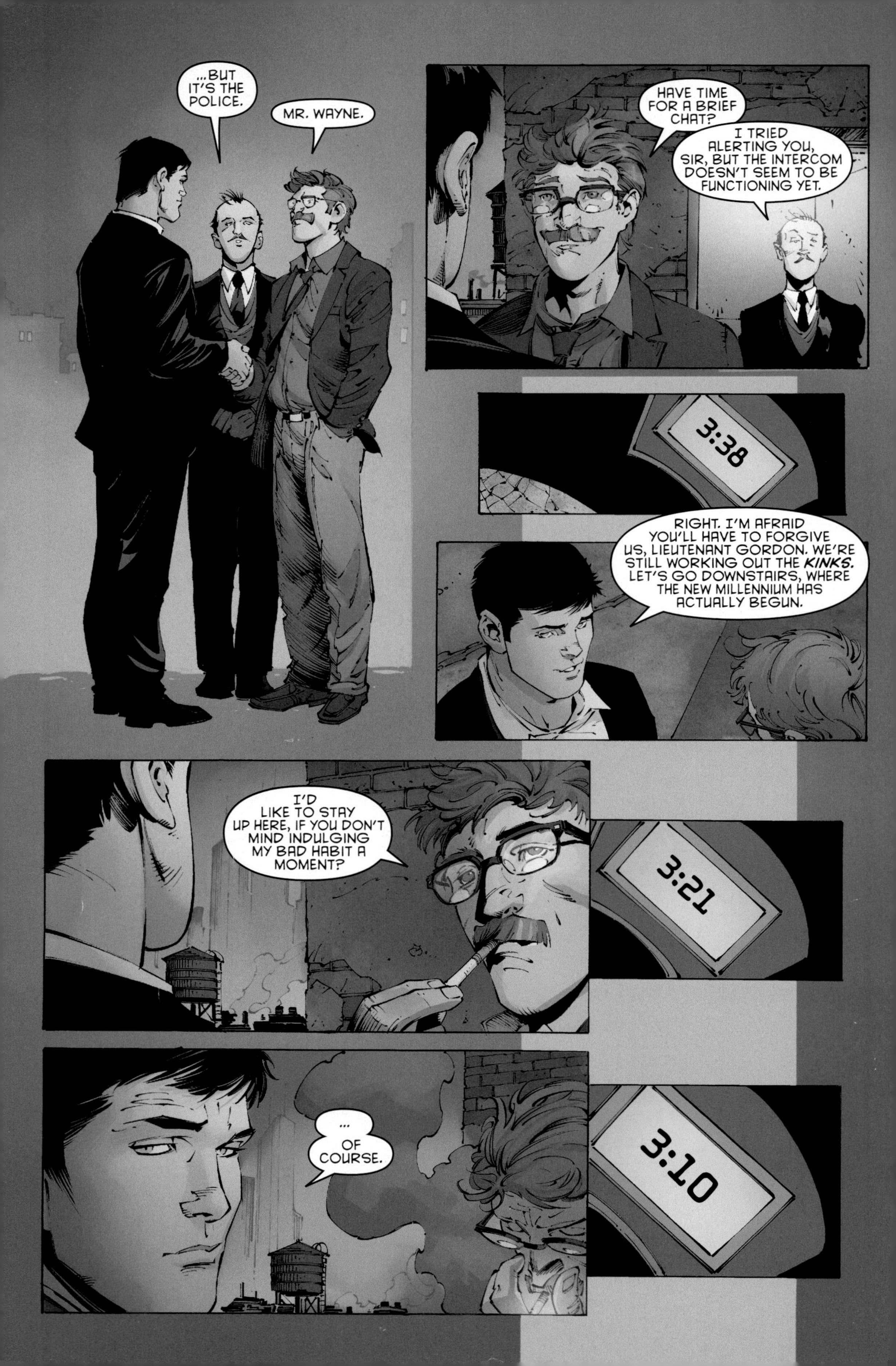
...BUT IT'S THE POLICE.
MR. WAYNE.
HAVE TIME FOR A BRIEF CHAT?
I TRIED ALERTING YOU, SIR, BUT THE INTERCOM DOESN'T SEEM TO BE FUNCTIONING YET.
3:38
RIGHT. I'M AFRAID YOU'LL HAVE TO FORGIVE US, LIEUTENANT GORDON. WE'RE STILL WORKING OUT THE KINKS. LET'S GO DOWNSTAIRS, WHERE THE NEW MILLENNIUM HAS ACTUALLY BEGUN.
I'D LIKE TO STAY UP HERE, IF YOU DON'T MIND INDULGING MY BAD HABIT A MOMENT?
3:21
... OF COURSE.
3:10

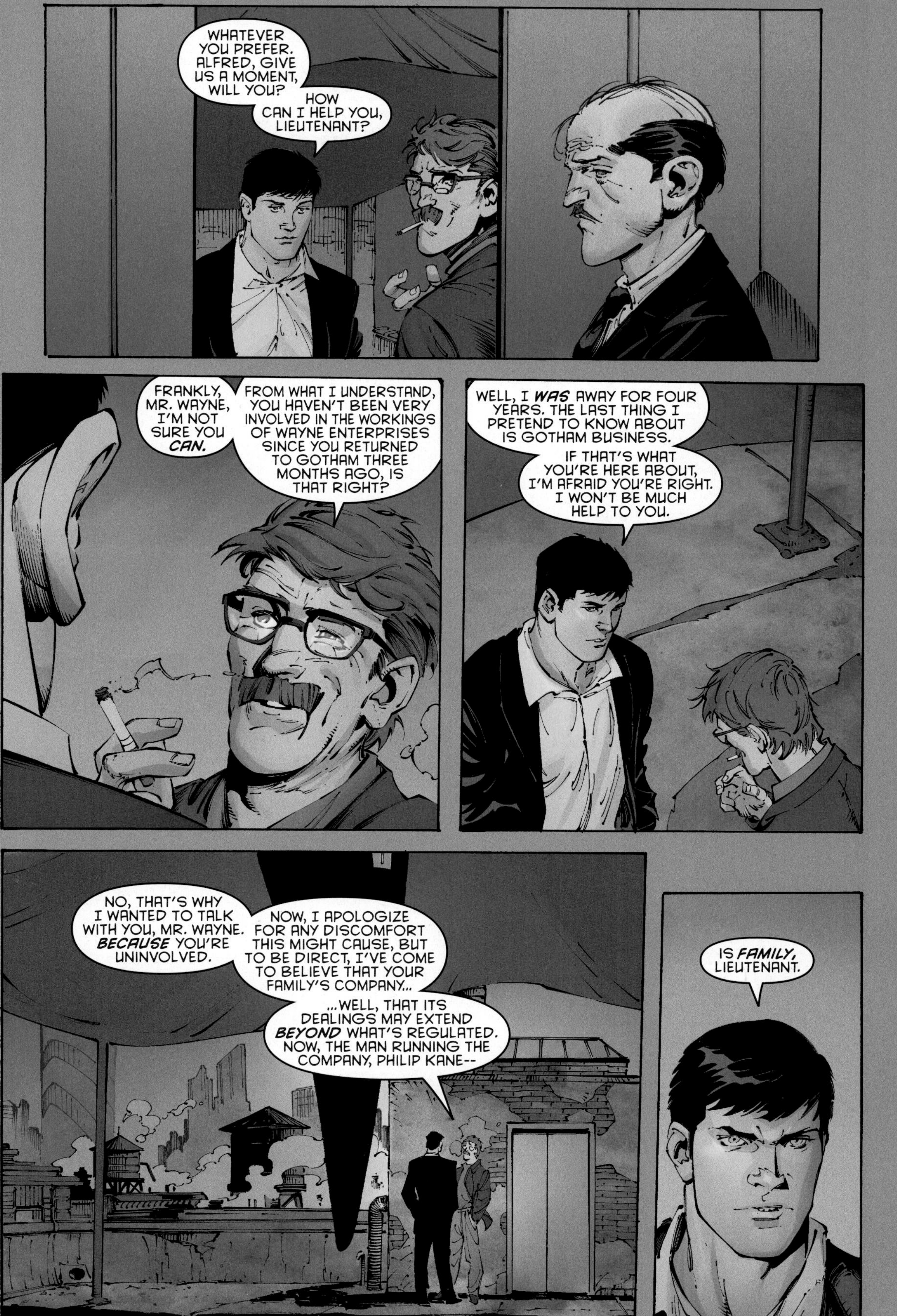
WHATEVER YOU PREFER. ALFRED, GIVE US A MOMENT, WILL YOU?
HOW CAN I HELP YOU, LIEUTENANT?
FRANKLY, MR. WAYNE, I'M NOT SURE YOU *CAN.*
FROM WHAT I UNDERSTAND, YOU HAVEN'T BEEN VERY INVOLVED IN THE WORKINGS OF WAYNE ENTERPRISES SINCE YOU RETURNED TO GOTHAM THREE MONTHS AGO, IS THAT RIGHT?
WELL, I *WAS* AWAY FOR FOUR YEARS. THE LAST THING I PRETEND TO KNOW ABOUT IS GOTHAM BUSINESS.
IF THAT'S WHAT YOU'RE HERE ABOUT, I'M AFRAID YOU'RE RIGHT. I WON'T BE MUCH HELP TO YOU.
NO, THAT'S WHY I WANTED TO TALK WITH YOU, MR. WAYNE. *BECAUSE* YOU'RE UNINVOLVED.
NOW, I APOLOGIZE FOR ANY DISCOMFORT THIS MIGHT CAUSE, BUT TO BE DIRECT, I'VE COME TO BELIEVE THAT YOUR FAMILY'S COMPANY...
...WELL, THAT ITS DEALINGS MAY EXTEND *BEYOND* WHAT'S REGULATED. NOW, THE MAN RUNNING THE COMPANY, PHILIP KANE--
IS *FAMILY,* LIEUTENANT.

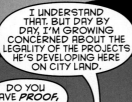

1:48

I UNDERSTAND THAT. BUT DAY BY DAY, I'M GROWING CONCERNED ABOUT THE LEGALITY OF THE PROJECTS HE'S DEVELOPING HERE ON CITY LAND.

DO YOU HAVE *PROOF,* LIEUTENANT?

-:SIGH:- NO. I DON'T. I HAVE WHISPERS AND A HUNCH. AND A HELL OF A LOT OF *RED TAPE.*

WELL, I'M SORRY, BUT I'M AFRAID I CAN'T HELP YOU. SO IF THAT'S ALL...

OF COURSE.

THOUGH THERE IS ONE MORE THING...

WE'VE HAD REPORTS OF A... *VIGILANTE* IN THE NEIGHBORHOOD. SOMEONE SNEAKING AROUND AT NIGHT, STOPPING CRIMES.

NEIGHBORHOOD WATCH, EH?

HEH. THIS GUY'S APPARENTLY A LITLE MORE *UPTOWN* THAN THAT. HE'S GOT RESOURCES. TECH THAT HAS OUR I.T. GUYS SWOONING LIKE TEENAGERS.

WHAT ARE YOU ASKING ME, LIEUTENANT?

I'M ASKING YOU IF YOU KNOW ANYTHING ABOUT IT, THAT'S ALL.

I'M AFRAID I CAN'T HELP YOU.

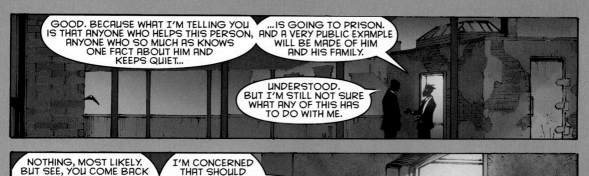

GOOD. BECAUSE WHAT I'M TELLING YOU IS THAT ANYONE WHO HELPS THIS PERSON, ANYONE WHO SO MUCH AS KNOWS ONE FACT ABOUT HIM AND KEEPS QUIET...

...IS GOING TO PRISON. AND A VERY PUBLIC EXAMPLE WILL BE MADE OF HIM AND HIS FAMILY.

UNDERSTOOD. BUT I'M STILL NOT SURE WHAT ANY OF THIS HAS TO DO WITH ME.

NOTHING, MOST LIKELY. BUT SEE, YOU COME BACK TO GOTHAM AND FIRST THING YOU DO IS PLANT YOUR FLAG HERE, IN CRIME ALLEY, THE WORST OF THE WORST, WHEN YOU COULD BE IN A COZY MANSION.

I'M CONCERNED THAT SHOULD YOU CROSS PATHS WITH THIS PERSON, THIS *VIGILANTE*, YOU MIGHT SYMPATHIZE WITH HIM. YOU SEEM TO BE ON A BIT OF A CRUSADE HERE, IS ALL.

HEH. WELL, YOU DON'T HAVE TO WORRY. I WON'T BE FRATERNIZING WITH ANY VIGILANTES. BUT IT'S FUNNY, I HEAR *YOU'RE* A BIT OF A CRUSADER YOURSELF.

IS THAT SO?

I'M AFRAID IT IS.

WELL, I BETTER DISPEL THAT RUMOR AS FAST AS POSSIBLE. I'VE HEARD CRUSADERS IN GOTHAM, THEY END UP PRETTY DAMN LONELY.

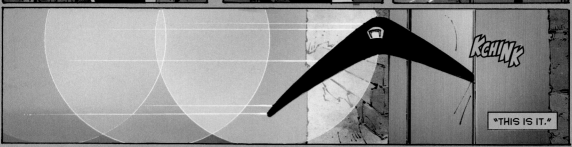

KCHINK

"THIS IS IT."

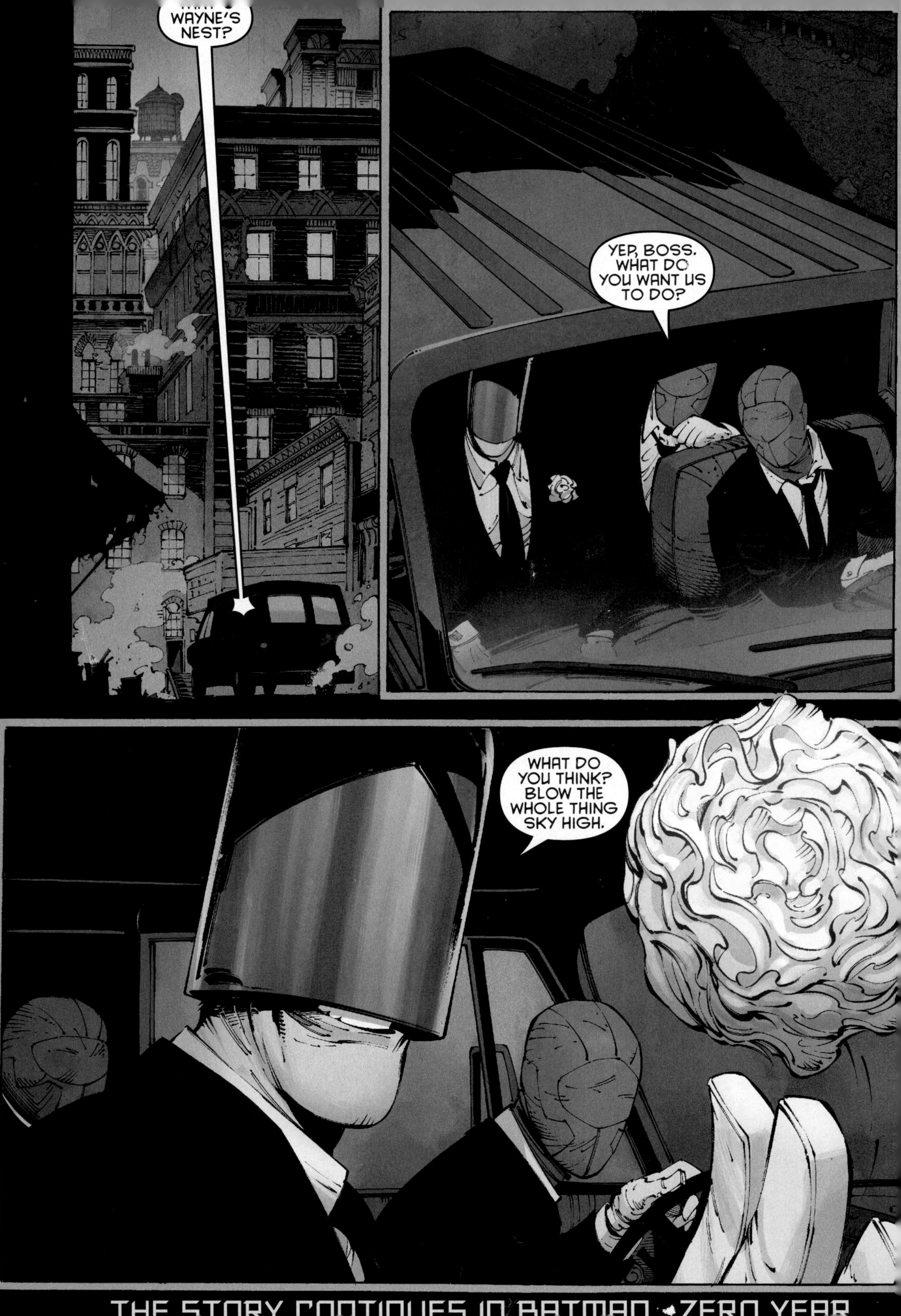
WAYNE'S NEST?
YEP, BOSS. WHAT DO YOU WANT US TO DO?
WHAT DO YOU THINK? BLOW THE WHOLE THING SKY HIGH.

THE STORY CONTINUES IN BATMAN: ZERO YEAR

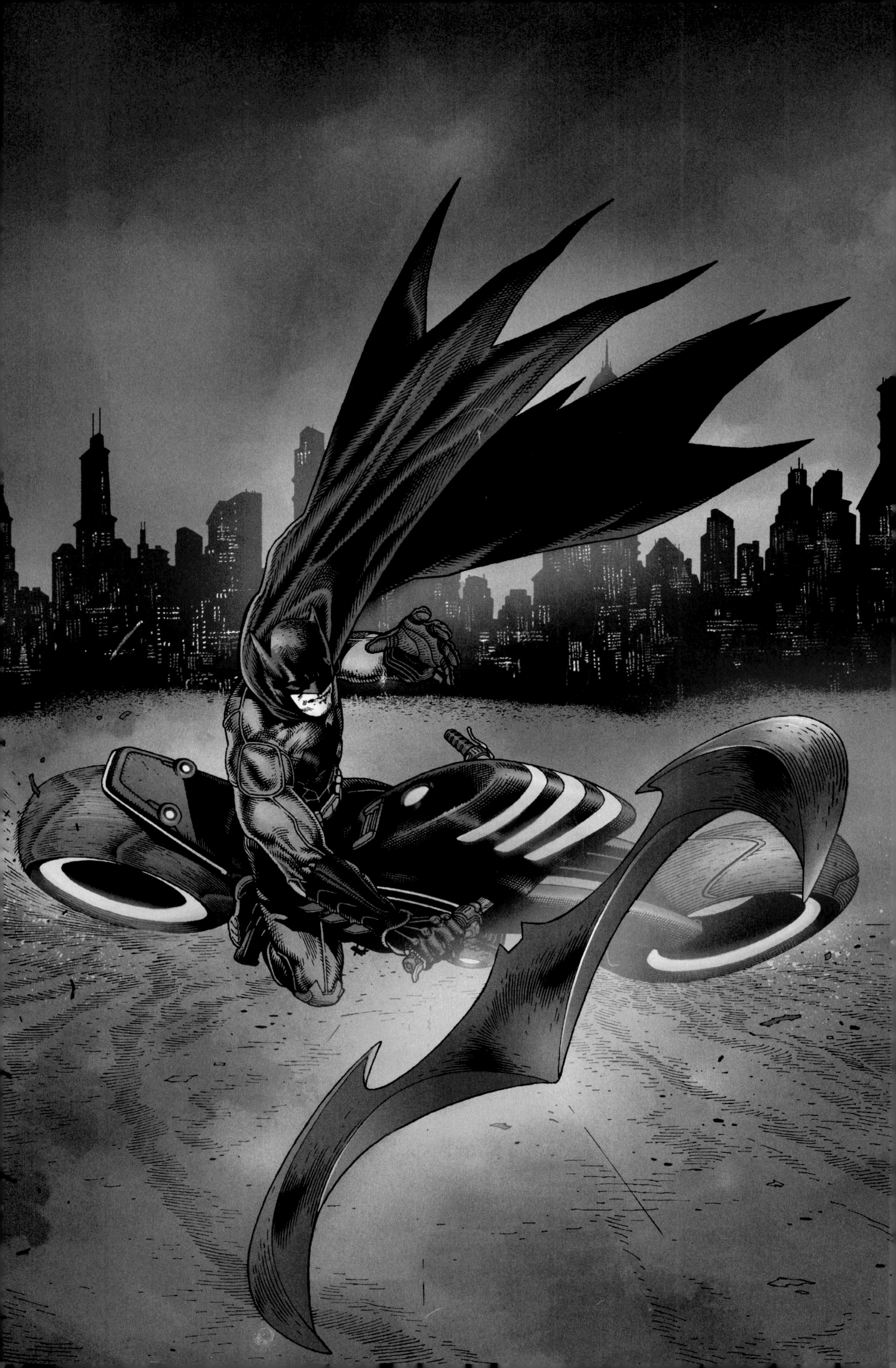

TOMORROW

JAMES TYNION IV writer ANDY CLARKE artist FCO PLASCENCIA colorist variant cover by ANDY CLARKE

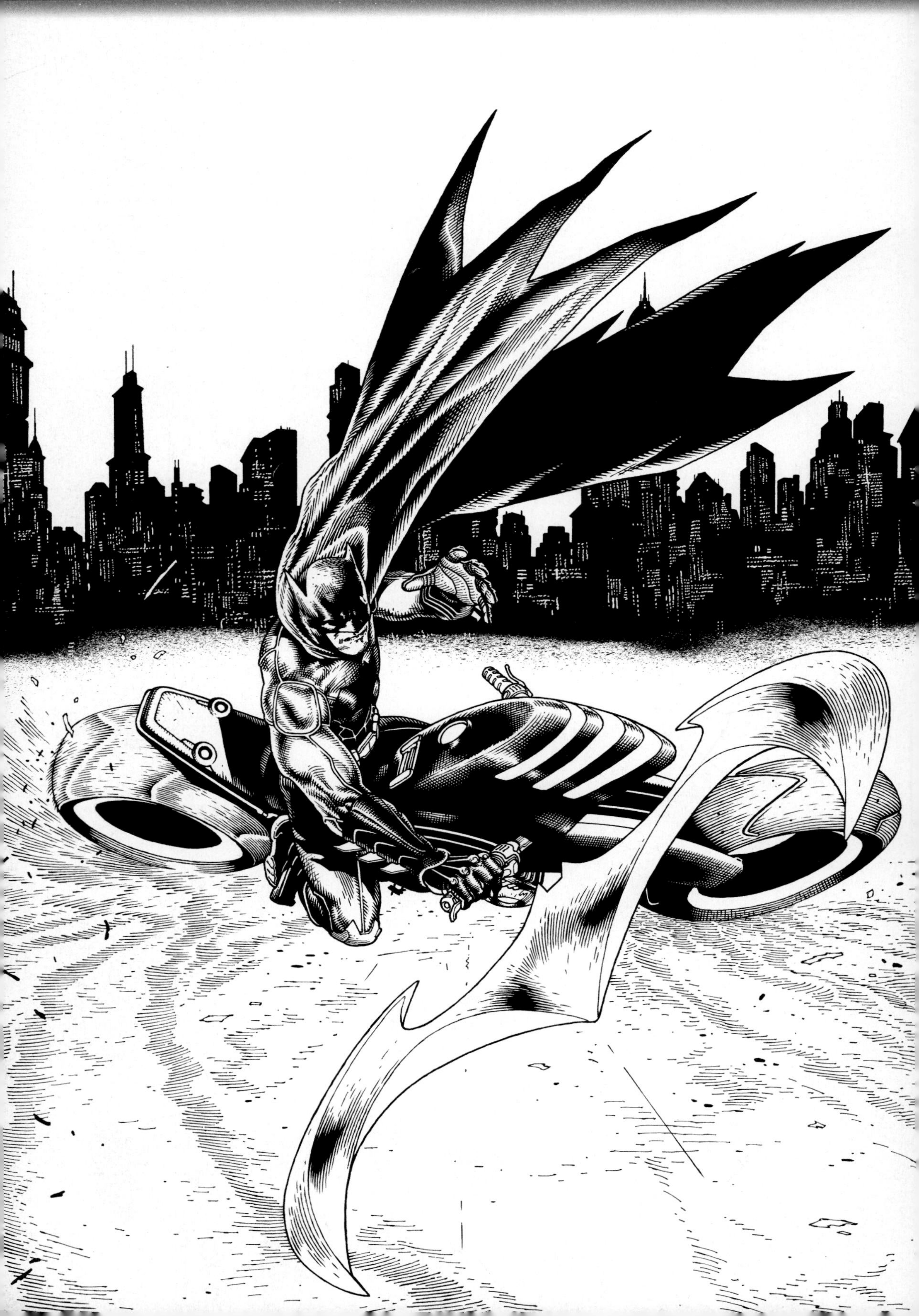

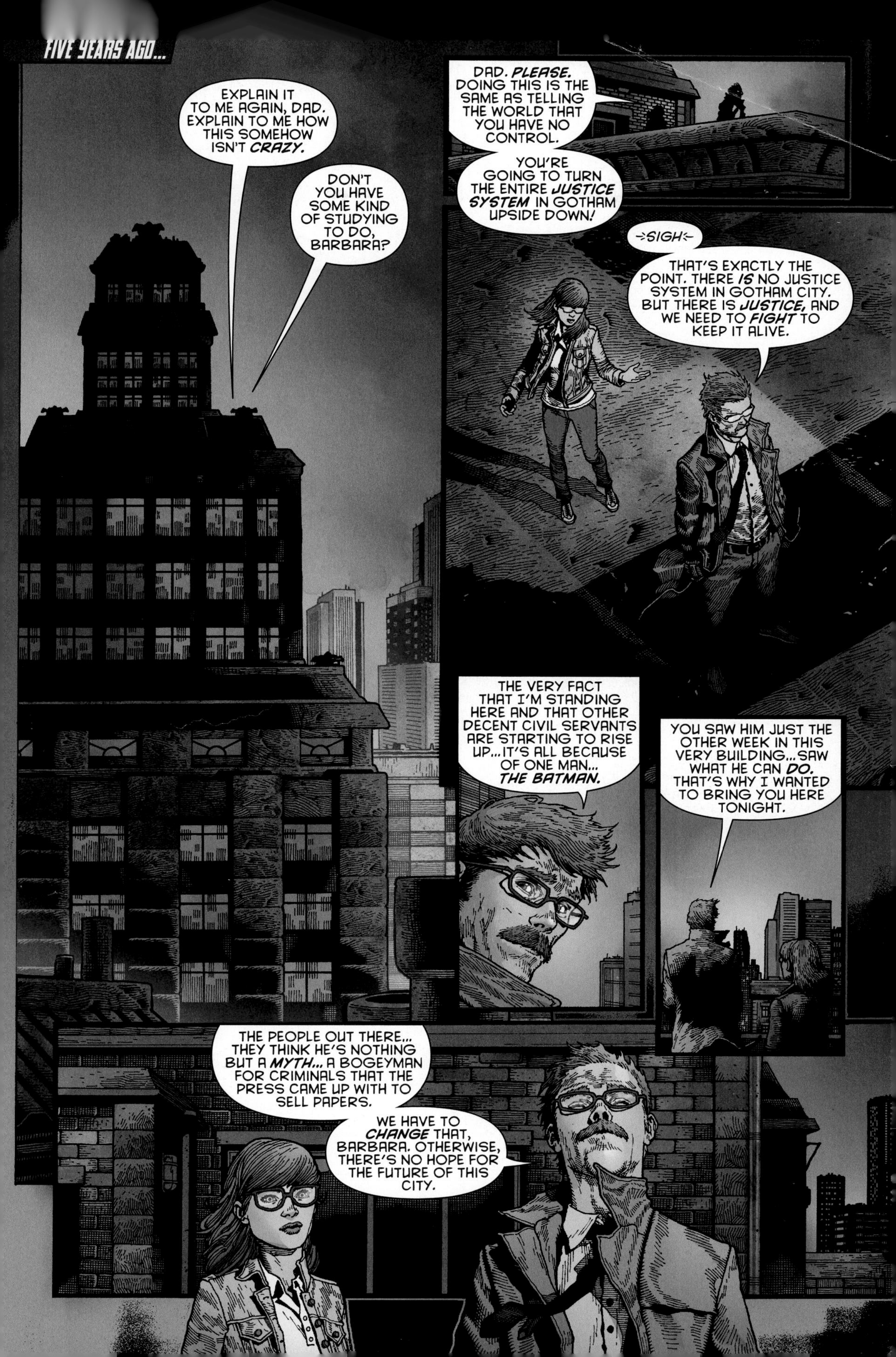
FIVE YEARS AGO...
EXPLAIN IT TO ME AGAIN, DAD. EXPLAIN TO ME HOW THIS SOMEHOW ISN'T CRAZY.
DON'T YOU HAVE SOME KIND OF STUDYING TO DO, BARBARA?
DAD. PLEASE. DOING THIS IS THE SAME AS TELLING THE WORLD THAT YOU HAVE NO CONTROL.
YOU'RE GOING TO TURN THE ENTIRE JUSTICE SYSTEM IN GOTHAM UPSIDE DOWN!
SIGH
THAT'S EXACTLY THE POINT. THERE IS NO JUSTICE SYSTEM IN GOTHAM CITY. BUT THERE IS JUSTICE, AND WE NEED TO FIGHT TO KEEP IT ALIVE.
THE VERY FACT THAT I'M STANDING HERE AND THAT OTHER DECENT CIVIL SERVANTS ARE STARTING TO RISE UP...IT'S ALL BECAUSE OF ONE MAN... THE BATMAN.
YOU SAW HIM JUST THE OTHER WEEK IN THIS VERY BUILDING...SAW WHAT HE CAN DO. THAT'S WHY I WANTED TO BRING YOU HERE TONIGHT.
THE PEOPLE OUT THERE... THEY THINK HE'S NOTHING BUT A MYTH... A BOGEYMAN FOR CRIMINALS THAT THE PRESS CAME UP WITH TO SELL PAPERS.
WE HAVE TO CHANGE THAT, BARBARA. OTHERWISE, THERE'S NO HOPE FOR THE FUTURE OF THIS CITY.

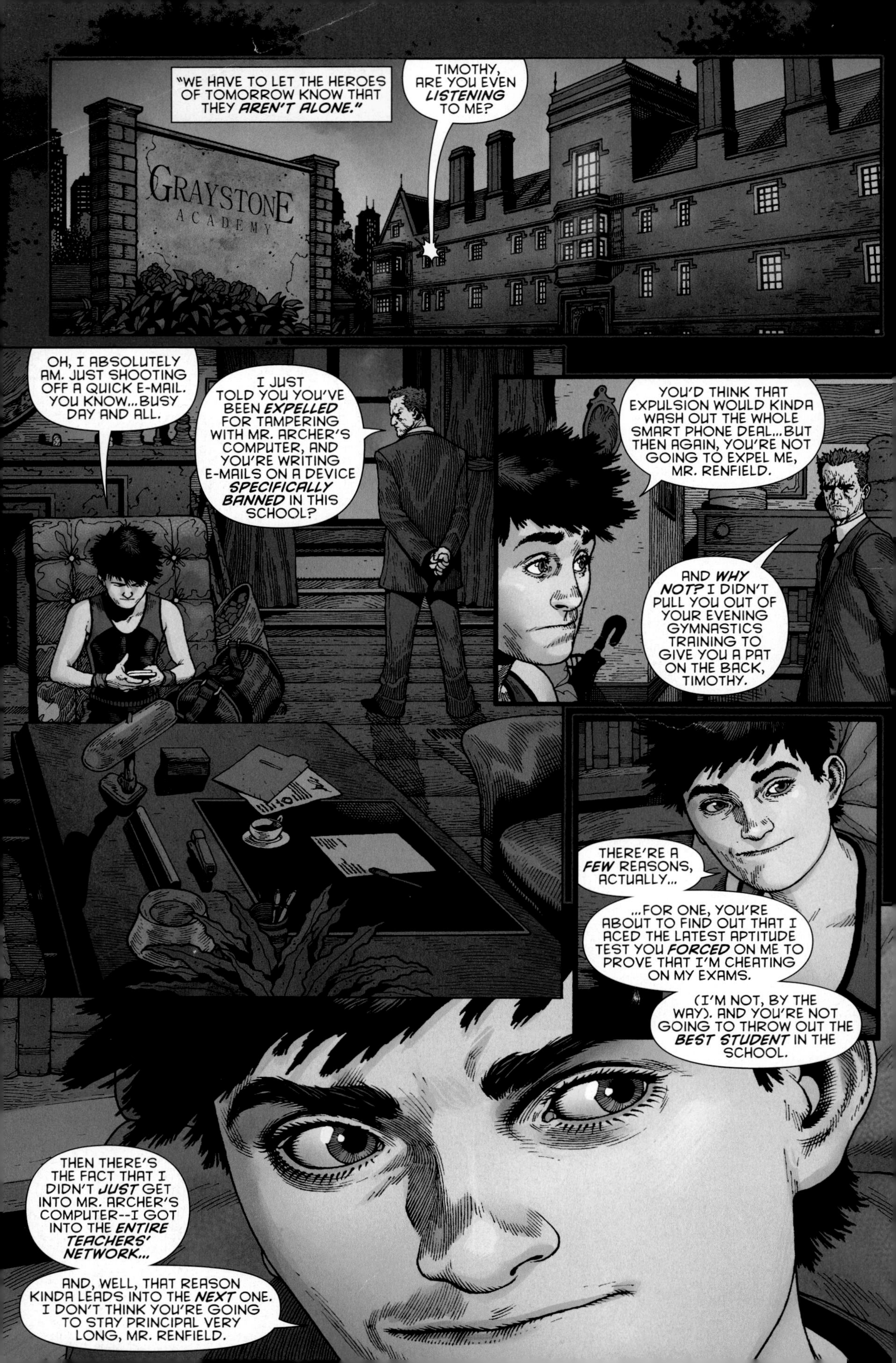
GRAYSTONE ACADEMY
"WE HAVE TO LET THE HEROES OF TOMORROW KNOW THAT THEY AREN'T ALONE."
TIMOTHY, ARE YOU EVEN LISTENING TO ME?
OH, I ABSOLUTELY AM. JUST SHOOTING OFF A QUICK E-MAIL. YOU KNOW...BUSY DAY AND ALL.
I JUST TOLD YOU YOU'VE BEEN EXPELLED FOR TAMPERING WITH MR. ARCHER'S COMPUTER, AND YOU'RE WRITING E-MAILS ON A DEVICE SPECIFICALLY BANNED IN THIS SCHOOL?
YOU'D THINK THAT EXPULSION WOULD KINDA WASH OUT THE WHOLE SMART PHONE DEAL...BUT THEN AGAIN, YOU'RE NOT GOING TO EXPEL ME, MR. RENFIELD.
AND WHY NOT? I DIDN'T PULL YOU OUT OF YOUR EVENING GYMNASTICS TRAINING TO GIVE YOU A PAT ON THE BACK, TIMOTHY.
THERE'RE A FEW REASONS, ACTUALLY...
...FOR ONE, YOU'RE ABOUT TO FIND OUT THAT I ACED THE LATEST APTITUDE TEST YOU FORCED ON ME TO PROVE THAT I'M CHEATING ON MY EXAMS.
(I'M NOT, BY THE WAY). AND YOU'RE NOT GOING TO THROW OUT THE BEST STUDENT IN THE SCHOOL.
THEN THERE'S THE FACT THAT I DIDN'T JUST GET INTO MR. ARCHER'S COMPUTER--I GOT INTO THE ENTIRE TEACHERS' NETWORK...
AND, WELL, THAT REASON KINDA LEADS INTO THE NEXT ONE. I DON'T THINK YOU'RE GOING TO STAY PRINCIPAL VERY LONG, MR. RENFIELD.

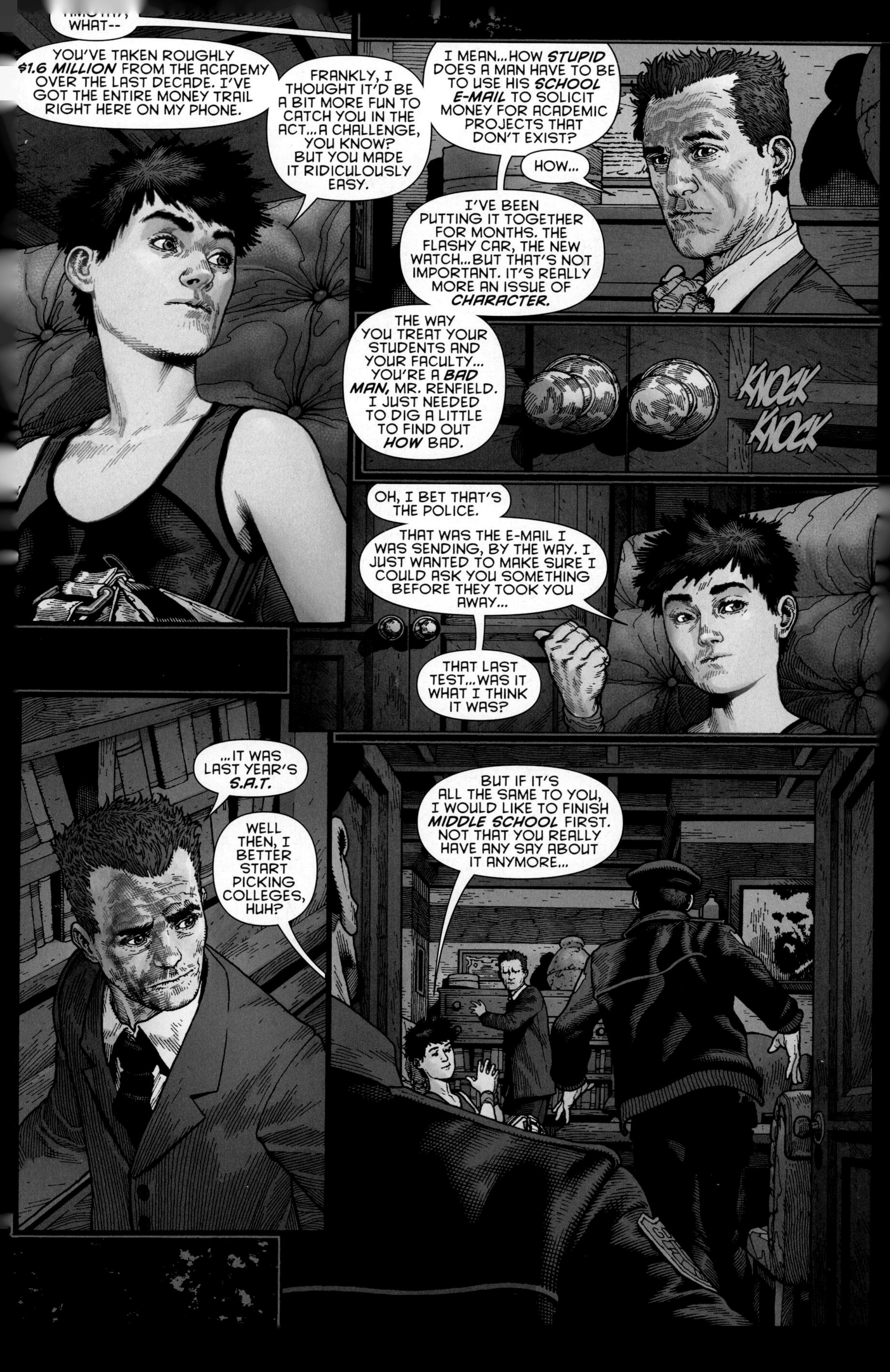

WHAT--
YOU'VE TAKEN ROUGHLY $1.6 MILLION FROM THE ACADEMY OVER THE LAST DECADE. I'VE GOT THE ENTIRE MONEY TRAIL RIGHT HERE ON MY PHONE.
FRANKLY, I THOUGHT IT'D BE A BIT MORE FUN TO CATCH YOU IN THE ACT...A CHALLENGE, YOU KNOW? BUT YOU MADE IT RIDICULOUSLY EASY.
I MEAN...HOW STUPID DOES A MAN HAVE TO BE TO USE HIS SCHOOL E-MAIL TO SOLICIT MONEY FOR ACADEMIC PROJECTS THAT DON'T EXIST?
HOW...
I'VE BEEN PUTTING IT TOGETHER FOR MONTHS. THE FLASHY CAR, THE NEW WATCH...BUT THAT'S NOT IMPORTANT. IT'S REALLY MORE AN ISSUE OF CHARACTER.
THE WAY YOU TREAT YOUR STUDENTS AND YOUR FACULTY... YOU'RE A BAD MAN, MR. RENFIELD. I JUST NEEDED TO DIG A LITTLE TO FIND OUT HOW BAD.
KNOCK KNOCK
OH, I BET THAT'S THE POLICE.
THAT WAS THE E-MAIL I WAS SENDING, BY THE WAY. I JUST WANTED TO MAKE SURE I COULD ASK YOU SOMETHING BEFORE THEY TOOK YOU AWAY...
THAT LAST TEST...WAS IT WHAT I THINK IT WAS?
...IT WAS LAST YEAR'S S.A.T.
WELL THEN, I BETTER START PICKING COLLEGES, HUH?
BUT IF IT'S ALL THE SAME TO YOU, I WOULD LIKE TO FINISH MIDDLE SCHOOL FIRST. NOT THAT YOU REALLY HAVE ANY SAY ABOUT IT ANYMORE...

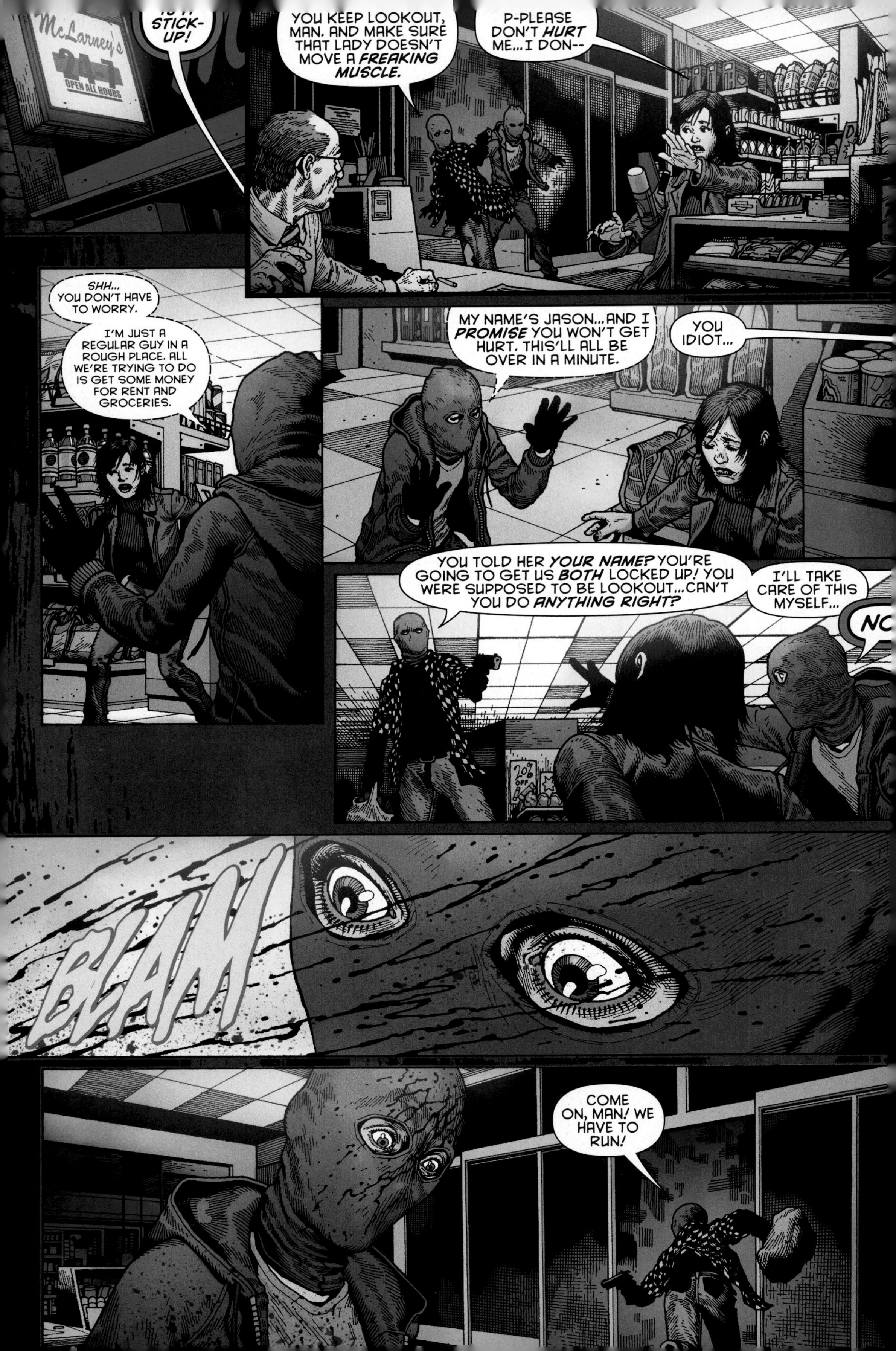
McLarney's
24-7
OPEN ALL HOURS
STICK-UP!
YOU KEEP LOOKOUT, MAN. AND MAKE SURE THAT LADY DOESN'T MOVE A FREAKING MUSCLE.
P-PLEASE DON'T HURT ME...I DON--
SHH... YOU DON'T HAVE TO WORRY.
I'M JUST A REGULAR GUY IN A ROUGH PLACE. ALL WE'RE TRYING TO DO IS GET SOME MONEY FOR RENT AND GROCERIES.
MY NAME'S JASON...AND I PROMISE YOU WON'T GET HURT. THIS'LL ALL BE OVER IN A MINUTE.
YOU IDIOT...
YOU TOLD HER YOUR NAME? YOU'RE GOING TO GET US BOTH LOCKED UP! YOU WERE SUPPOSED TO BE LOOKOUT...CAN'T YOU DO ANYTHING RIGHT?
I'LL TAKE CARE OF THIS MYSELF...
20% OFF
BLAM
COME ON, MAN! WE HAVE TO RUN!

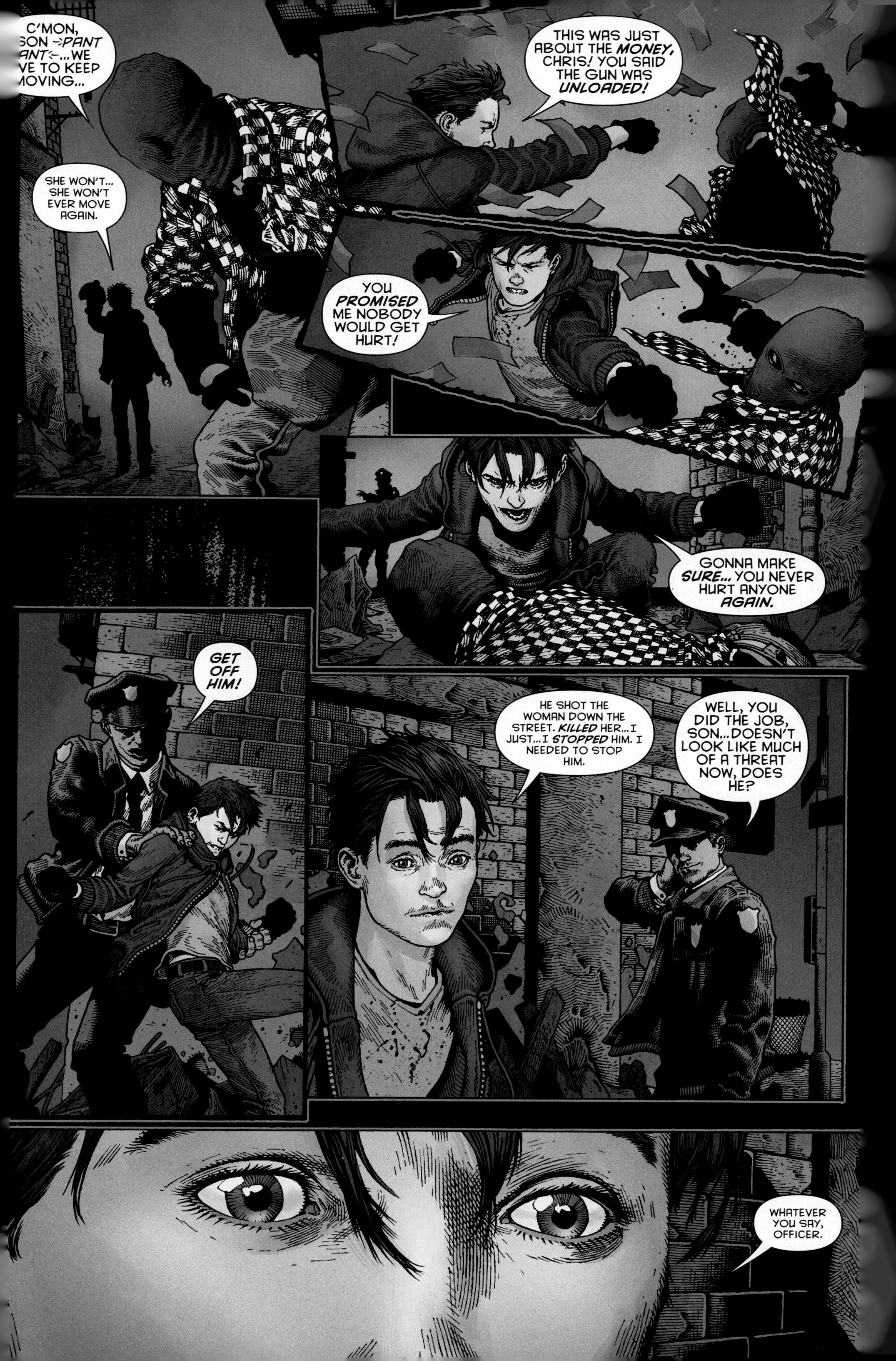
C'MON, SON ⇒PANT ANT⇐...WE VE TO KEEP MOVING...
THIS WAS JUST ABOUT THE MONEY, CHRIS! YOU SAID THE GUN WAS UNLOADED!
SHE WON'T... SHE WON'T EVER MOVE AGAIN.
YOU PROMISED ME NOBODY WOULD GET HURT!
GONNA MAKE SURE... YOU NEVER HURT ANYONE AGAIN.
GET OFF HIM!
HE SHOT THE WOMAN DOWN THE STREET. KILLED HER... I JUST... I STOPPED HIM. I NEEDED TO STOP HIM.
WELL, YOU DID THE JOB, SON... DOESN'T LOOK LIKE MUCH OF A THREAT NOW, DOES HE?
WHATEVER YOU SAY, OFFICER.

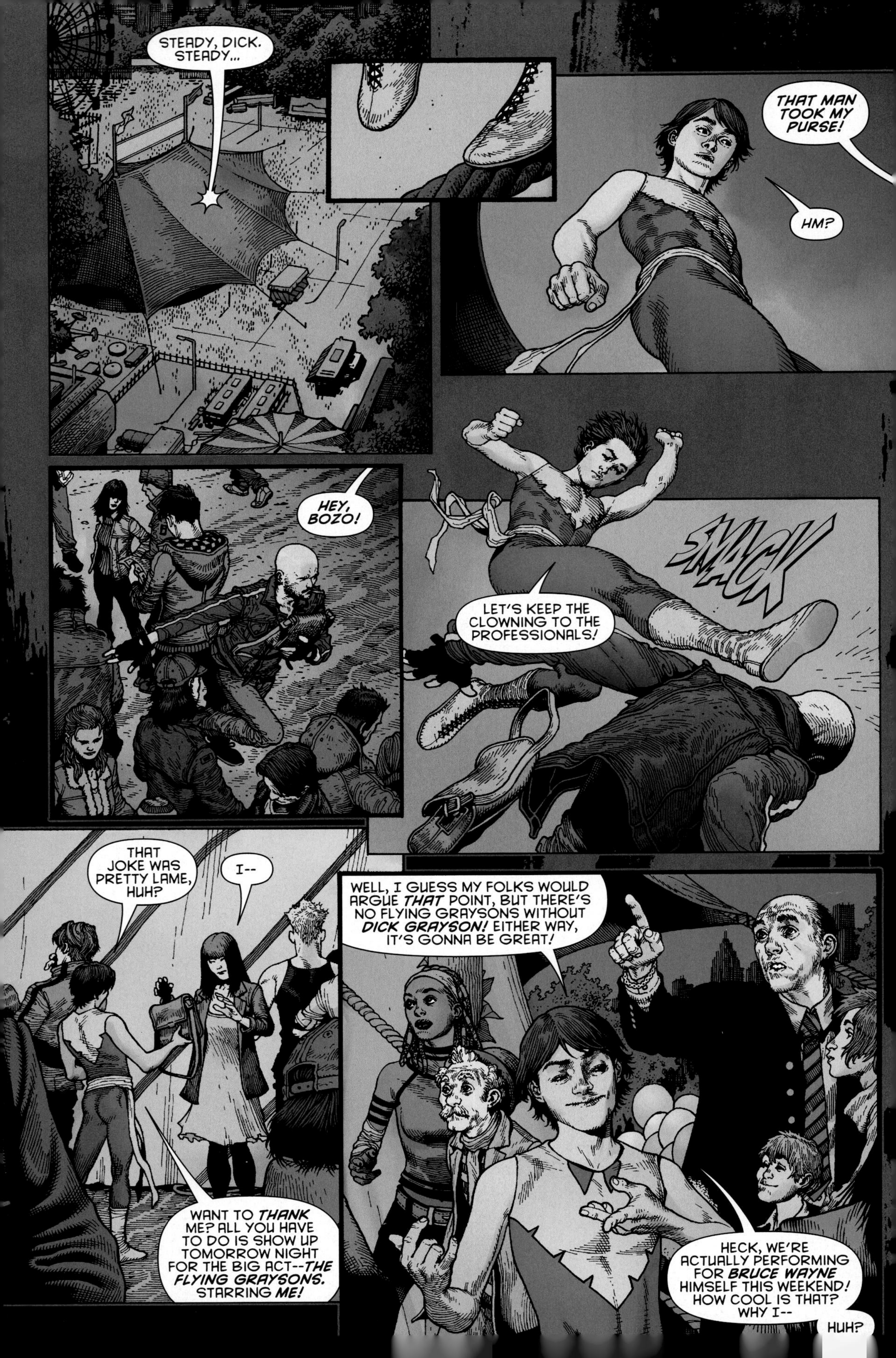
STEADY, DICK. STEADY...
THAT MAN TOOK MY PURSE!
HM?
HEY, BOZO!
SMACK
LET'S KEEP THE CLOWNING TO THE PROFESSIONALS!
THAT JOKE WAS PRETTY LAME, HUH?
I--
WANT TO THANK ME? ALL YOU HAVE TO DO IS SHOW UP TOMORROW NIGHT FOR THE BIG ACT--THE FLYING GRAYSONS. STARRING ME!
WELL, I GUESS MY FOLKS WOULD ARGUE THAT POINT, BUT THERE'S NO FLYING GRAYSONS WITHOUT DICK GRAYSON! EITHER WAY, IT'S GONNA BE GREAT!
HECK, WE'RE ACTUALLY PERFORMING FOR BRUCE WAYNE HIMSELF THIS WEEKEND! HOW COOL IS THAT? WHY I--
HUH?

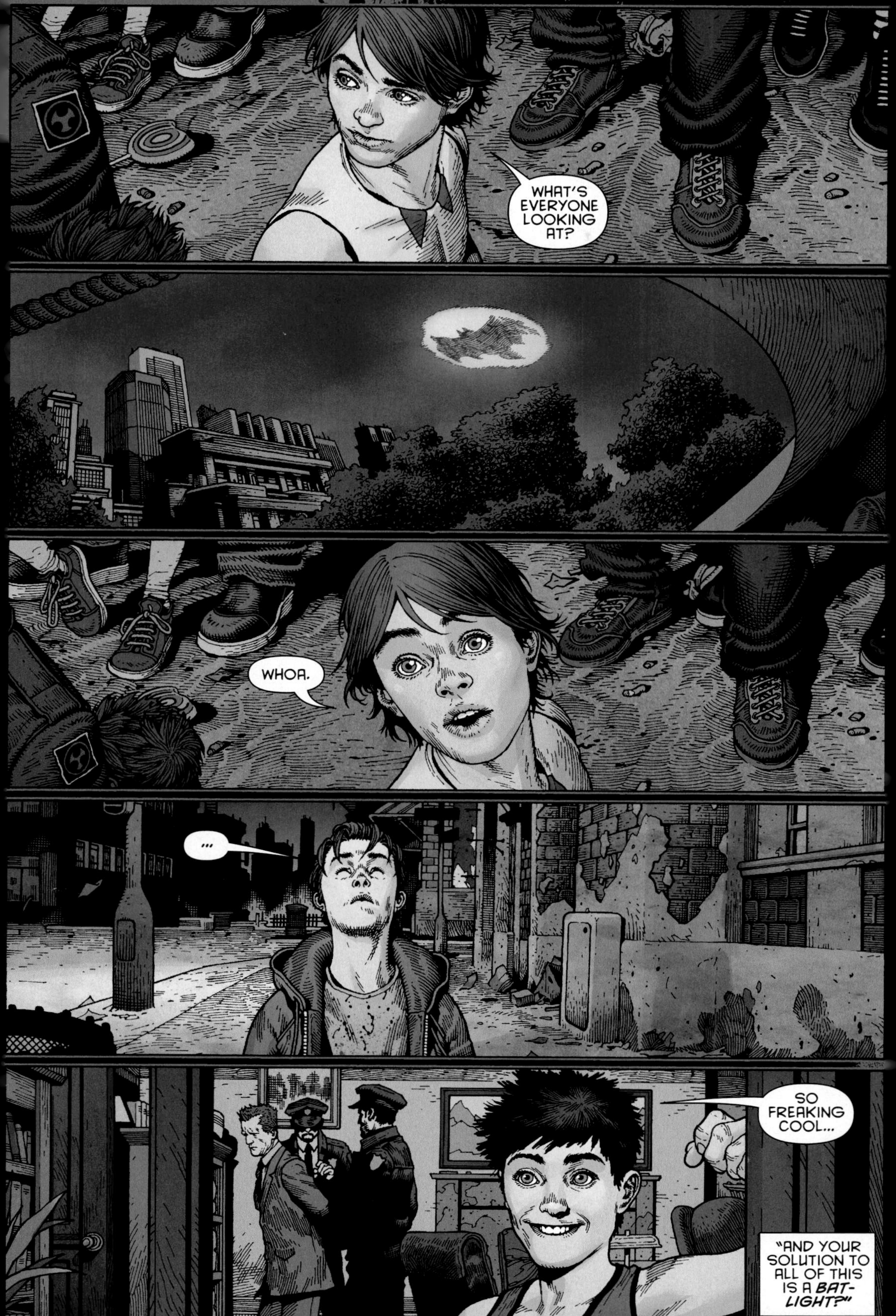
WHAT'S EVERYONE LOOKING AT?
WHOA.
...
SO FREAKING COOL...
"AND YOUR SOLUTION TO ALL OF THIS IS A BAT-LIGHT?"

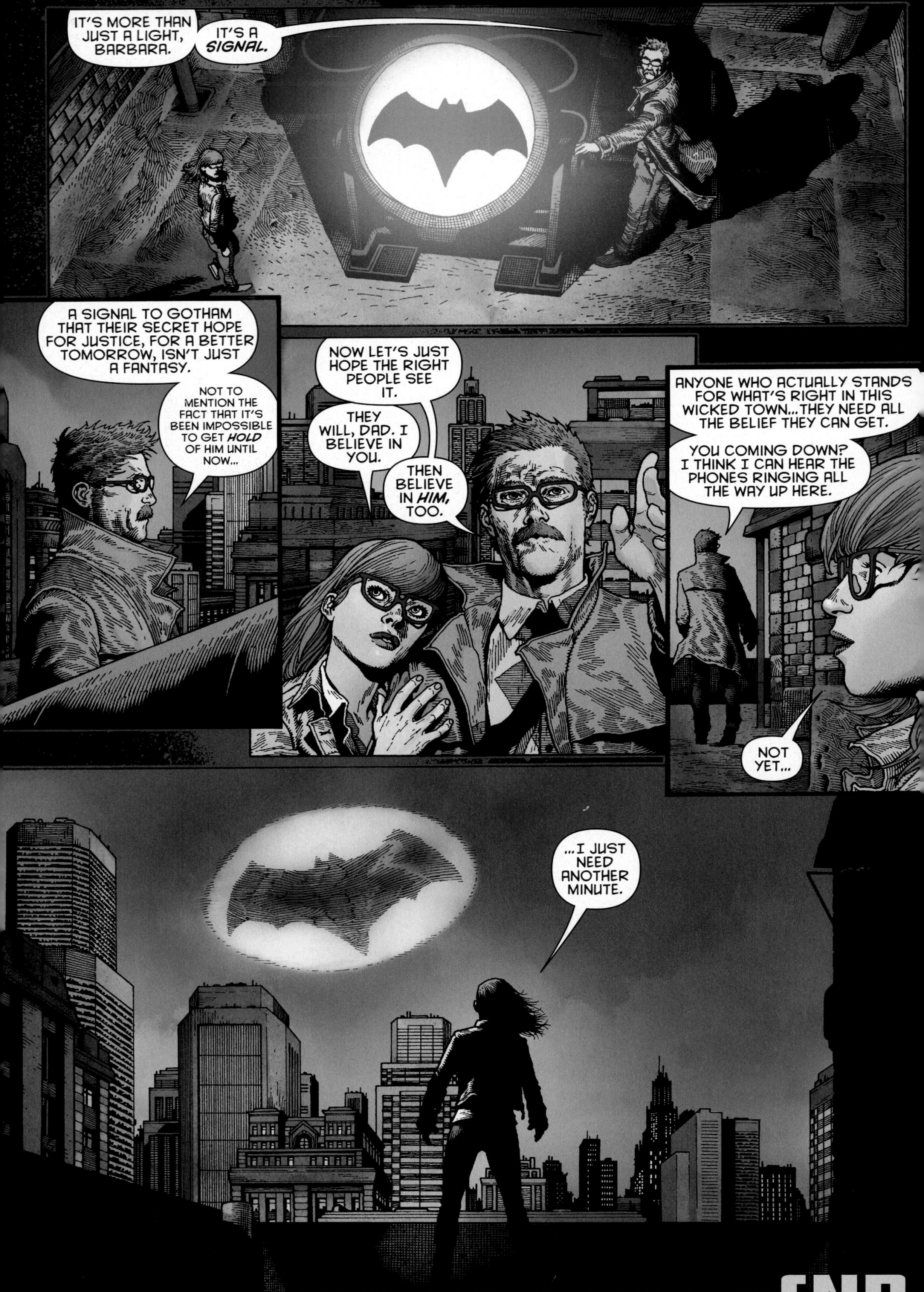
IT'S MORE THAN JUST A LIGHT, BARBARA.
IT'S A *SIGNAL.*
A SIGNAL TO GOTHAM THAT THEIR SECRET HOPE FOR JUSTICE, FOR A BETTER TOMORROW, ISN'T JUST A FANTASY.
NOT TO MENTION THE FACT THAT IT'S BEEN IMPOSSIBLE TO GET *HOLD* OF HIM UNTIL NOW...
NOW LET'S JUST HOPE THE RIGHT PEOPLE SEE IT.
THEY WILL, DAD. I BELIEVE IN YOU.
THEN BELIEVE IN *HIM,* TOO.
ANYONE WHO ACTUALLY STANDS FOR WHAT'S RIGHT IN THIS WICKED TOWN...THEY NEED ALL THE BELIEF THEY CAN GET.
YOU COMING DOWN? I THINK I CAN HEAR THE PHONES RINGING ALL THE WAY UP HERE.
NOT YET...
...I JUST NEED ANOTHER MINUTE.
END

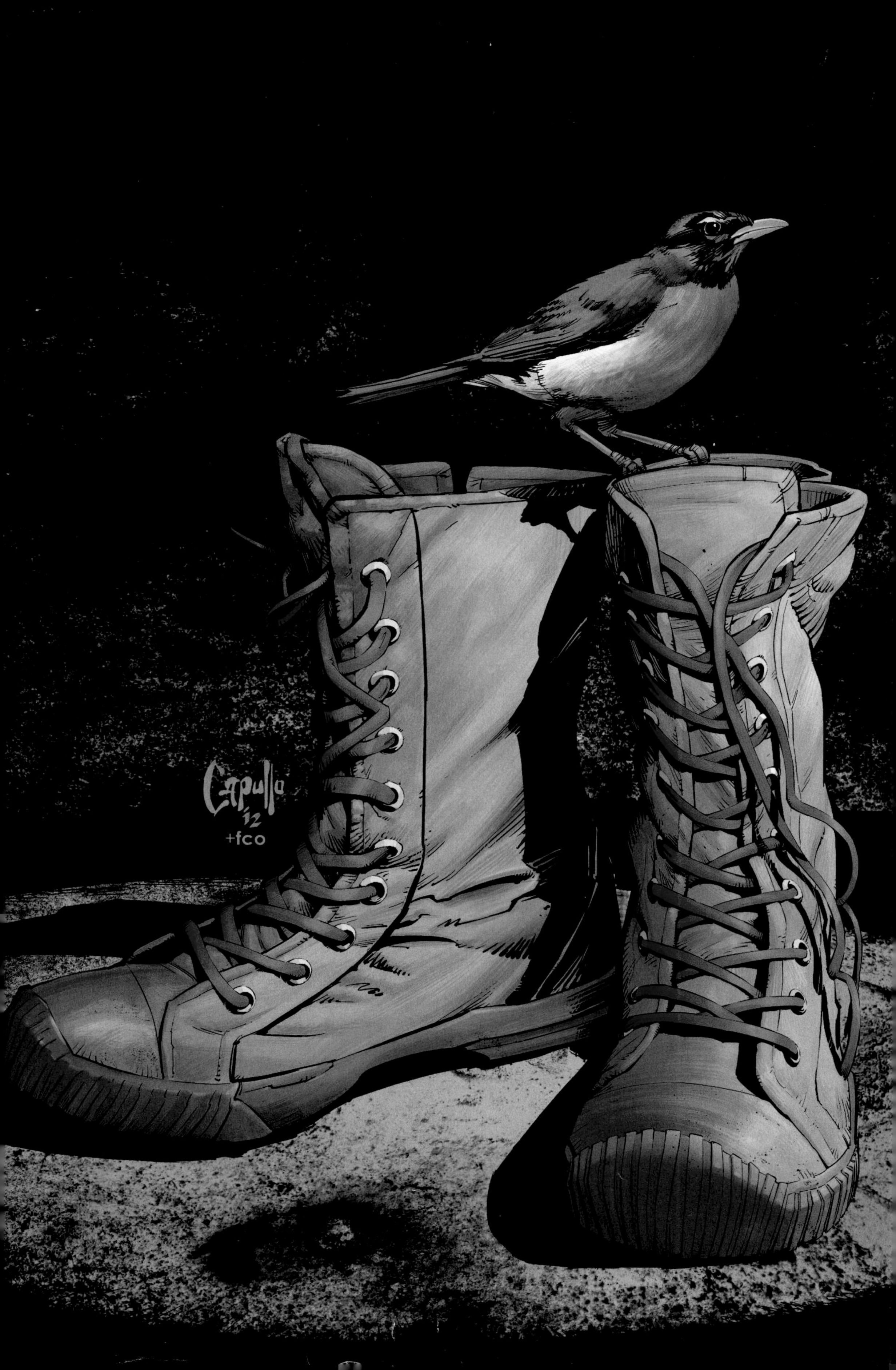
Capullo '12
+fco

RESOLVE

Chapter One **SCOTT SNYDER** writer **ANDY KUBERT** penciller **SANDRA HOPE** inker **BRAD ANDERSON** colorist
Chapter Two **SCOTT SNYDER JAMES TYNION IV** writers **ALEX MALEEV** artist **NATHAN FAIRBAIRN** colorist
cover by **GREG CAPULLO & FCO PLASCENCIA**

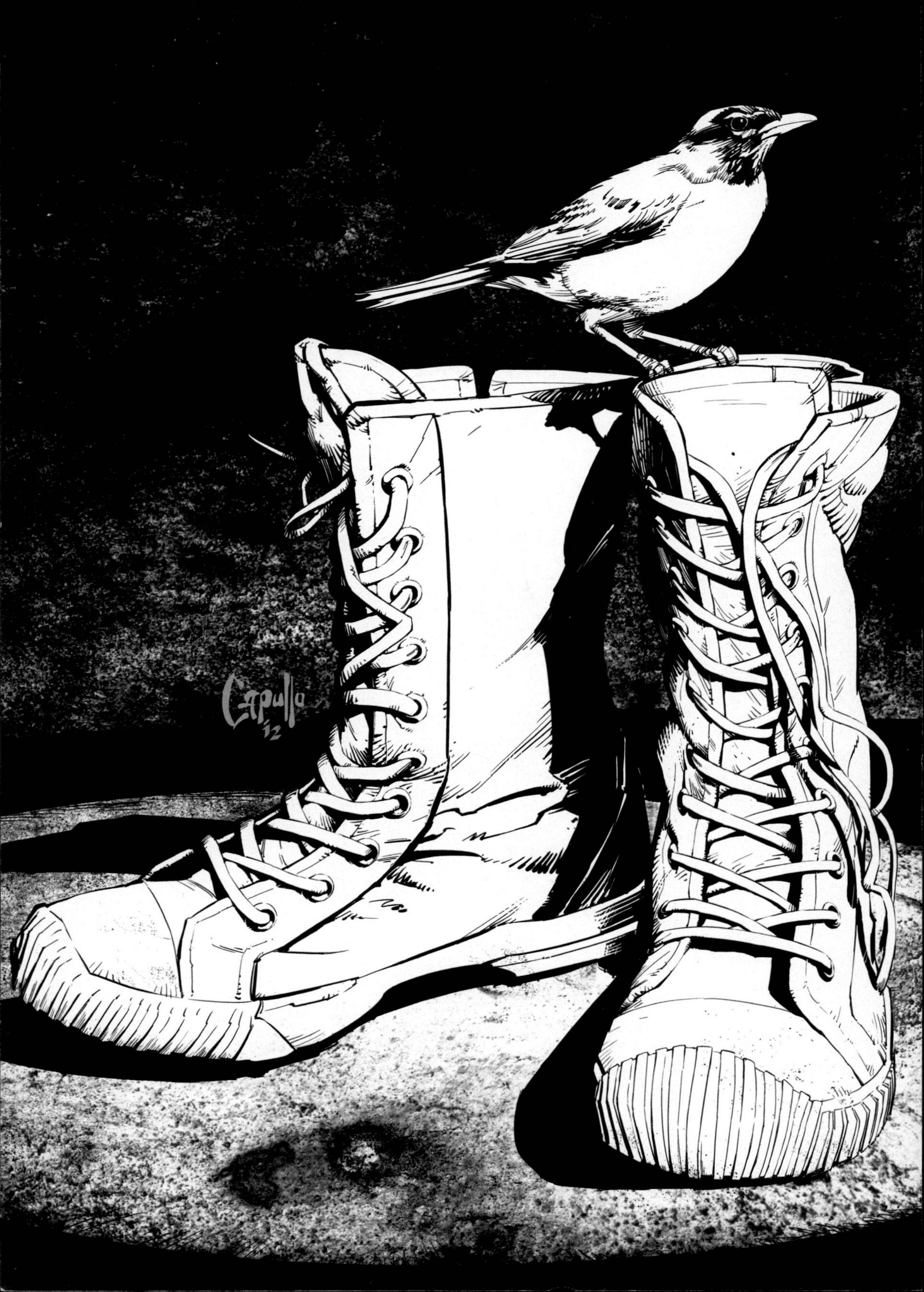
Capullo '12

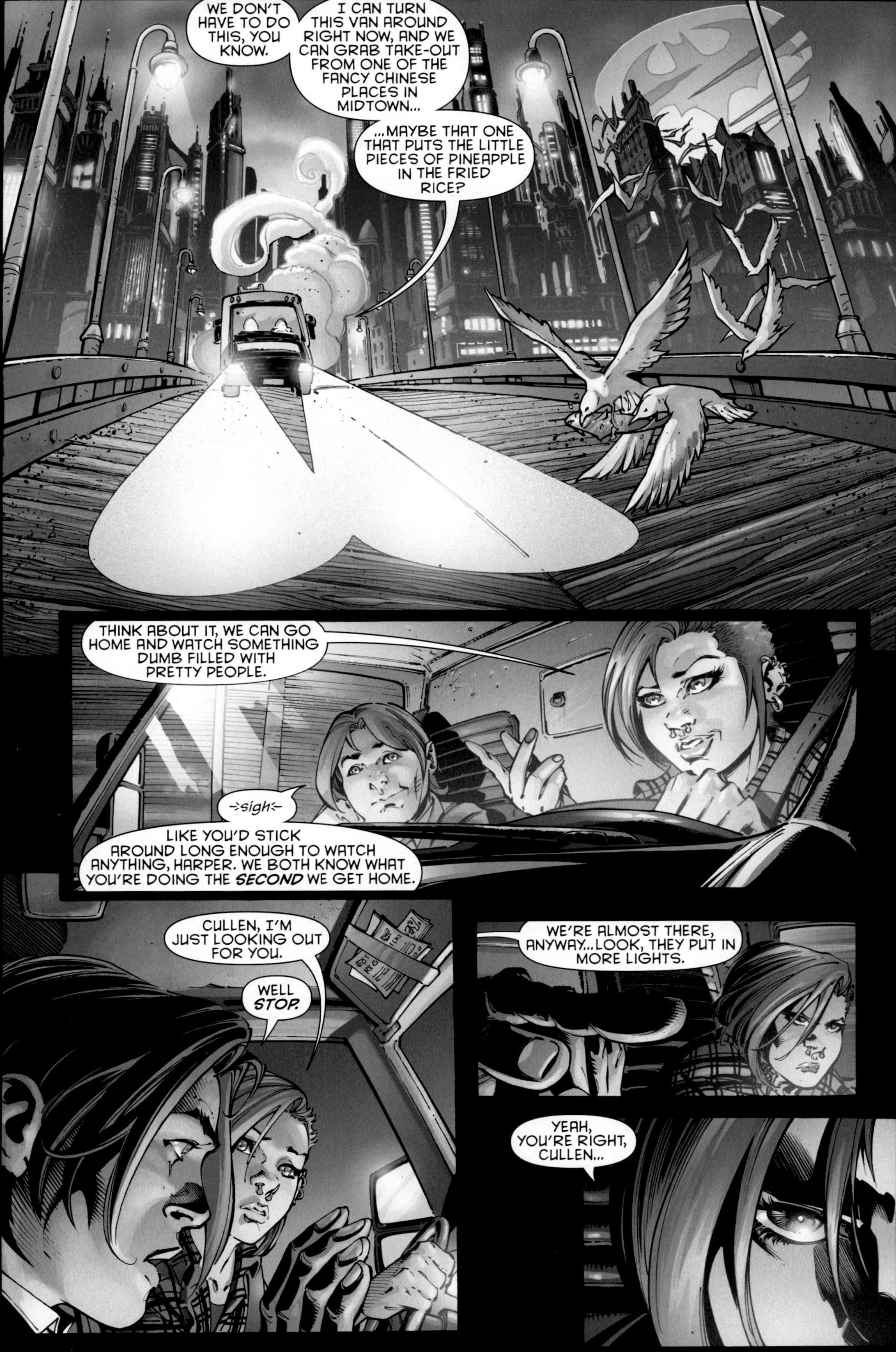
WE DON'T HAVE TO DO THIS, YOU KNOW.
I CAN TURN THIS VAN AROUND RIGHT NOW, AND WE CAN GRAB TAKE-OUT FROM ONE OF THE FANCY CHINESE PLACES IN MIDTOWN...
...MAYBE THAT ONE THAT PUTS THE LITTLE PIECES OF PINEAPPLE IN THE FRIED RICE?
THINK ABOUT IT, WE CAN GO HOME AND WATCH SOMETHING DUMB FILLED WITH PRETTY PEOPLE.
-sigh-
LIKE YOU'D STICK AROUND LONG ENOUGH TO WATCH ANYTHING, HARPER. WE BOTH KNOW WHAT YOU'RE DOING THE SECOND WE GET HOME.
CULLEN, I'M JUST LOOKING OUT FOR YOU.
WELL STOP.
WE'RE ALMOST THERE, ANYWAY...LOOK, THEY PUT IN MORE LIGHTS.
YEAH, YOU'RE RIGHT, CULLEN...

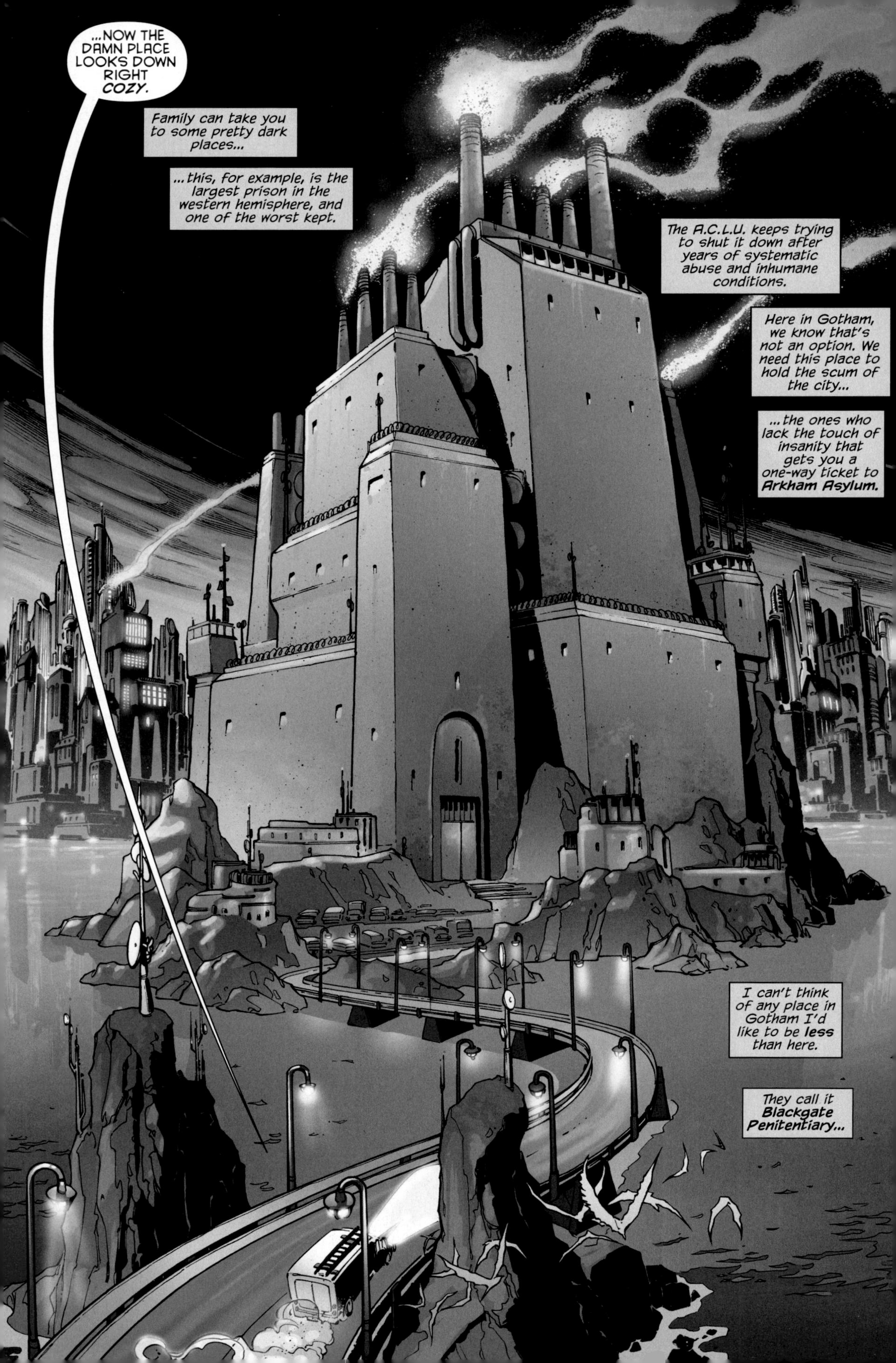
...NOW THE DAMN PLACE LOOKS DOWN RIGHT COZY.
Family can take you to some pretty dark places...
...this, for example, is the largest prison in the western hemisphere, and one of the worst kept.
The A.C.L.U. keeps trying to shut it down after years of systematic abuse and inhumane conditions.
Here in Gotham, we know that's not an option. We need this place to hold the scum of the city...
...the ones who lack the touch of insanity that gets you a one-way ticket to Arkham Asylum.
I can't think of any place in Gotham I'd like to be less than here.
They call it Blackgate Penitentiary...

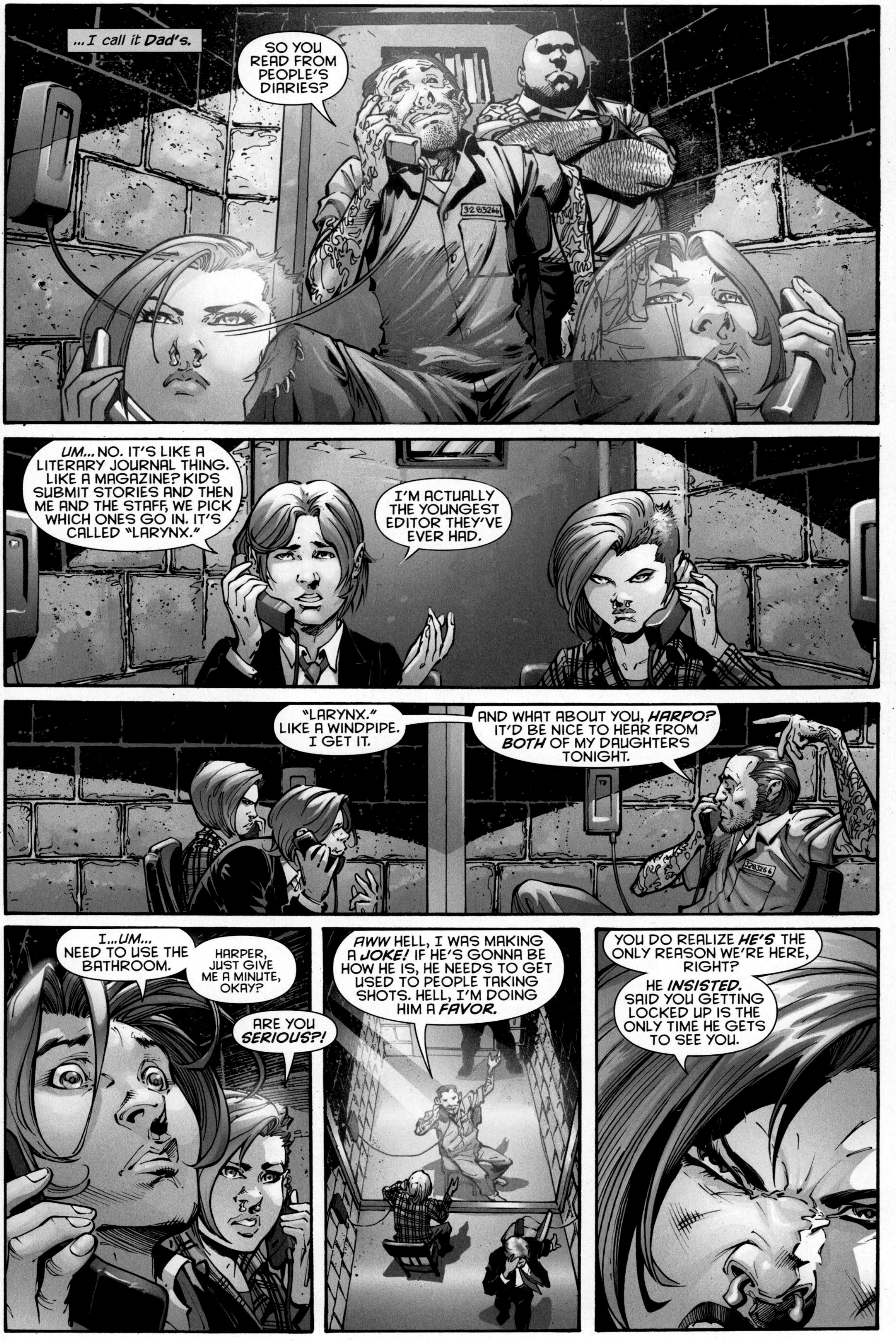
...I call it Dad's.
SO YOU READ FROM PEOPLE'S DIARIES?
UM... NO. IT'S LIKE A LITERARY JOURNAL THING. LIKE A MAGAZINE? KIDS SUBMIT STORIES AND THEN ME AND THE STAFF, WE PICK WHICH ONES GO IN. IT'S CALLED "LARYNX."
I'M ACTUALLY THE YOUNGEST EDITOR THEY'VE EVER HAD.
"LARYNX." LIKE A WINDPIPE. I GET IT.
AND WHAT ABOUT YOU, HARPO? IT'D BE NICE TO HEAR FROM BOTH OF MY DAUGHTERS TONIGHT.
I...UM... NEED TO USE THE BATHROOM.
HARPER, JUST GIVE ME A MINUTE, OKAY?
ARE YOU SERIOUS?!
AWW HELL, I WAS MAKING A JOKE! IF HE'S GONNA BE HOW HE IS, HE NEEDS TO GET USED TO PEOPLE TAKING SHOTS. HELL, I'M DOING HIM A FAVOR.
YOU DO REALIZE HE'S THE ONLY REASON WE'RE HERE, RIGHT?
HE INSISTED. SAID YOU GETTING LOCKED UP IS THE ONLY TIME HE GETS TO SEE YOU.

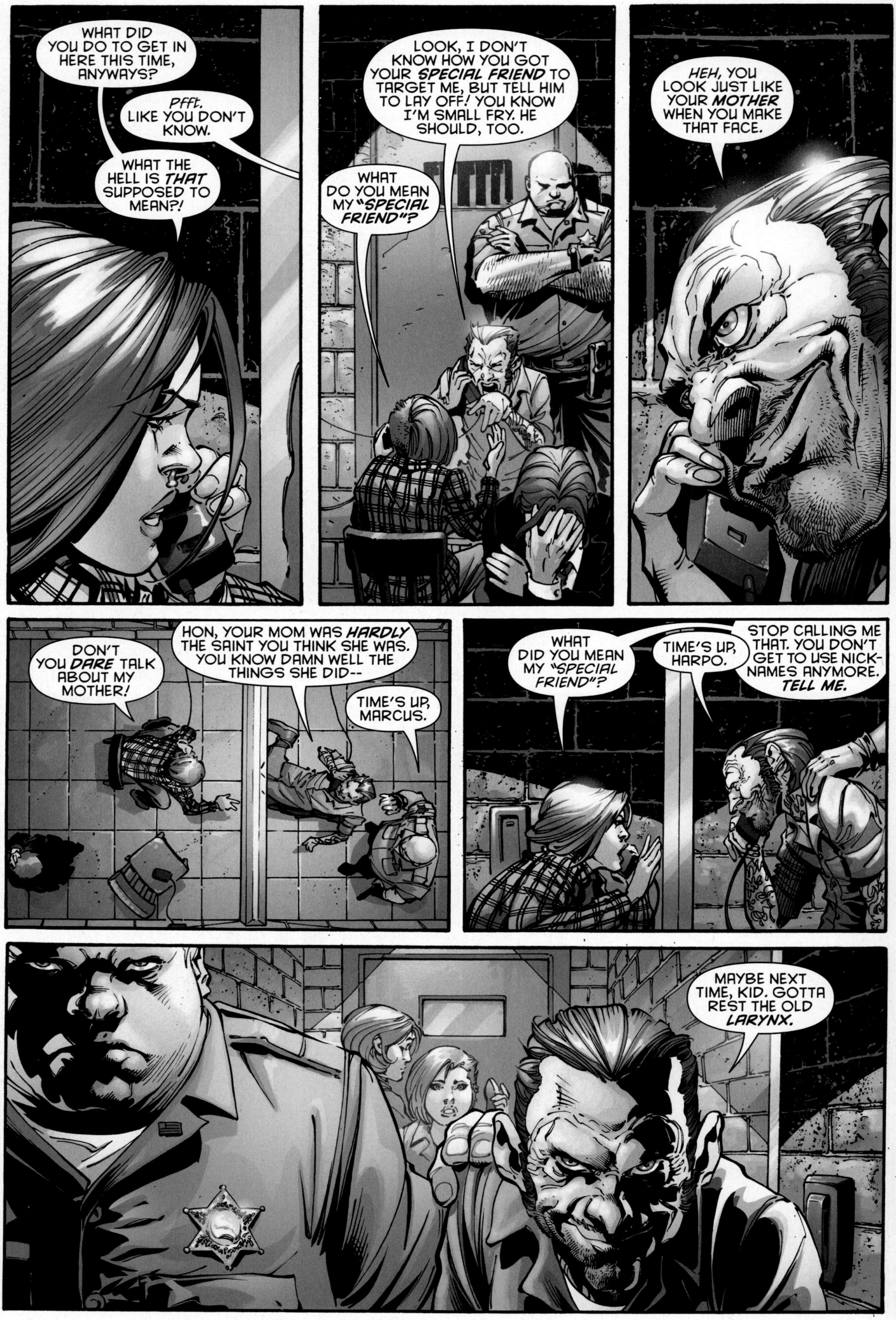
WHAT DID YOU DO TO GET IN HERE THIS TIME, ANYWAYS?
PFFT. LIKE YOU DON'T KNOW.
WHAT THE HELL IS *THAT* SUPPOSED TO MEAN?!
LOOK, I DON'T KNOW HOW YOU GOT YOUR *SPECIAL FRIEND* TO TARGET ME, BUT TELL HIM TO LAY OFF! YOU KNOW I'M SMALL FRY. HE SHOULD, TOO.
WHAT DO YOU MEAN MY "*SPECIAL FRIEND*"?
HEH, YOU LOOK JUST LIKE YOUR *MOTHER* WHEN YOU MAKE THAT FACE.
DON'T YOU *DARE* TALK ABOUT MY MOTHER!
HON, YOUR MOM WAS *HARDLY* THE SAINT YOU THINK SHE WAS. YOU KNOW DAMN WELL THE THINGS SHE DID--
TIME'S UP, MARCUS.
WHAT DID YOU MEAN MY "*SPECIAL FRIEND*"?
TIME'S UP, HARPO.
STOP CALLING ME THAT. YOU DON'T GET TO USE NICK-NAMES ANYMORE. ***TELL ME.***
MAYBE NEXT TIME, KID. GOTTA REST THE OLD *LARYNX.*

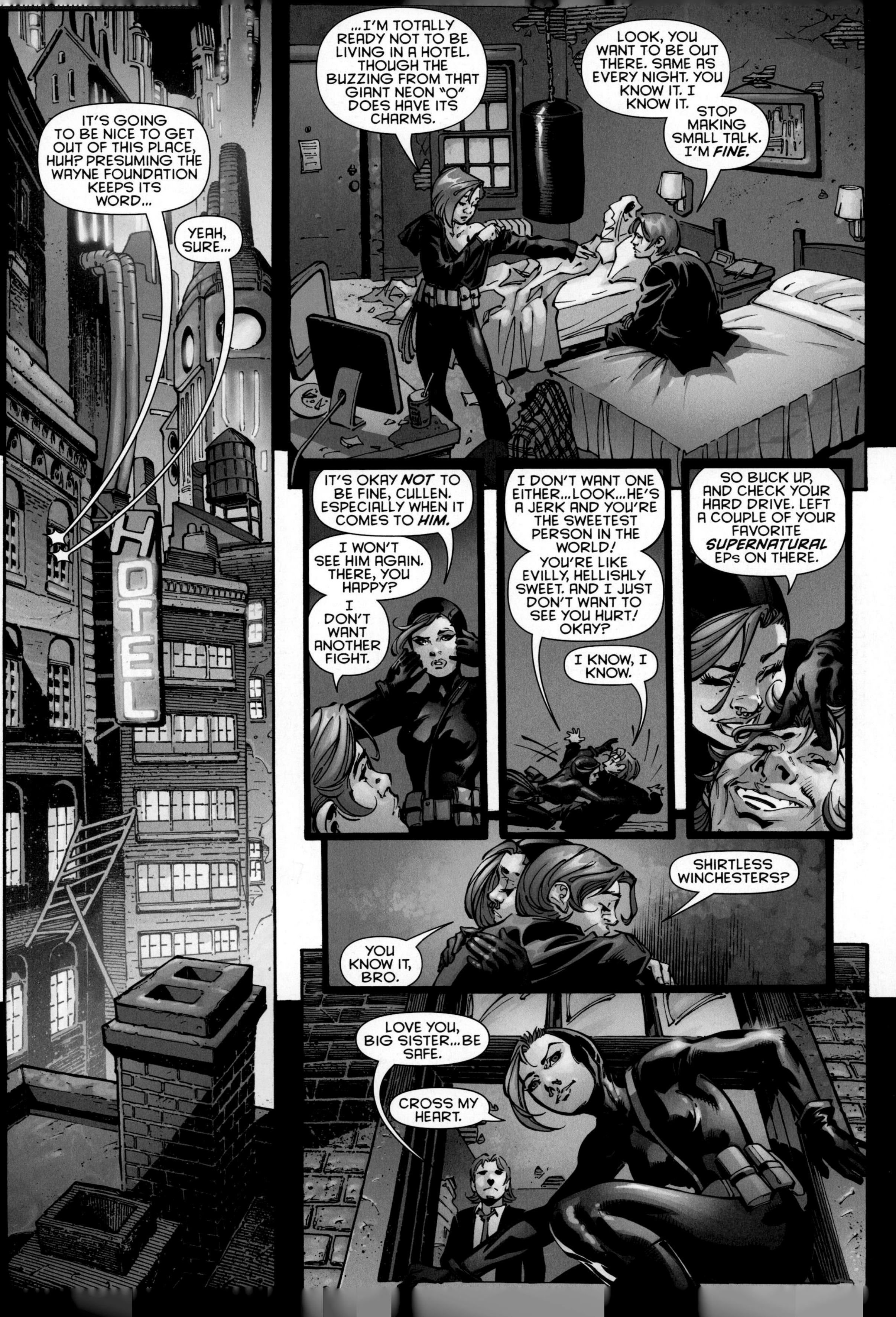
IT'S GOING TO BE NICE TO GET OUT OF THIS PLACE, HUH? PRESUMING THE WAYNE FOUNDATION KEEPS ITS WORD...
YEAH, SURE...
HOTEL
...I'M TOTALLY READY NOT TO BE LIVING IN A HOTEL. THOUGH THE BUZZING FROM THAT GIANT NEON "O" DOES HAVE ITS CHARMS.
LOOK, YOU WANT TO BE OUT THERE. SAME AS EVERY NIGHT. YOU KNOW IT. I KNOW IT.
STOP MAKING SMALL TALK. I'M FINE.
IT'S OKAY NOT TO BE FINE, CULLEN. ESPECIALLY WHEN IT COMES TO HIM.
I WON'T SEE HIM AGAIN. THERE, YOU HAPPY?
I DON'T WANT ANOTHER FIGHT.
I DON'T WANT ONE EITHER...LOOK...HE'S A JERK AND YOU'RE THE SWEETEST PERSON IN THE WORLD!
YOU'RE LIKE EVILLY, HELLISHLY SWEET. AND I JUST DON'T WANT TO SEE YOU HURT! OKAY?
I KNOW, I KNOW.
SO BUCK UP, AND CHECK YOUR HARD DRIVE. LEFT A COUPLE OF YOUR FAVORITE SUPERNATURAL EPs ON THERE.
SHIRTLESS WINCHESTERS?
YOU KNOW IT, BRO.
LOVE YOU, BIG SISTER...BE SAFE.
CROSS MY HEART.

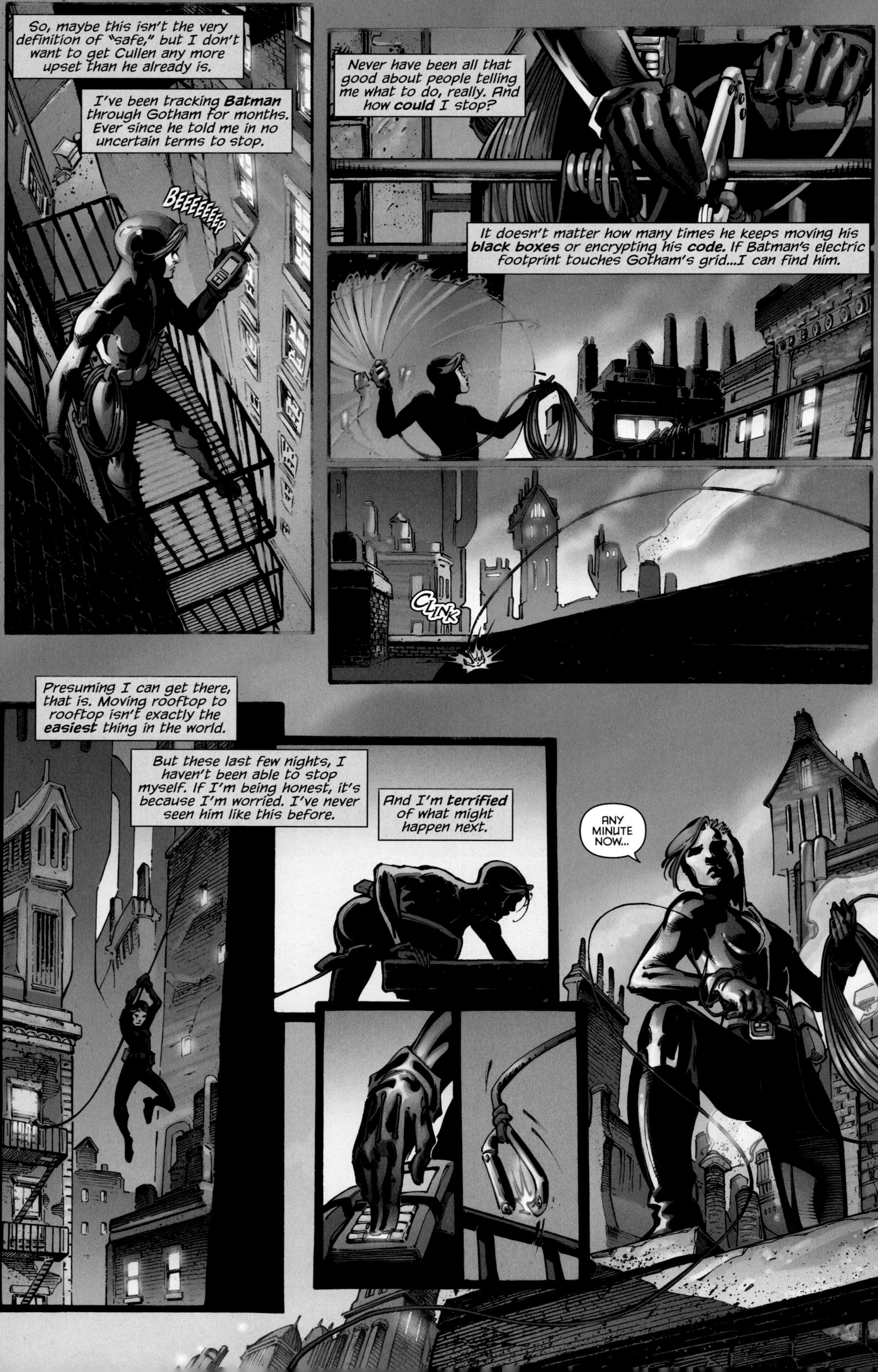

So, maybe this isn't the very definition of "safe," but I don't want to get Cullen any more upset than he already is.
I've been tracking Batman through Gotham for months. Ever since he told me in no uncertain terms to stop.
BEEEEEEEP
Never have been all that good about people telling me what to do, really. And how could I stop?
It doesn't matter how many times he keeps moving his black boxes or encrypting his code. If Batman's electric footprint touches Gotham's grid...I can find him.
CLINK
Presuming I can get there, that is. Moving rooftop to rooftop isn't exactly the easiest thing in the world.
But these last few nights, I haven't been able to stop myself. If I'm being honest, it's because I'm worried. I've never seen him like this before.
And I'm terrified of what might happen next.
ANY MINUTE NOW...

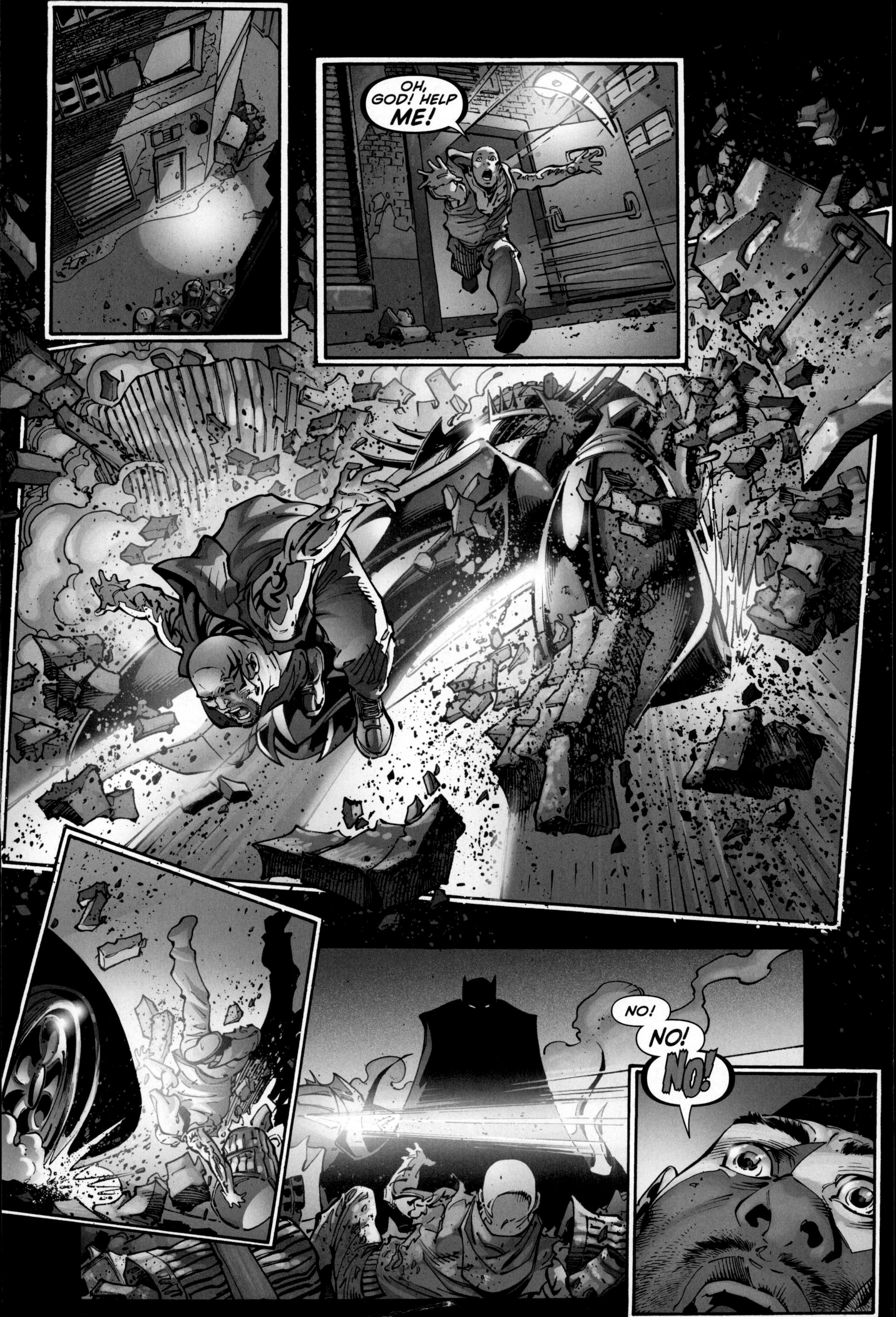
OH, GOD! HELP ME!
NO!
NO!
NO!

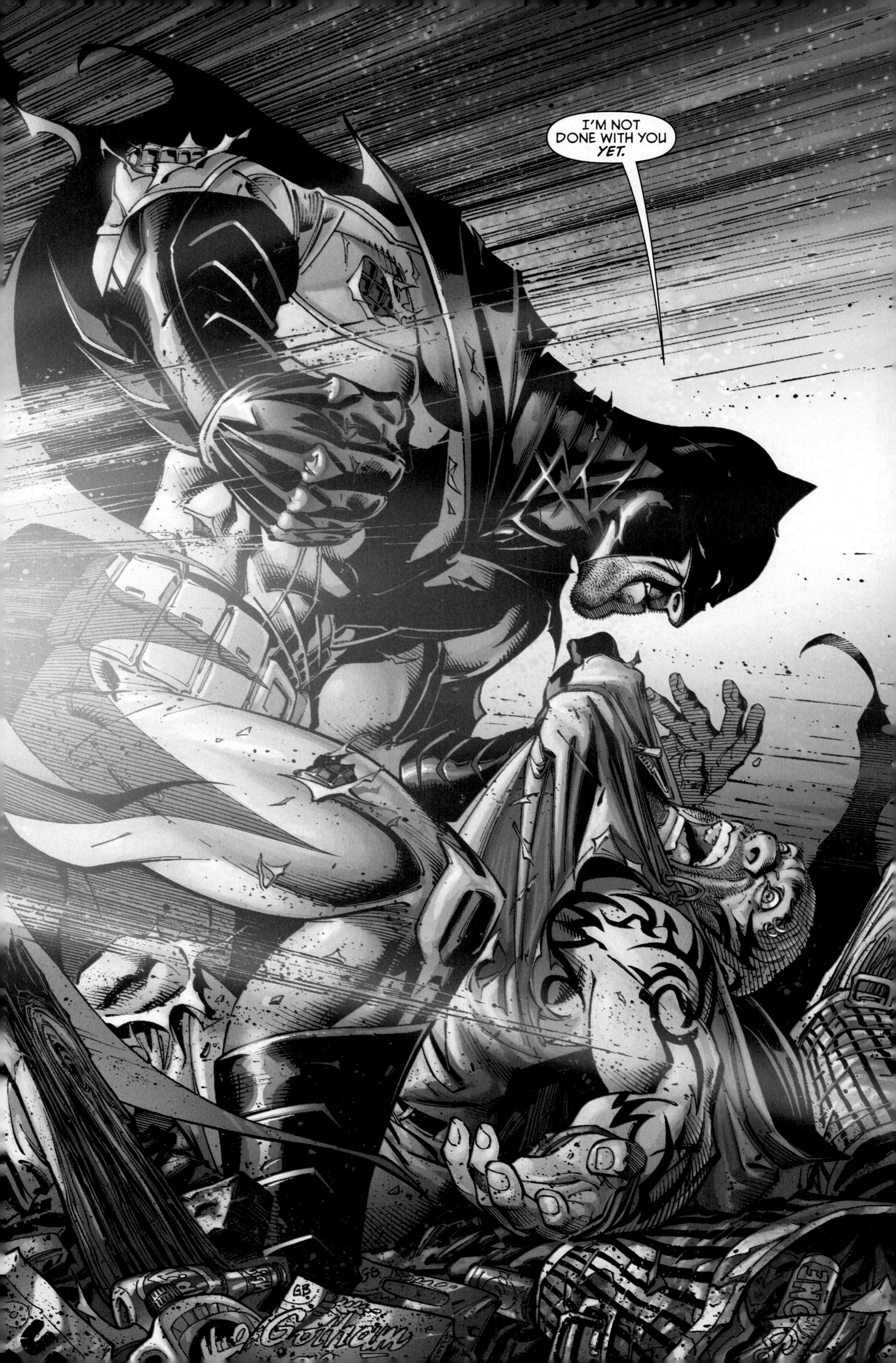
I'M NOT DONE WITH YOU *YET.*

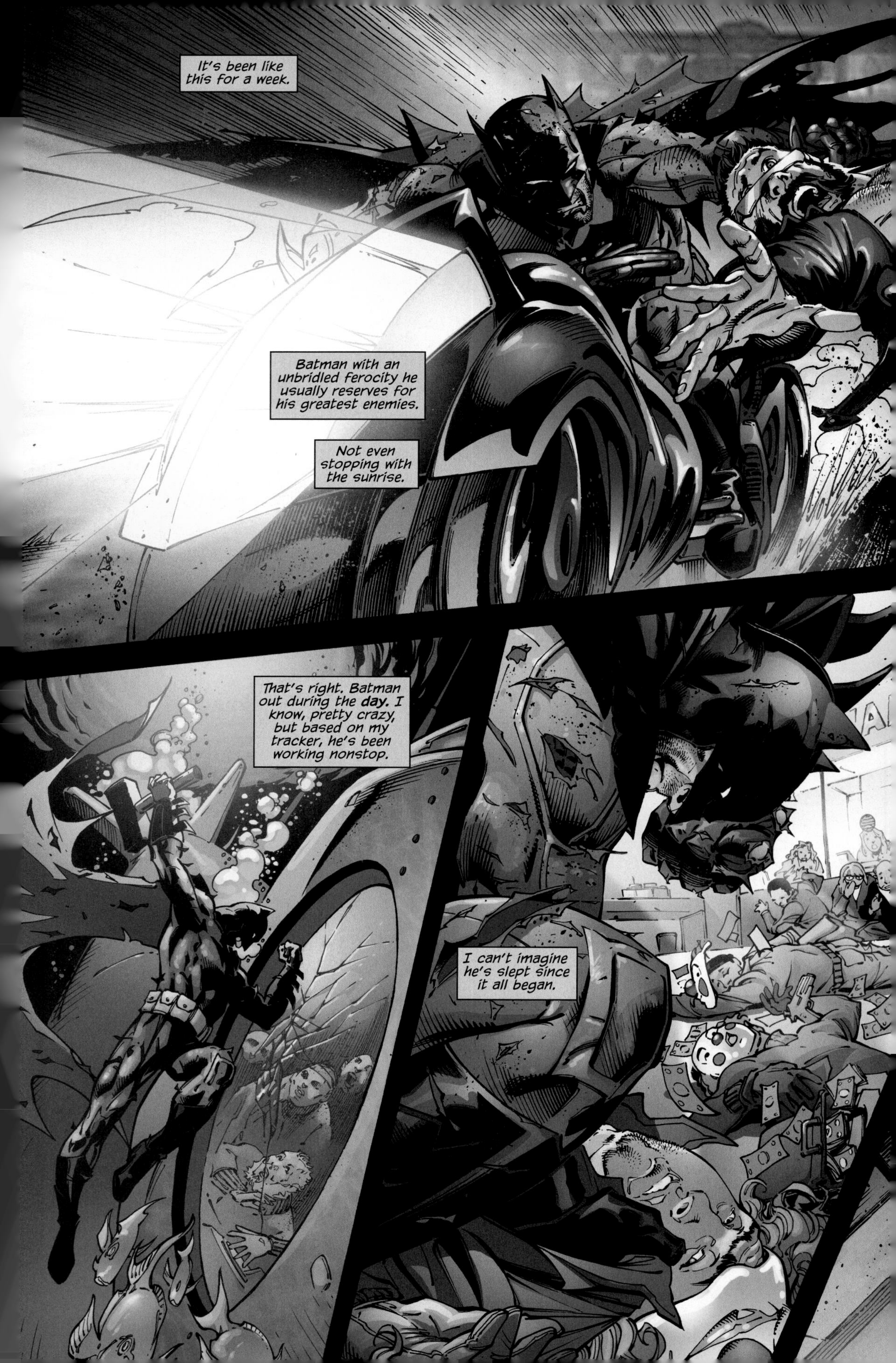
It's been like this for a week.
Batman with an unbridled ferocity he usually reserves for his greatest enemies.
Not even stopping with the sunrise.
That's right. Batman out during the day. I know, pretty crazy, but based on my tracker, he's been working nonstop.
I can't imagine he's slept since it all began.

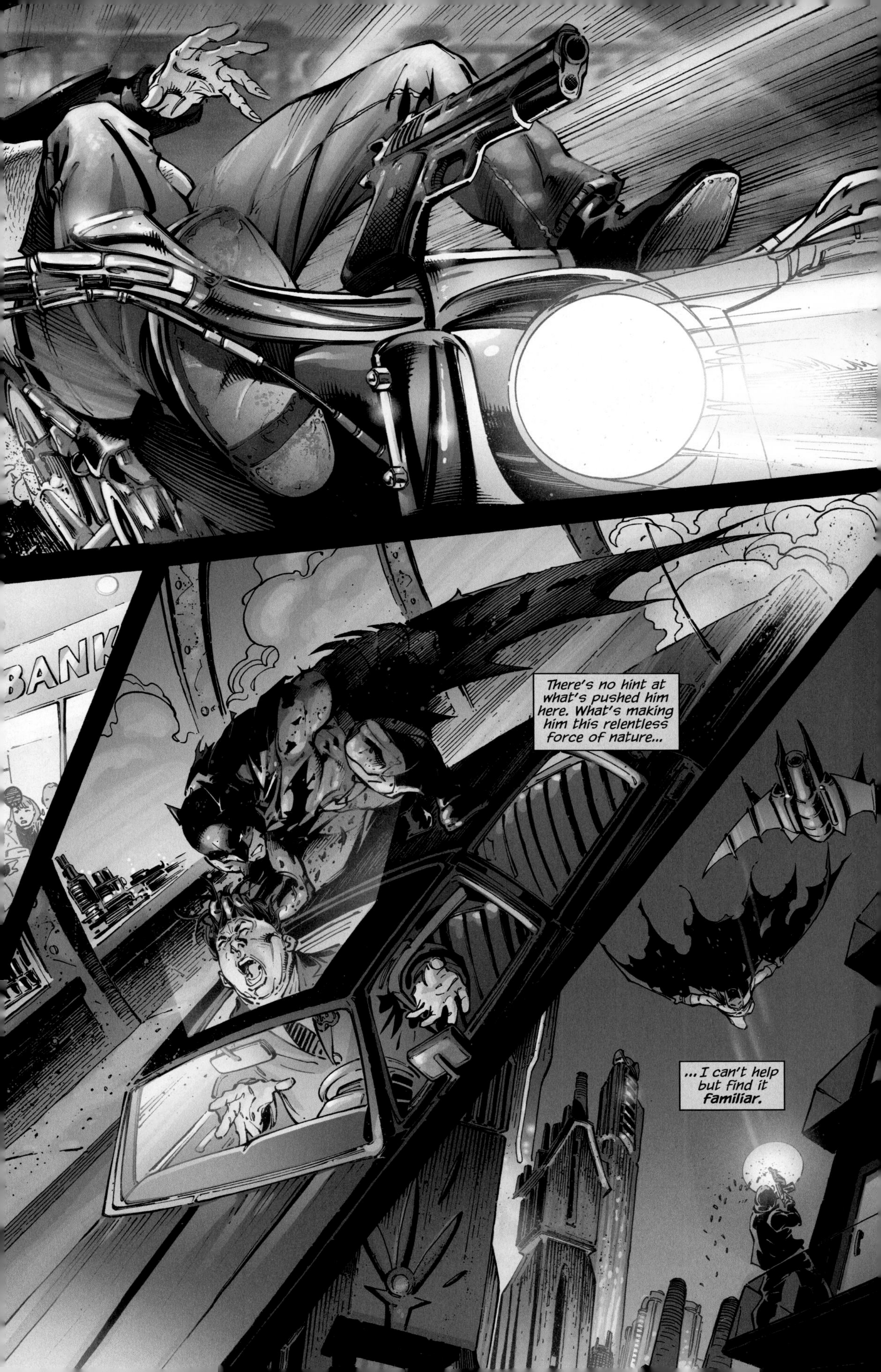
BANK
There's no hint at what's pushed him here. What's making him this relentless force of nature...
...I can't help but find it familiar.

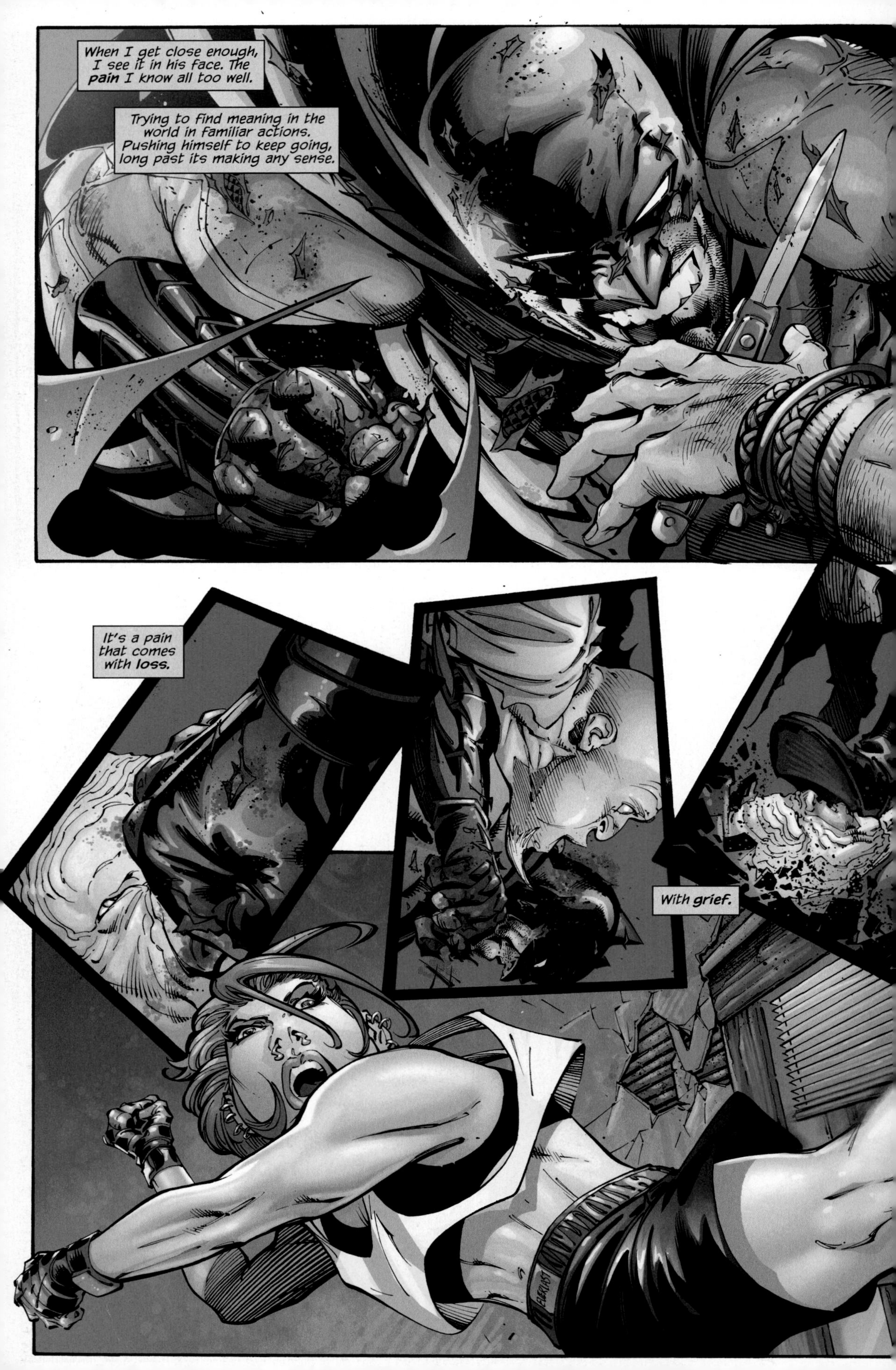
When I get close enough, I see it in his face. The pain I know all too well.
Trying to find meaning in the world in familiar actions. Pushing himself to keep going, long past its making any sense.
It's a pain that comes with loss.
With grief.

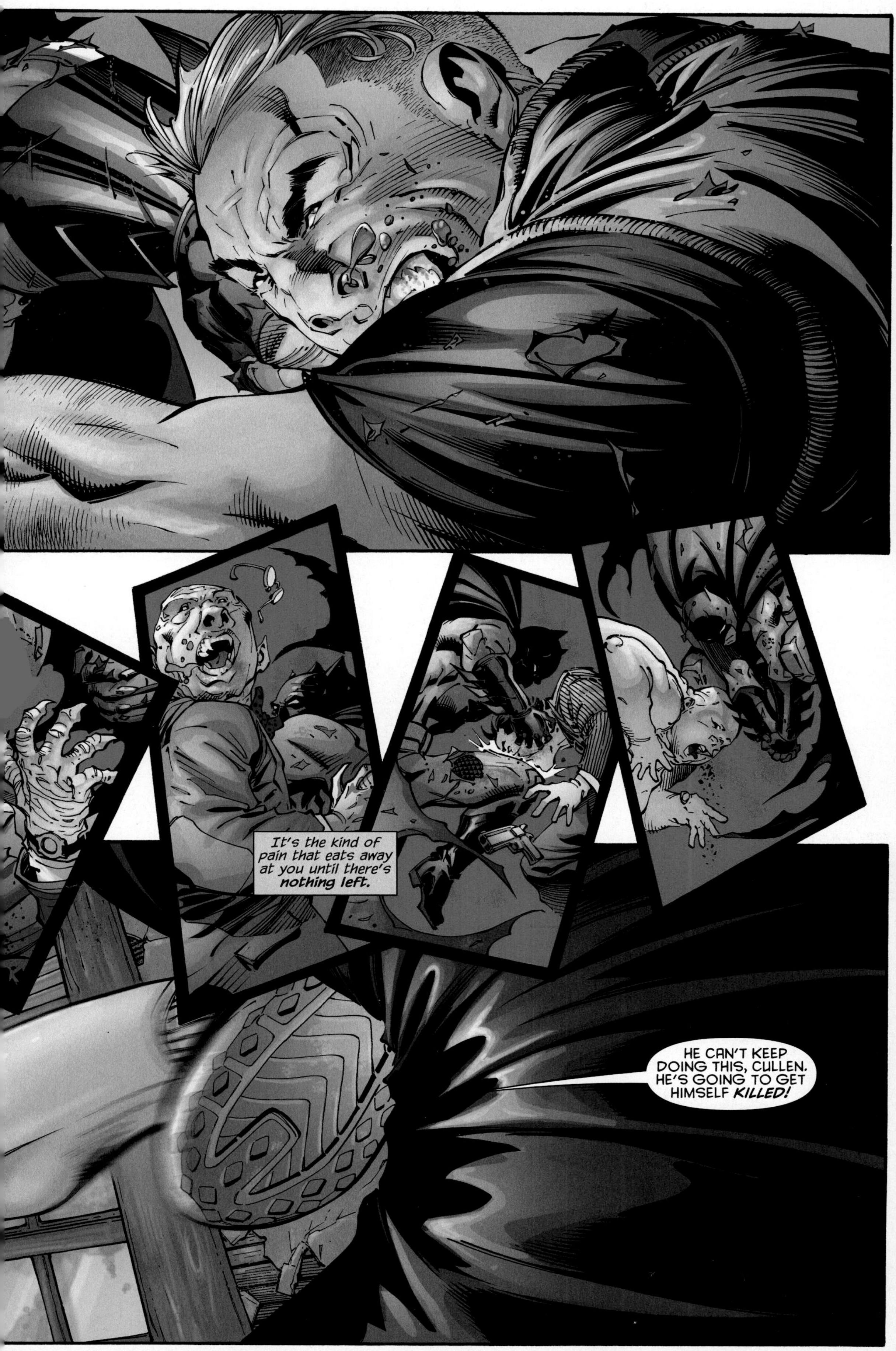
It's the kind of pain that eats away at you until there's nothing left.
HE CAN'T KEEP DOING THIS, CULLEN. HE'S GOING TO GET HIMSELF KILLED!

WAIT, WHAT ARE WE *TALKING* ABOUT?

BATMAN, CULLEN. WE'RE ALWAYS TALKING ABOUT BATMAN. THIS TIME IS NO DIFFERENT.

WELL, I'M NOT EXACTLY SURE THAT YOU WATCHING HIM FOR A FEW MONTHS MAKES YOU AN *EXPERT.*

I'M BEING *SERIOUS!*

EVERY DAY IT'S A LITTLE WORSE. YESTERDAY, I SAW HIM GET STABBED IN THE LEG BY A MUGGER...

I'M SURE HE GETS HIT LIKE THAT ALL THE TIME.

BY NINJA CYBORG ASSASSINS! NOT HALF-DRUNK, BACK ALLEY MUGGERS!

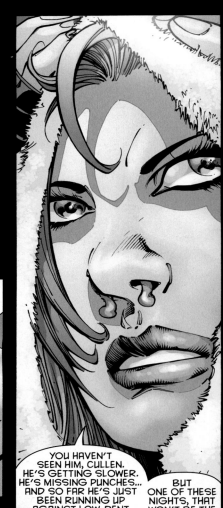

THE IDEA THAT SOME *NOBODY* COULD GET THAT CLOSE, AND HURT HIM...ACTUALLY *HURT* HIM...IT'S *TERRIFYING.*

HE'S *BATMAN!* HE'S GOING TO BE FINE.

YOU HAVEN'T SEEN HIM, CULLEN. HE'S GETTING SLOWER. HE'S MISSING PUNCHES... AND SO FAR HE'S JUST BEEN RUNNING UP AGAINST LOW-RENT NOBODIES.

BUT ONE OF THESE NIGHTS, THAT WON'T BE THE CASE.

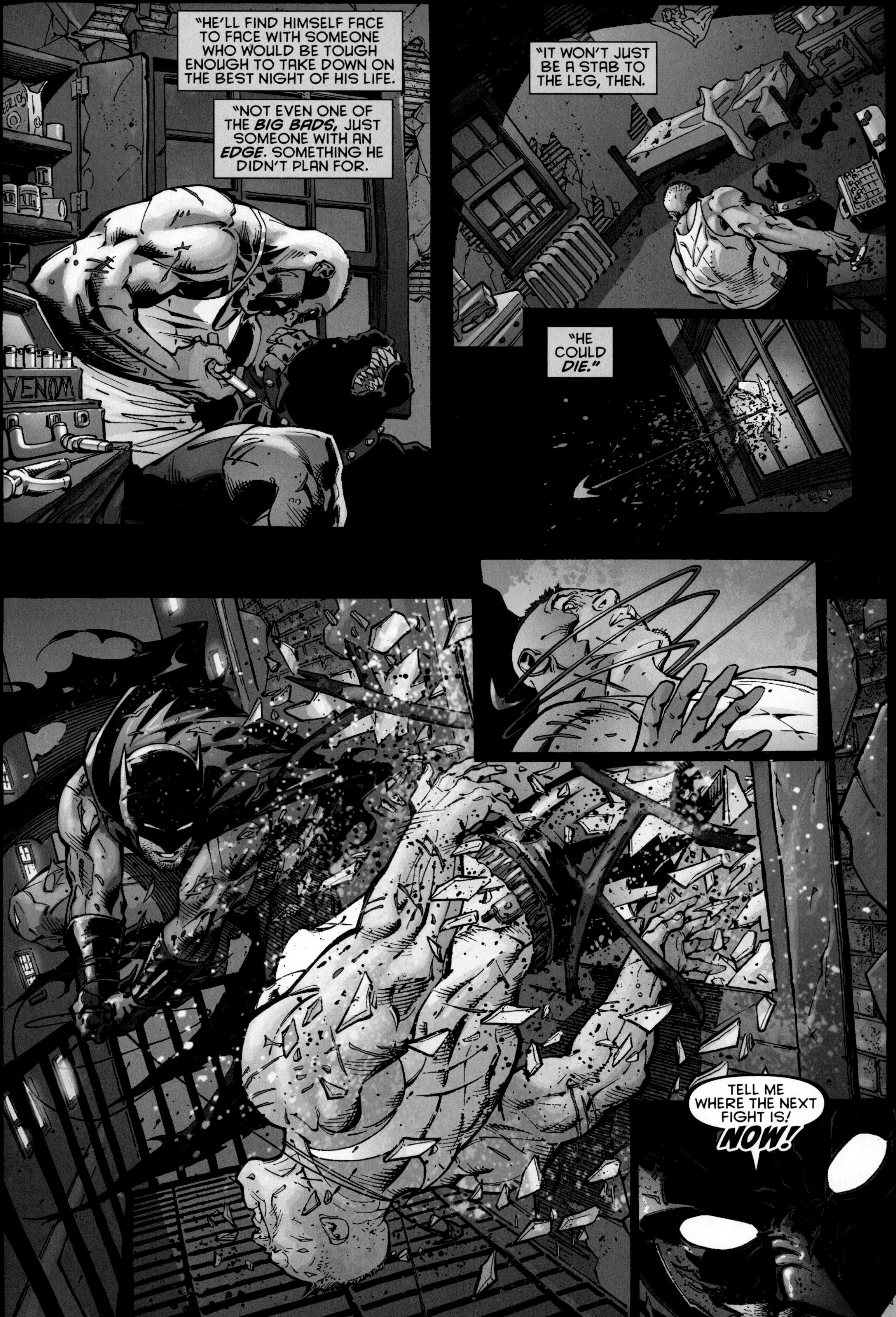
"HE'LL FIND HIMSELF FACE TO FACE WITH SOMEONE WHO WOULD BE TOUGH ENOUGH TO TAKE DOWN ON THE BEST NIGHT OF HIS LIFE.
"NOT EVEN ONE OF THE *BIG BADS,* JUST SOMEONE WITH AN *EDGE*. SOMETHING HE DIDN'T PLAN FOR.
VENOM
"IT WON'T JUST BE A STAB TO THE LEG, THEN.
"HE COULD *DIE.*"
TELL ME WHERE THE NEXT FIGHT IS! *NOW!*

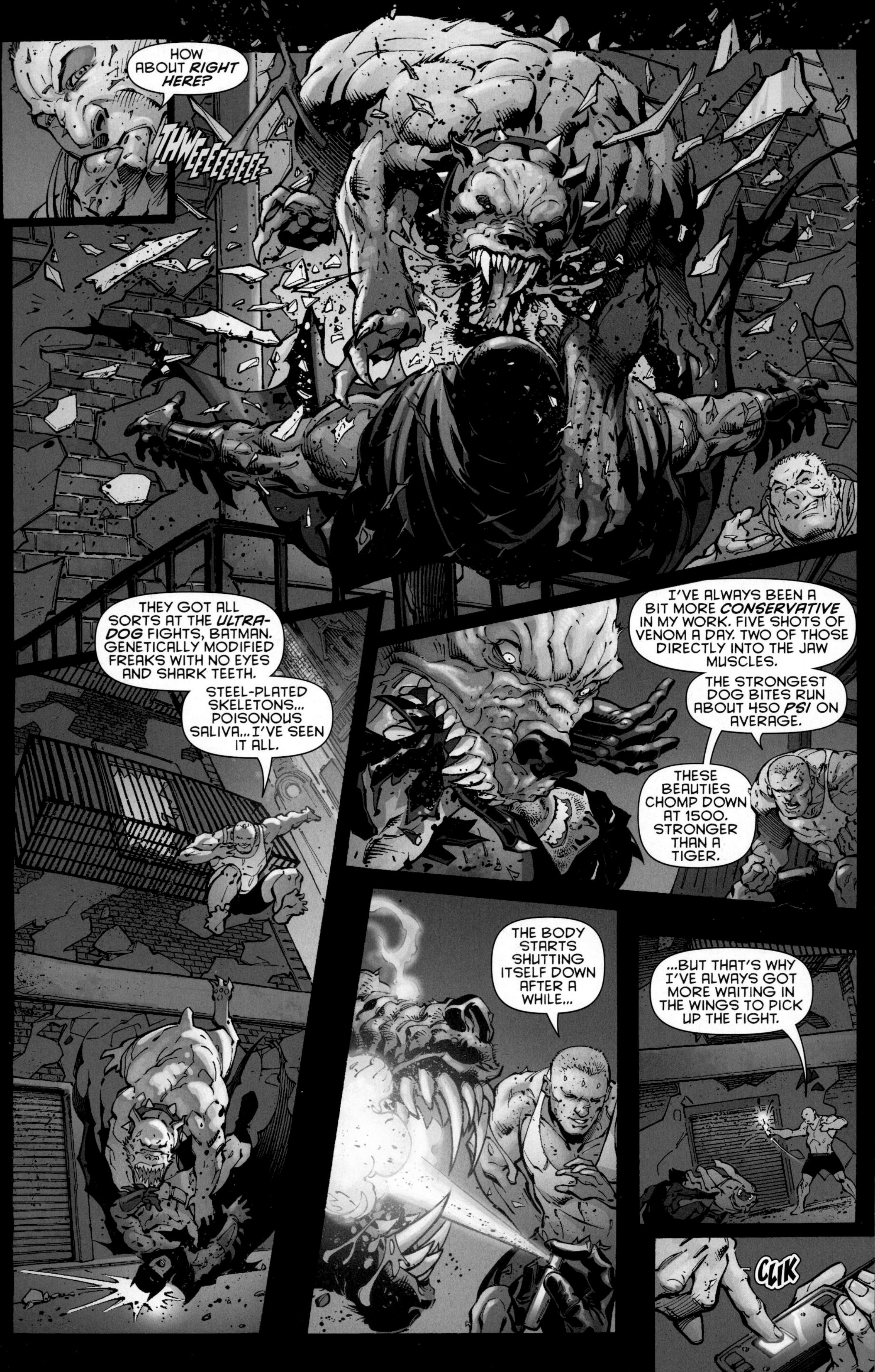

HOW ABOUT *RIGHT* HERE?
THWEEEEEEEE
THEY GOT ALL SORTS AT THE *ULTRA-DOG* FIGHTS, BATMAN. GENETICALLY MODIFIED FREAKS WITH NO EYES AND SHARK TEETH.
STEEL-PLATED SKELETONS... POISONOUS SALIVA... I'VE SEEN IT ALL.
I'VE ALWAYS BEEN A BIT MORE *CONSERVATIVE* IN MY WORK. FIVE SHOTS OF VENOM A DAY. TWO OF THOSE DIRECTLY INTO THE JAW MUSCLES.
THE STRONGEST DOG BITES RUN ABOUT 450 *PSI* ON AVERAGE.
THESE BEAUTIES CHOMP DOWN AT 1500. STRONGER THAN A TIGER.
THE BODY STARTS SHUTTING ITSELF DOWN AFTER A WHILE...
...BUT THAT'S WHY I'VE ALWAYS GOT MORE WAITING IN THE WINGS TO PICK UP THE FIGHT.
CLIK

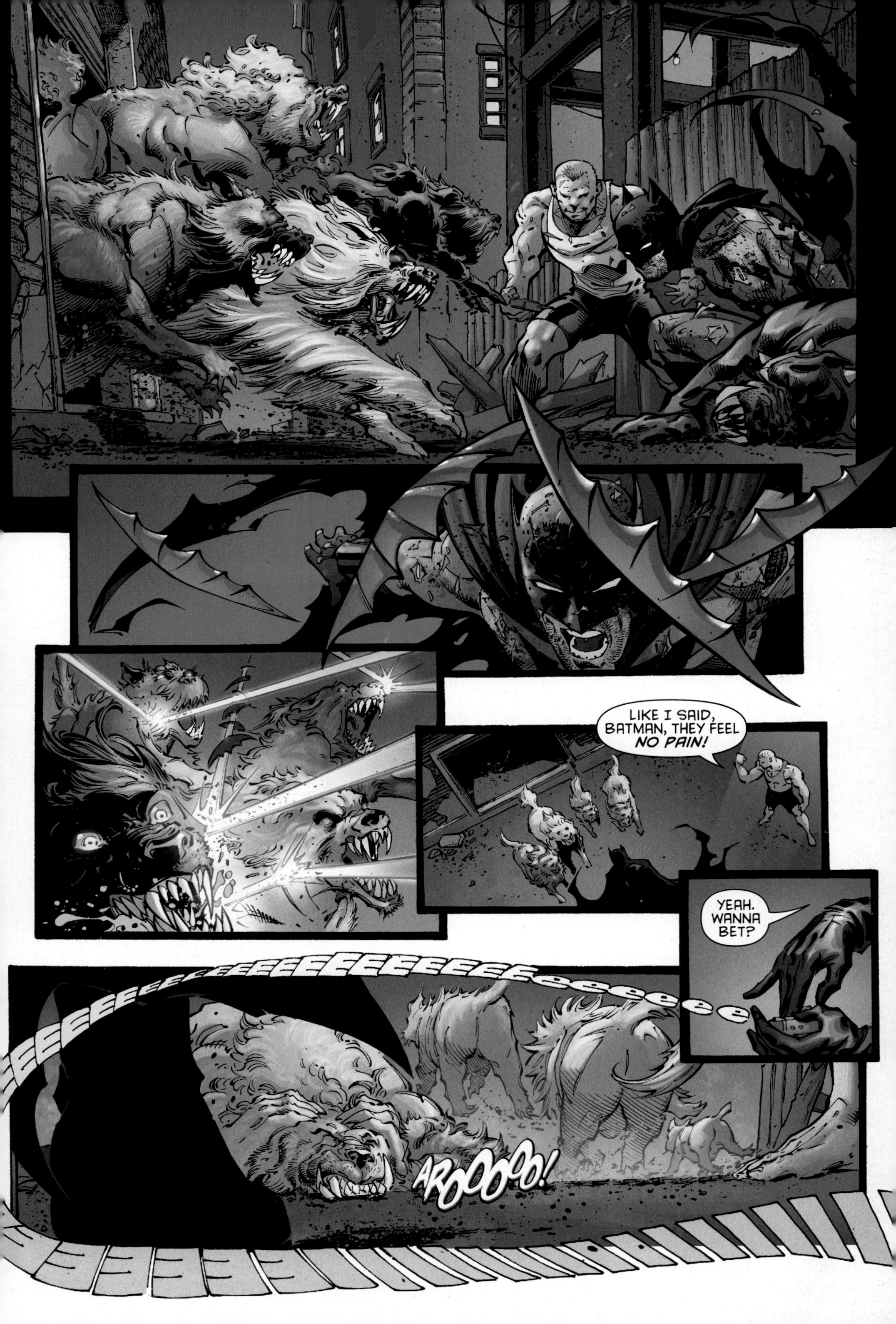
LIKE I SAID, BATMAN, THEY FEEL NO PAIN!
YEAH. WANNA BET?
AROOOOO!

WHO THE
HELL--?

YOUR WORST
NIGHTMARE.
A TEENAGE
GIRL WHO IS
ALMOST CERTAINLY
GOING TO KICK
YOUR BUTT.

OR ZAP
AWAY YOUR
FATHERING
PROSPECTS AT
THE VERY
LEAST.

...KILL...
YOU....

DON'T
THINK SO, BIG
BOY.

HUH?

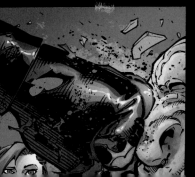

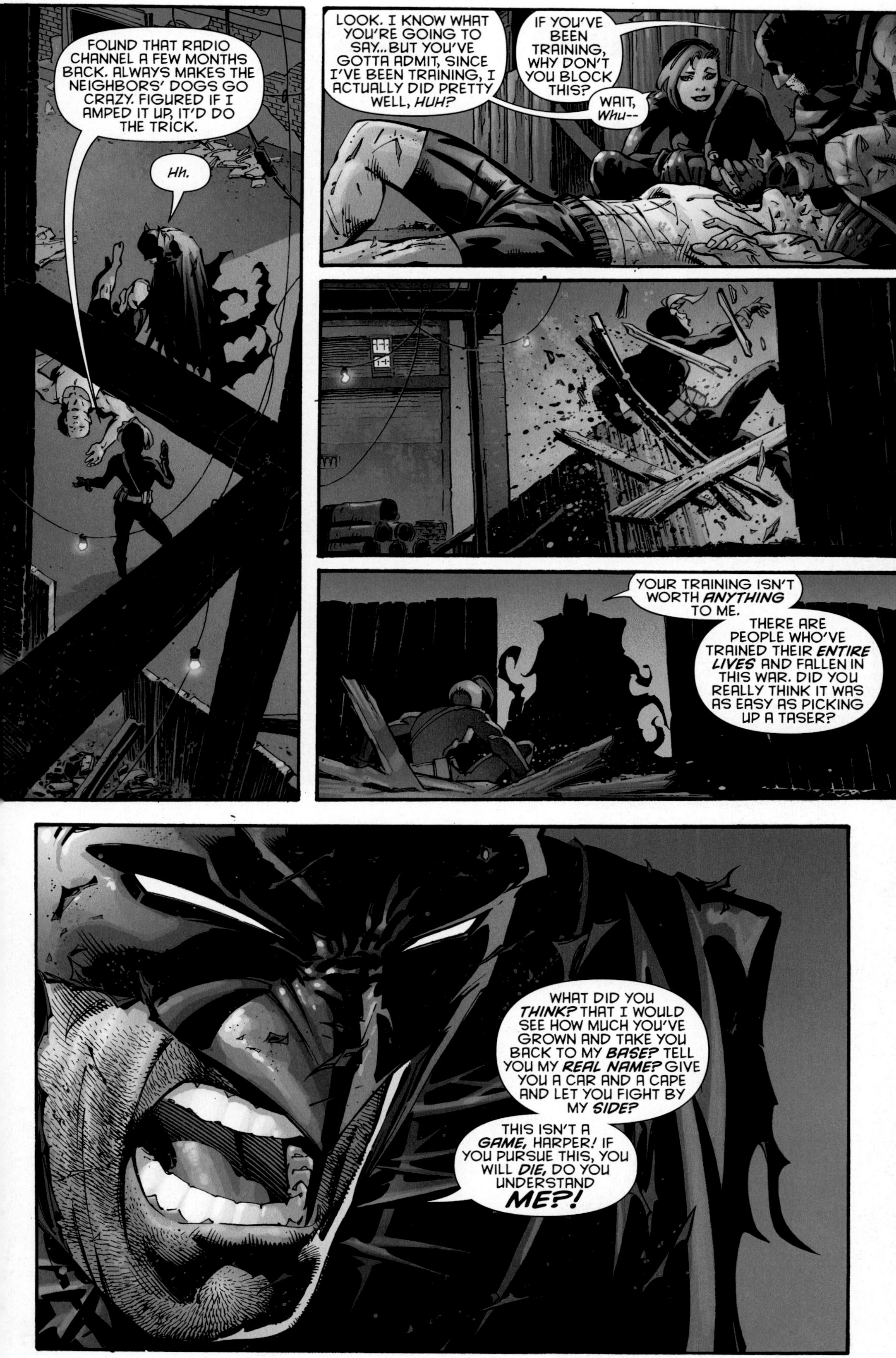
FOUND THAT RADIO CHANNEL A FEW MONTHS BACK. ALWAYS MAKES THE NEIGHBORS' DOGS GO CRAZY. FIGURED IF I AMPED IT UP, IT'D DO THE TRICK.
Hh.
LOOK. I KNOW WHAT YOU'RE GOING TO SAY...BUT YOU'VE GOTTA ADMIT, SINCE I'VE BEEN TRAINING, I ACTUALLY DID PRETTY WELL, HUH?
IF YOU'VE BEEN TRAINING, WHY DON'T YOU BLOCK THIS?
WAIT, Whu--
YOUR TRAINING ISN'T WORTH ANYTHING TO ME.
THERE ARE PEOPLE WHO'VE TRAINED THEIR ENTIRE LIVES AND FALLEN IN THIS WAR. DID YOU REALLY THINK IT WAS AS EASY AS PICKING UP A TASER?
WHAT DID YOU THINK? THAT I WOULD SEE HOW MUCH YOU'VE GROWN AND TAKE YOU BACK TO MY BASE? TELL YOU MY REAL NAME? GIVE YOU A CAR AND A CAPE AND LET YOU FIGHT BY MY SIDE?
THIS ISN'T A GAME, HARPER! IF YOU PURSUE THIS, YOU WILL DIE, DO YOU UNDERSTAND ME?!

I'M NOT AN *IDIOT,* BATMAN. I KNOW I'M NOT READY. NOT YET. BUT THAT DOESN'T MEAN I'M GOING TO STOP. YOU KNOW YOU CAN'T MAKE ME.

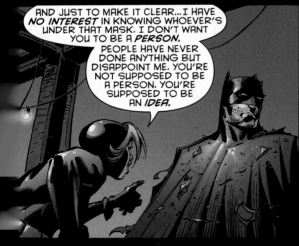

AND JUST TO MAKE IT CLEAR... I HAVE *NO INTEREST* IN KNOWING WHOEVER'S UNDER THAT MASK. I DON'T WANT YOU TO BE A *PERSON.*

PEOPLE HAVE NEVER DONE ANYTHING BUT DISAPPOINT ME. YOU'RE NOT SUPPOSED TO BE A PERSON. YOU'RE SUPPOSED TO BE AN *IDEA.*

BUT YOU CAN'T BE THAT IF YOU'RE *DEAD.* THAT'S WHY I STEPPED IN TONIGHT. YOU DO REALIZE THAT YOU COULD HAVE *DIED,* RIGHT? OR ARE YOU THAT FAR GONE?

YOU NEED TO FACE WHATEVER YOU'RE TRYING NOT TO FACE. YOU NEED TO DO IT *RIGHT NOW!*

BATMAN DOESN'T *GET* TO DIE.

I COULDN'T SIT BY AND WATCH MY HERO FALL IN SOME BACK ALLEY LIKE A COMMON THUG.

I DON'T *CARE* WHO YOU ARE. I DON'T CARE IF YOU APPROVE OF WHAT I'M DOING. BUT I'M DOING IT *BECAUSE* OF YOU.

AND YOU CAN JUST FREAKING *DEAL.*

AND DON'T PRETEND LIKE I'M *NOTHING* TO YOU, ALL RIGHT? I KNOW IT WAS YOU. I KNOW YOU LOCKED UP MY FATHER.

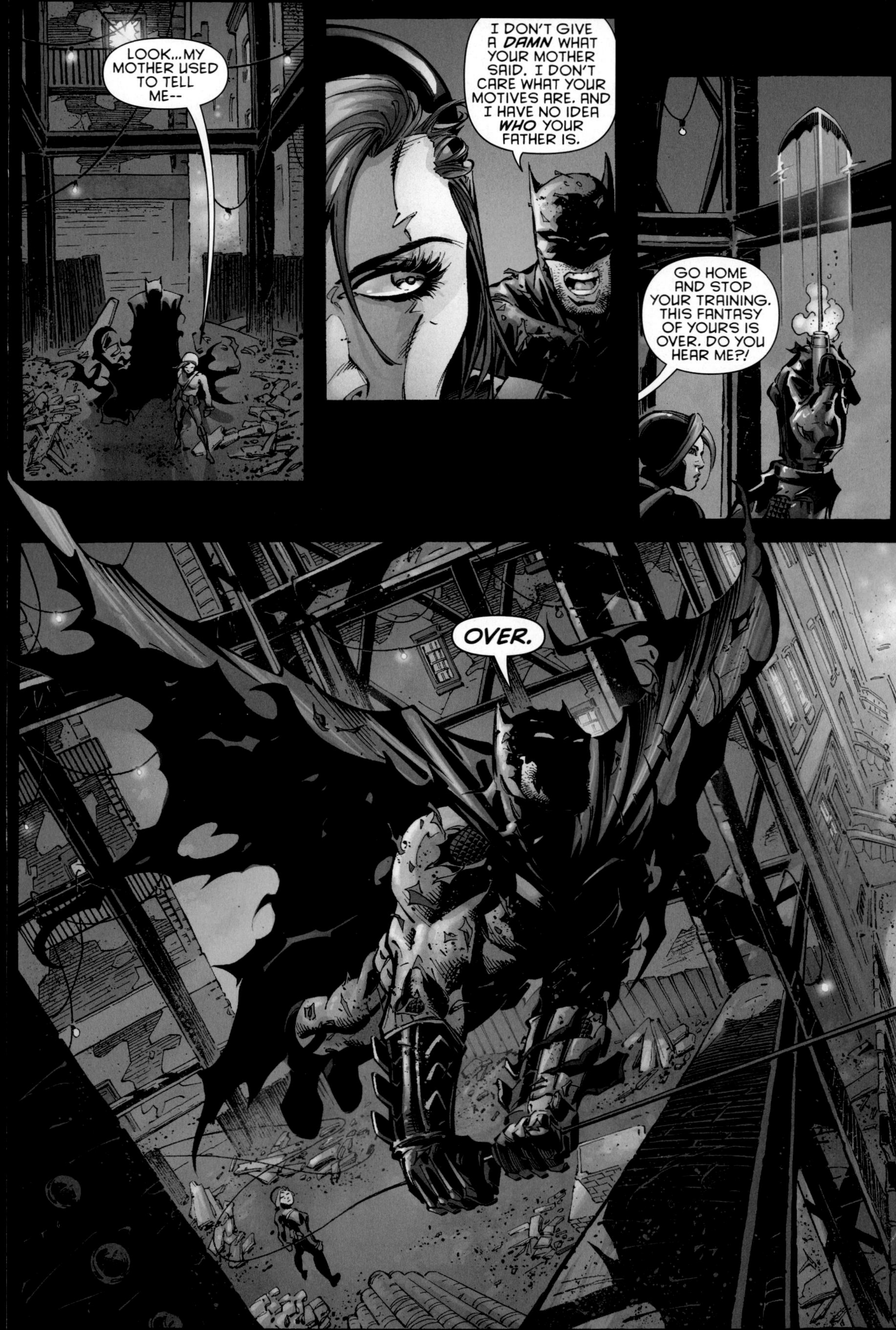
LOOK...MY MOTHER USED TO TELL ME--
I DON'T GIVE A DAMN WHAT YOUR MOTHER SAID. I DON'T CARE WHAT YOUR MOTIVES ARE. AND I HAVE NO IDEA WHO YOUR FATHER IS.
GO HOME AND STOP YOUR TRAINING. THIS FANTASY OF YOURS IS OVER. DO YOU HEAR ME?!
OVER.

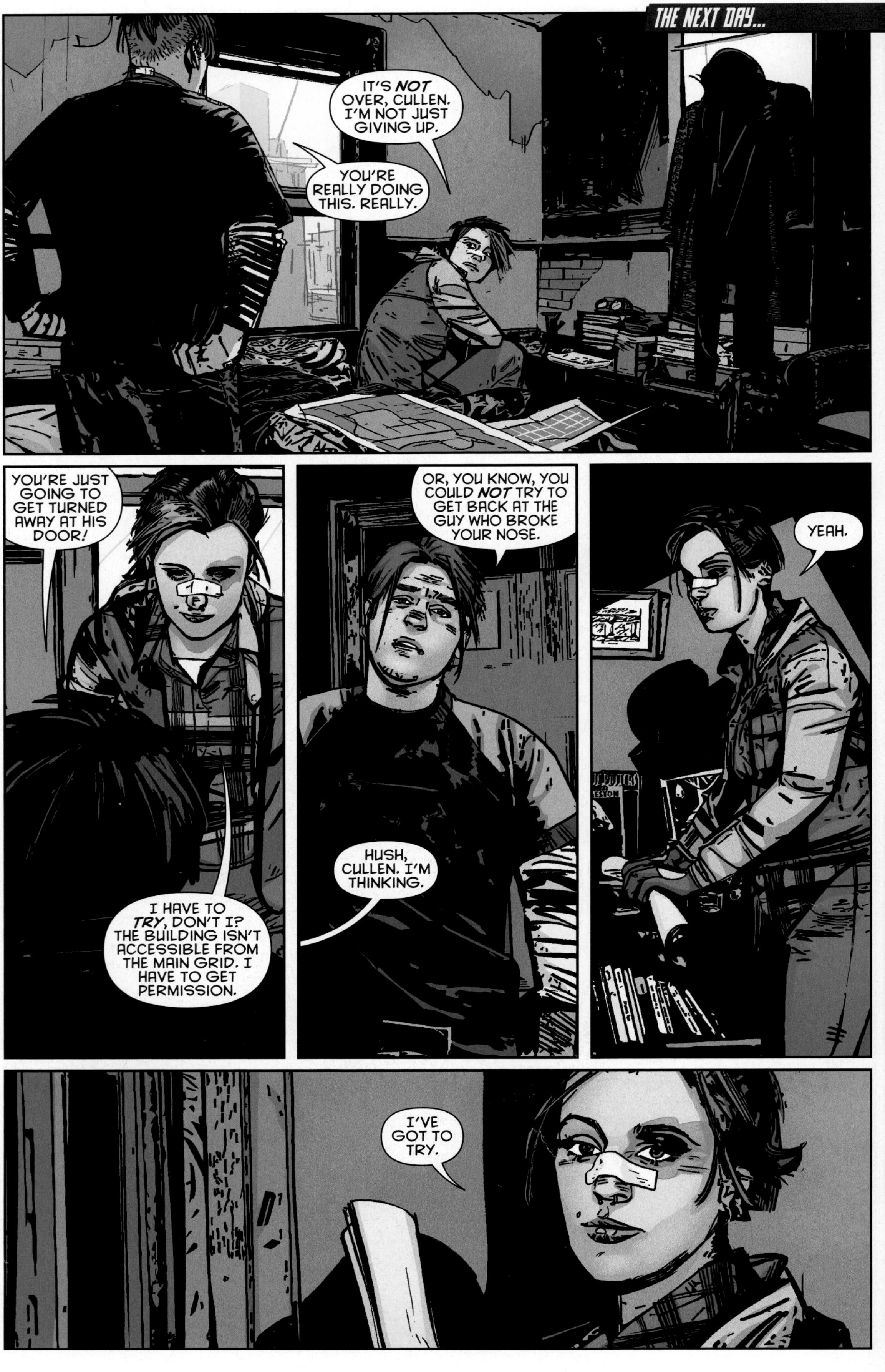
THE NEXT DAY...
IT'S NOT OVER, CULLEN. I'M NOT JUST GIVING UP.
YOU'RE REALLY DOING THIS. REALLY.
YOU'RE JUST GOING TO GET TURNED AWAY AT HIS DOOR!
I HAVE TO TRY, DON'T I? THE BUILDING ISN'T ACCESSIBLE FROM THE MAIN GRID. I HAVE TO GET PERMISSION.
OR, YOU KNOW, YOU COULD NOT TRY TO GET BACK AT THE GUY WHO BROKE YOUR NOSE.
HUSH, CULLEN. I'M THINKING.
YEAH.
I'VE GOT TO TRY.

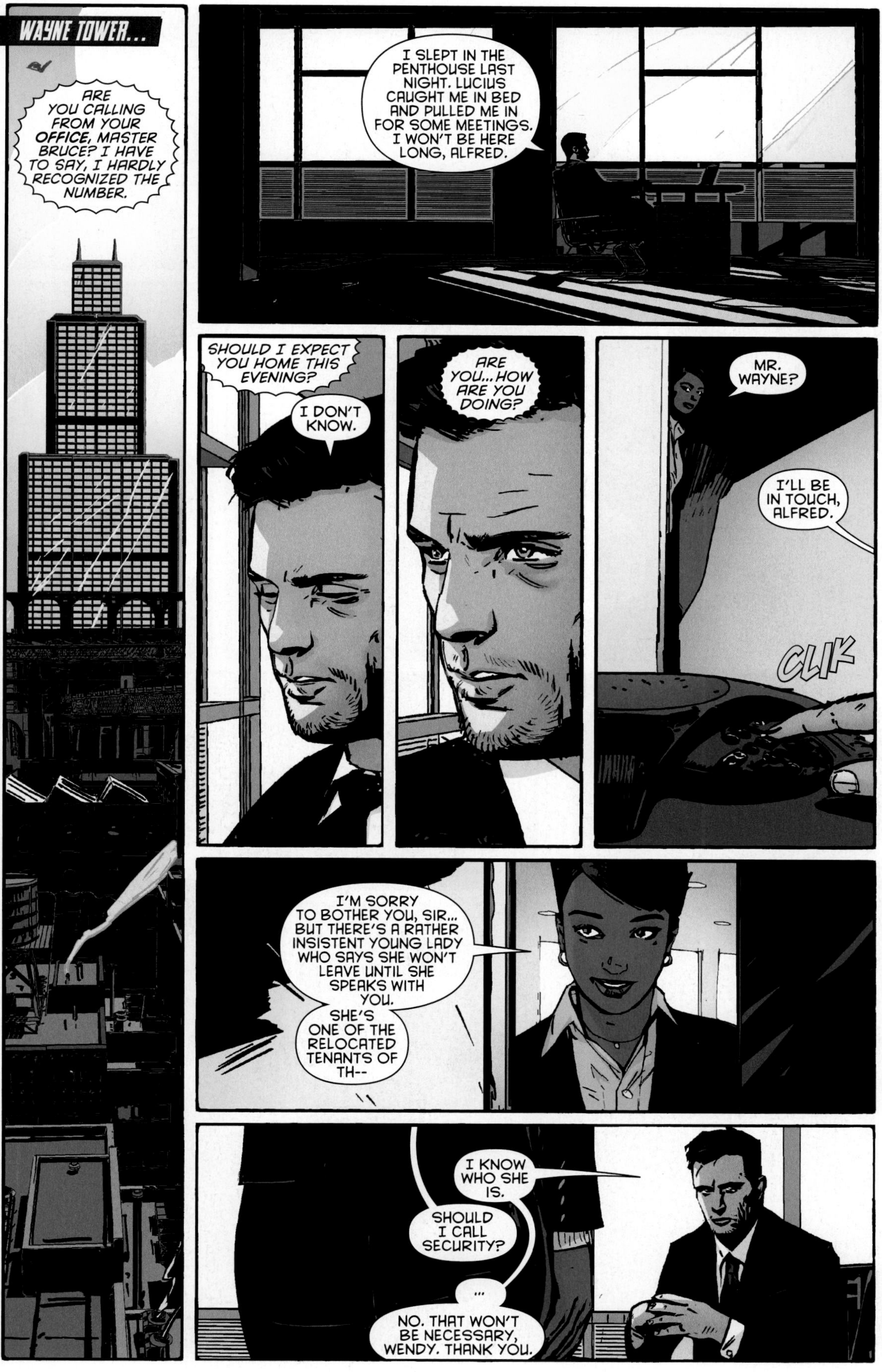
WAYNE TOWER...
ARE YOU CALLING FROM YOUR OFFICE, MASTER BRUCE? I HAVE TO SAY, I HARDLY RECOGNIZED THE NUMBER.
I SLEPT IN THE PENTHOUSE LAST NIGHT. LUCIUS CAUGHT ME IN BED AND PULLED ME IN FOR SOME MEETINGS. I WON'T BE HERE LONG, ALFRED.
SHOULD I EXPECT YOU HOME THIS EVENING?
I DON'T KNOW.
ARE YOU... HOW ARE YOU DOING?
MR. WAYNE?
I'LL BE IN TOUCH, ALFRED.
CLIK
I'M SORRY TO BOTHER YOU, SIR... BUT THERE'S A RATHER INSISTENT YOUNG LADY WHO SAYS SHE WON'T LEAVE UNTIL SHE SPEAKS WITH YOU.
SHE'S ONE OF THE RELOCATED TENANTS OF TH--
I KNOW WHO SHE IS.
SHOULD I CALL SECURITY?
...
NO. THAT WON'T BE NECESSARY, WENDY. THANK YOU.

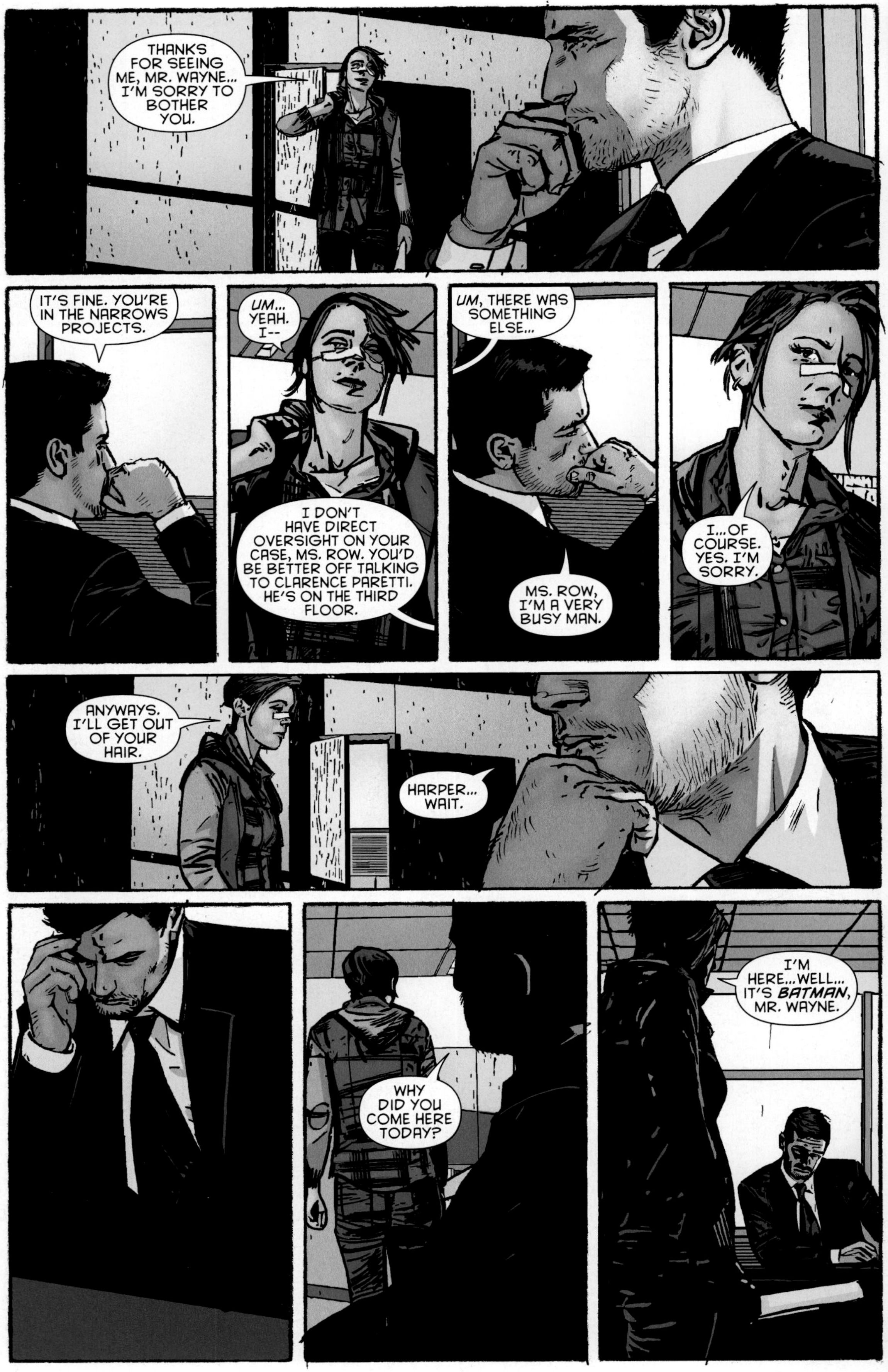
THANKS FOR SEEING ME, MR. WAYNE... I'M SORRY TO BOTHER YOU.
IT'S FINE. YOU'RE IN THE NARROWS PROJECTS.
UM... YEAH. I--
I DON'T HAVE DIRECT OVERSIGHT ON YOUR CASE, MS. ROW. YOU'D BE BETTER OFF TALKING TO CLARENCE PARETTI. HE'S ON THE THIRD FLOOR.
UM, THERE WAS SOMETHING ELSE...
MS. ROW, I'M A VERY BUSY MAN.
I...OF COURSE. YES. I'M SORRY.
ANYWAYS. I'LL GET OUT OF YOUR HAIR.
HARPER... WAIT.
WHY DID YOU COME HERE TODAY?
I'M HERE...WELL... IT'S BATMAN, MR. WAYNE.

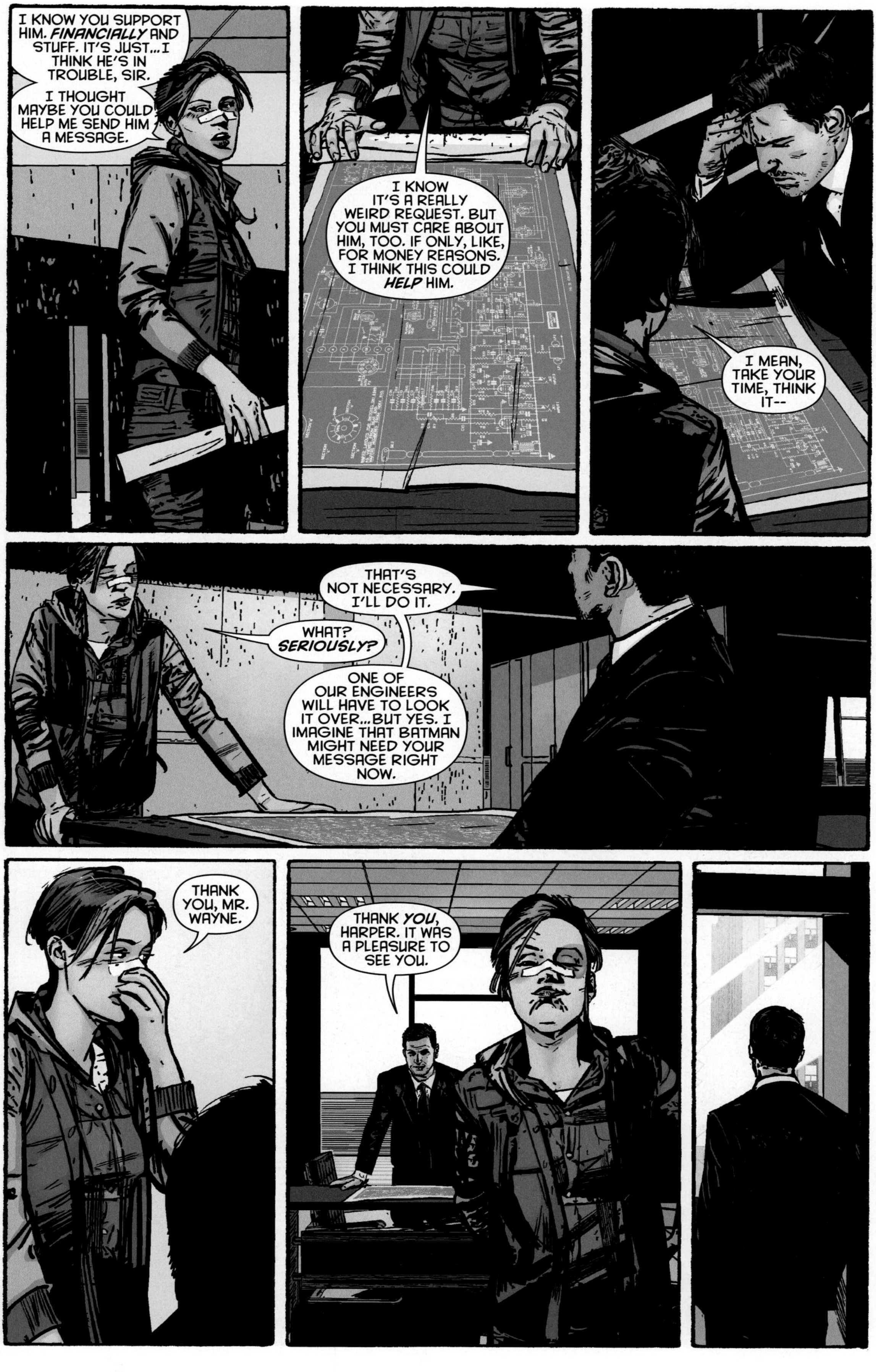

I KNOW YOU SUPPORT HIM. FINANCIALLY AND STUFF. IT'S JUST... I THINK HE'S IN TROUBLE, SIR.
I THOUGHT MAYBE YOU COULD HELP ME SEND HIM A MESSAGE.
I KNOW IT'S A REALLY WEIRD REQUEST. BUT YOU MUST CARE ABOUT HIM, TOO. IF ONLY, LIKE, FOR MONEY REASONS. I THINK THIS COULD HELP HIM.
I MEAN, TAKE YOUR TIME, THINK IT--
THAT'S NOT NECESSARY. I'LL DO IT.
WHAT? SERIOUSLY?
ONE OF OUR ENGINEERS WILL HAVE TO LOOK IT OVER... BUT YES. I IMAGINE THAT BATMAN MIGHT NEED YOUR MESSAGE RIGHT NOW.
THANK YOU, MR. WAYNE.
THANK YOU, HARPER. IT WAS A PLEASURE TO SEE YOU.

I ACTED... *RASHLY* THE OTHER NIGHT.

IS THAT WHAT YOU CALL AN *APOLOGY?* YOU BROKE MY NOSE.

I'M SORRY, HARPER.

EH, IT'S FINE. SEEMS LIKE IT WAS BOUND TO HAPPEN SOONER OR LATER. THE NOSE-BREAKING PART. NOT YOU PUNCHING ME. THAT WAS A BIT OF A SURPRISE.

HARPER... THERE ARE THINGS HAPPENING IN MY LIFE RIGHT NOW YOU COULDN'T UNDER-STAND.

HMM. MAYBE NOT THE DETAILS, BUT I CAN SEE YOUR PAIN. EVEN NOW. AND I'VE DEFINITELY BEEN THERE BEFORE.

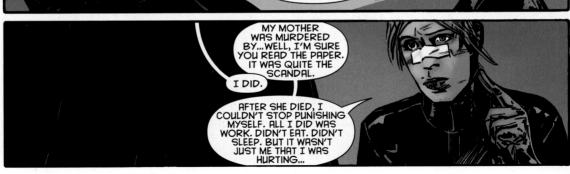

MY MOTHER WAS MURDERED BY...WELL, I'M SURE YOU READ THE PAPER. IT WAS QUITE THE SCANDAL.

I DID.

AFTER SHE DIED, I COULDN'T STOP PUNISHING MYSELF. ALL I DID WAS WORK. DIDN'T EAT. DIDN'T SLEEP. BUT IT WASN'T JUST ME THAT I WAS HURTING...

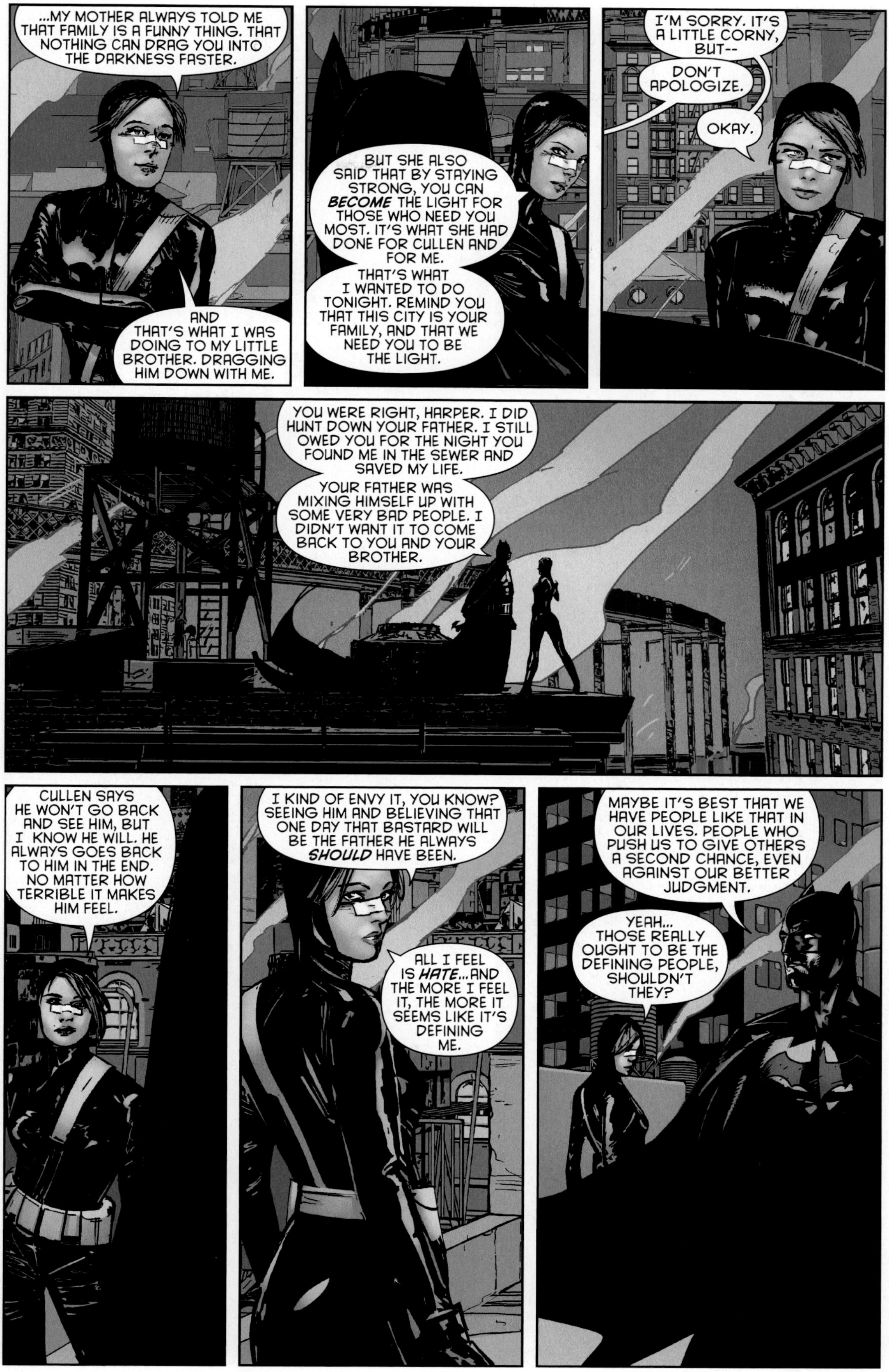
...MY MOTHER ALWAYS TOLD ME THAT FAMILY IS A FUNNY THING. THAT NOTHING CAN DRAG YOU INTO THE DARKNESS FASTER.
AND THAT'S WHAT I WAS DOING TO MY LITTLE BROTHER. DRAGGING HIM DOWN WITH ME.
BUT SHE ALSO SAID THAT BY STAYING STRONG, YOU CAN BECOME THE LIGHT FOR THOSE WHO NEED YOU MOST. IT'S WHAT SHE HAD DONE FOR CULLEN AND FOR ME.
THAT'S WHAT I WANTED TO DO TONIGHT. REMIND YOU THAT THIS CITY IS YOUR FAMILY, AND THAT WE NEED YOU TO BE THE LIGHT.
I'M SORRY. IT'S A LITTLE CORNY, BUT--
DON'T APOLOGIZE.
OKAY.
YOU WERE RIGHT, HARPER. I DID HUNT DOWN YOUR FATHER. I STILL OWED YOU FOR THE NIGHT YOU FOUND ME IN THE SEWER AND SAVED MY LIFE.
YOUR FATHER WAS MIXING HIMSELF UP WITH SOME VERY BAD PEOPLE. I DIDN'T WANT IT TO COME BACK TO YOU AND YOUR BROTHER.
CULLEN SAYS HE WON'T GO BACK AND SEE HIM, BUT I KNOW HE WILL. HE ALWAYS GOES BACK TO HIM IN THE END. NO MATTER HOW TERRIBLE IT MAKES HIM FEEL.
I KIND OF ENVY IT, YOU KNOW? SEEING HIM AND BELIEVING THAT ONE DAY THAT BASTARD WILL BE THE FATHER HE ALWAYS SHOULD HAVE BEEN.
ALL I FEEL IS HATE...AND THE MORE I FEEL IT, THE MORE IT SEEMS LIKE IT'S DEFINING ME.
MAYBE IT'S BEST THAT WE HAVE PEOPLE LIKE THAT IN OUR LIVES. PEOPLE WHO PUSH US TO GIVE OTHERS A SECOND CHANCE, EVEN AGAINST OUR BETTER JUDGMENT.
YEAH... THOSE REALLY OUGHT TO BE THE DEFINING PEOPLE, SHOULDN'T THEY?

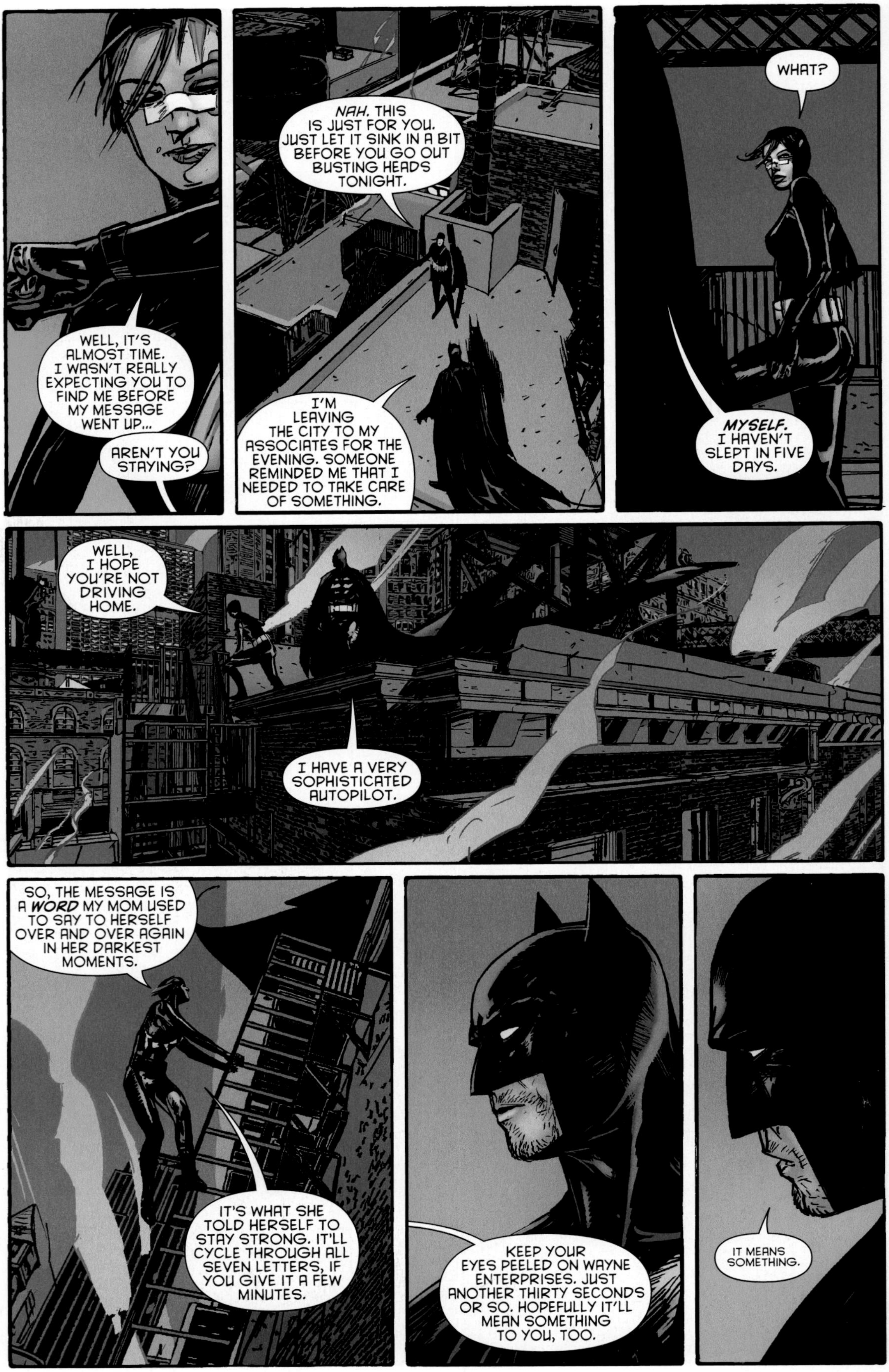

WELL, IT'S ALMOST TIME. I WASN'T REALLY EXPECTING YOU TO FIND ME BEFORE MY MESSAGE WENT UP...
AREN'T YOU STAYING?
NAH. THIS IS JUST FOR YOU. JUST LET IT SINK IN A BIT BEFORE YOU GO OUT BUSTING HEADS TONIGHT.
I'M LEAVING THE CITY TO MY ASSOCIATES FOR THE EVENING. SOMEONE REMINDED ME THAT I NEEDED TO TAKE CARE OF SOMETHING.
WHAT?
MYSELF. I HAVEN'T SLEPT IN FIVE DAYS.
WELL, I HOPE YOU'RE NOT DRIVING HOME.
I HAVE A VERY SOPHISTICATED AUTOPILOT.
SO, THE MESSAGE IS A WORD MY MOM USED TO SAY TO HERSELF OVER AND OVER AGAIN IN HER DARKEST MOMENTS.
IT'S WHAT SHE TOLD HERSELF TO STAY STRONG. IT'LL CYCLE THROUGH ALL SEVEN LETTERS, IF YOU GIVE IT A FEW MINUTES.
KEEP YOUR EYES PEELED ON WAYNE ENTERPRISES. JUST ANOTHER THIRTY SECONDS OR SO. HOPEFULLY IT'LL MEAN SOMETHING TO YOU, TOO.
IT MEANS SOMETHING.

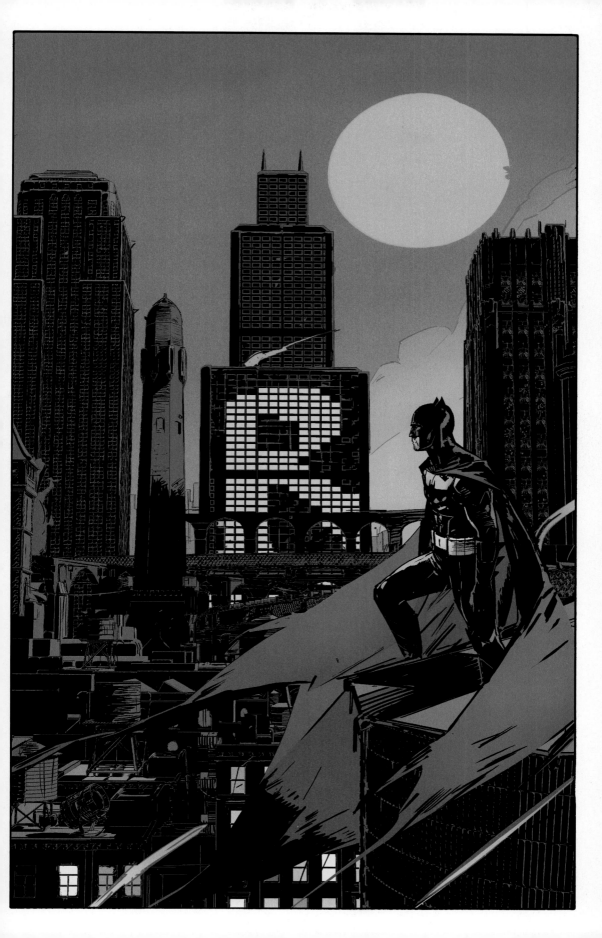

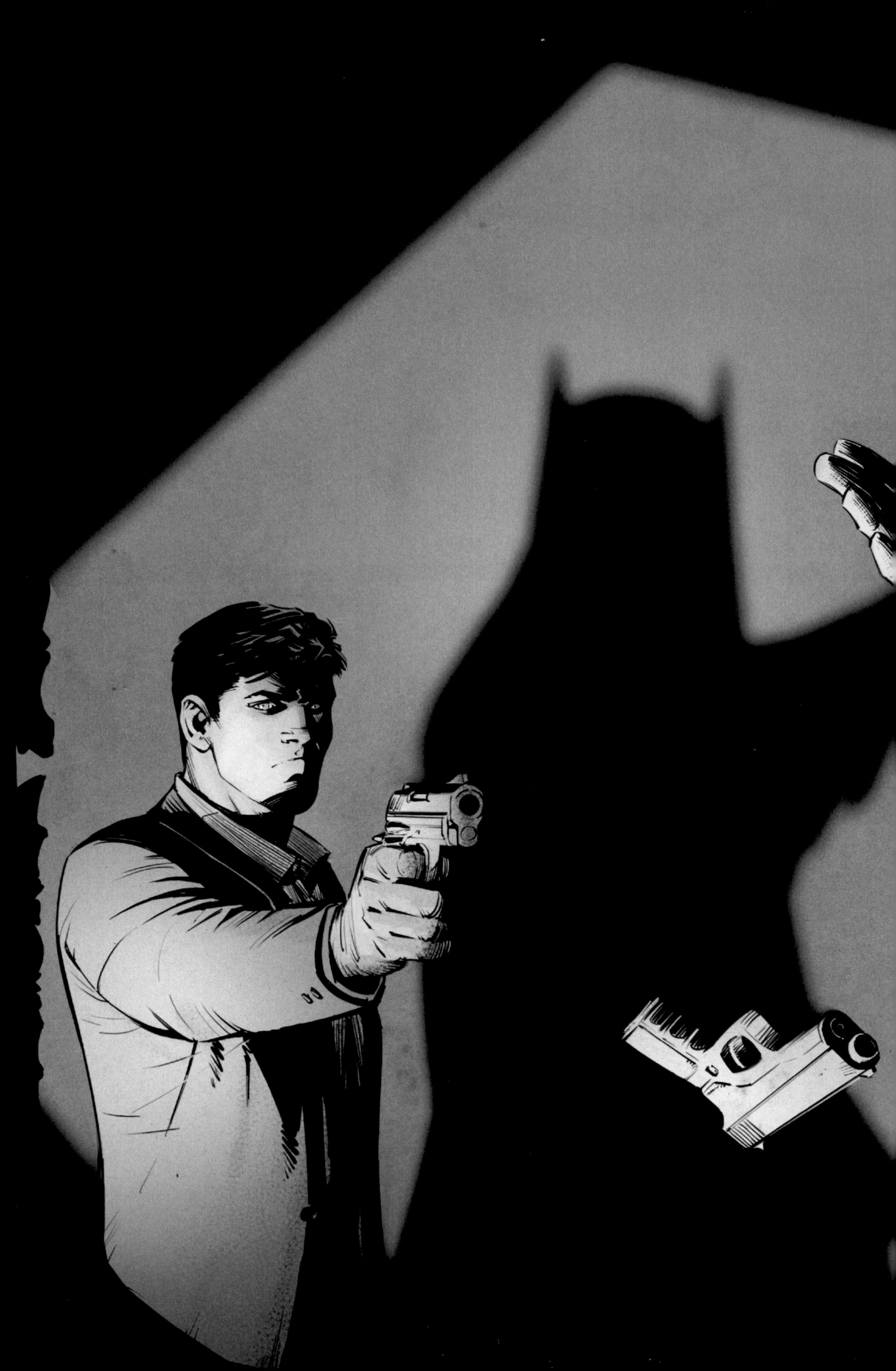

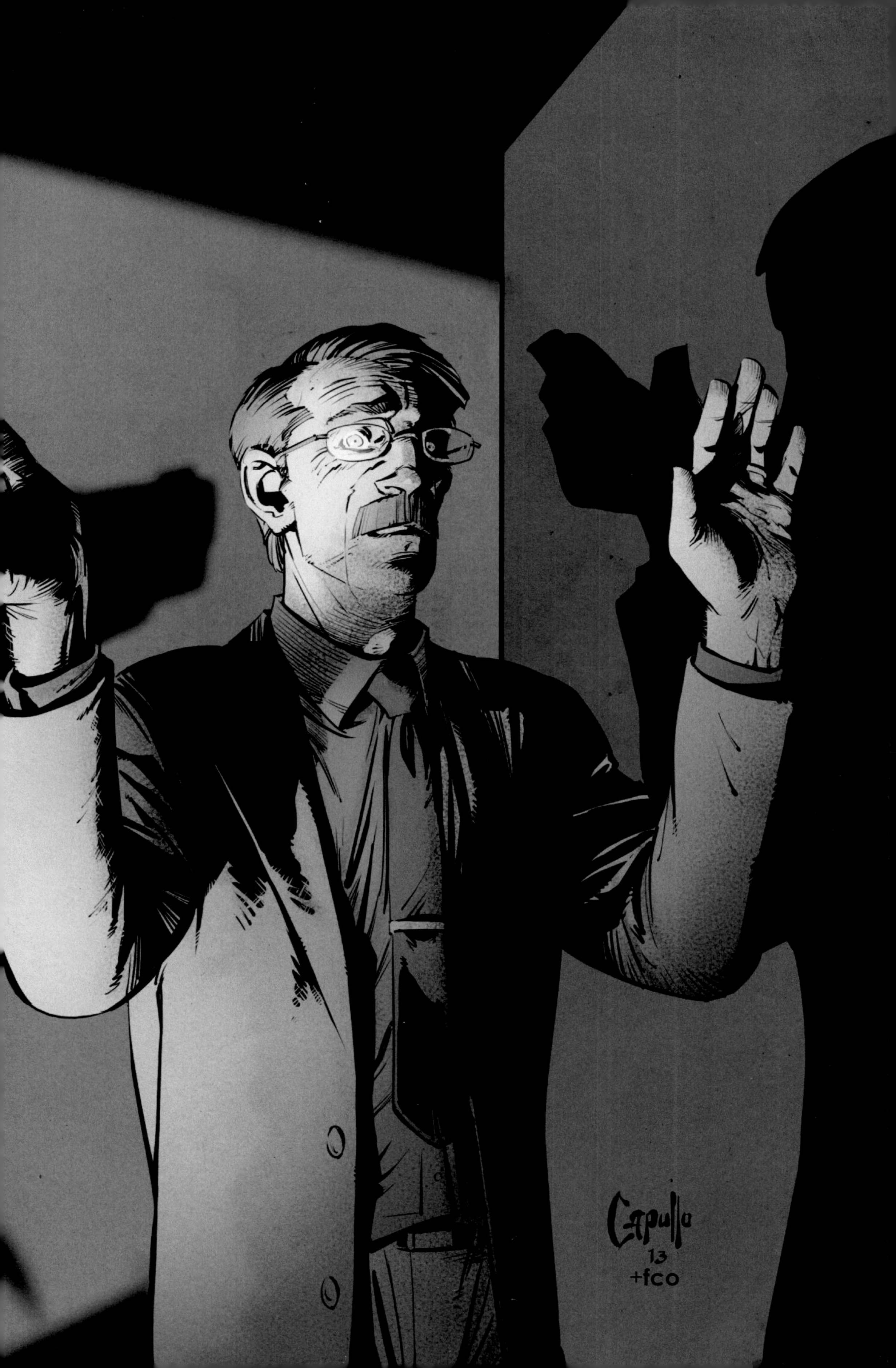
Capullo
13
+fco

NOWHERE MAN

SCOTT SNYDER writer **GREG CAPULLO** penciller **DANNY MIKI** inker **FCO PLASCENCIA** colorist cover by **GREG CAPULLO & FCO PLASCENCIA**

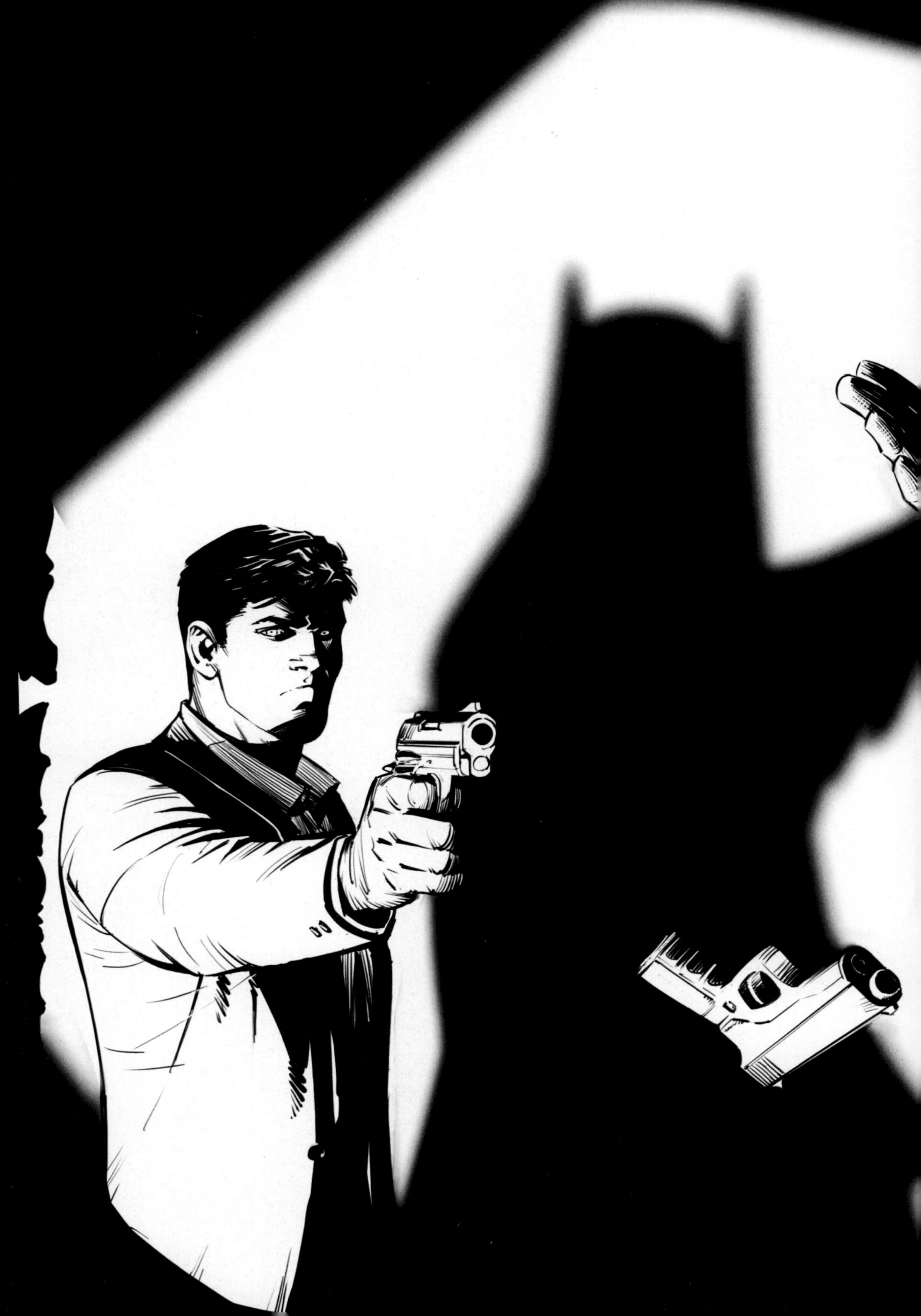

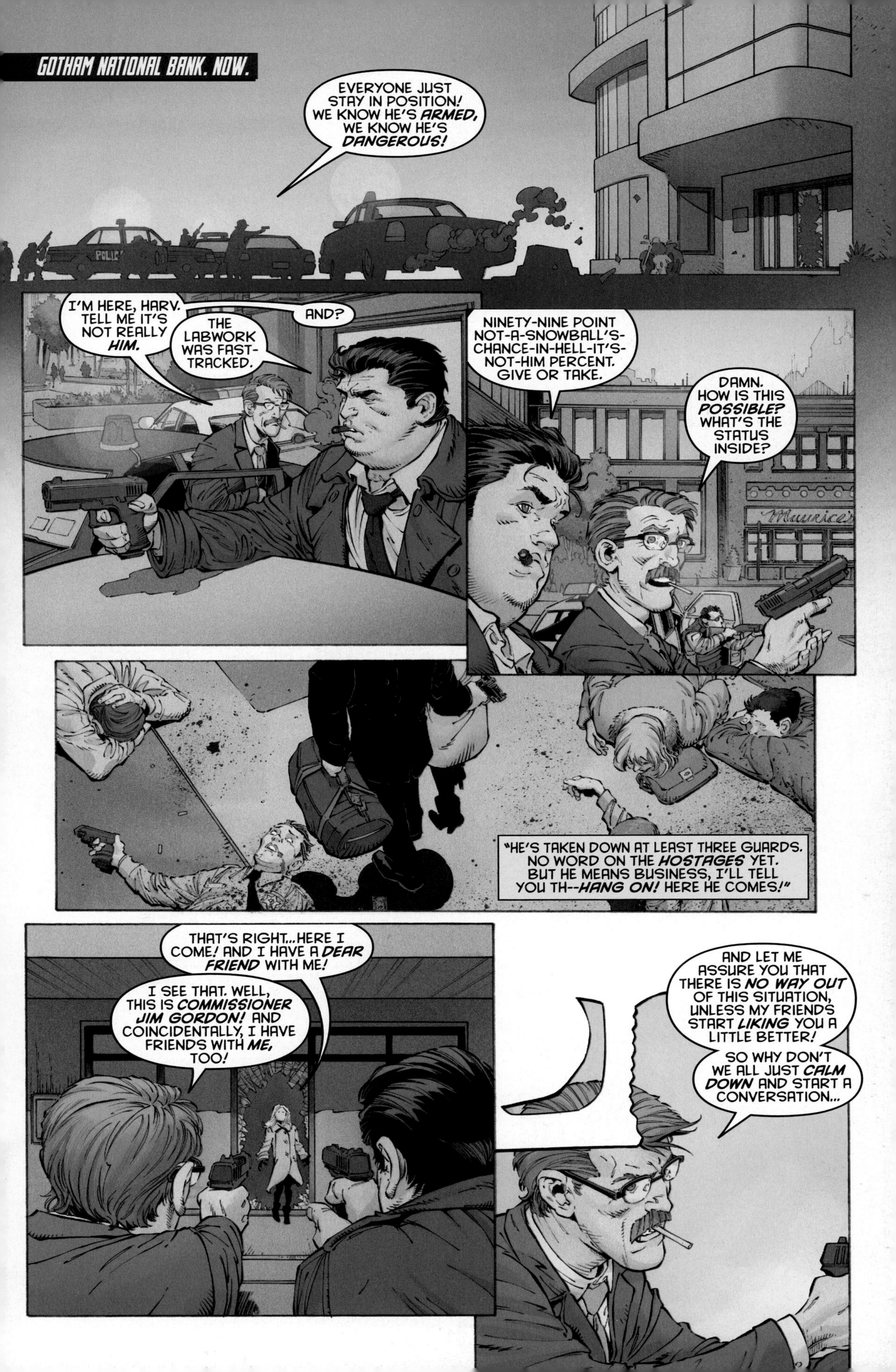
GOTHAM NATIONAL BANK. NOW.
EVERYONE JUST STAY IN POSITION! WE KNOW HE'S ARMED, WE KNOW HE'S DANGEROUS!
POLICE
I'M HERE, HARV. TELL ME IT'S NOT REALLY HIM.
THE LABWORK WAS FAST-TRACKED.
AND?
NINETY-NINE POINT NOT-A-SNOWBALL'S-CHANCE-IN-HELL-IT'S-NOT-HIM PERCENT. GIVE OR TAKE.
DAMN. HOW IS THIS POSSIBLE? WHAT'S THE STATUS INSIDE?
Maurice's
"HE'S TAKEN DOWN AT LEAST THREE GUARDS. NO WORD ON THE HOSTAGES YET. BUT HE MEANS BUSINESS, I'LL TELL YOU TH--HANG ON! HERE HE COMES!"
THAT'S RIGHT...HERE I COME! AND I HAVE A DEAR FRIEND WITH ME!
I SEE THAT. WELL, THIS IS COMMISSIONER JIM GORDON! AND COINCIDENTALLY, I HAVE FRIENDS WITH ME, TOO!
AND LET ME ASSURE YOU THAT THERE IS NO WAY OUT OF THIS SITUATION, UNLESS MY FRIENDS START LIKING YOU A LITTLE BETTER!
SO WHY DON'T WE ALL JUST CALM DOWN AND START A CONVERSATION...

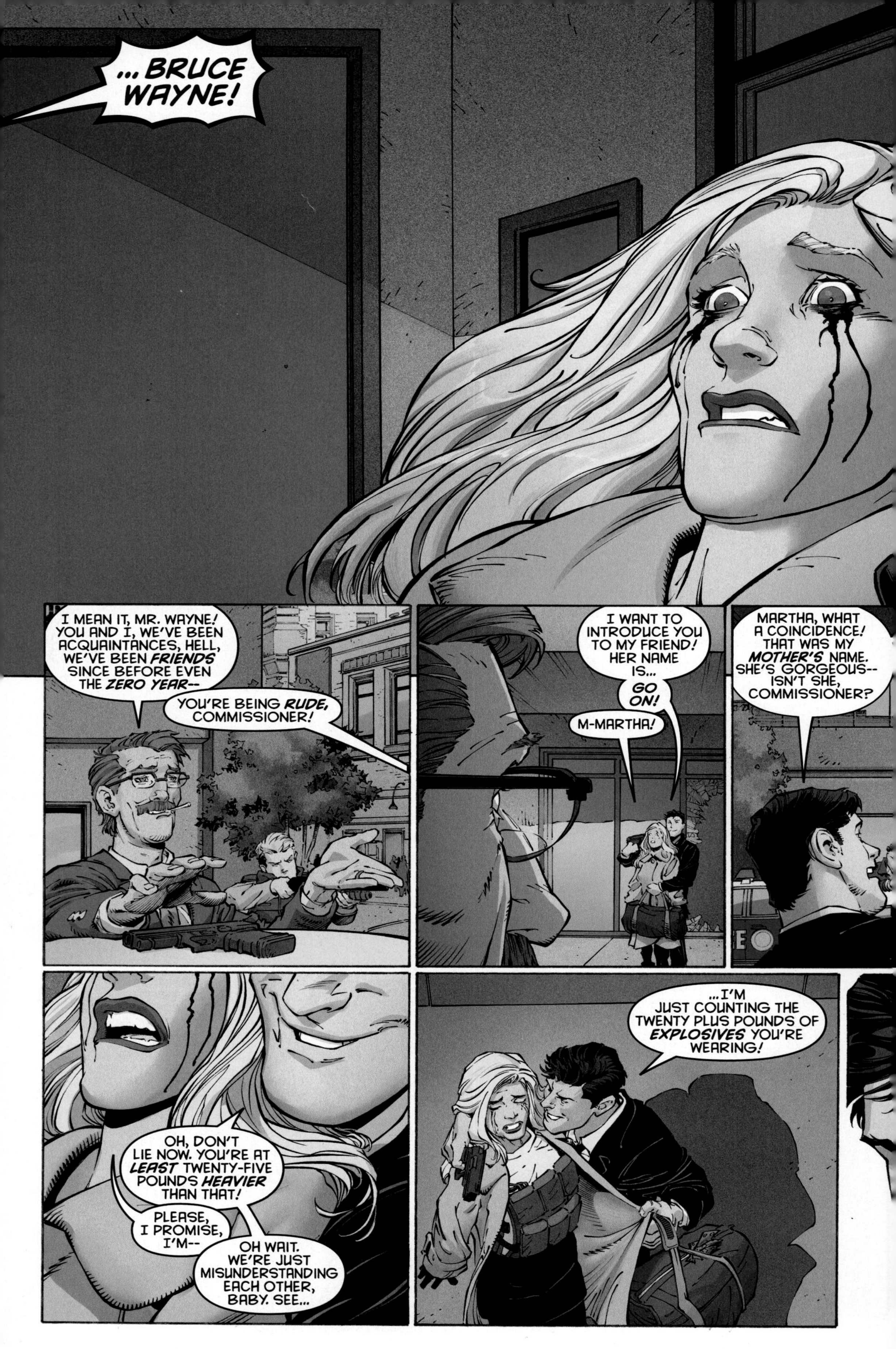
...BRUCE WAYNE!
I MEAN IT, MR. WAYNE! YOU AND I, WE'VE BEEN ACQUAINTANCES, HELL, WE'VE BEEN FRIENDS SINCE BEFORE EVEN THE ZERO YEAR--
YOU'RE BEING RUDE, COMMISSIONER!
I WANT TO INTRODUCE YOU TO MY FRIEND! HER NAME IS...
GO ON!
M-MARTHA!
MARTHA, WHAT A COINCIDENCE! THAT WAS MY MOTHER'S NAME. SHE'S GORGEOUS--ISN'T SHE, COMMISSIONER?
OH, DON'T LIE NOW. YOU'RE AT LEAST TWENTY-FIVE POUNDS HEAVIER THAN THAT!
PLEASE, I PROMISE, I'M--
OH WAIT. WE'RE JUST MISUNDERSTANDING EACH OTHER, BABY. SEE...
...I'M JUST COUNTING THE TWENTY PLUS POUNDS OF EXPLOSIVES YOU'RE WEARING!

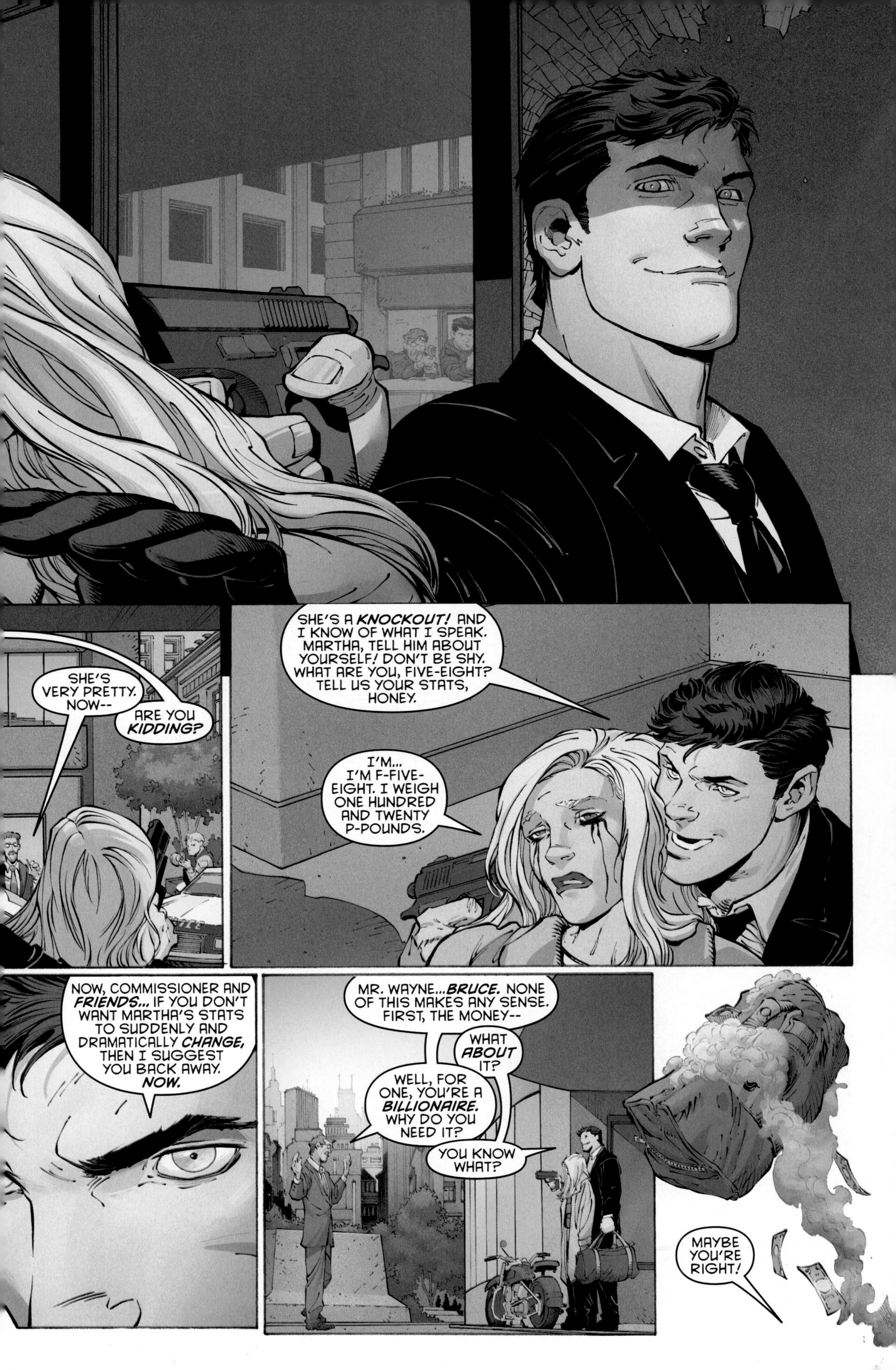
SHE'S VERY PRETTY. NOW--
ARE YOU KIDDING?
SHE'S A KNOCKOUT! AND I KNOW OF WHAT I SPEAK. MARTHA, TELL HIM ABOUT YOURSELF! DON'T BE SHY. WHAT ARE YOU, FIVE-EIGHT? TELL US YOUR STATS, HONEY.
I'M... I'M F-FIVE-EIGHT. I WEIGH ONE HUNDRED AND TWENTY P-POUNDS.
NOW, COMMISSIONER AND FRIENDS... IF YOU DON'T WANT MARTHA'S STATS TO SUDDENLY AND DRAMATICALLY CHANGE, THEN I SUGGEST YOU BACK AWAY. NOW.
MR. WAYNE...BRUCE. NONE OF THIS MAKES ANY SENSE. FIRST, THE MONEY--
WHAT ABOUT IT?
WELL, FOR ONE, YOU'RE A BILLIONAIRE. WHY DO YOU NEED IT?
YOU KNOW WHAT?
MAYBE YOU'RE RIGHT!

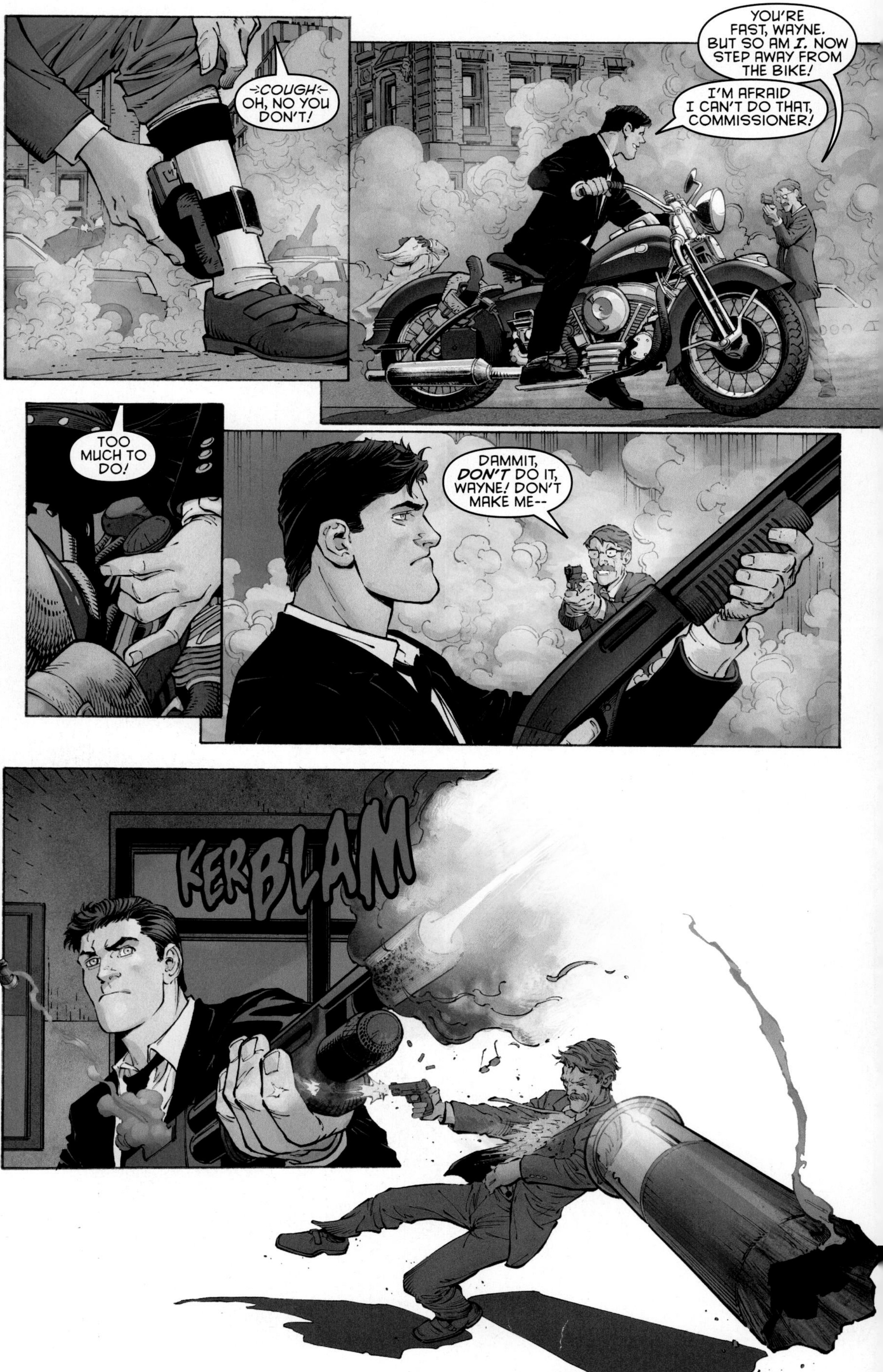

-COUGH- OH, NO YOU DON'T!
YOU'RE FAST, WAYNE. BUT SO AM I. NOW STEP AWAY FROM THE BIKE!
I'M AFRAID I CAN'T DO THAT, COMMISSIONER!
TOO MUCH TO DO!
DAMMIT, DON'T DO IT, WAYNE! DON'T MAKE ME--
KERBLAM

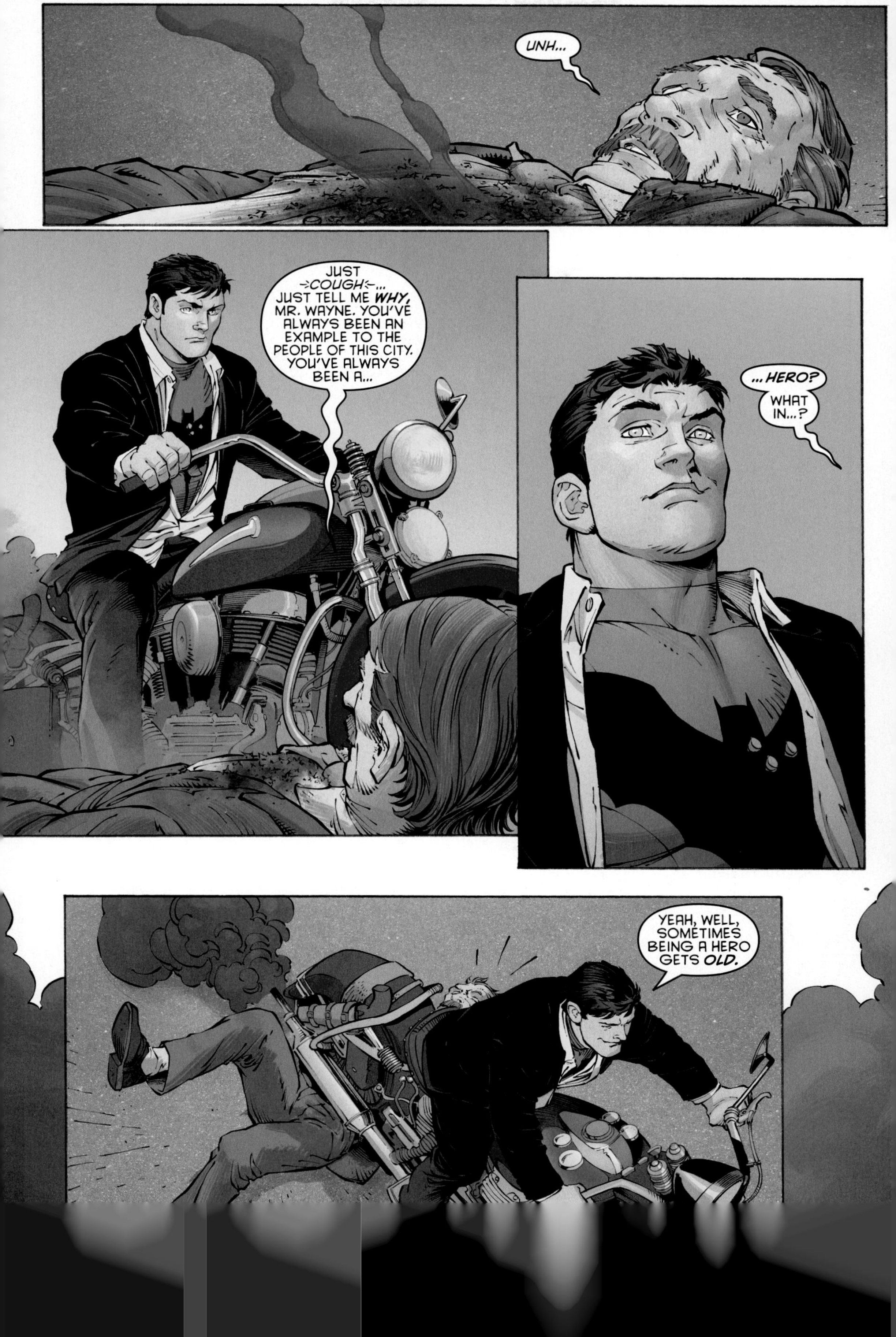
UNH...
JUST -COUGH-... JUST TELL ME WHY, MR. WAYNE. YOU'VE ALWAYS BEEN AN EXAMPLE TO THE PEOPLE OF THIS CITY. YOU'VE ALWAYS BEEN A...
...HERO? WHAT IN...?
YEAH, WELL, SOMETIMES BEING A HERO GETS OLD.

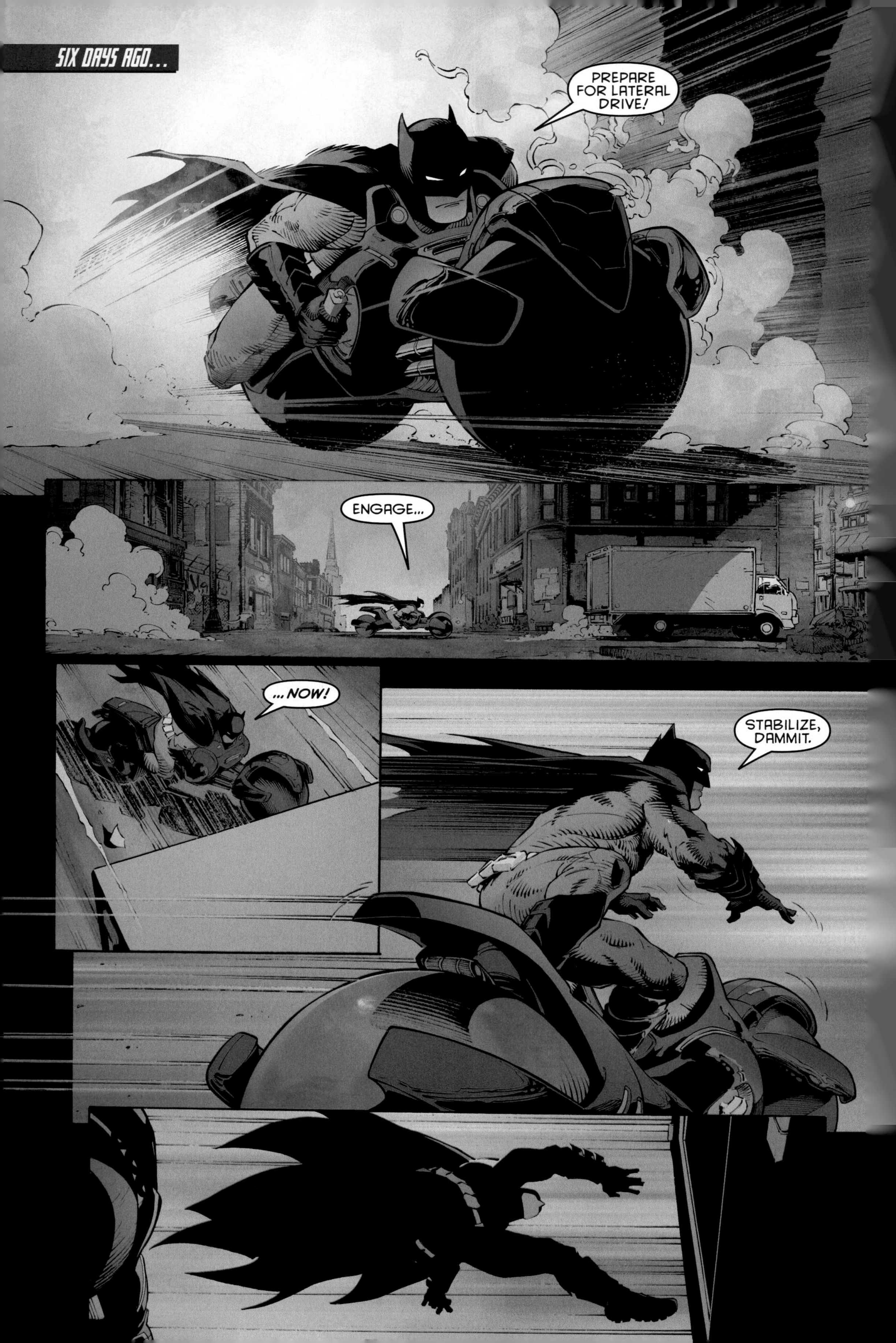
SIX DAYS AGO...
PREPARE FOR LATERAL DRIVE!
ENGAGE...
...NOW!
STABILIZE, DAMMIT.

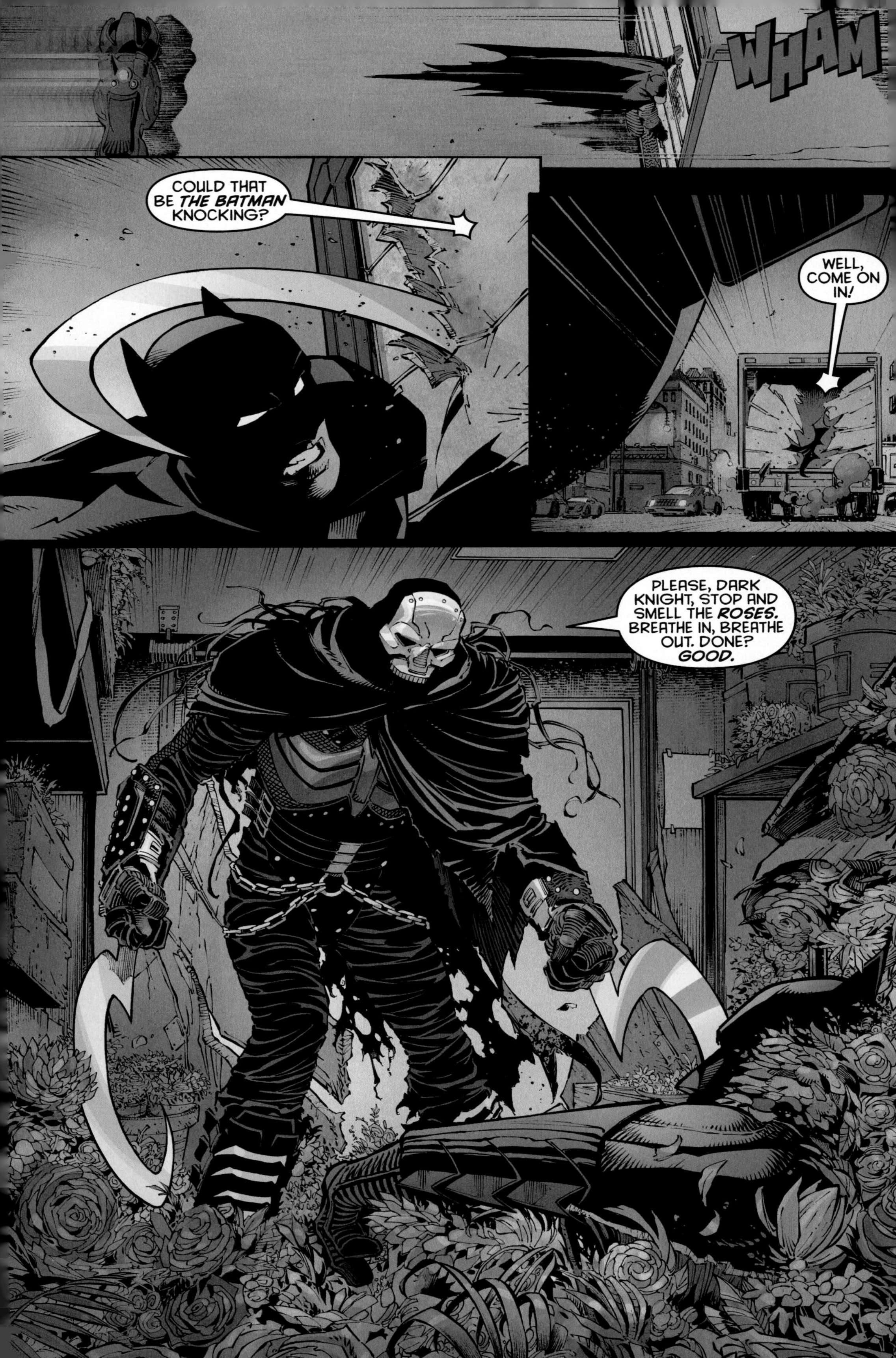
WHAM
COULD THAT BE THE BATMAN KNOCKING?
WELL, COME ON IN!
PLEASE, DARK KNIGHT, STOP AND SMELL THE ROSES. BREATHE IN, BREATHE OUT. DONE? GOOD.

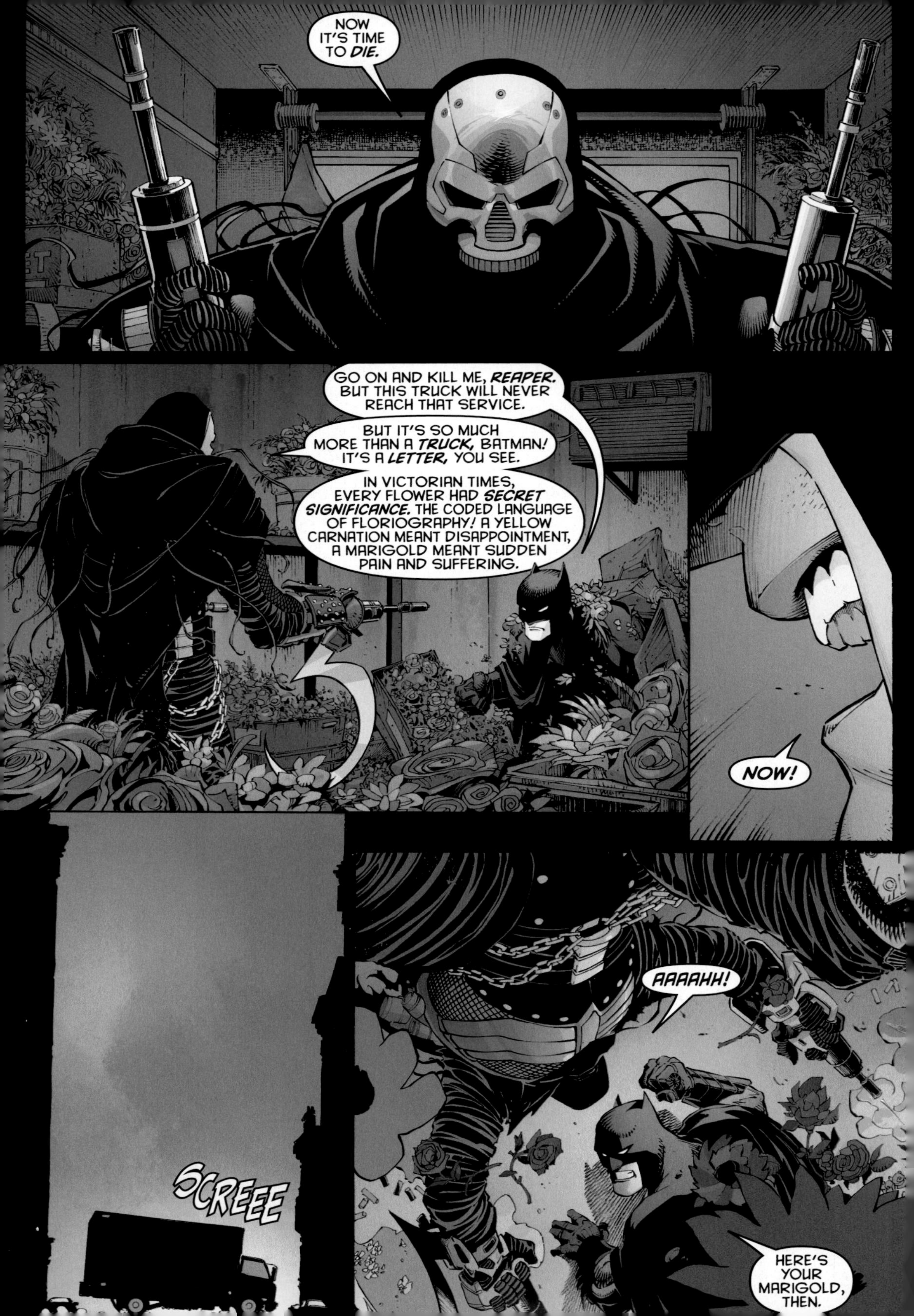
NOW IT'S TIME TO DIE.
GO ON AND KILL ME, REAPER. BUT THIS TRUCK WILL NEVER REACH THAT SERVICE.
BUT IT'S SO MUCH MORE THAN A TRUCK, BATMAN! IT'S A LETTER, YOU SEE.
IN VICTORIAN TIMES, EVERY FLOWER HAD SECRET SIGNIFICANCE. THE CODED LANGUAGE OF FLORIOGRAPHY! A YELLOW CARNATION MEANT DISAPPOINTMENT, A MARIGOLD MEANT SUDDEN PAIN AND SUFFERING.
NOW!
SCREEE
AAAAHH!
HERE'S YOUR MARIGOLD, THEN.

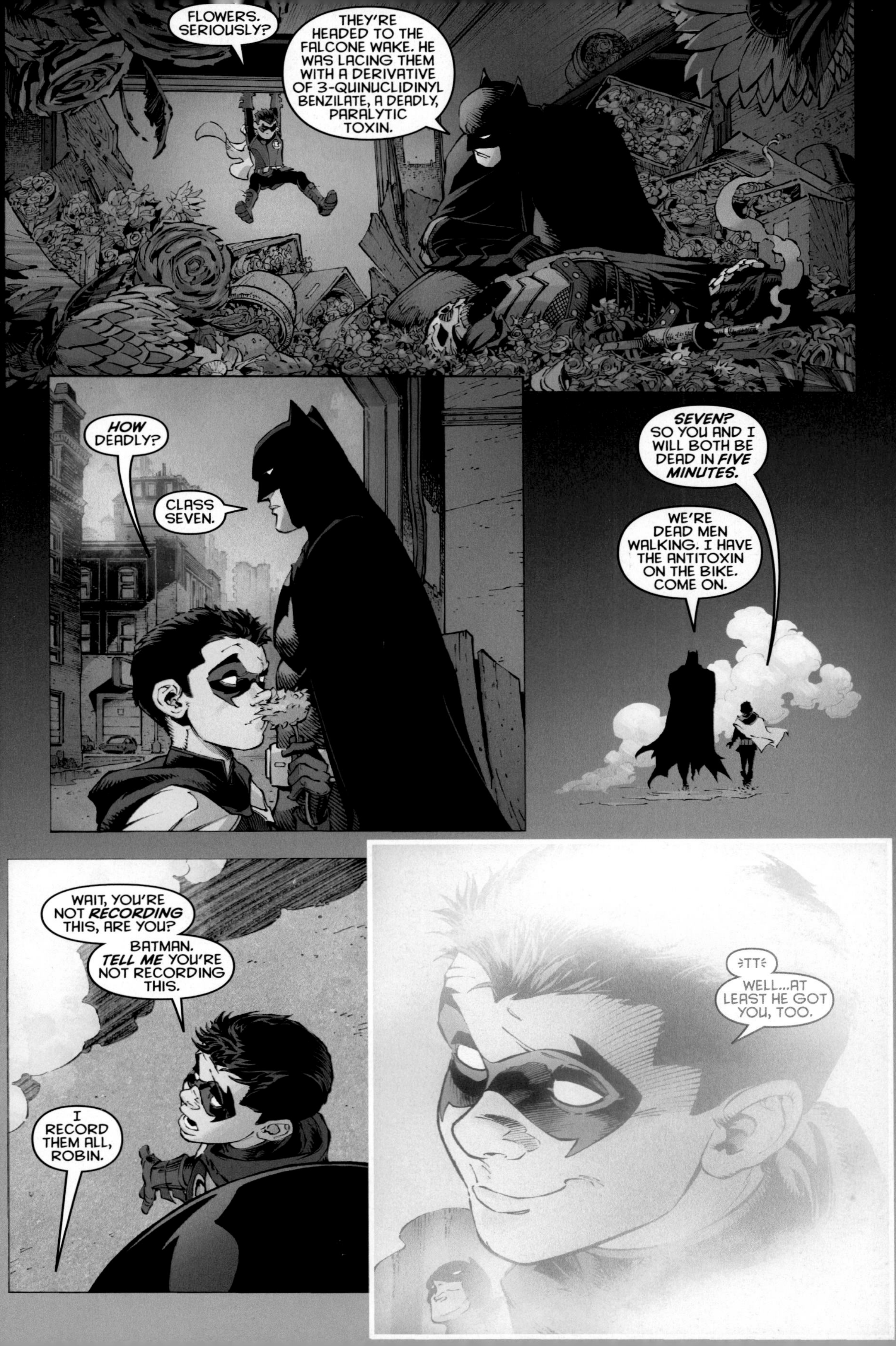
FLOWERS. SERIOUSLY?
THEY'RE HEADED TO THE FALCONE WAKE. HE WAS LACING THEM WITH A DERIVATIVE OF 3-QUINUCLIDINYL BENZILATE, A DEADLY, PARALYTIC TOXIN.
HOW DEADLY?
CLASS SEVEN.
SEVEN? SO YOU AND I WILL BOTH BE DEAD IN *FIVE MINUTES.*
WE'RE DEAD MEN WALKING. I HAVE THE ANTITOXIN ON THE BIKE. COME ON.
WAIT, YOU'RE NOT *RECORDING* THIS, ARE YOU?
BATMAN. *TELL ME* YOU'RE NOT RECORDING THIS.
I RECORD THEM ALL, ROBIN.
TT
WELL...AT LEAST HE GOT YOU, TOO.

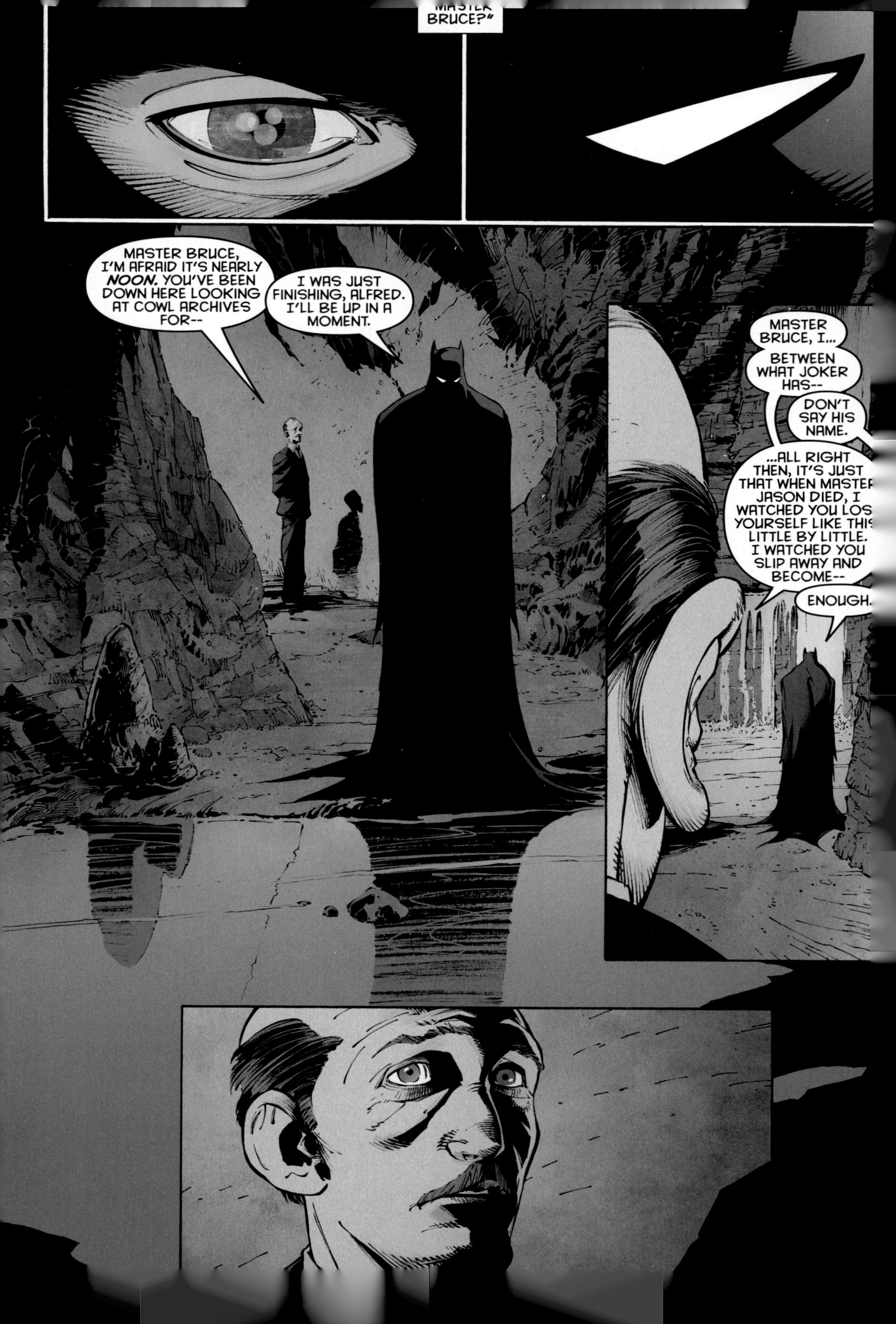
MASTER BRUCE?"
MASTER BRUCE, I'M AFRAID IT'S NEARLY **NOON.** YOU'VE BEEN DOWN HERE LOOKING AT COWL ARCHIVES FOR--
I WAS JUST FINISHING, ALFRED. I'LL BE UP IN A MOMENT.
MASTER BRUCE, I...
BETWEEN WHAT JOKER HAS--
DON'T SAY HIS NAME.
...ALL RIGHT THEN, IT'S JUST THAT WHEN MASTER JASON DIED, I WATCHED YOU LOSE YOURSELF LIKE THIS LITTLE BY LITTLE. I WATCHED YOU SLIP AWAY AND BECOME--
ENOUGH.

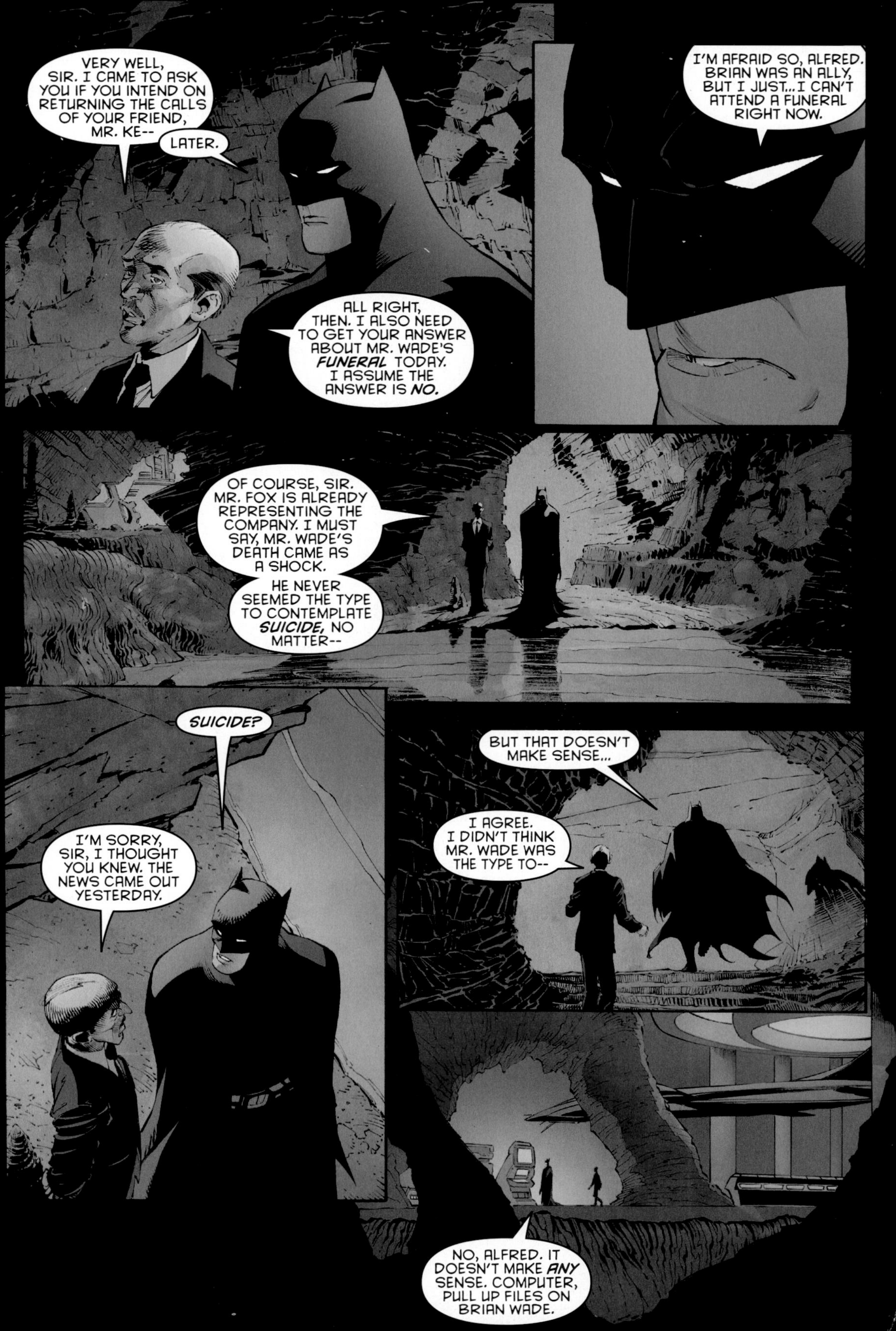
VERY WELL, SIR. I CAME TO ASK YOU IF YOU INTEND ON RETURNING THE CALLS OF YOUR FRIEND, MR. KE--
LATER.
ALL RIGHT, THEN. I ALSO NEED TO GET YOUR ANSWER ABOUT MR. WADE'S FUNERAL TODAY. I ASSUME THE ANSWER IS NO.
I'M AFRAID SO, ALFRED. BRIAN WAS AN ALLY, BUT I JUST... I CAN'T ATTEND A FUNERAL RIGHT NOW.
OF COURSE, SIR. MR. FOX IS ALREADY REPRESENTING THE COMPANY. I MUST SAY, MR. WADE'S DEATH CAME AS A SHOCK.
HE NEVER SEEMED THE TYPE TO CONTEMPLATE SUICIDE, NO MATTER--
SUICIDE?
I'M SORRY, SIR, I THOUGHT YOU KNEW. THE NEWS CAME OUT YESTERDAY.
BUT THAT DOESN'T MAKE SENSE...
I AGREE. I DIDN'T THINK MR. WADE WAS THE TYPE TO--
NO, ALFRED. IT DOESN'T MAKE ANY SENSE. COMPUTER, PULL UP FILES ON BRIAN WADE.

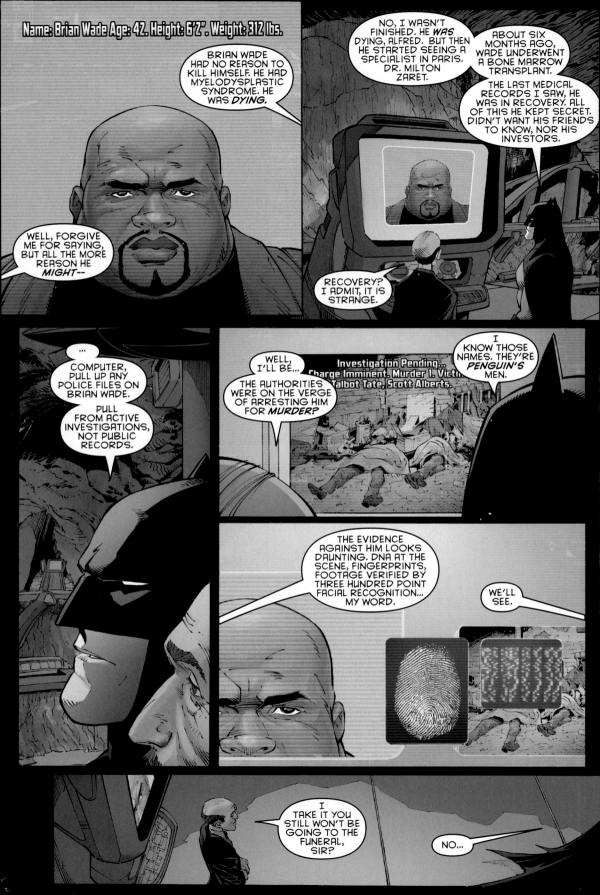

Name: Brian Wade Age: 42. Height: 6'2". Weight: 312 lbs.

BRIAN WADE HAD NO REASON TO KILL HIMSELF. HE HAD MYELODYSPLASTIC SYNDROME. HE WAS *DYING*.

NO, I WASN'T FINISHED. HE *WAS* DYING, ALFRED. BUT THEN HE STARTED SEEING A SPECIALIST IN PARIS. DR. MILTON ZARET.

ABOUT SIX MONTHS AGO, WADE UNDERWENT A BONE MARROW TRANSPLANT.

THE LAST MEDICAL RECORDS I SAW, HE WAS IN RECOVERY. ALL OF THIS HE KEPT SECRET. DIDN'T WANT HIS FRIENDS TO KNOW, NOR HIS INVESTORS.

WELL, FORGIVE ME FOR SAYING, BUT ALL THE MORE REASON HE *MIGHT--*

RECOVERY? I ADMIT, IT IS STRANGE.

...

COMPUTER, PULL UP ANY POLICE FILES ON BRIAN WADE.

PULL FROM ACTIVE INVESTIGATIONS, NOT PUBLIC RECORDS.

WELL, I'LL BE... THE AUTHORITIES WERE ON THE VERGE OF ARRESTING HIM FOR *MURDER?*

Investigation Pending... Charge Imminent. Murder I. Victim. Talbot Tate, Scott Alberts.

I KNOW THOSE NAMES. THEY'RE *PENGUIN'S* MEN.

THE EVIDENCE AGAINST HIM LOOKS DAUNTING. DNA AT THE SCENE, FINGERPRINTS, FOOTAGE VERIFIED BY THREE HUNDRED POINT FACIAL RECOGNITION... MY WORD.

WE'LL SEE.

I TAKE IT YOU STILL WON'T BE GOING TO THE FUNERAL, SIR?

NO...

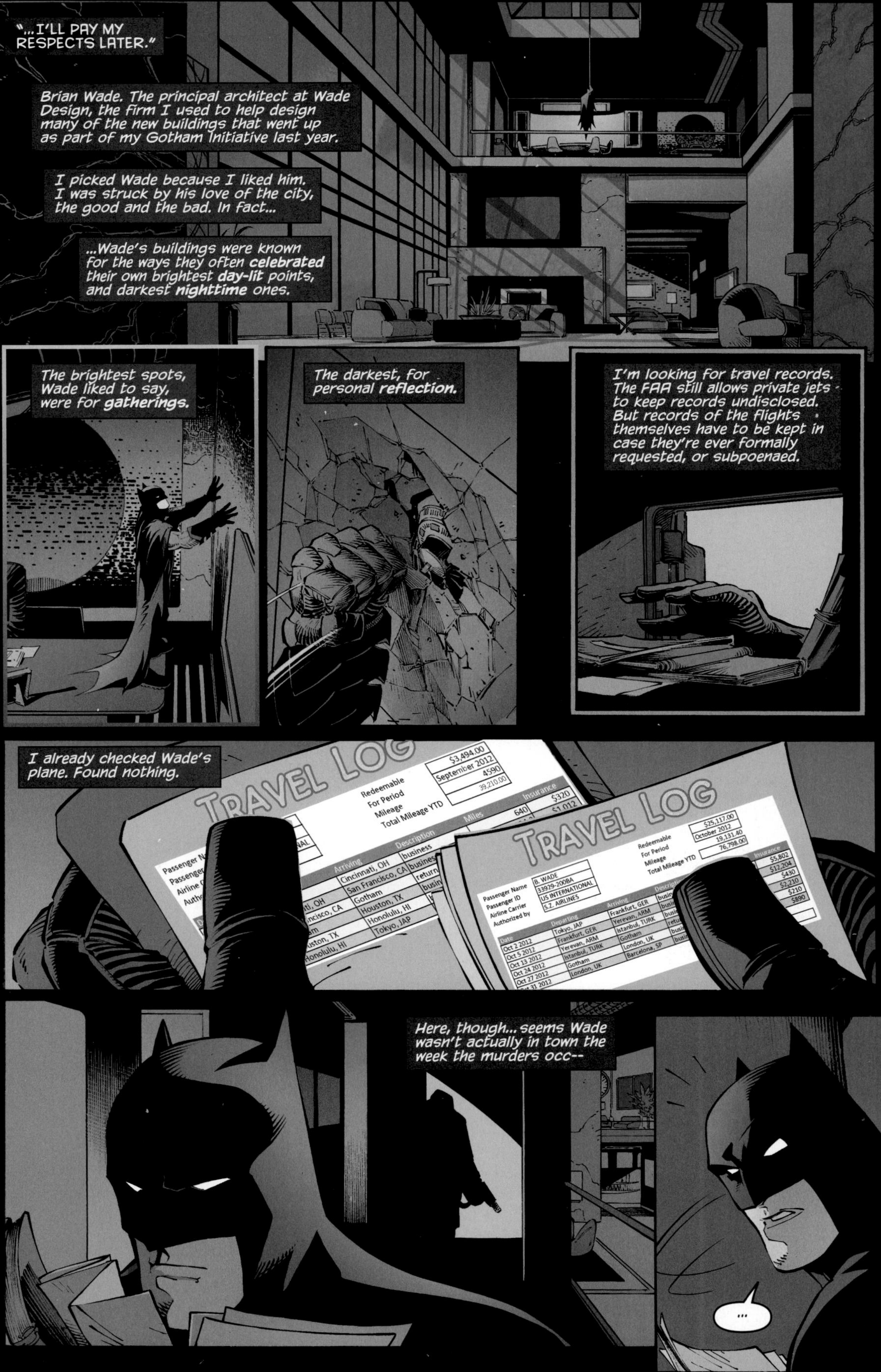
"...I'LL PAY MY RESPECTS LATER."
Brian Wade. The principal architect at Wade Design, the firm I used to help design many of the new buildings that went up as part of my Gotham Initiative last year.
I picked Wade because I liked him. I was struck by his love of the city, the good and the bad. In fact...
...Wade's buildings were known for the ways they often celebrated their own brightest day-lit points, and darkest nighttime ones.
The brightest spots, Wade liked to say, were for gatherings.
The darkest, for personal reflection.
I'm looking for travel records. The FAA still allows private jets to keep records undisclosed. But records of the flights themselves have to be kept in case they're ever formally requested, or subpoenaed.
I already checked Wade's plane. Found nothing.
TRAVEL LOG
Redeemable $3,494.00
For Period September 2012
Mileage 4590
Total Mileage YTD 39,210.00
TRAVEL LOG
Redeemable $25,117.00
For Period October 2012
Mileage 19,131.40
Total Mileage YTD 76,798.00
Passenger Name B. WADE
Passenger ID 33929-200BA
Airline Carrier US INTERNATIONAL
Authorized by S.Z. AIRLINES
Here, though...seems Wade wasn't actually in town the week the murders occ--
...

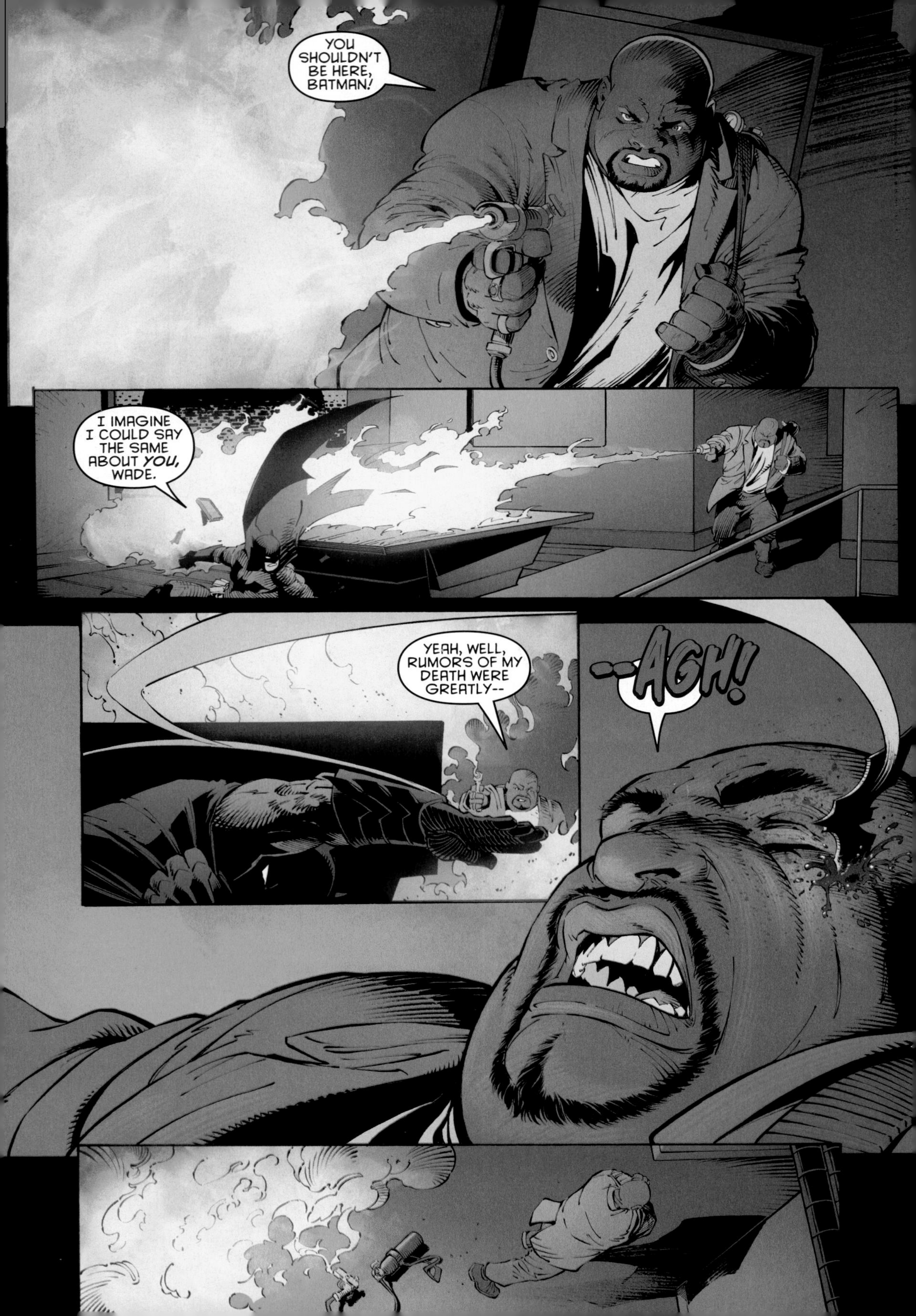
YOU SHOULDN'T BE HERE, BATMAN!
I IMAGINE I COULD SAY THE SAME ABOUT *YOU,* WADE.
YEAH, WELL, RUMORS OF MY DEATH WERE GREATLY--
--AGH!

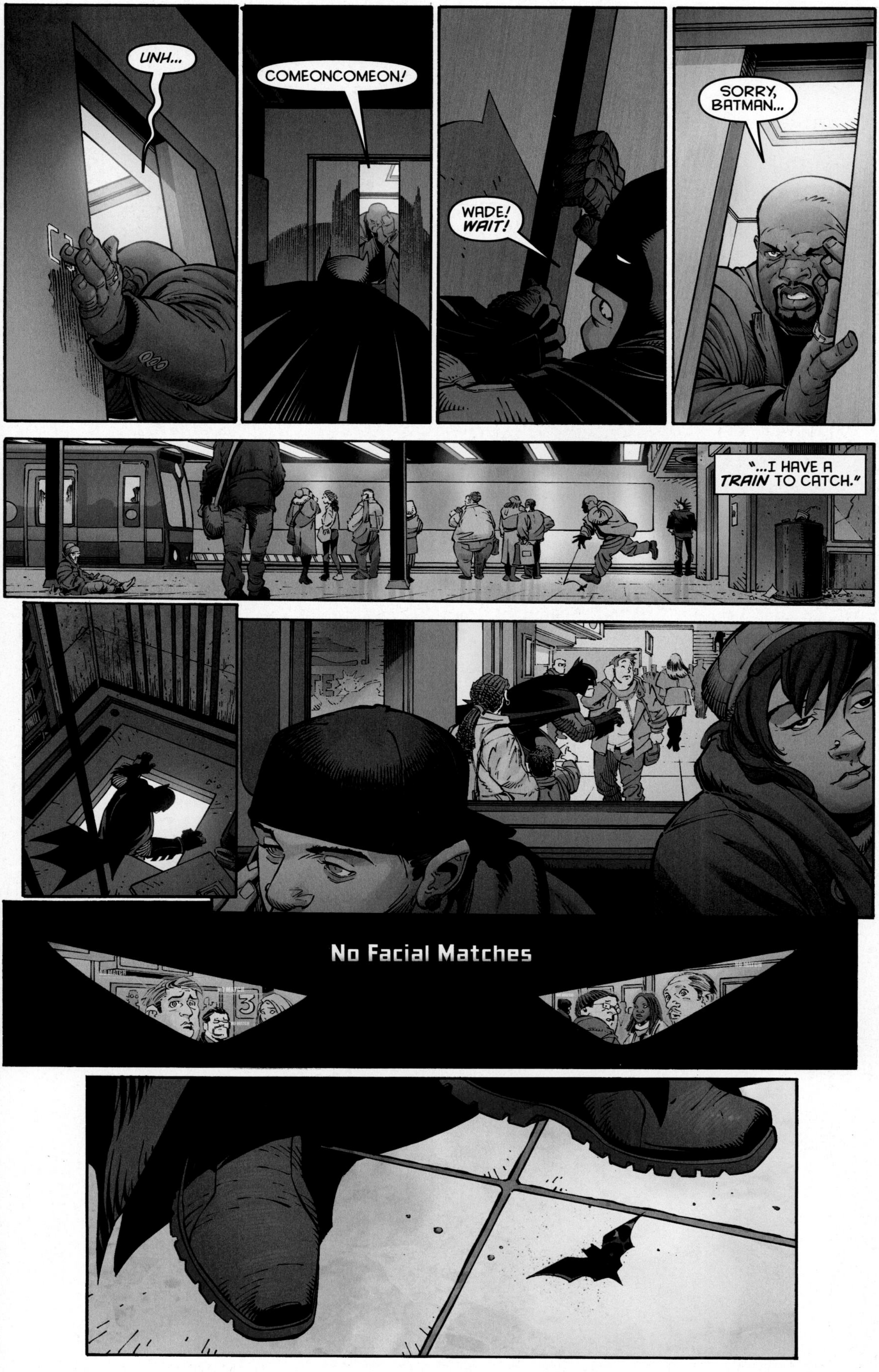
UNH...
COMEONCOMEON!
WADE! WAIT!
SORRY, BATMAN...
"...I HAVE A TRAIN TO CATCH."
No Facial Matches

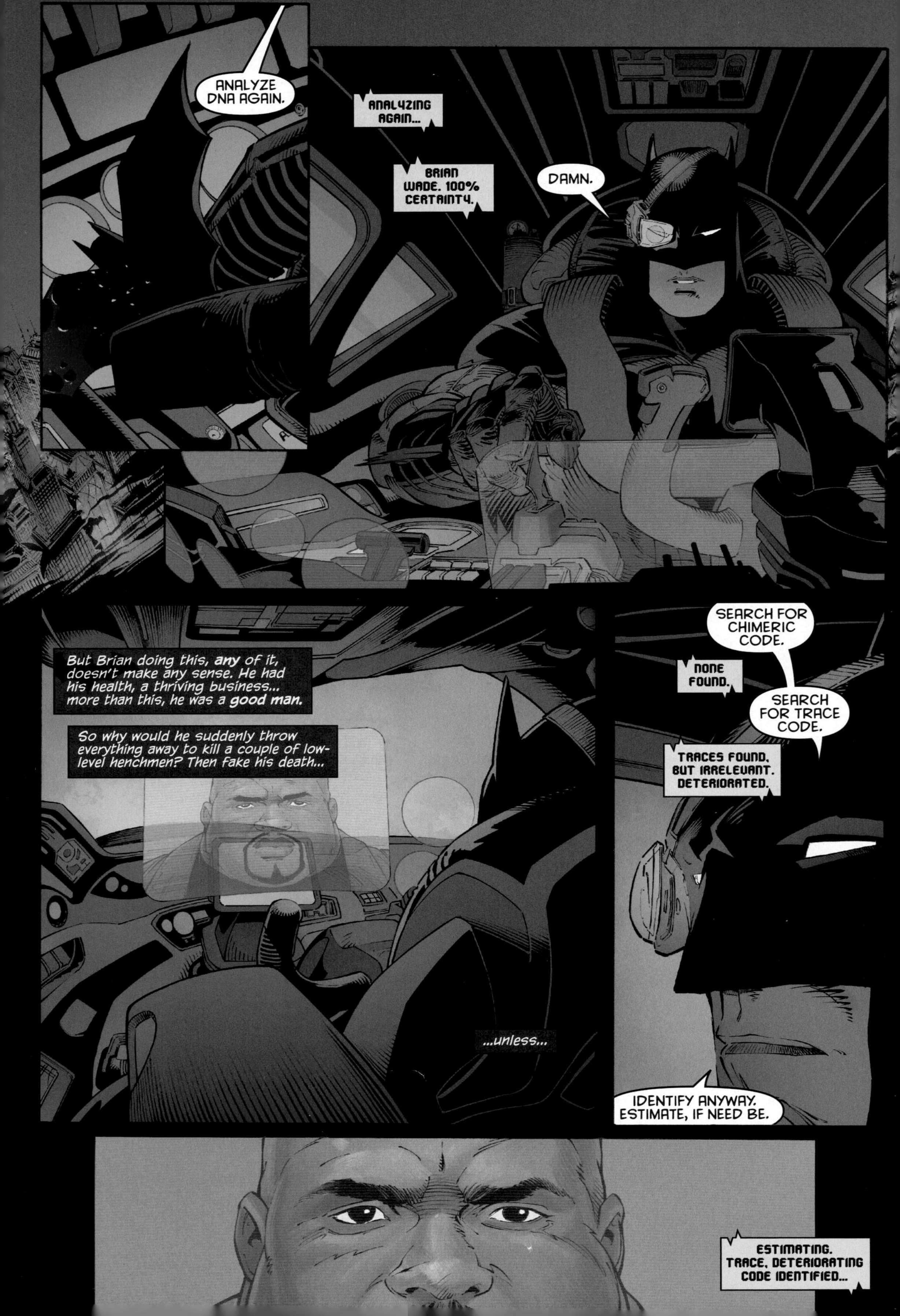
ANALYZE DNA AGAIN.
ANALYZING AGAIN...
BRIAN WADE. 100% CERTAINTY.
DAMN.
But Brian doing this, any of it, doesn't make any sense. He had his health, a thriving business... more than this, he was a good man.
So why would he suddenly throw everything away to kill a couple of low-level henchmen? Then fake his death...
...unless...
SEARCH FOR CHIMERIC CODE.
NONE FOUND.
SEARCH FOR TRACE CODE.
TRACES FOUND, BUT IRRELEVANT. DETERIORATED.
IDENTIFY ANYWAY. ESTIMATE, IF NEED BE.
ESTIMATING. TRACE, DETERIORATING CODE IDENTIFIED...

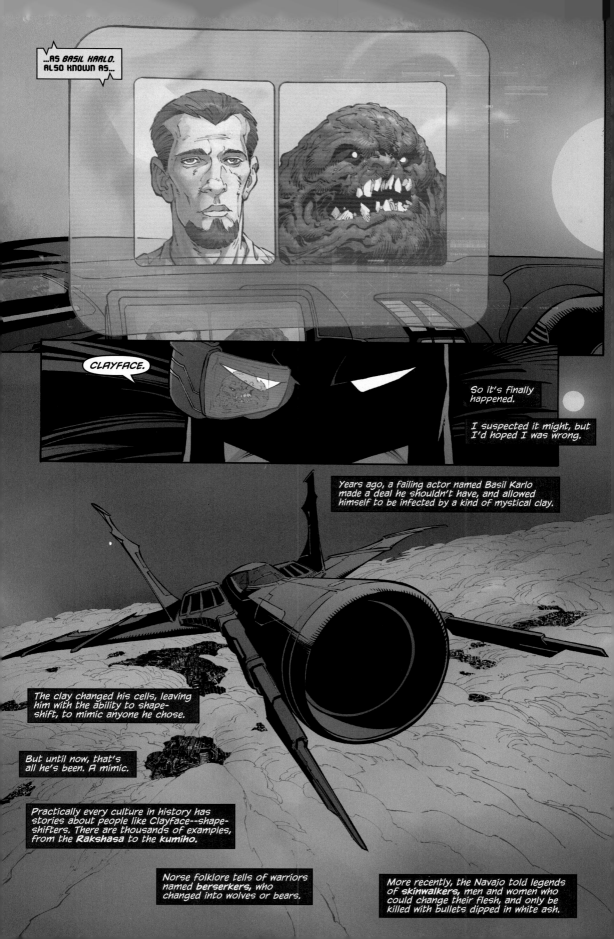

...AS *BASIL KARLO.* ALSO KNOWN AS...

CLAYFACE.

So it's finally happened.

I suspected it might, but I'd hoped I was wrong.

Years ago, a failing actor named Basil Karlo made a deal he shouldn't have, and allowed himself to be infected by a kind of mystical clay.

The clay changed his cells, leaving him with the ability to shape-shift, to mimic anyone he chose.

But until now, that's all he's been. A mimic.

Practically every culture in history has stories about people like Clayface--shape-shifters. There are thousands of examples, from the *Rakshasa* to the *kumiho.*

Norse folklore tells of warriors named *berserkers,* who changed into wolves or bears.

More recently, the Navajo told legends of *skinwalkers,* men and women who could change their flesh, and only be killed with bullets dipped in white ash.

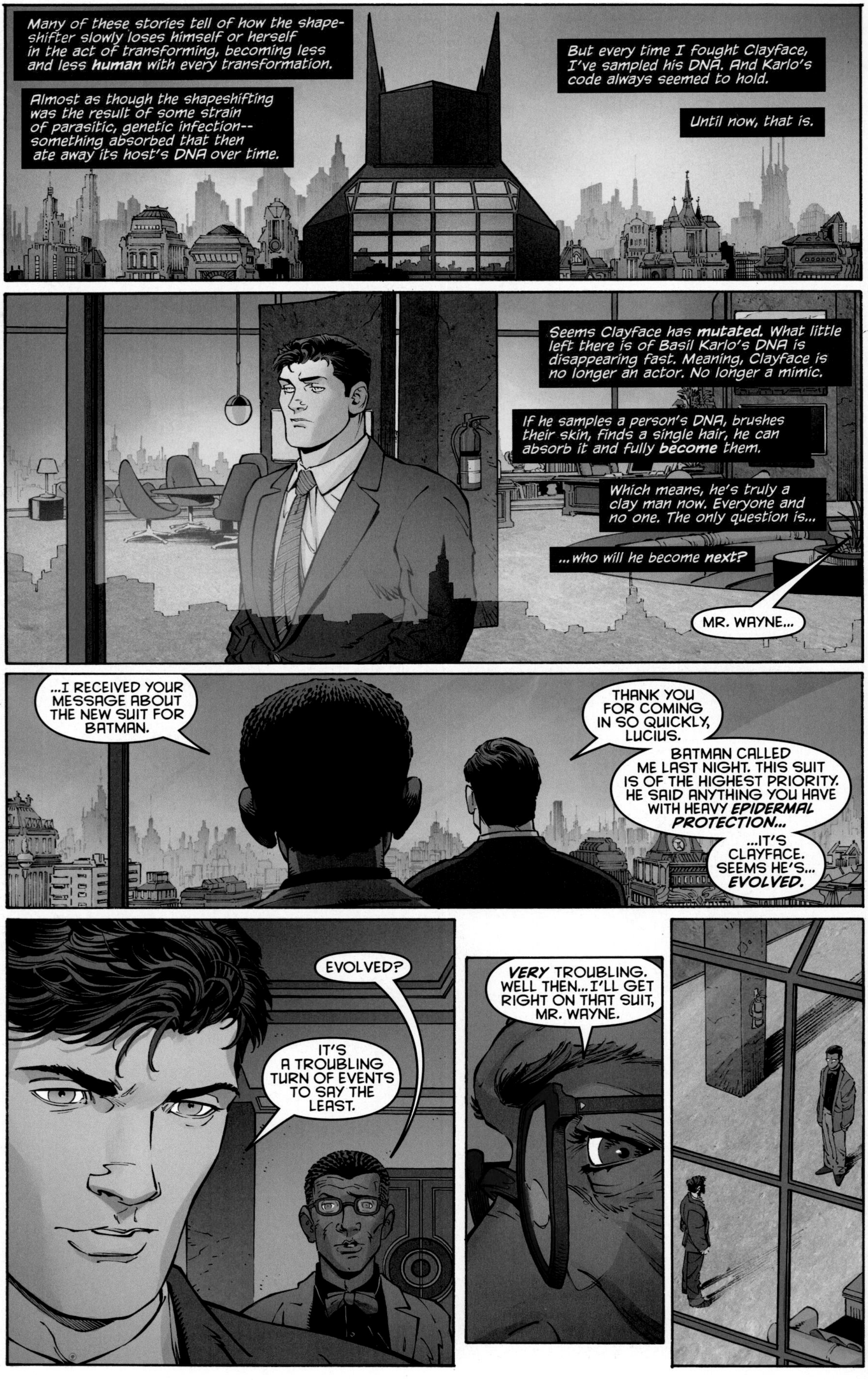

Many of these stories tell of how the shape-shifter slowly loses himself or herself in the act of transforming, becoming less and less **human** with every transformation.
Almost as though the shapeshifting was the result of some strain of parasitic, genetic infection--something absorbed that then ate away its host's DNA over time.
But every time I fought Clayface, I've sampled his DNA. And Karlo's code always seemed to hold.
Until now, that is.
Seems Clayface has **mutated.** What little left there is of Basil Karlo's DNA is disappearing fast. Meaning, Clayface is no longer an actor. No longer a mimic.
If he samples a person's DNA, brushes their skin, finds a single hair, he can absorb it and fully **become** them.
Which means, he's truly a clay man now. Everyone and no one. The only question is...
...who will he become **next?**
MR. WAYNE...
...I RECEIVED YOUR MESSAGE ABOUT THE NEW SUIT FOR BATMAN.
THANK YOU FOR COMING IN SO QUICKLY, LUCIUS.
BATMAN CALLED ME LAST NIGHT. THIS SUIT IS OF THE HIGHEST PRIORITY. HE SAID ANYTHING YOU HAVE WITH HEAVY ***EPIDERMAL PROTECTION...***
...IT'S CLAYFACE. SEEMS HE'S... ***EVOLVED.***
EVOLVED?
IT'S A TROUBLING TURN OF EVENTS TO SAY THE LEAST.
VERY TROUBLING. WELL THEN...I'LL GET RIGHT ON THAT SUIT, MR. WAYNE.

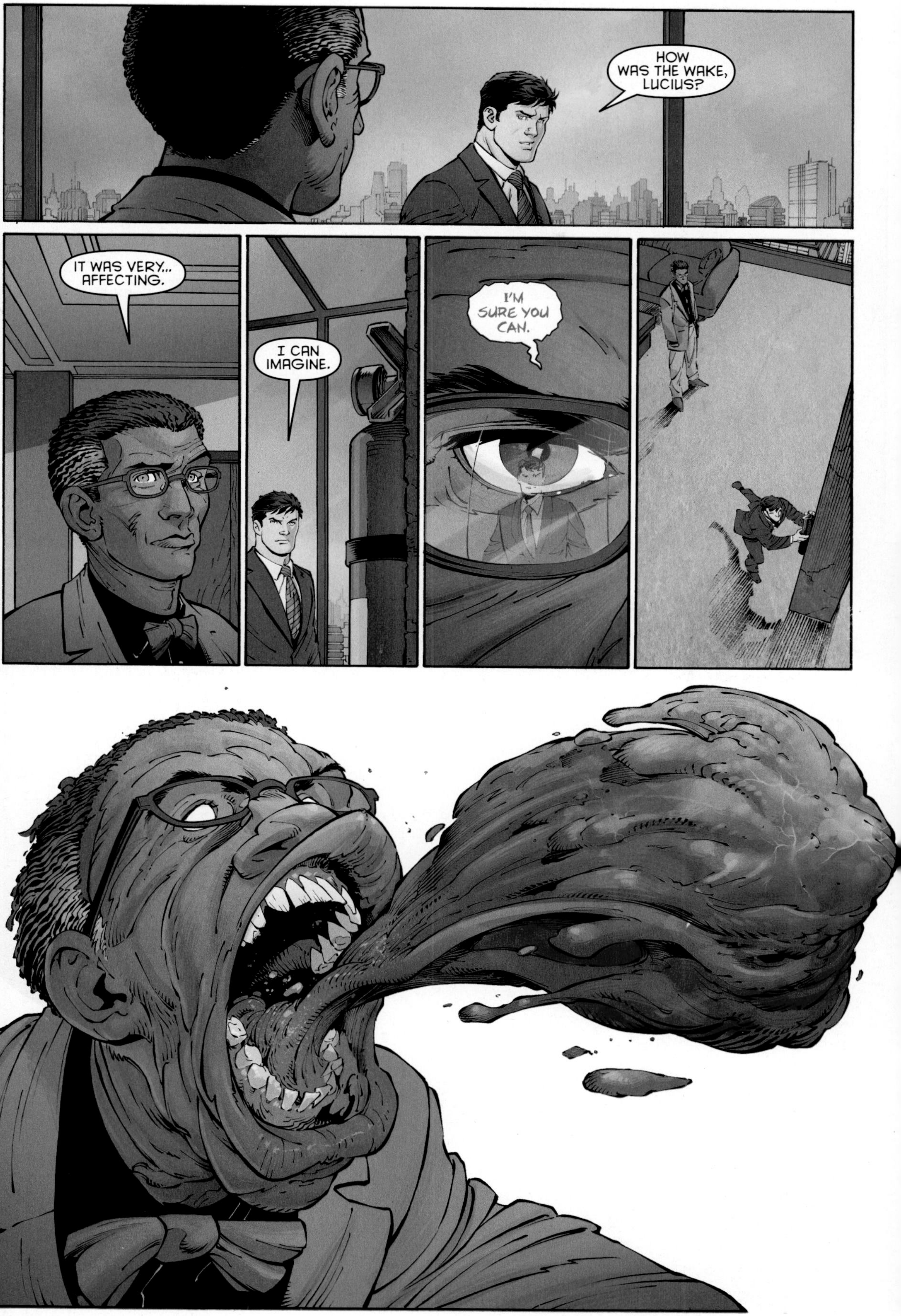
HOW WAS THE WAKE, LUCIUS?
IT WAS VERY... AFFECTING.
I CAN IMAGINE.
I'M SURE YOU CAN.

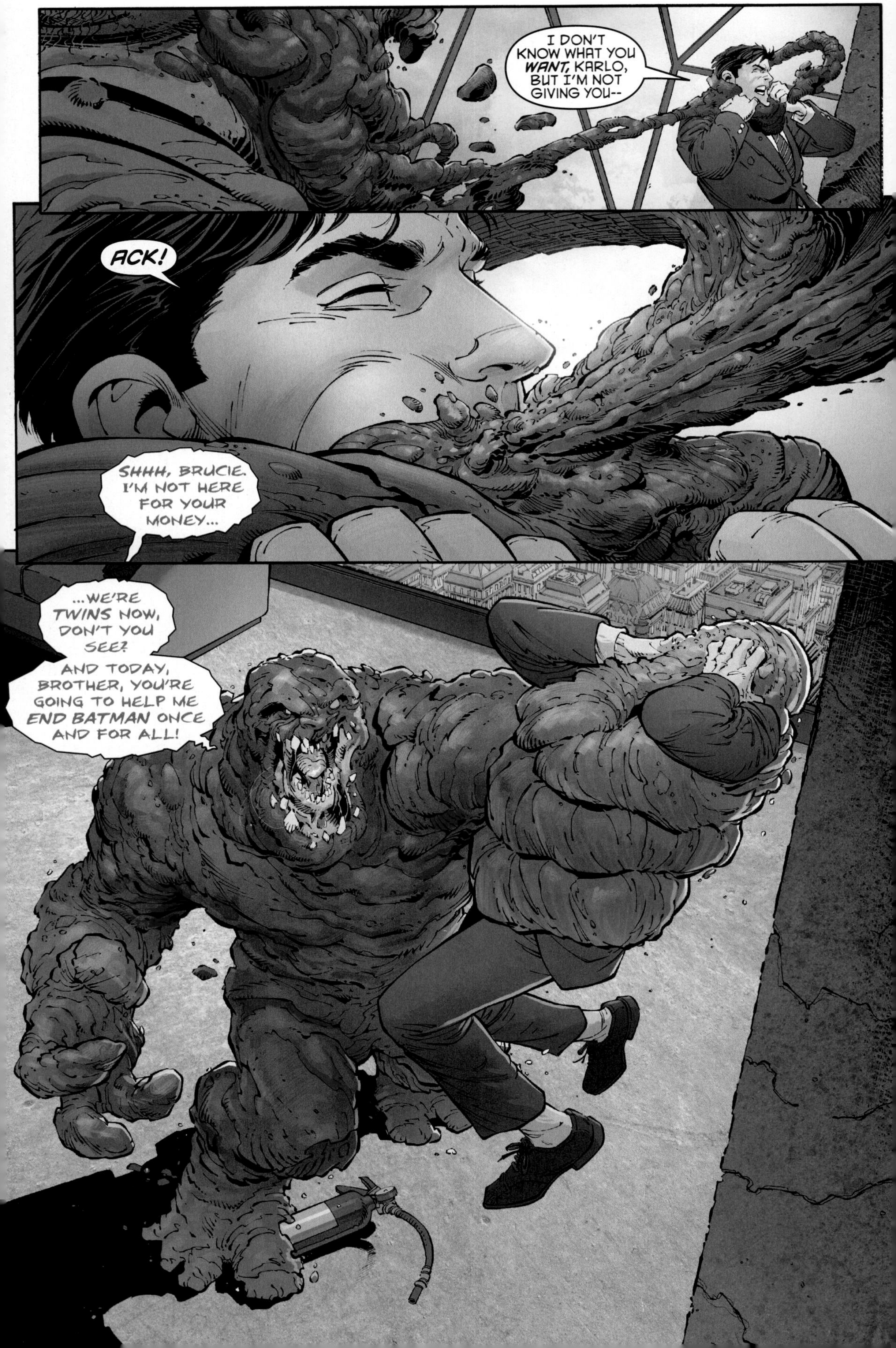
I DON'T KNOW WHAT YOU WANT, KARLO, BUT I'M NOT GIVING YOU--
ACK!
SHHH, BRUCIE. I'M NOT HERE FOR YOUR MONEY...
...WE'RE TWINS NOW, DON'T YOU SEE?
AND TODAY, BROTHER, YOU'RE GOING TO HELP ME END BATMAN ONCE AND FOR ALL!

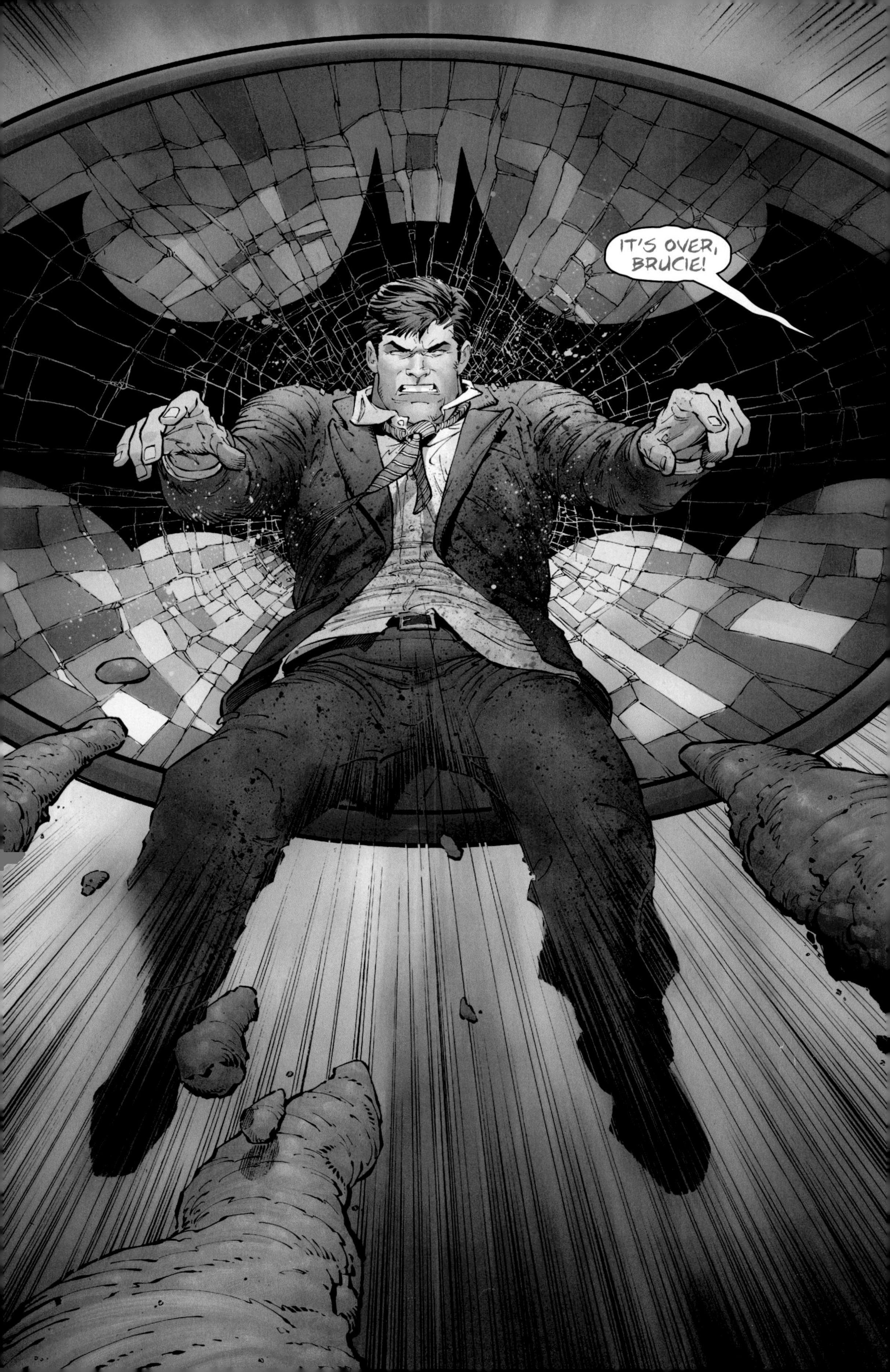
IT'S OVER, BRUCIE!

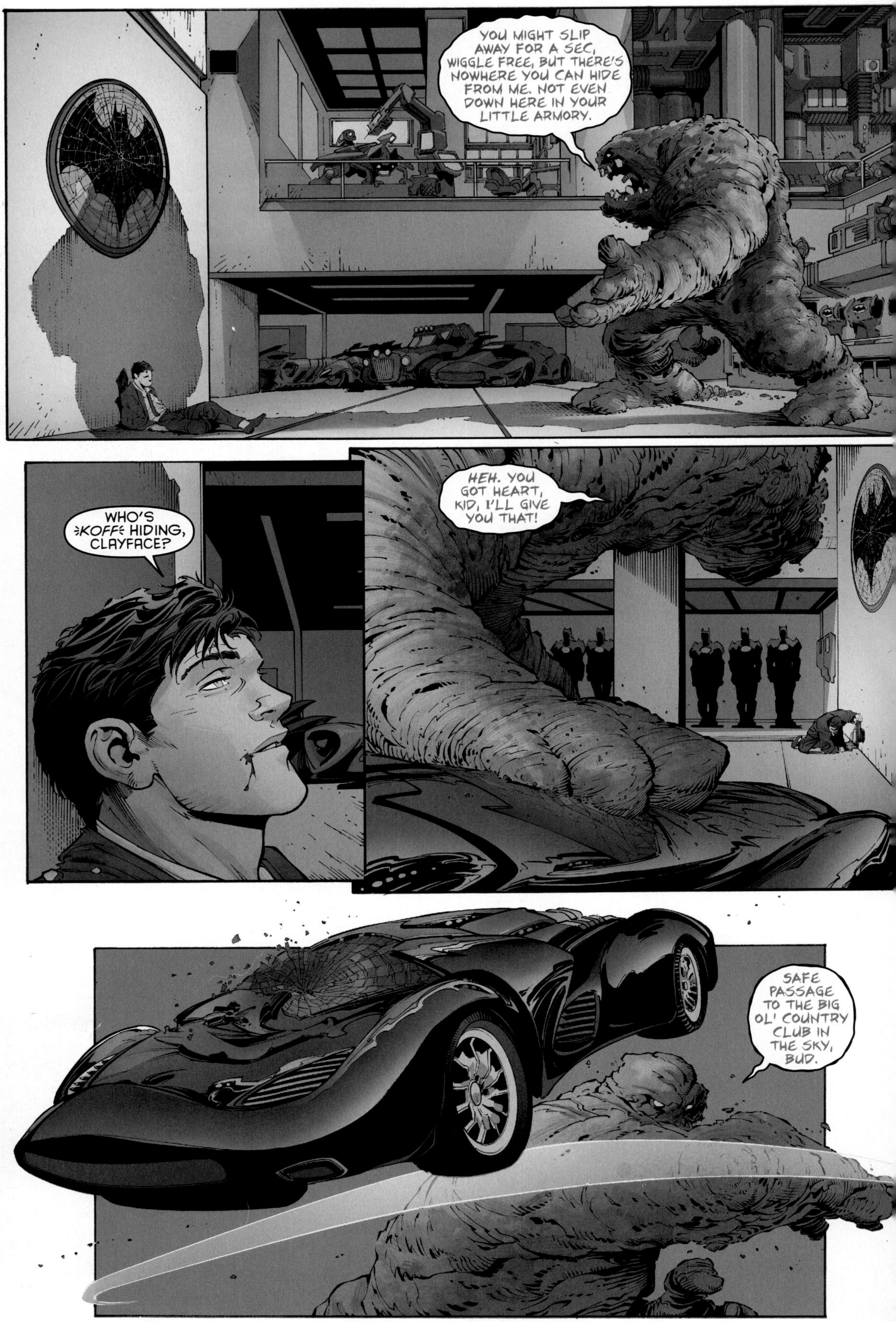
YOU MIGHT SLIP AWAY FOR A SEC, WIGGLE FREE, BUT THERE'S NOWHERE YOU CAN HIDE FROM ME. NOT EVEN DOWN HERE IN YOUR LITTLE ARMORY.
WHO'S *KOFF* HIDING, CLAYFACE?
HEH. YOU GOT HEART, KID, I'LL GIVE YOU THAT!
SAFE PASSAGE TO THE BIG OL' COUNTRY CLUB IN THE SKY, BUD.

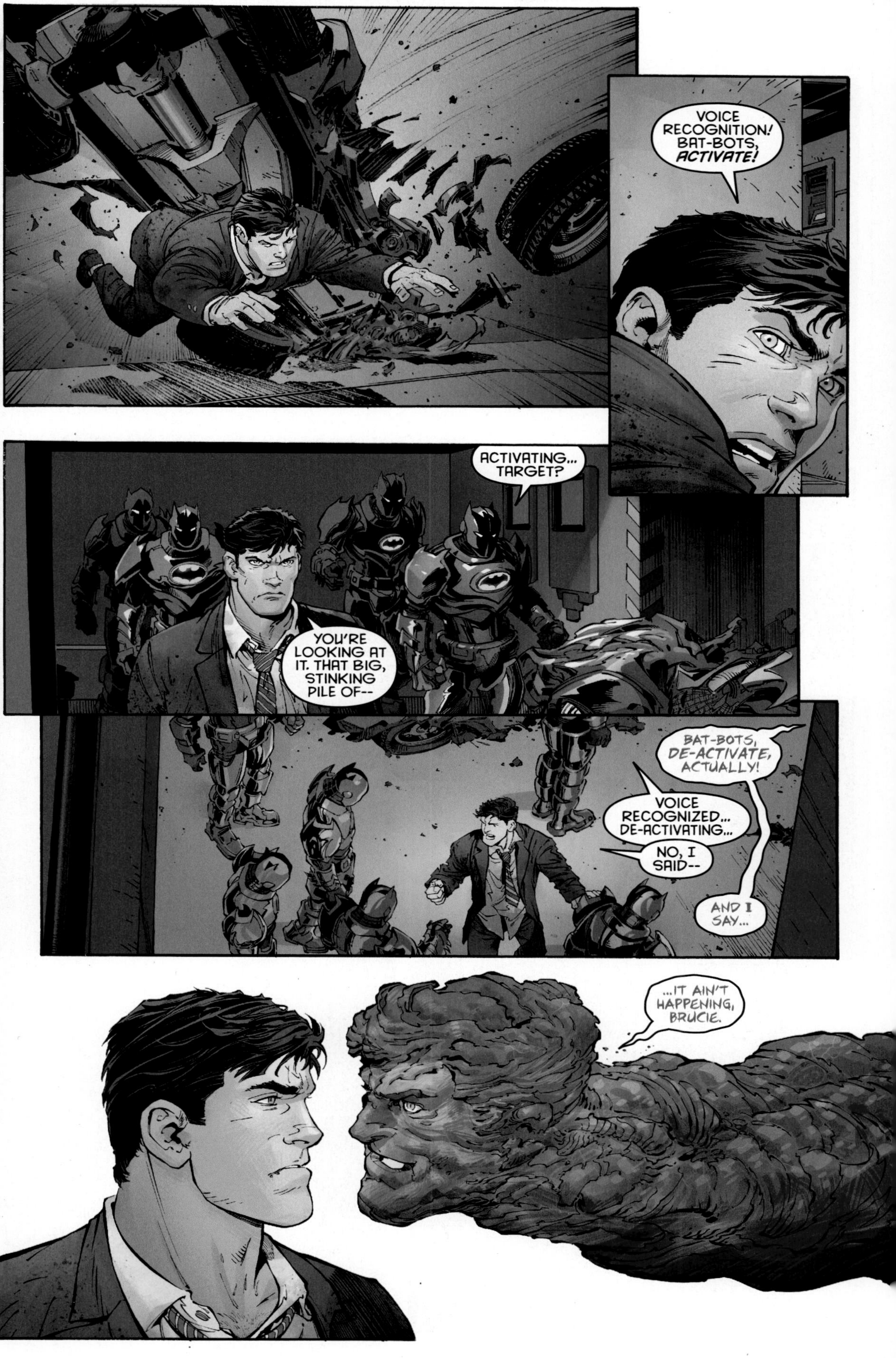
VOICE RECOGNITION! BAT-BOTS, ACTIVATE!
ACTIVATING... TARGET?
YOU'RE LOOKING AT IT. THAT BIG, STINKING PILE OF--
BAT-BOTS, DE-ACTIVATE, ACTUALLY!
VOICE RECOGNIZED... DE-ACTIVATING...
NO, I SAID--
AND I SAY...
...IT AIN'T HAPPENING, BRUCIE.

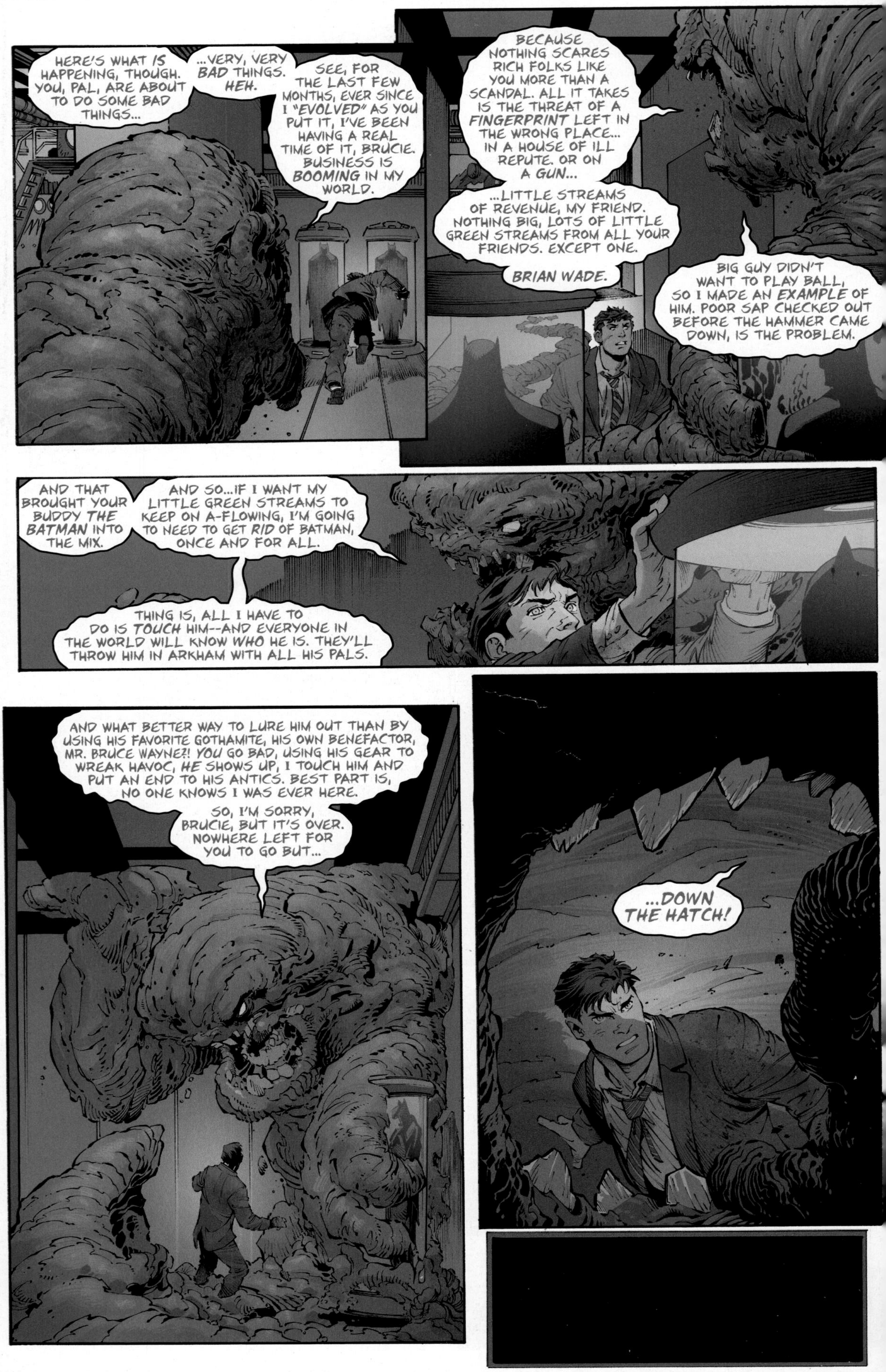
HERE'S WHAT IS HAPPENING, THOUGH. YOU, PAL, ARE ABOUT TO DO SOME BAD THINGS...
...VERY, VERY BAD THINGS. HEH.
SEE, FOR THE LAST FEW MONTHS, EVER SINCE I "EVOLVED" AS YOU PUT IT, I'VE BEEN HAVING A REAL TIME OF IT, BRUCIE. BUSINESS IS BOOMING IN MY WORLD.
BECAUSE NOTHING SCARES RICH FOLKS LIKE YOU MORE THAN A SCANDAL. ALL IT TAKES IS THE THREAT OF A FINGERPRINT LEFT IN THE WRONG PLACE... IN A HOUSE OF ILL REPUTE. OR ON A GUN...
...LITTLE STREAMS OF REVENUE, MY FRIEND. NOTHING BIG, LOTS OF LITTLE GREEN STREAMS FROM ALL YOUR FRIENDS. EXCEPT ONE.
BRIAN WADE.
BIG GUY DIDN'T WANT TO PLAY BALL, SO I MADE AN EXAMPLE OF HIM. POOR SAP CHECKED OUT BEFORE THE HAMMER CAME DOWN, IS THE PROBLEM.
AND THAT BROUGHT YOUR BUDDY THE BATMAN INTO THE MIX.
AND SO...IF I WANT MY LITTLE GREEN STREAMS TO KEEP ON A-FLOWING, I'M GOING TO NEED TO GET RID OF BATMAN, ONCE AND FOR ALL.
THING IS, ALL I HAVE TO DO IS TOUCH HIM--AND EVERYONE IN THE WORLD WILL KNOW WHO HE IS. THEY'LL THROW HIM IN ARKHAM WITH ALL HIS PALS.
AND WHAT BETTER WAY TO LURE HIM OUT THAN BY USING HIS FAVORITE GOTHAMITE, HIS OWN BENEFACTOR, MR. BRUCE WAYNE?! YOU GO BAD, USING HIS GEAR TO WREAK HAVOC, HE SHOWS UP, I TOUCH HIM AND PUT AN END TO HIS ANTICS. BEST PART IS, NO ONE KNOWS I WAS EVER HERE.
SO, I'M SORRY, BRUCIE, BUT IT'S OVER. NOWHERE LEFT FOR YOU TO GO BUT...
...DOWN THE HATCH!

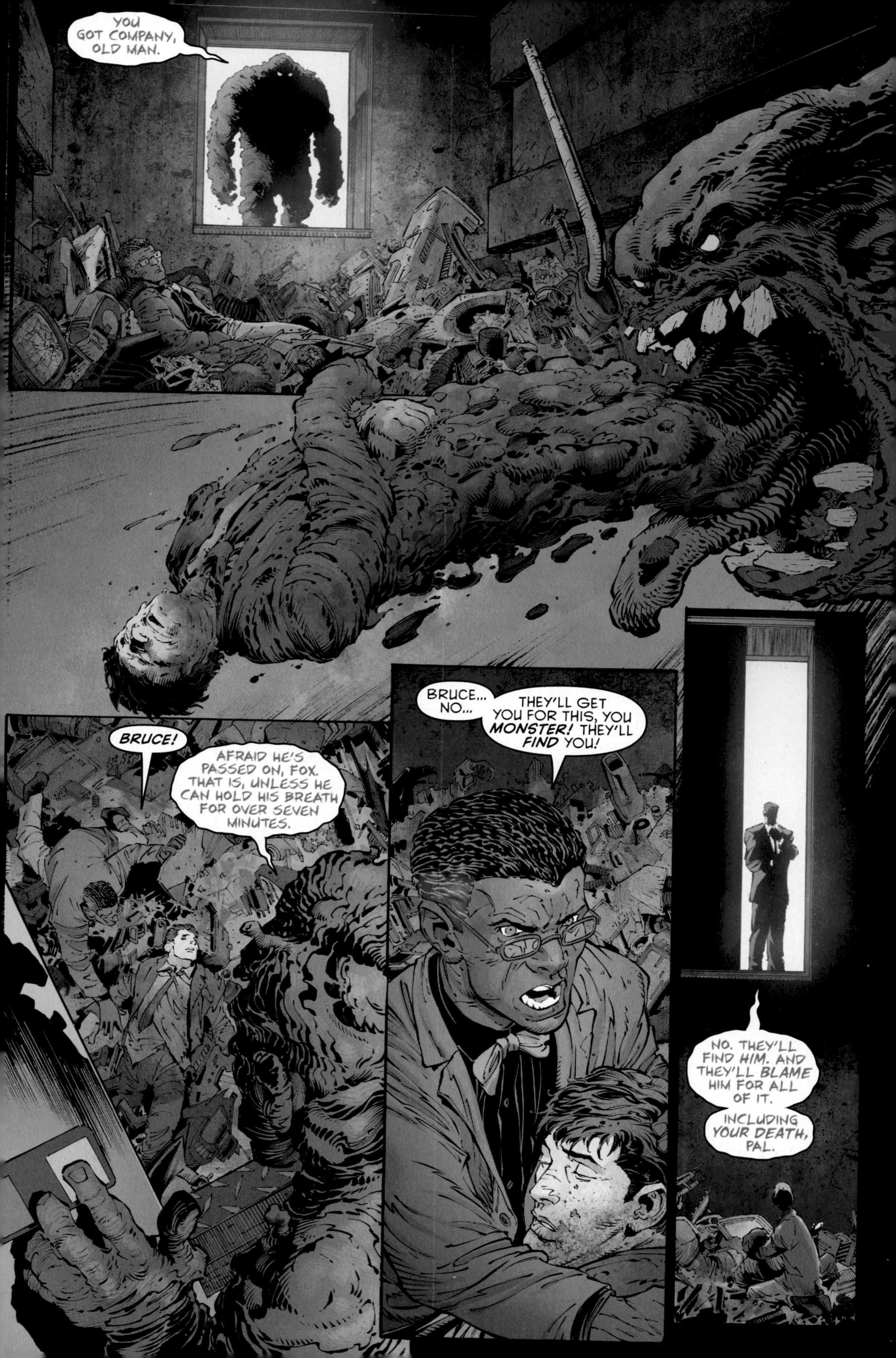
YOU GOT COMPANY, OLD MAN.
BRUCE!
AFRAID HE'S PASSED ON, FOX. THAT IS, UNLESS HE CAN HOLD HIS BREATH FOR OVER SEVEN MINUTES.
BRUCE... NO...
THEY'LL GET YOU FOR THIS, YOU MONSTER! THEY'LL FIND YOU!
NO. THEY'LL FIND HIM. AND THEY'LL BLAME HIM FOR ALL OF IT.
INCLUDING YOUR DEATH, PAL.

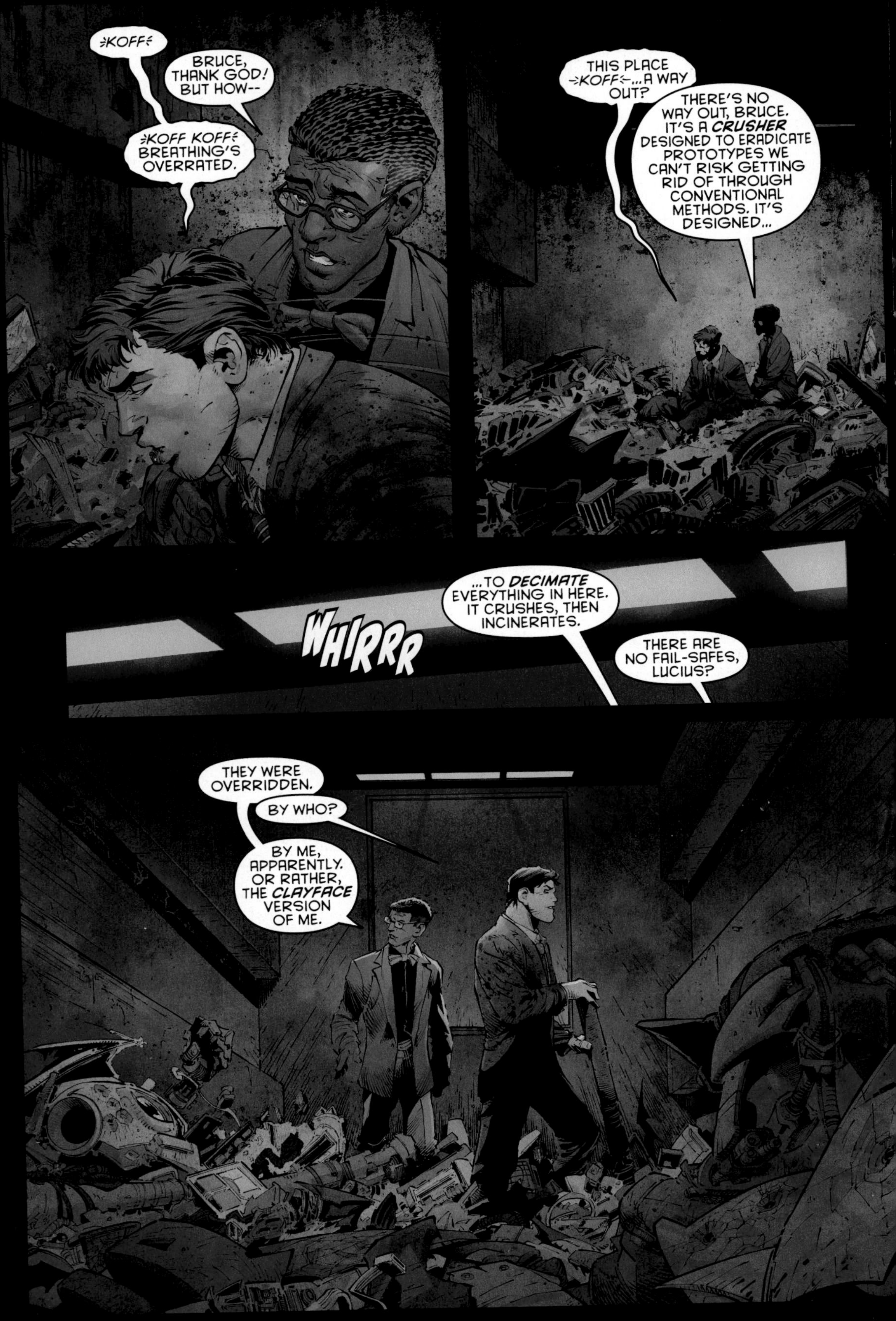

KOFF
BRUCE, THANK GOD! BUT HOW--
KOFF KOFF BREATHING'S OVERRATED.
THIS PLACE -*KOFF*-...A WAY OUT?
THERE'S NO WAY OUT, BRUCE. IT'S A CRUSHER DESIGNED TO ERADICATE PROTOTYPES WE CAN'T RISK GETTING RID OF THROUGH CONVENTIONAL METHODS. IT'S DESIGNED...
WHIRRR
...TO DECIMATE EVERYTHING IN HERE. IT CRUSHES, THEN INCINERATES.
THERE ARE NO FAIL-SAFES, LUCIUS?
THEY WERE OVERRIDDEN.
BY WHO?
BY ME, APPARENTLY. OR RATHER, THE CLAYFACE VERSION OF ME.

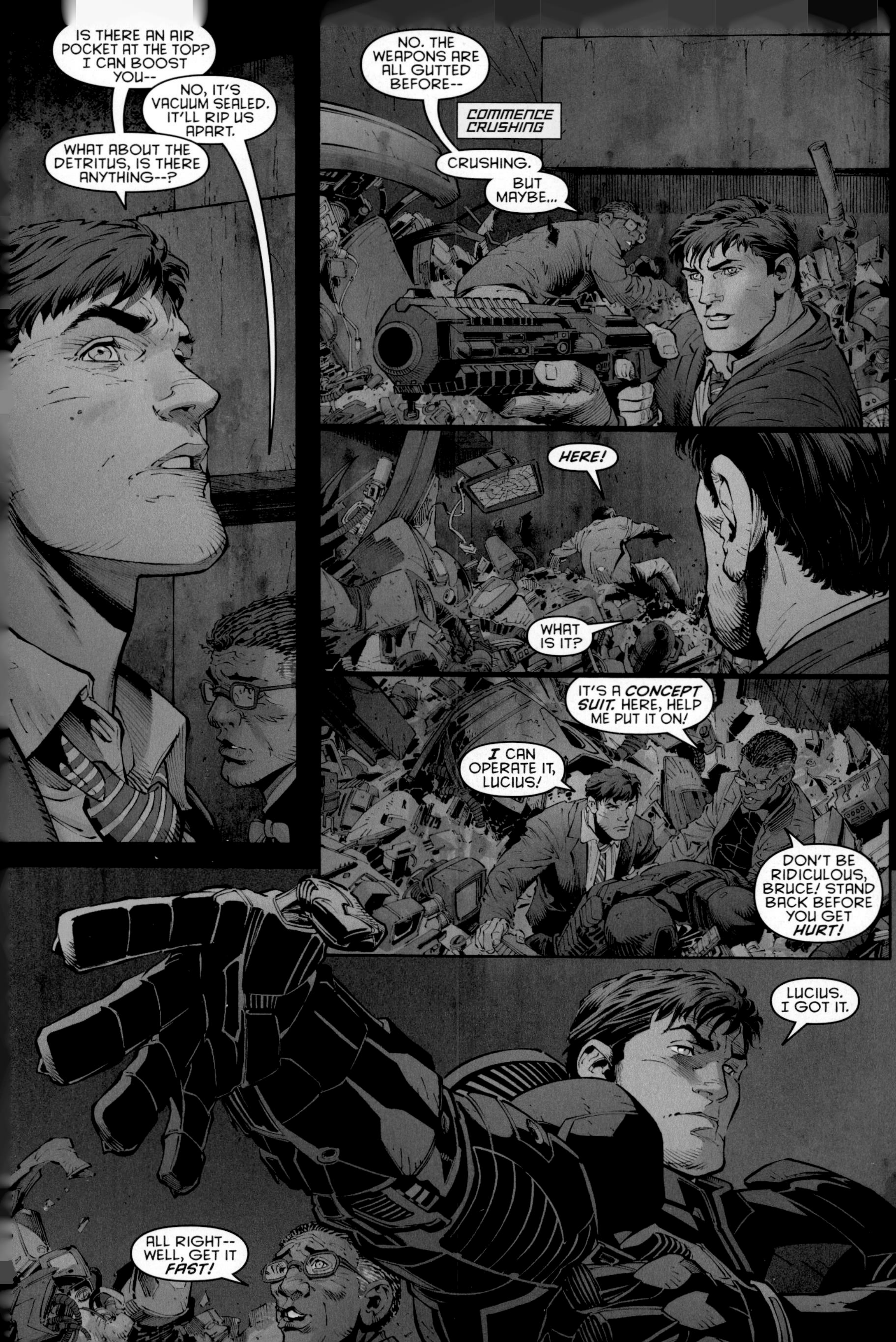
IS THERE AN AIR POCKET AT THE TOP? I CAN BOOST YOU--
NO, IT'S VACUUM SEALED. IT'LL RIP US APART.
WHAT ABOUT THE DETRITUS, IS THERE ANYTHING--?
NO. THE WEAPONS ARE ALL GUTTED BEFORE--
COMMENCE CRUSHING
CRUSHING.
BUT MAYBE...
HERE!
WHAT IS IT?
IT'S A CONCEPT SUIT. HERE, HELP ME PUT IT ON!
I CAN OPERATE IT, LUCIUS!
DON'T BE RIDICULOUS, BRUCE! STAND BACK BEFORE YOU GET HURT!
LUCIUS. I GOT IT.
ALL RIGHT-- WELL, GET IT FAST!

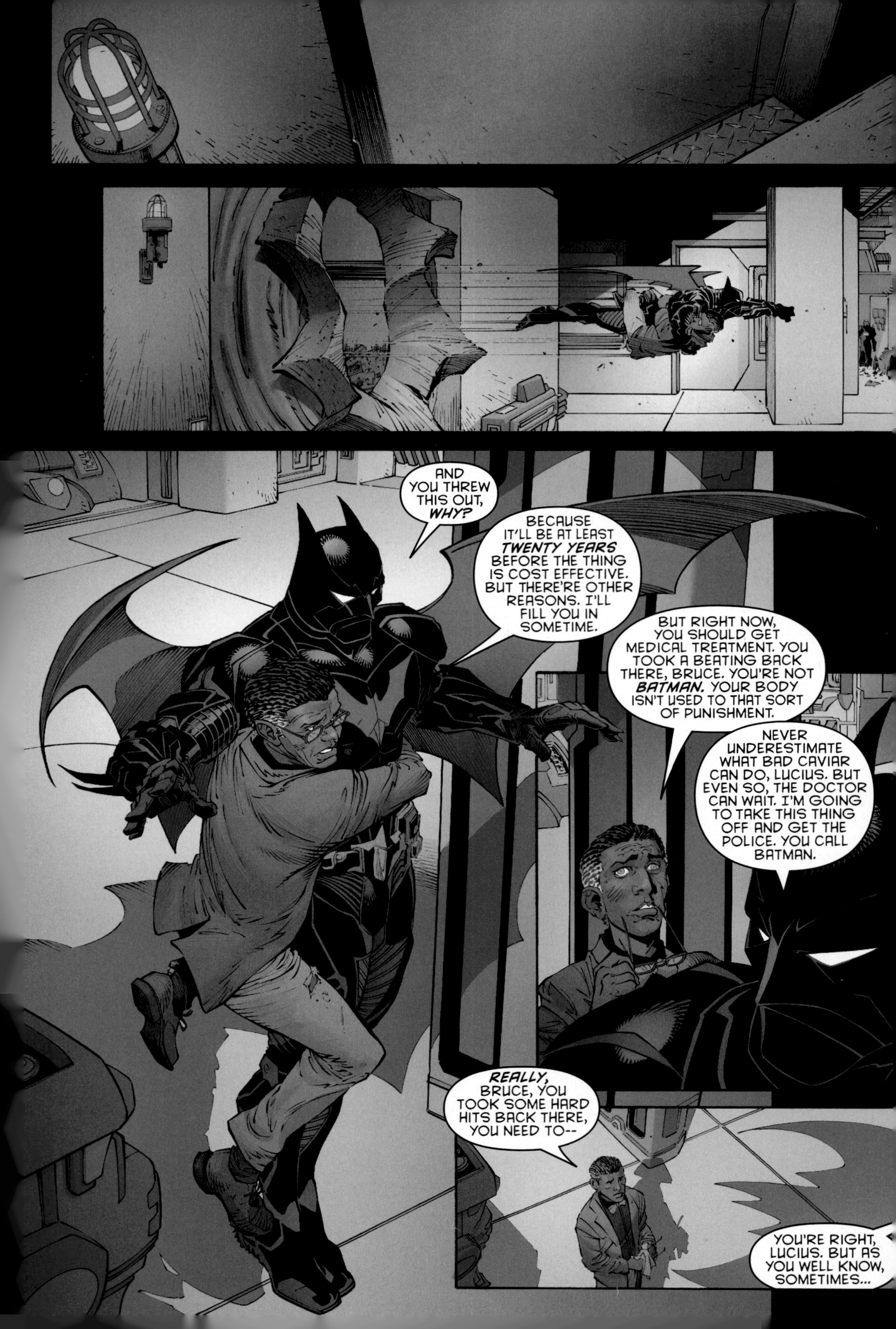
AND YOU THREW THIS OUT, *WHY?*
BECAUSE IT'LL BE AT LEAST *TWENTY YEARS* BEFORE THE THING IS COST EFFECTIVE. BUT THERE'RE OTHER REASONS. I'LL FILL YOU IN SOMETIME.
BUT RIGHT NOW, YOU SHOULD GET MEDICAL TREATMENT. YOU TOOK A BEATING BACK THERE, BRUCE. YOU'RE NOT *BATMAN.* YOUR BODY ISN'T USED TO THAT SORT OF PUNISHMENT.
NEVER UNDERESTIMATE WHAT BAD CAVIAR CAN DO, LUCIUS. BUT EVEN SO, THE DOCTOR CAN WAIT. I'M GOING TO TAKE THIS THING OFF AND GET THE POLICE. YOU CALL BATMAN.
REALLY, BRUCE, YOU TOOK SOME HARD HITS BACK THERE, YOU NEED TO--
YOU'RE RIGHT, LUCIUS. BUT AS YOU WELL KNOW, SOMETIMES...

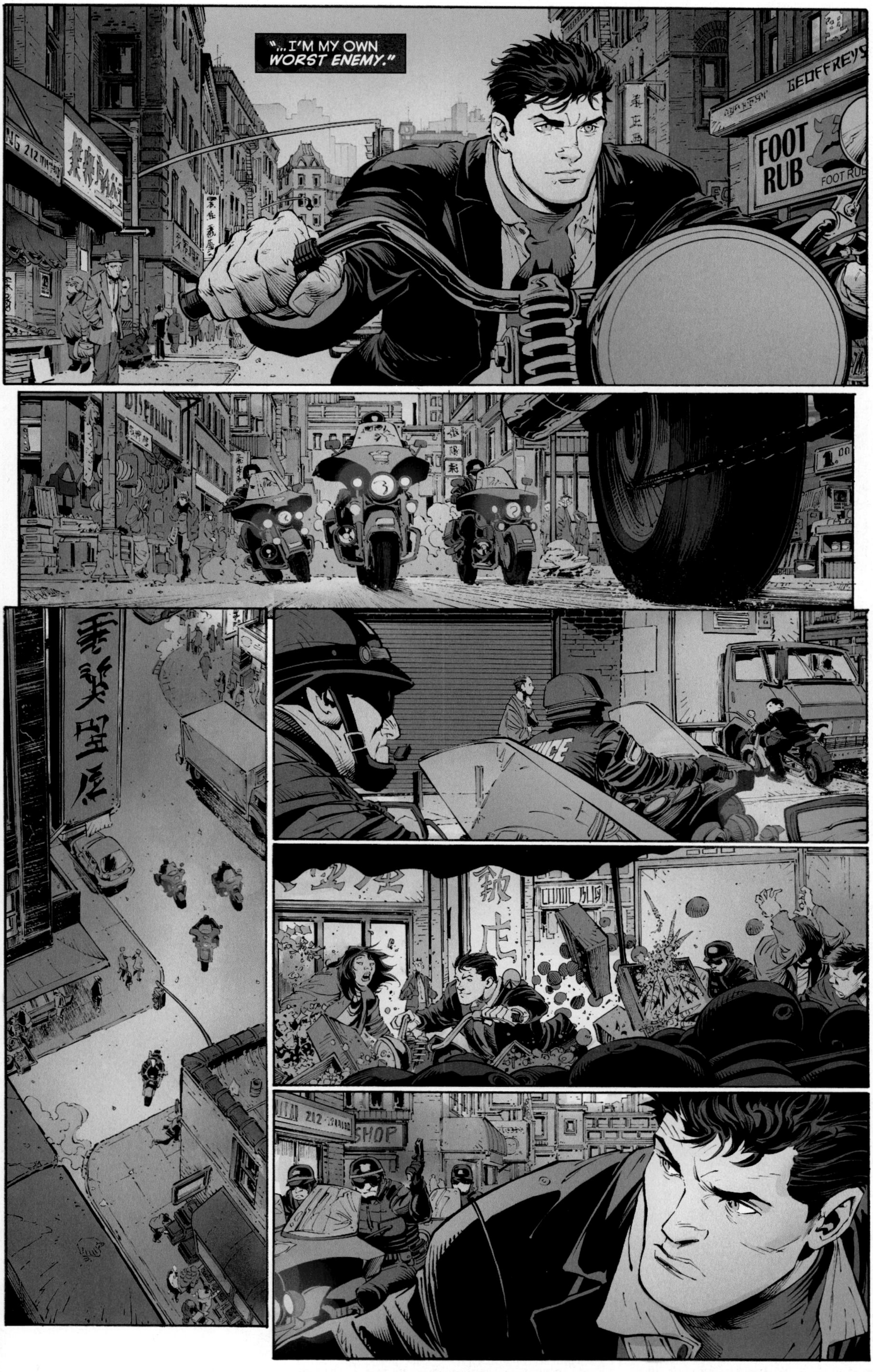
"...I'M MY OWN WORST ENEMY."
GEOFFREYS
FOOT RUB
SHOP

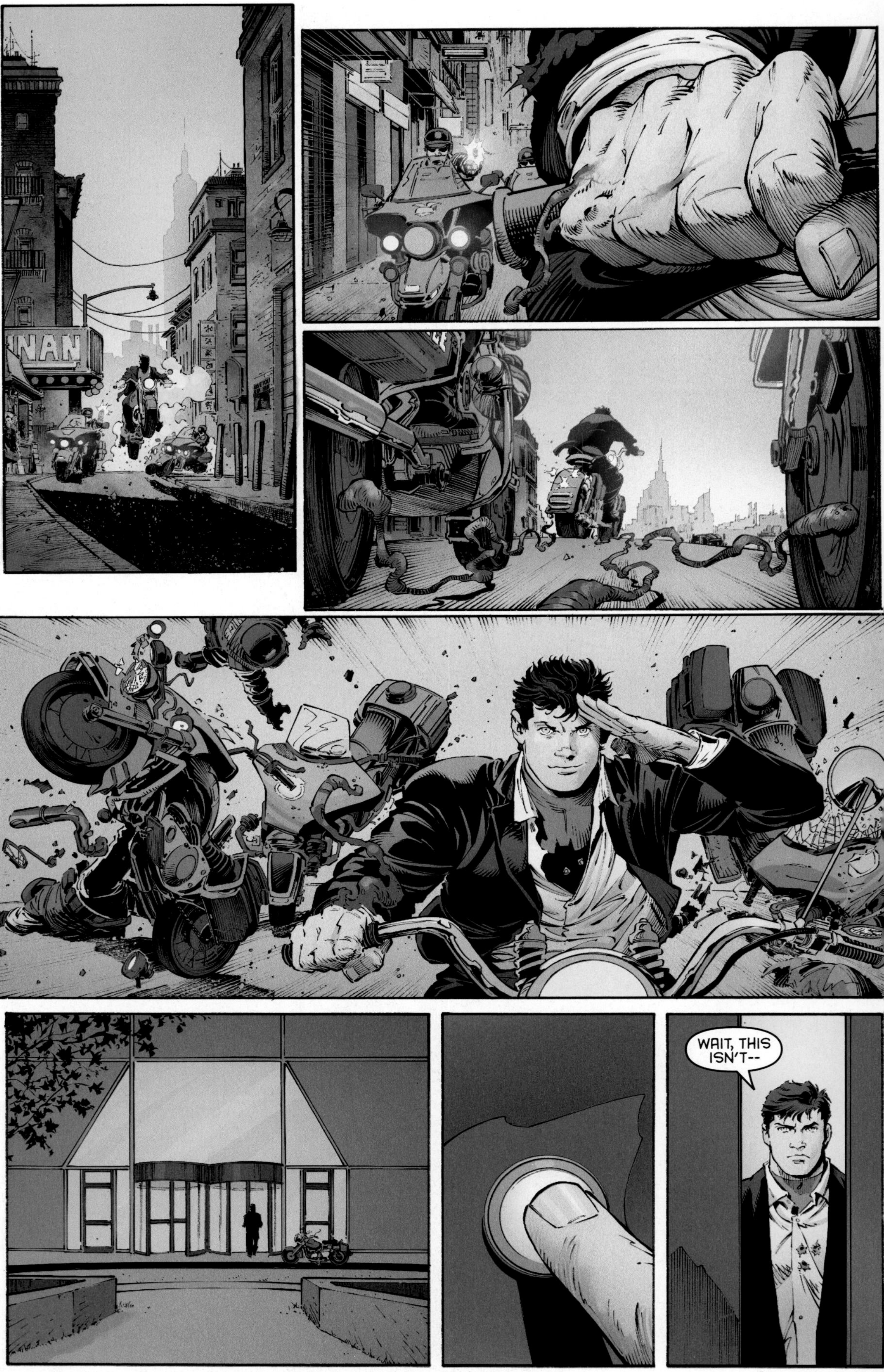

INAN
WAIT, THIS ISN'T--

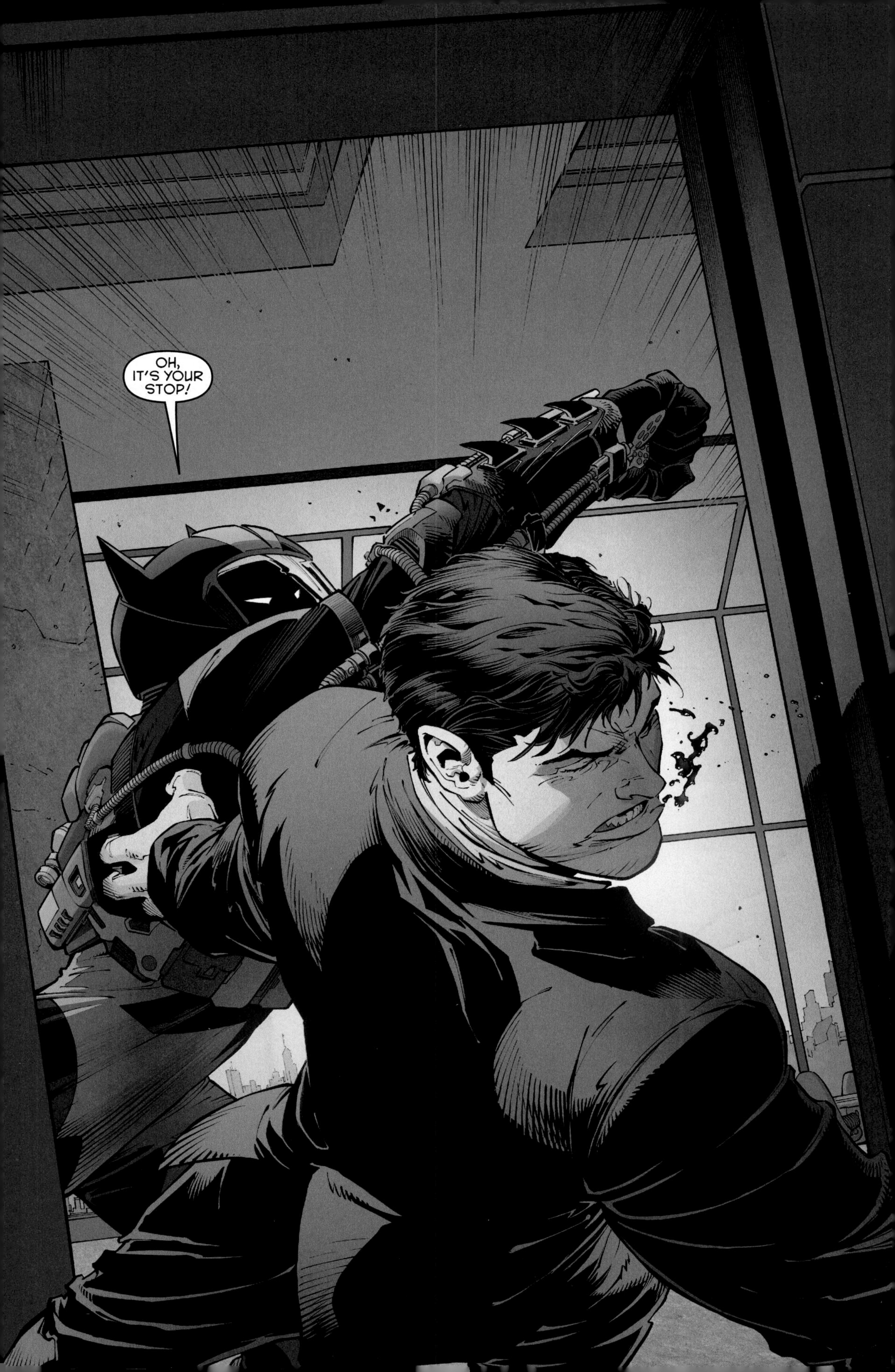
OH, IT'S YOUR STOP!

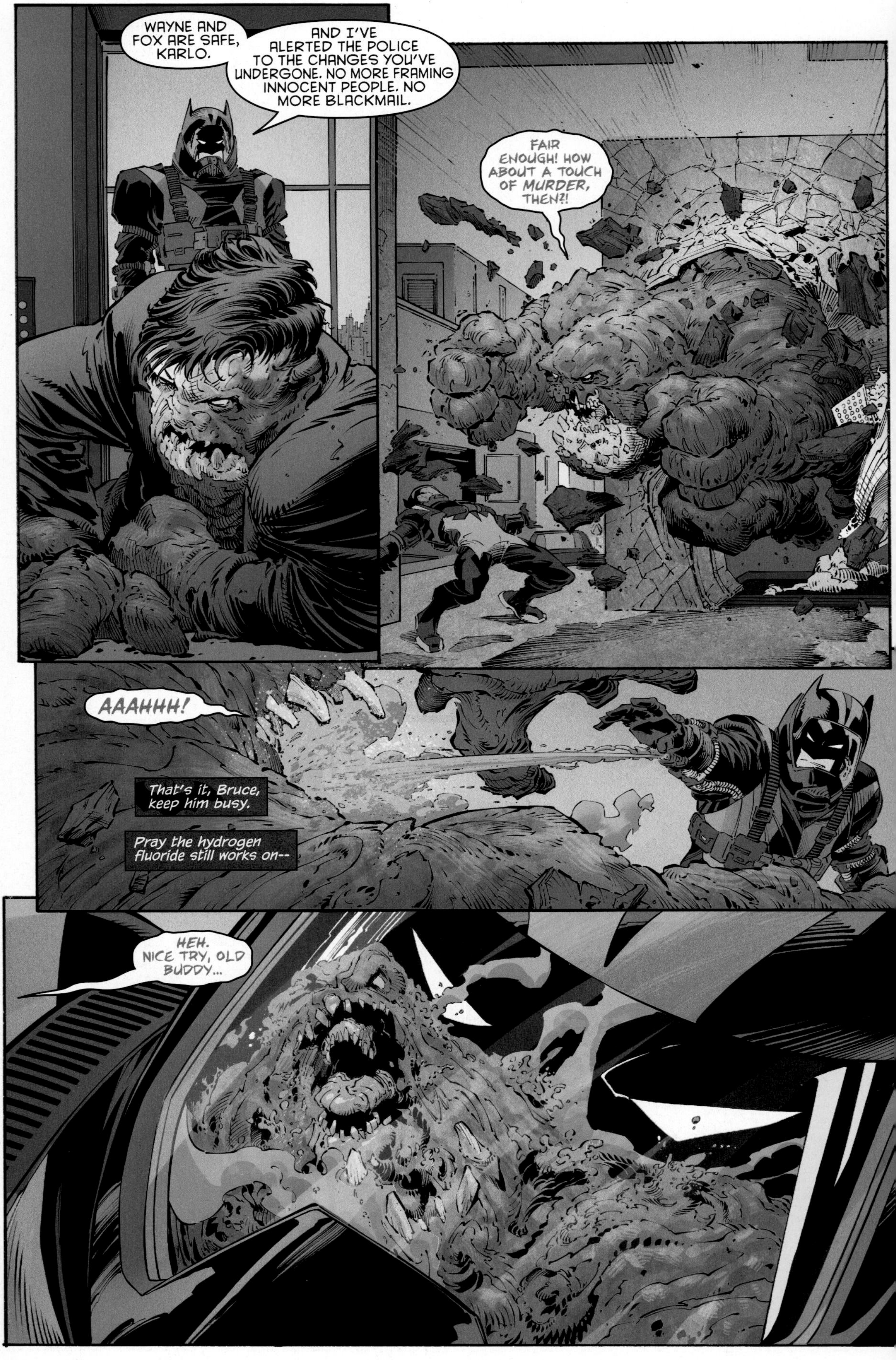
WAYNE AND FOX ARE SAFE, KARLO.
AND I'VE ALERTED THE POLICE TO THE CHANGES YOU'VE UNDERGONE. NO MORE FRAMING INNOCENT PEOPLE. NO MORE BLACKMAIL.
FAIR ENOUGH! HOW ABOUT A TOUCH OF *MURDER*, THEN?!
AAAHHH!
That's it, Bruce, keep him busy.
Pray the hydrogen fluoride still works on--
HEH. NICE TRY, OLD BUDDY...

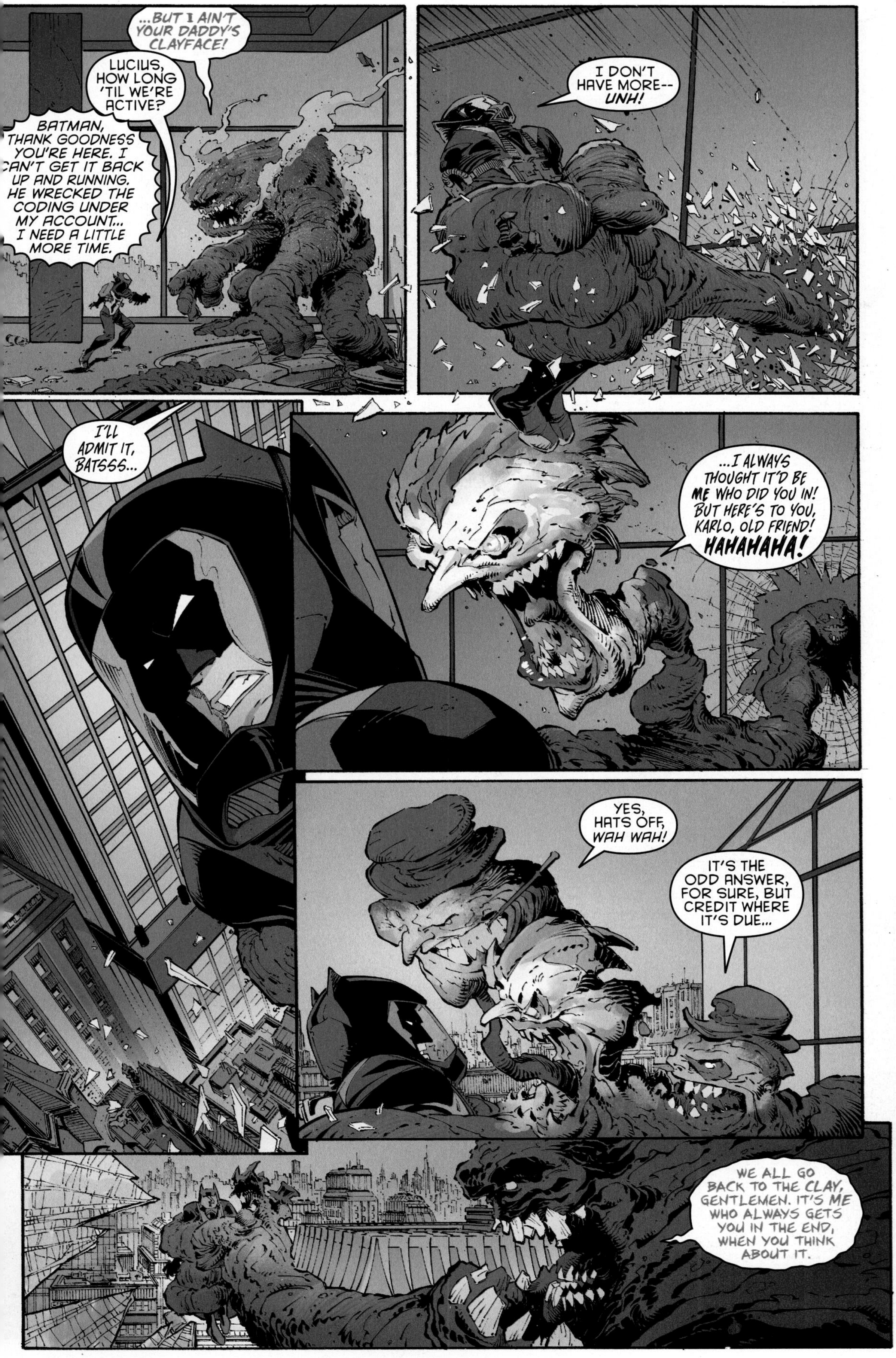

...BUT I AIN'T YOUR DADDY'S CLAYFACE!
LUCIUS, HOW LONG 'TIL WE'RE ACTIVE?
BATMAN, THANK GOODNESS YOU'RE HERE. I CAN'T GET IT BACK UP AND RUNNING. HE WRECKED THE CODING UNDER MY ACCOUNT... I NEED A LITTLE MORE TIME.
I DON'T HAVE MORE-- UNH!
I'LL ADMIT IT, BATSSS...
...I ALWAYS THOUGHT IT'D BE ME WHO DID YOU IN! BUT HERE'S TO YOU, KARLO, OLD FRIEND! HAHAHAHA!
YES, HATS OFF, WAH WAH!
IT'S THE ODD ANSWER, FOR SURE, BUT CREDIT WHERE IT'S DUE...
WE ALL GO BACK TO THE CLAY, GENTLEMEN. IT'S ME WHO ALWAYS GETS YOU IN THE END, WHEN YOU THINK ABOUT IT.

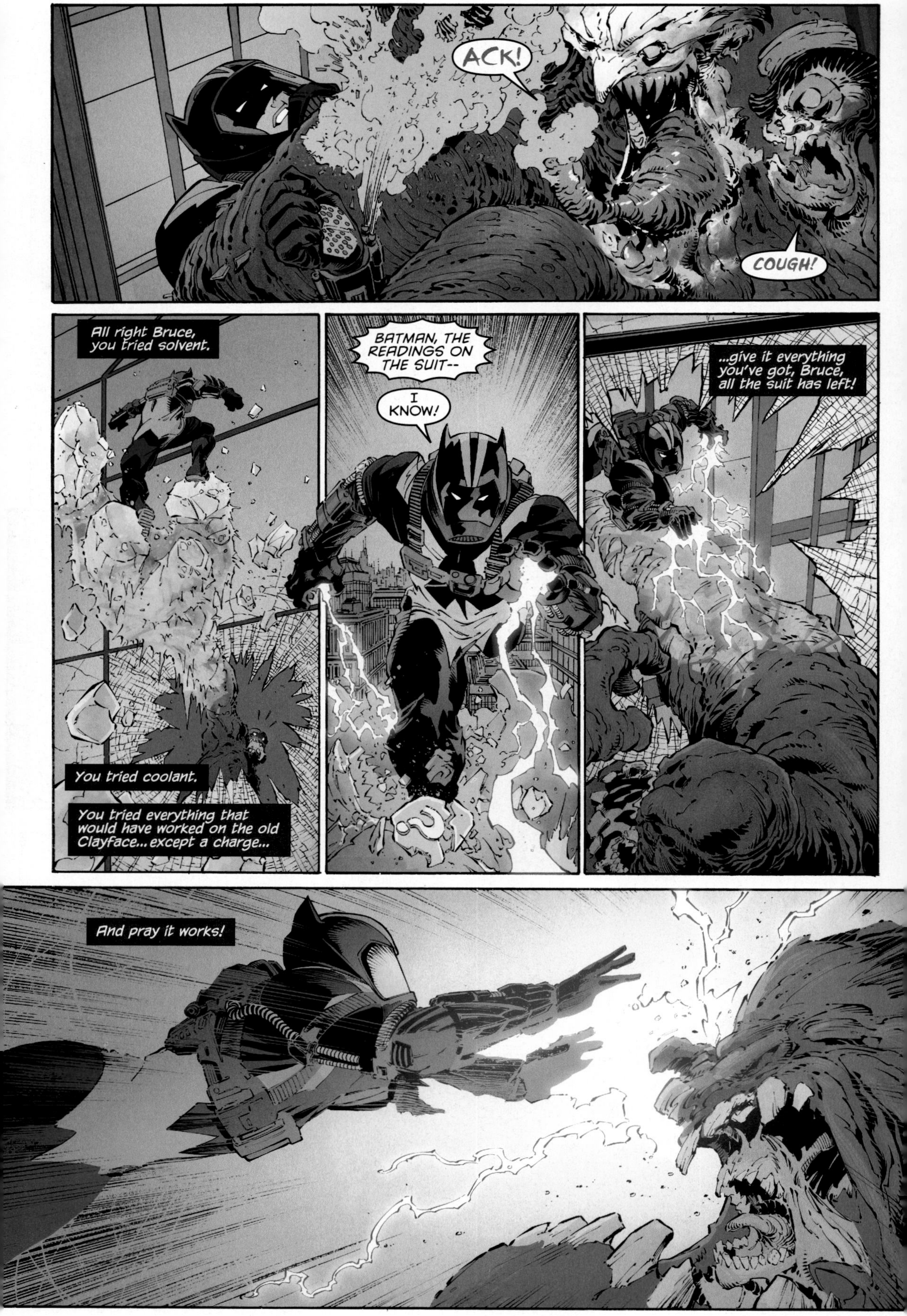
ACK!
COUGH!
All right Bruce, you tried solvent.
You tried coolant.
You tried everything that would have worked on the old Clayface... except a charge...
BATMAN, THE READINGS ON THE SUIT--
I KNOW!
...give it everything you've got, Bruce, all the suit has left!
And pray it works!

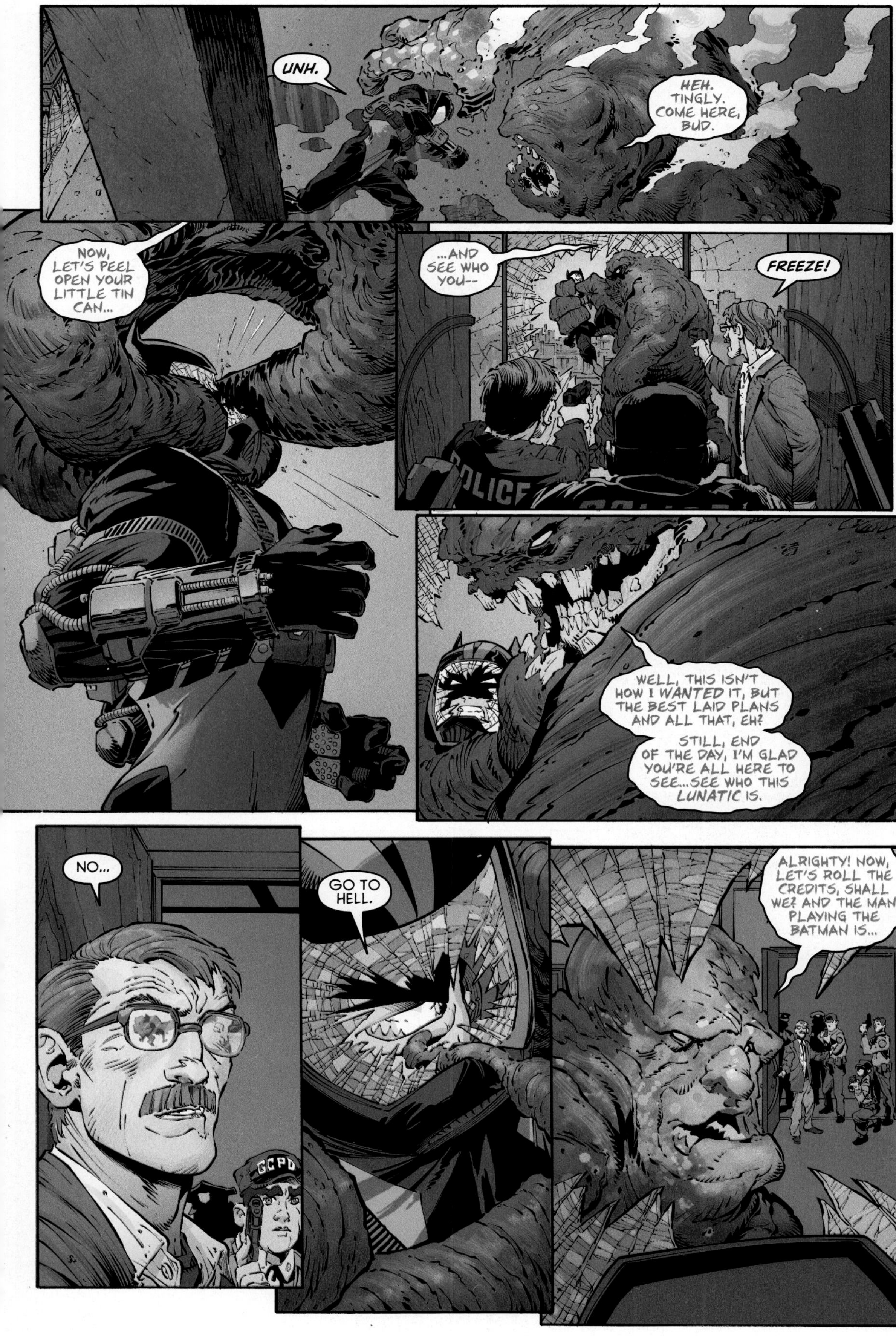
UNH.
HEH. TINGLY. COME HERE, BUD.
NOW, LET'S PEEL OPEN YOUR LITTLE TIN CAN...
...AND SEE WHO YOU--
FREEZE!
WELL, THIS ISN'T HOW I WANTED IT, BUT THE BEST LAID PLANS AND ALL THAT, EH?
STILL, END OF THE DAY, I'M GLAD YOU'RE ALL HERE TO SEE...SEE WHO THIS LUNATIC IS.
NO...
GO TO HELL.
ALRIGHTY! NOW, LET'S ROLL THE CREDITS, SHALL WE? AND THE MAN PLAYING THE BATMAN IS...
POLICE
GCPD

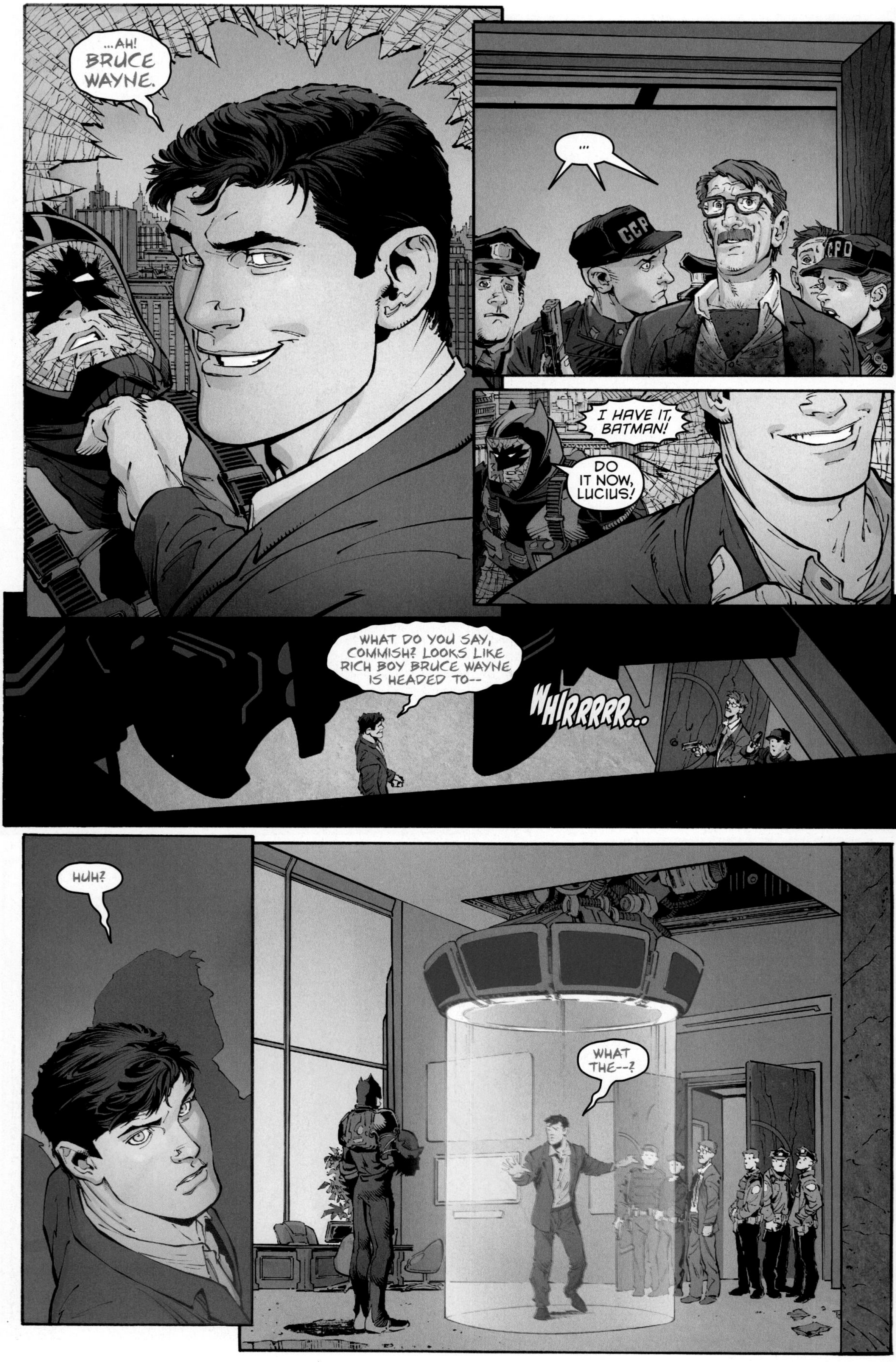

...AH! BRUCE WAYNE.
...
I HAVE IT, BATMAN!
DO IT NOW, LUCIUS!
WHAT DO YOU SAY, COMMISH? LOOKS LIKE RICH BOY BRUCE WAYNE IS HEADED TO--
WHIRRRRR...
HUH?
WHAT THE--?

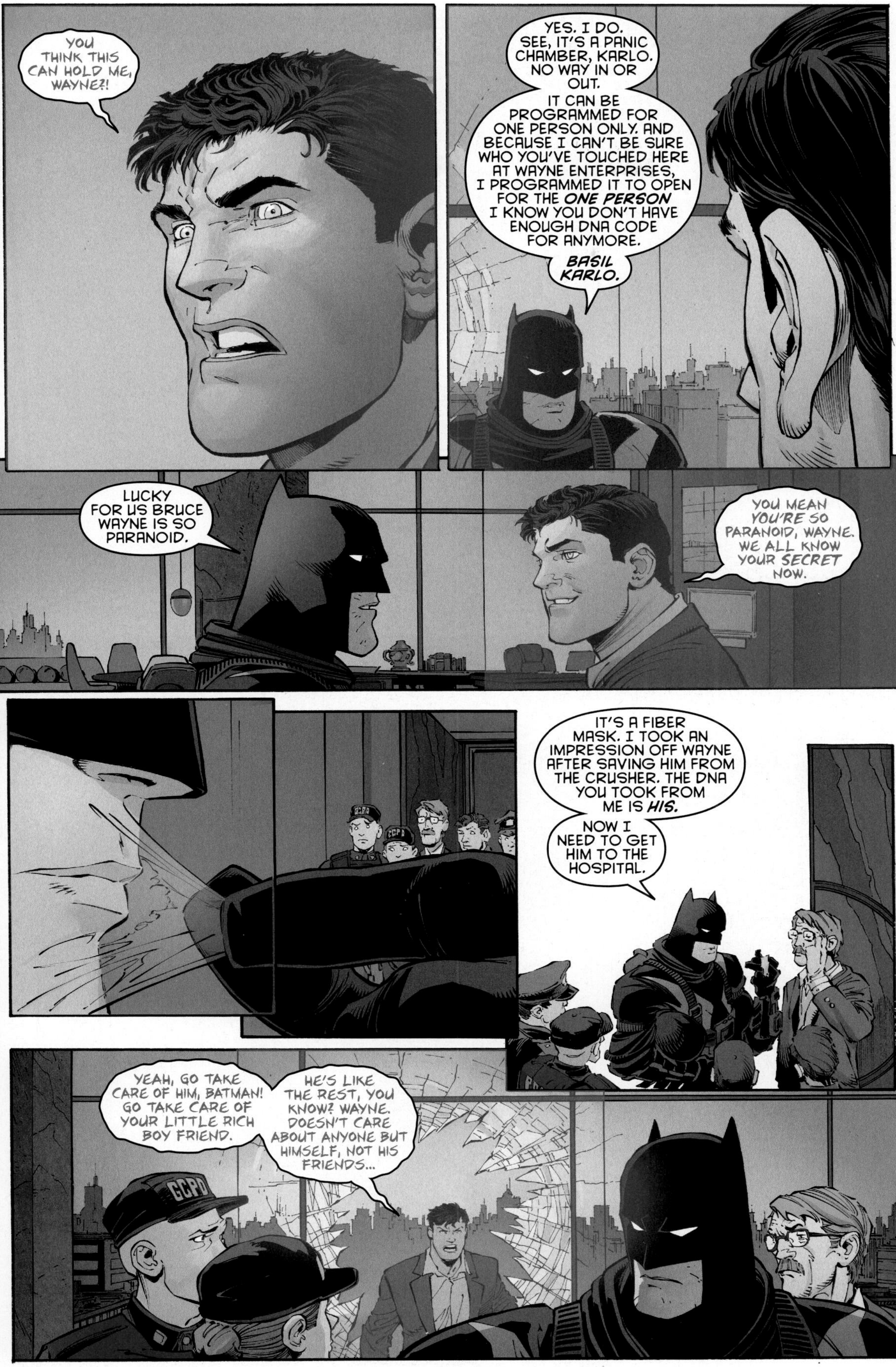
YOU THINK THIS CAN HOLD ME, WAYNE?!
YES. I DO. SEE, IT'S A PANIC CHAMBER, KARLO. NO WAY IN OR OUT.
IT CAN BE PROGRAMMED FOR ONE PERSON ONLY. AND BECAUSE I CAN'T BE SURE WHO YOU'VE TOUCHED HERE AT WAYNE ENTERPRISES, I PROGRAMMED IT TO OPEN FOR THE ONE PERSON I KNOW YOU DON'T HAVE ENOUGH DNA CODE FOR ANYMORE.
BASIL KARLO.
LUCKY FOR US BRUCE WAYNE IS SO PARANOID.
YOU MEAN YOU'RE SO PARANOID, WAYNE. WE ALL KNOW YOUR SECRET NOW.
IT'S A FIBER MASK. I TOOK AN IMPRESSION OFF WAYNE AFTER SAVING HIM FROM THE CRUSHER. THE DNA YOU TOOK FROM ME IS HIS.
NOW I NEED TO GET HIM TO THE HOSPITAL.
YEAH, GO TAKE CARE OF HIM, BATMAN! GO TAKE CARE OF YOUR LITTLE RICH BOY FRIEND.
HE'S LIKE THE REST, YOU KNOW? WAYNE. DOESN'T CARE ABOUT ANYONE BUT HIMSELF, NOT HIS FRIENDS...

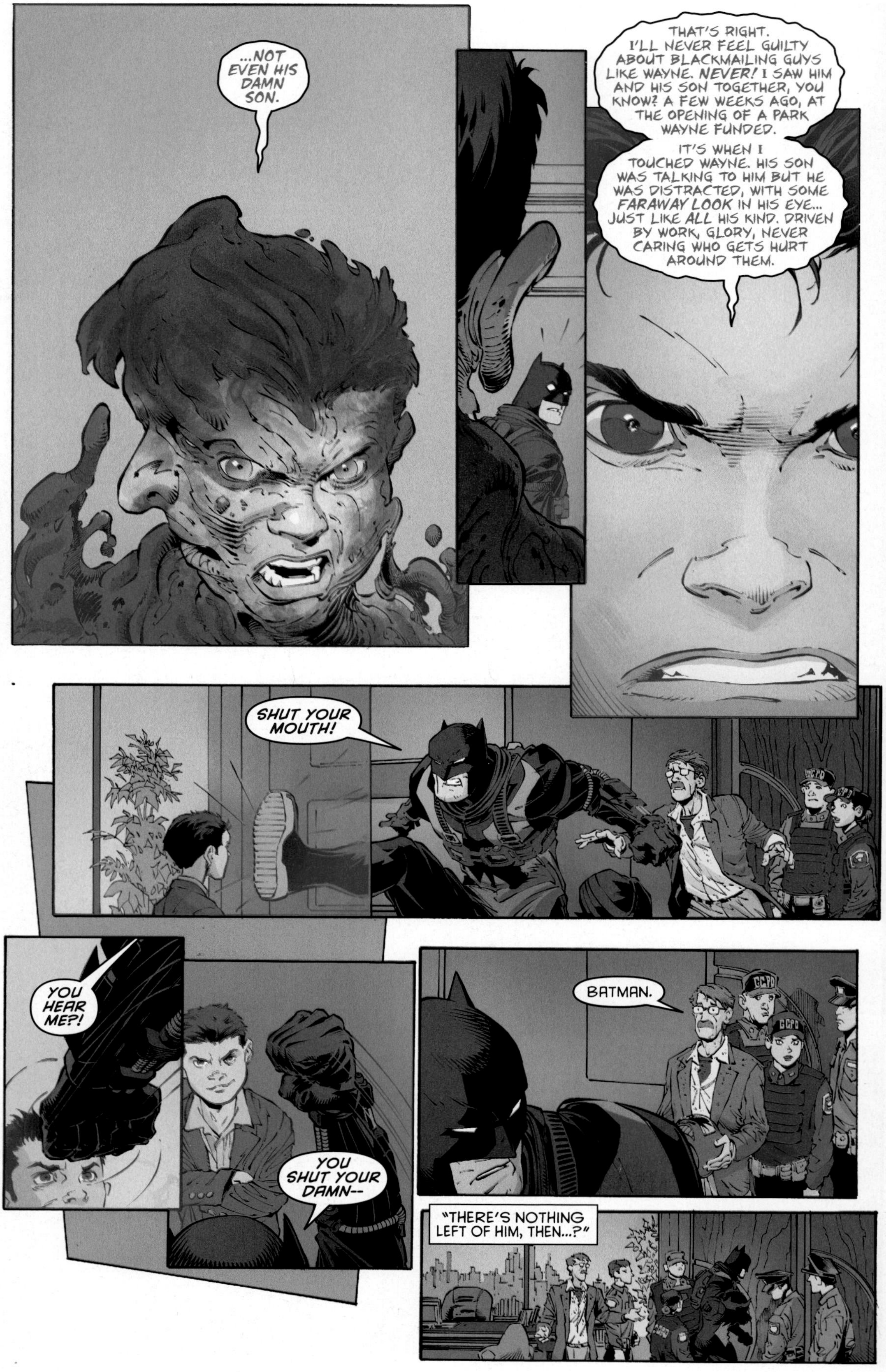
...NOT EVEN HIS DAMN SON.
THAT'S RIGHT. I'LL NEVER FEEL GUILTY ABOUT BLACKMAILING GUYS LIKE WAYNE. NEVER! I SAW HIM AND HIS SON TOGETHER, YOU KNOW? A FEW WEEKS AGO, AT THE OPENING OF A PARK WAYNE FUNDED.
IT'S WHEN I TOUCHED WAYNE. HIS SON WAS TALKING TO HIM BUT HE WAS DISTRACTED, WITH SOME FARAWAY LOOK IN HIS EYE... JUST LIKE ALL HIS KIND. DRIVEN BY WORK, GLORY, NEVER CARING WHO GETS HURT AROUND THEM.
SHUT YOUR MOUTH!
YOU HEAR ME?!
YOU SHUT YOUR DAMN--
BATMAN.
"THERE'S NOTHING LEFT OF HIM, THEN...?"

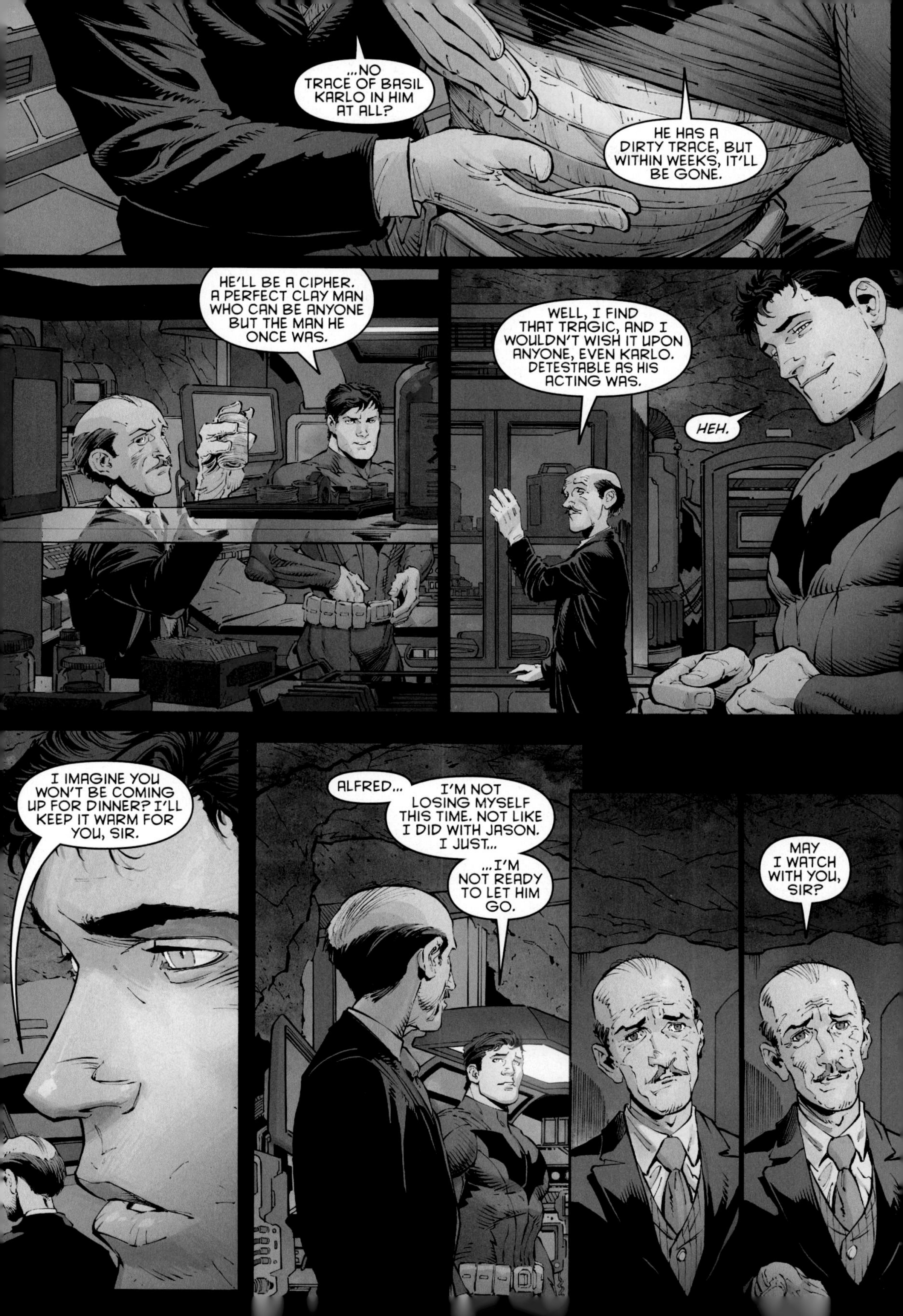

...NO TRACE OF BASIL KARLO IN HIM AT ALL?
HE HAS A DIRTY TRACE, BUT WITHIN WEEKS, IT'LL BE GONE.
HE'LL BE A CIPHER. A PERFECT CLAY MAN WHO CAN BE ANYONE BUT THE MAN HE ONCE WAS.
WELL, I FIND THAT TRAGIC, AND I WOULDN'T WISH IT UPON ANYONE, EVEN KARLO. DETESTABLE AS HIS ACTING WAS.
HEH.
I IMAGINE YOU WON'T BE COMING UP FOR DINNER? I'LL KEEP IT WARM FOR YOU, SIR.
ALFRED...
I'M NOT LOSING MYSELF THIS TIME. NOT LIKE I DID WITH JASON. I JUST...
...I'M NOT READY TO LET HIM GO.
MAY I WATCH WITH YOU, SIR?

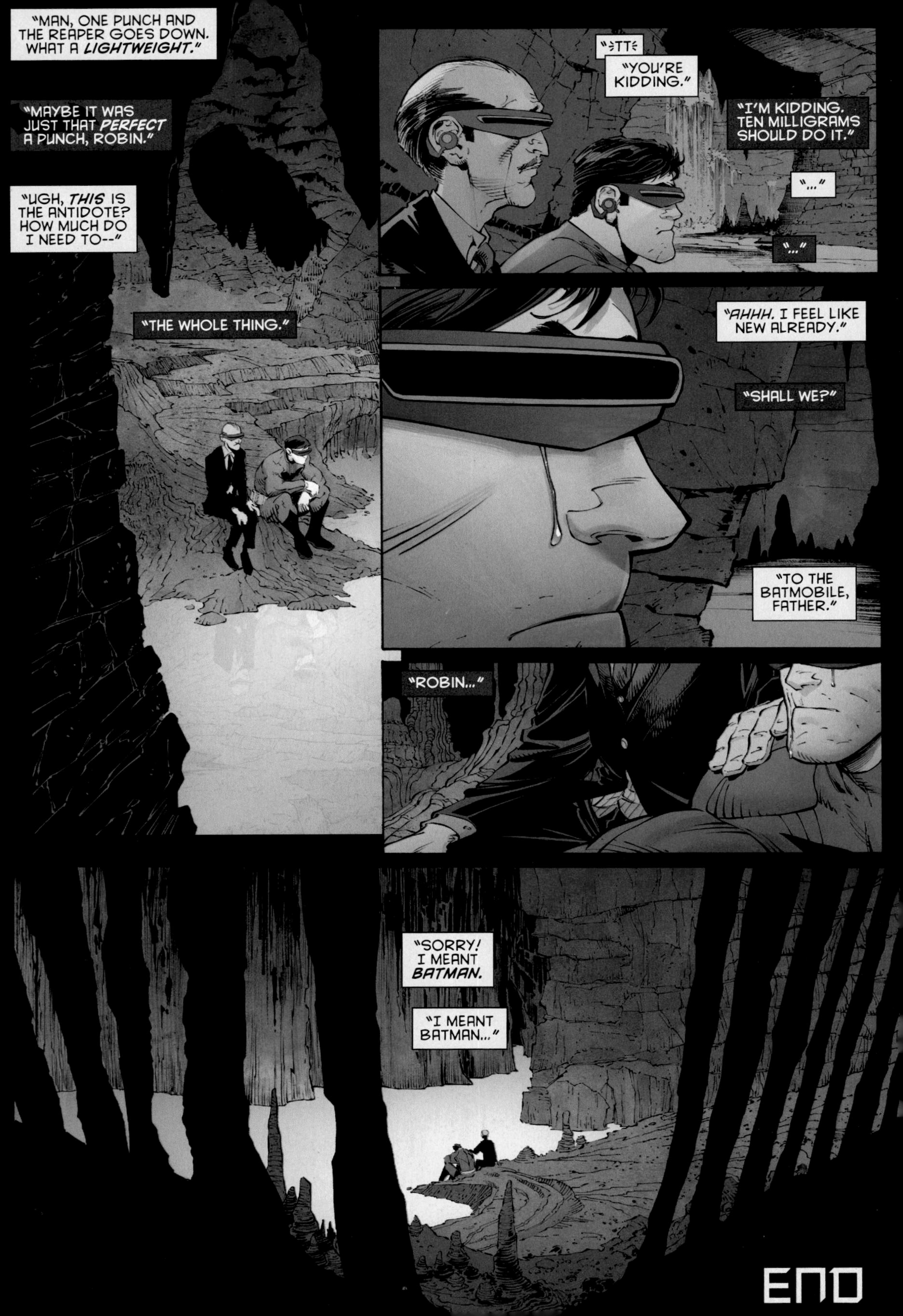
"MAN, ONE PUNCH AND THE REAPER GOES DOWN. WHAT A *LIGHTWEIGHT*."
"MAYBE IT WAS JUST THAT *PERFECT* A PUNCH, ROBIN."
"UGH, *THIS* IS THE ANTIDOTE? HOW MUCH DO I NEED TO--"
"THE WHOLE THING."
"TT"
"YOU'RE KIDDING."
"I'M KIDDING. TEN MILLIGRAMS SHOULD DO IT."
"..."
"..."
"*AHHH*. I FEEL LIKE NEW ALREADY."
"SHALL WE?"
"TO THE BATMOBILE, FATHER."
"ROBIN..."
"SORRY! I MEANT *BATMAN*.
"I MEANT BATMAN..."
END

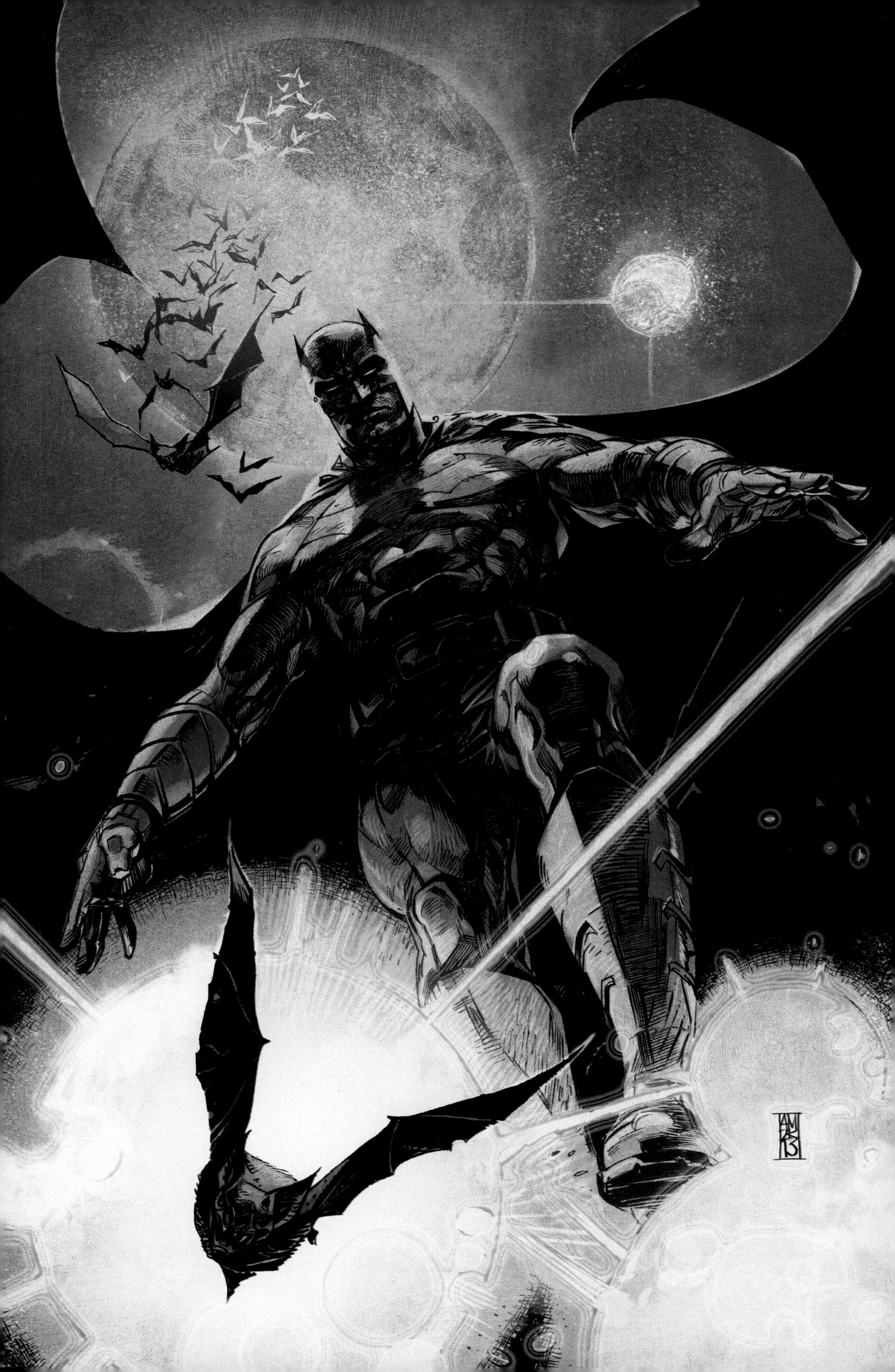

GHOST LIGHTS

JAMES TYNION IV writer ALEX MALEEV artist BRAD ANDERSON NATHAN FAIRBAIRN colorists variant cover by ALEX MALEEV
SUPERMAN created by JERRY SIEGEL & JOE SHUSTER By special arrangement with the JERRY SIEGEL family

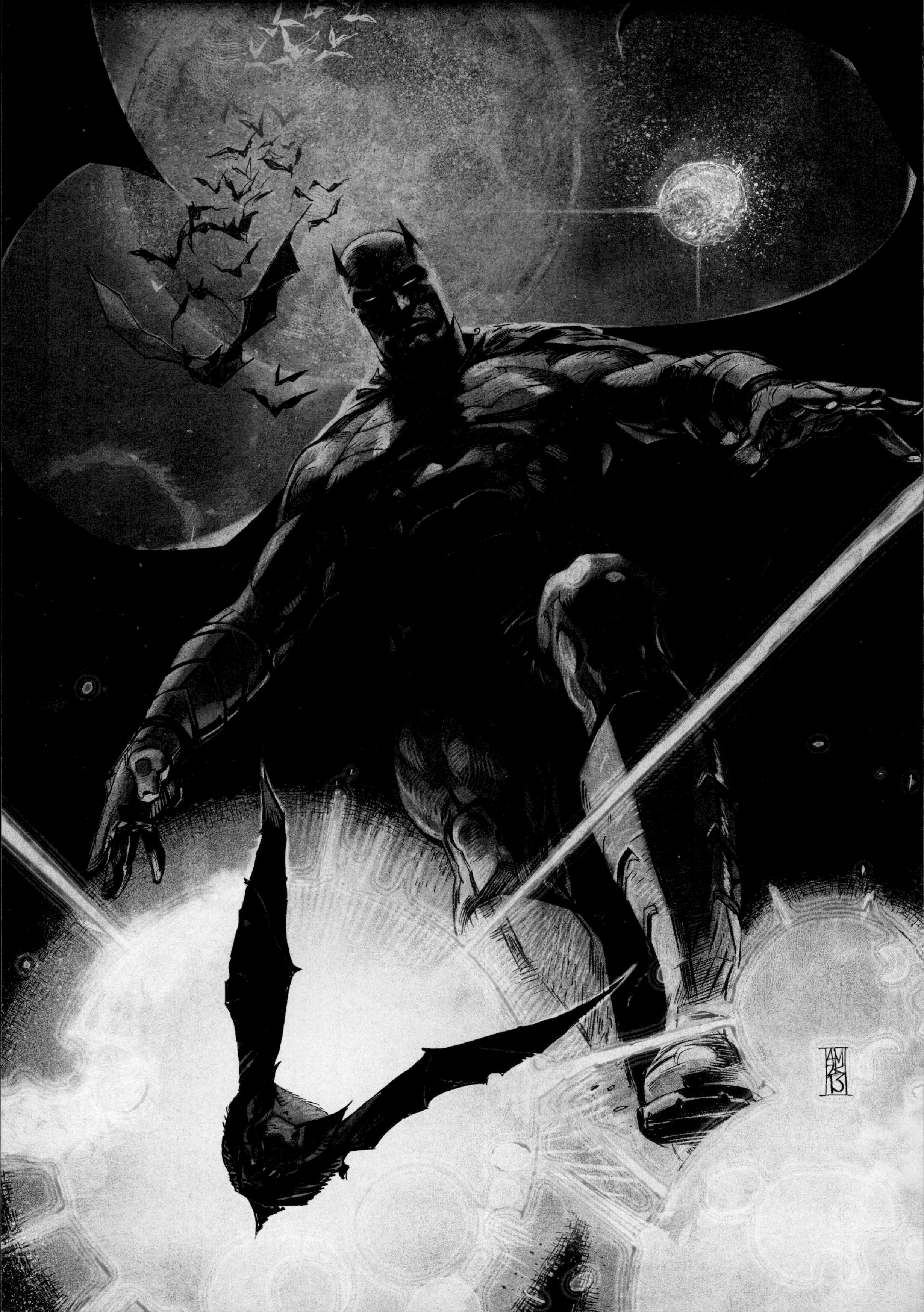

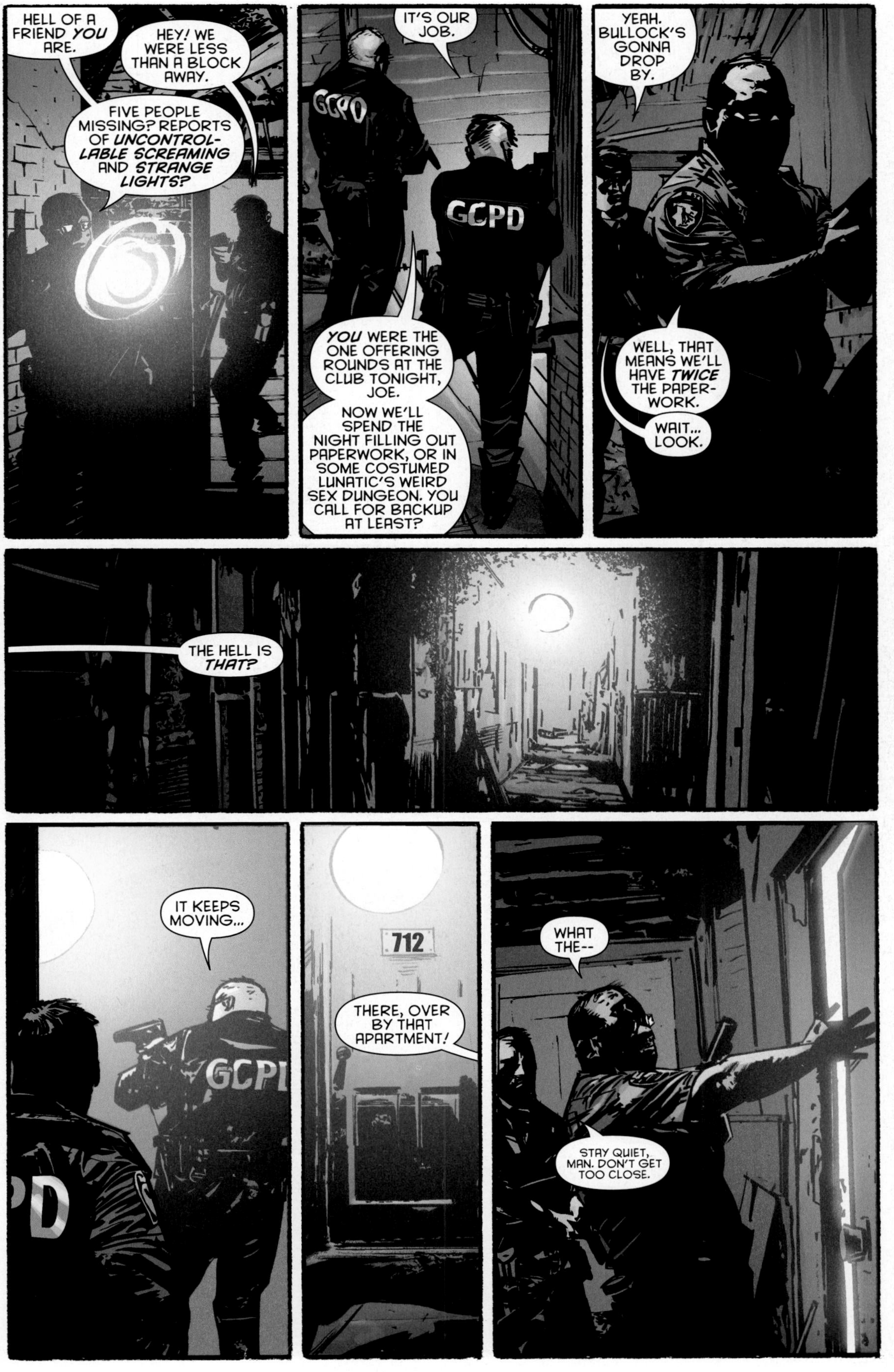
HELL OF A FRIEND YOU ARE.
HEY! WE WERE LESS THAN A BLOCK AWAY.
FIVE PEOPLE MISSING? REPORTS OF UNCONTROL-LABLE SCREAMING AND STRANGE LIGHTS?
IT'S OUR JOB.
GCPD
GCPD
YOU WERE THE ONE OFFERING ROUNDS AT THE CLUB TONIGHT, JOE.
NOW WE'LL SPEND THE NIGHT FILLING OUT PAPERWORK, OR IN SOME COSTUMED LUNATIC'S WEIRD SEX DUNGEON. YOU CALL FOR BACKUP AT LEAST?
YEAH. BULLOCK'S GONNA DROP BY.
WELL, THAT MEANS WE'LL HAVE TWICE THE PAPER-WORK.
WAIT... LOOK.
THE HELL IS THAT?
IT KEEPS MOVING...
GCPD
PD
712
THERE, OVER BY THAT APARTMENT!
WHAT THE--
STAY QUIET, MAN. DON'T GET TOO CLOSE.

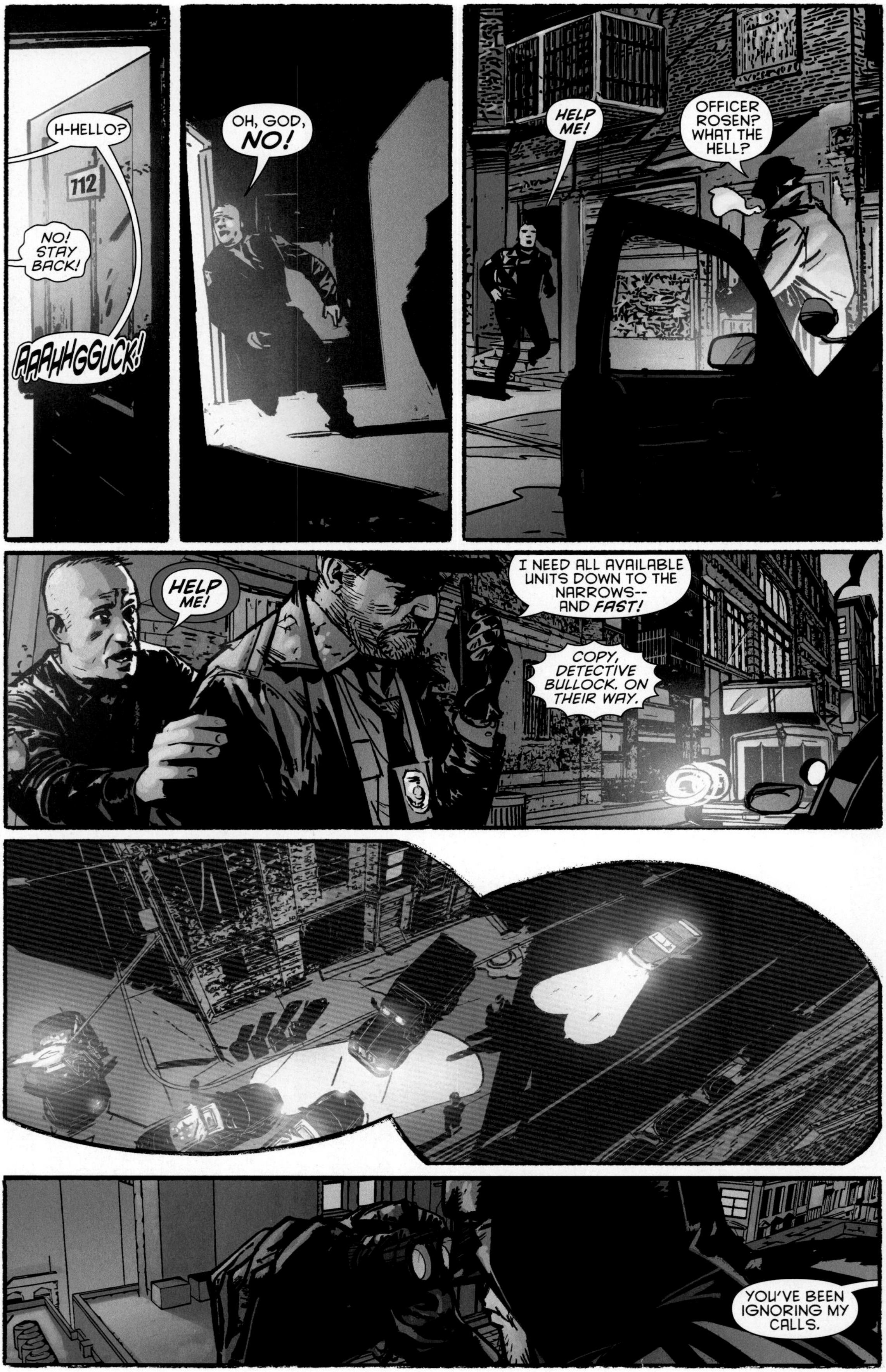
H-HELLO?
NO! STAY BACK!
AAAHHGGUCK!
OH, GOD, NO!
HELP ME!
OFFICER ROSEN? WHAT THE HELL?
HELP ME!
I NEED ALL AVAILABLE UNITS DOWN TO THE NARROWS-- AND FAST!
COPY, DETECTIVE BULLOCK. ON THEIR WAY.
YOU'VE BEEN IGNORING MY CALLS.

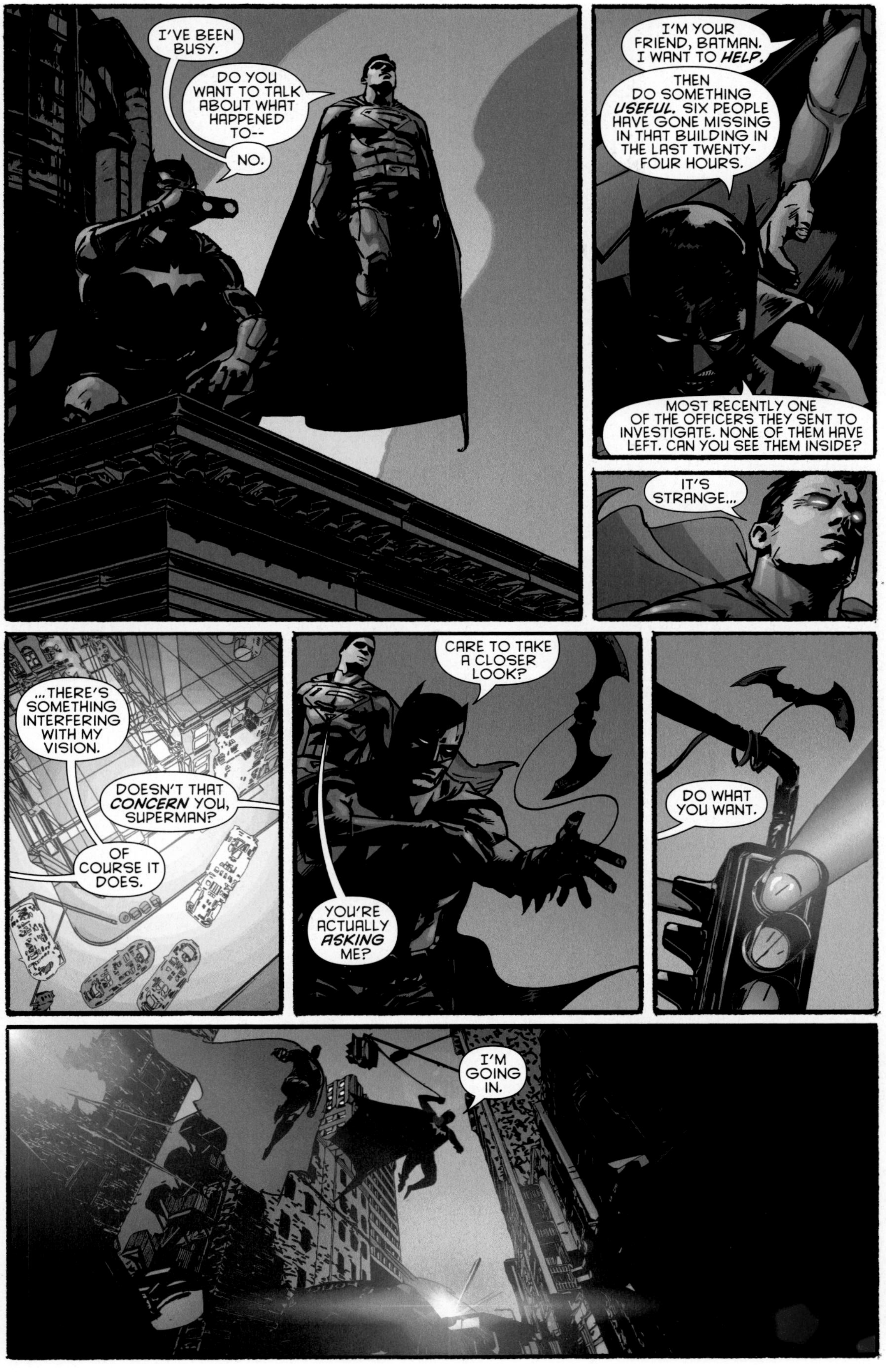
I'VE BEEN BUSY.
DO YOU WANT TO TALK ABOUT WHAT HAPPENED TO--
NO.
I'M YOUR FRIEND, BATMAN. I WANT TO *HELP.*
THEN DO SOMETHING *USEFUL.* SIX PEOPLE HAVE GONE MISSING IN THAT BUILDING IN THE LAST TWENTY-FOUR HOURS.
MOST RECENTLY ONE OF THE OFFICERS THEY SENT TO INVESTIGATE. NONE OF THEM HAVE LEFT. CAN YOU SEE THEM INSIDE?
IT'S STRANGE...
...THERE'S SOMETHING INTERFERING WITH MY VISION.
DOESN'T THAT *CONCERN* YOU, SUPERMAN?
OF COURSE IT DOES.
CARE TO TAKE A CLOSER LOOK?
YOU'RE ACTUALLY *ASKING* ME?
DO WHAT YOU WANT.
I'M GOING IN.

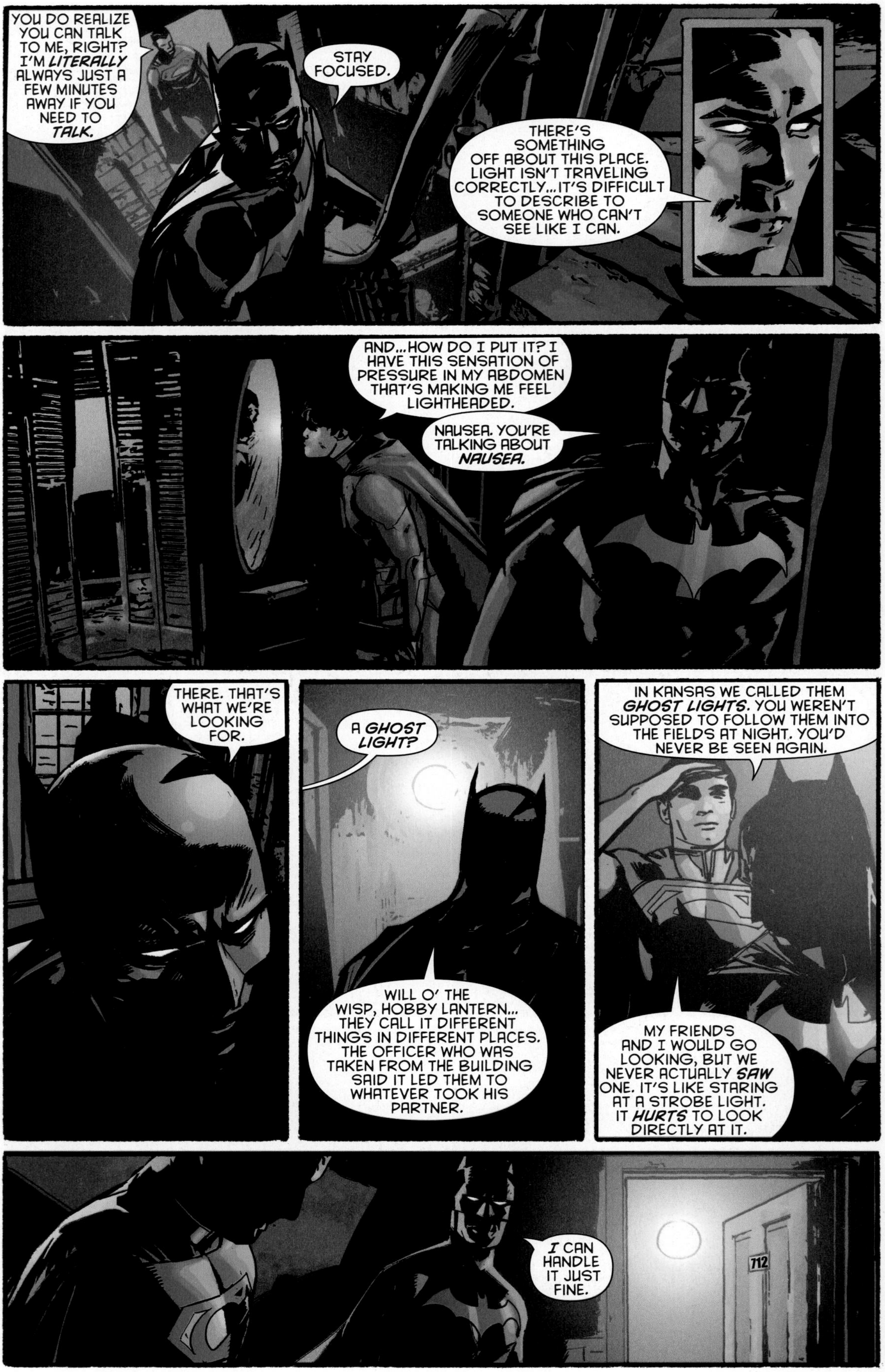
YOU DO REALIZE YOU CAN TALK TO ME, RIGHT? I'M *LITERALLY* ALWAYS JUST A FEW MINUTES AWAY IF YOU NEED TO *TALK.*
STAY FOCUSED.
THERE'S SOMETHING OFF ABOUT THIS PLACE. LIGHT ISN'T TRAVELING CORRECTLY...IT'S DIFFICULT TO DESCRIBE TO SOMEONE WHO CAN'T SEE LIKE I CAN.
AND...HOW DO I PUT IT? I HAVE THIS SENSATION OF PRESSURE IN MY ABDOMEN THAT'S MAKING ME FEEL LIGHTHEADED.
NAUSEA. YOU'RE TALKING ABOUT *NAUSEA.*
THERE. THAT'S WHAT WE'RE LOOKING FOR.
A *GHOST LIGHT?*
WILL O' THE WISP, HOBBY LANTERN... THEY CALL IT DIFFERENT THINGS IN DIFFERENT PLACES. THE OFFICER WHO WAS TAKEN FROM THE BUILDING SAID IT LED THEM TO WHATEVER TOOK HIS PARTNER.
IN KANSAS WE CALLED THEM *GHOST LIGHTS.* YOU WEREN'T SUPPOSED TO FOLLOW THEM INTO THE FIELDS AT NIGHT. YOU'D NEVER BE SEEN AGAIN.
MY FRIENDS AND I WOULD GO LOOKING, BUT WE NEVER ACTUALLY *SAW* ONE. IT'S LIKE STARING AT A STROBE LIGHT. IT *HURTS* TO LOOK DIRECTLY AT IT.
712
I CAN HANDLE IT JUST FINE.

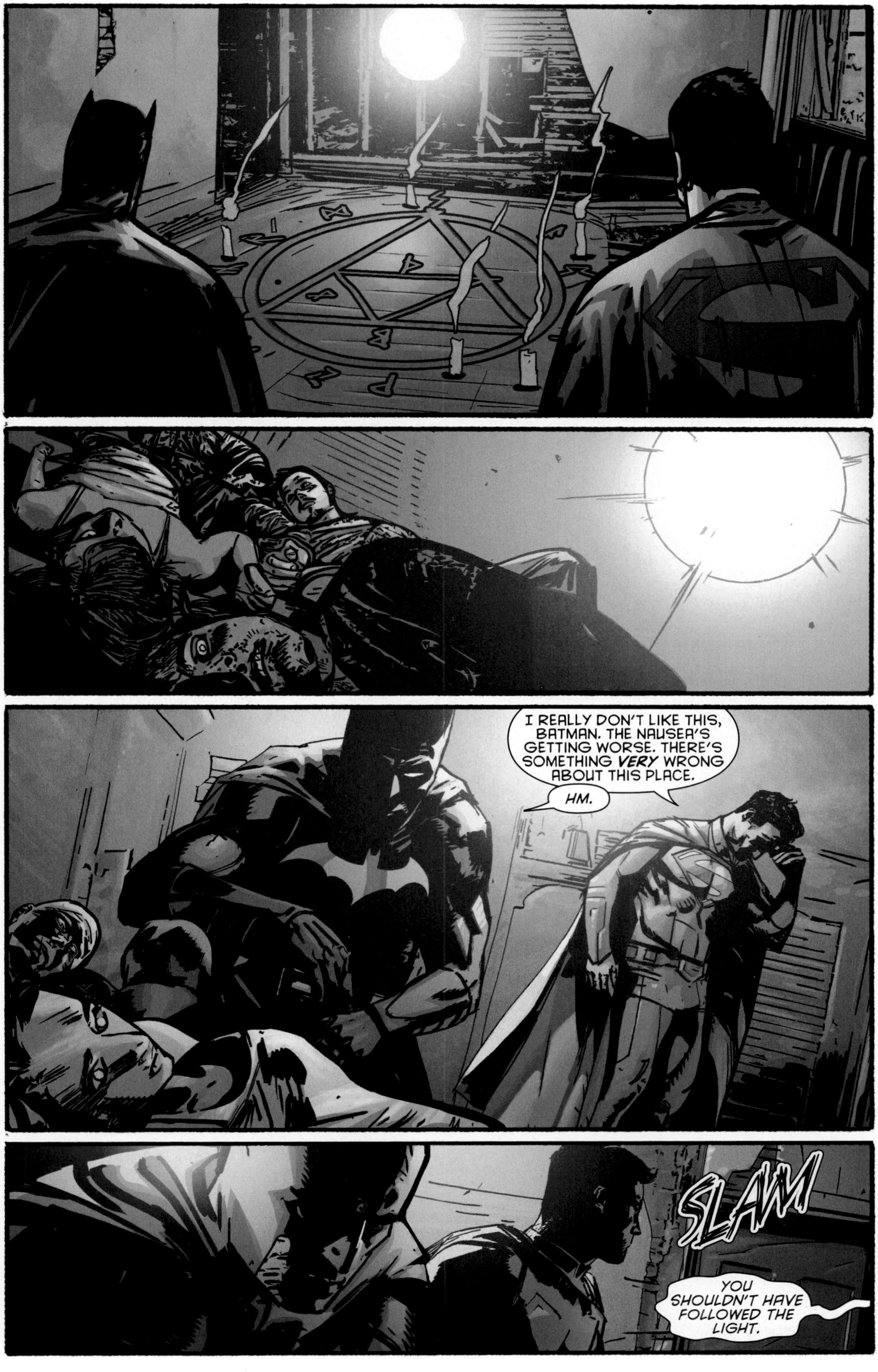
I REALLY DON'T LIKE THIS, BATMAN. THE NAUSEA'S GETTING WORSE. THERE'S SOMETHING *VERY* WRONG ABOUT THIS PLACE.
HM.
SLAM
YOU SHOULDN'T HAVE FOLLOWED THE LIGHT.

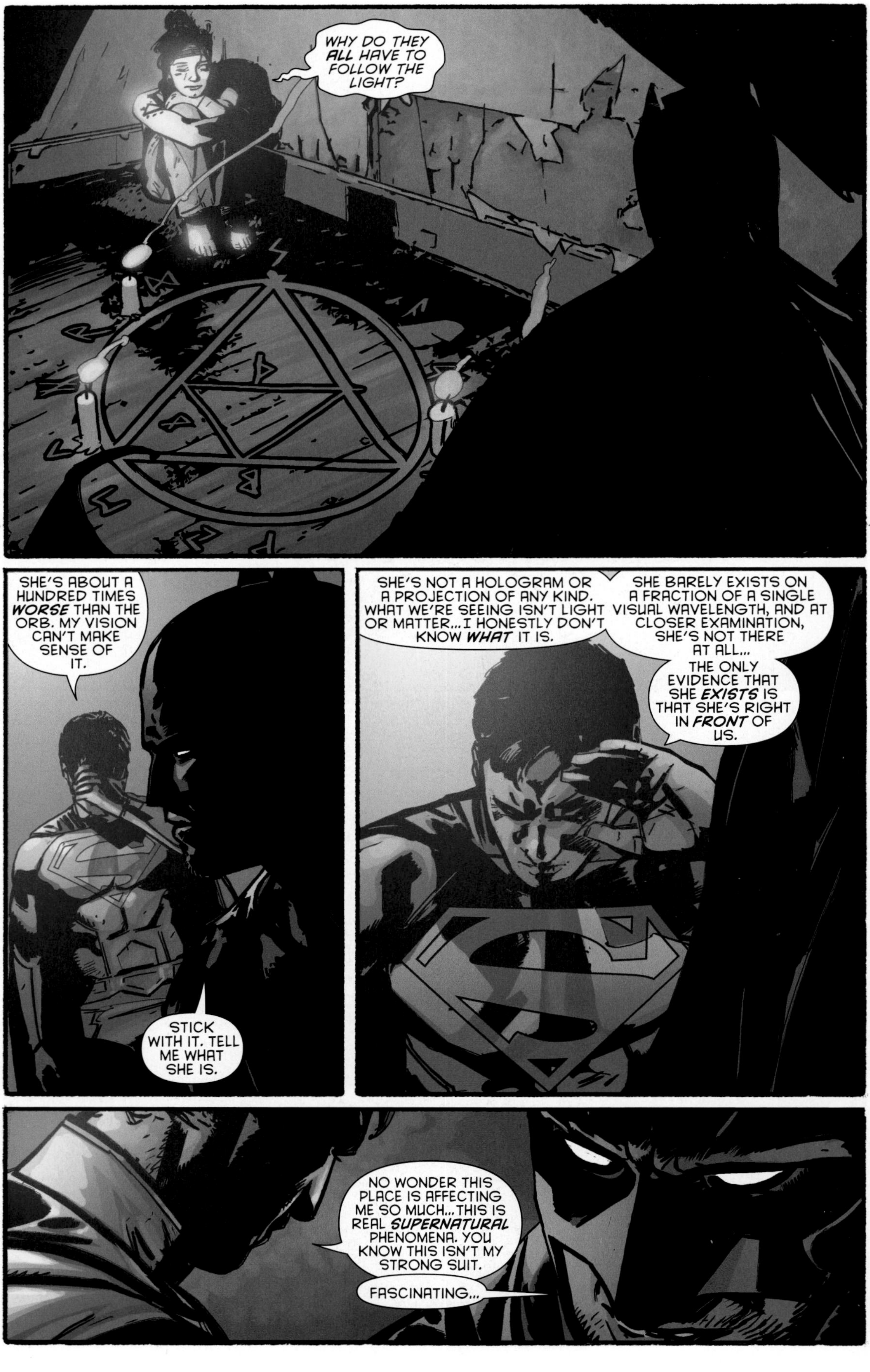

WHY DO THEY ALL HAVE TO FOLLOW THE LIGHT?
SHE'S ABOUT A HUNDRED TIMES WORSE THAN THE ORB. MY VISION CAN'T MAKE SENSE OF IT.
STICK WITH IT. TELL ME WHAT SHE IS.
SHE'S NOT A HOLOGRAM OR A PROJECTION OF ANY KIND. WHAT WE'RE SEEING ISN'T LIGHT OR MATTER... I HONESTLY DON'T KNOW WHAT IT IS.
SHE BARELY EXISTS ON A FRACTION OF A SINGLE VISUAL WAVELENGTH, AND AT CLOSER EXAMINATION, SHE'S NOT THERE AT ALL...
THE ONLY EVIDENCE THAT SHE EXISTS IS THAT SHE'S RIGHT IN FRONT OF US.
NO WONDER THIS PLACE IS AFFECTING ME SO MUCH... THIS IS REAL SUPERNATURAL PHENOMENA. YOU KNOW THIS ISN'T MY STRONG SUIT.
FASCINATING...

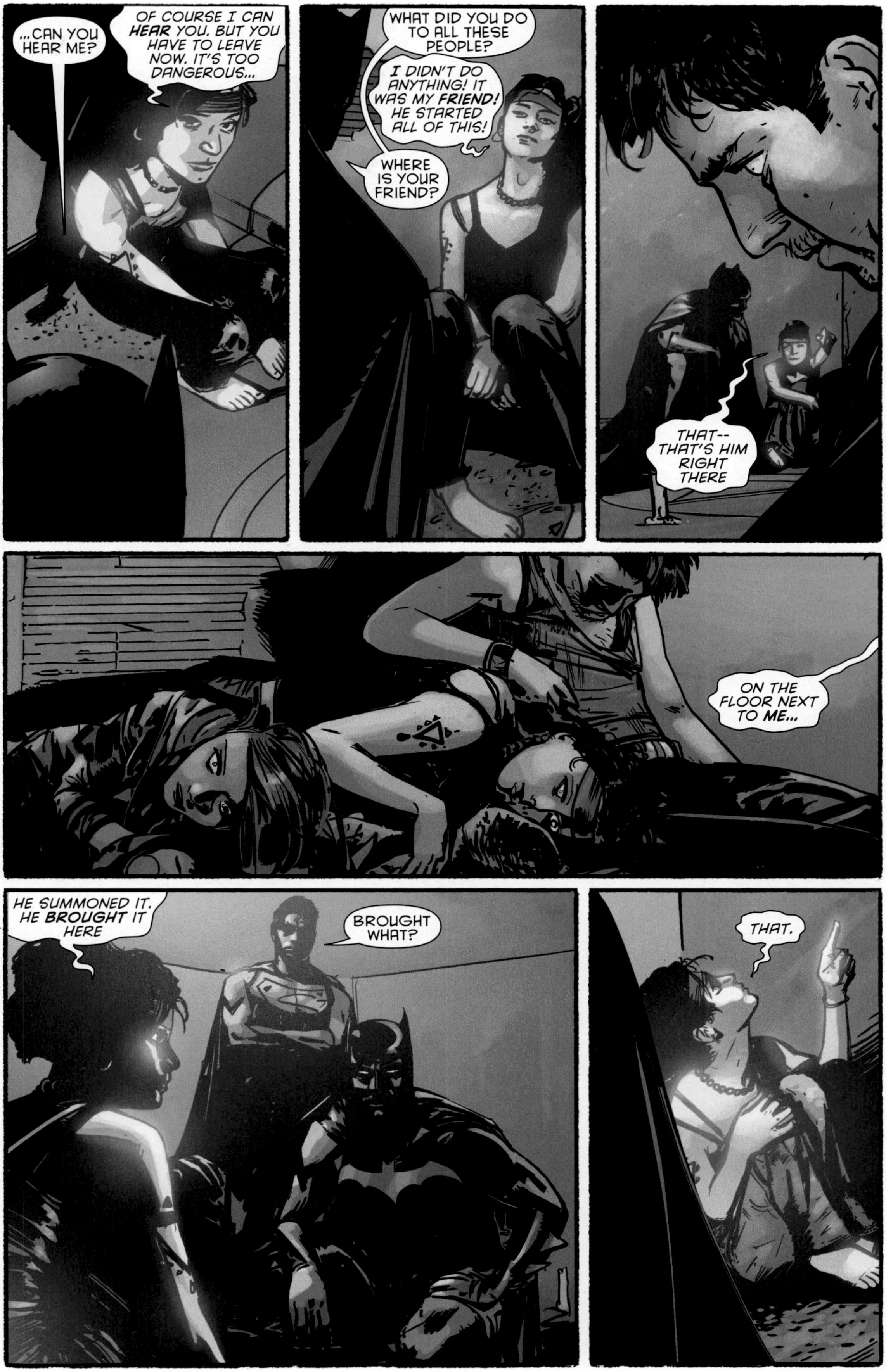

...CAN YOU HEAR ME?
OF COURSE I CAN HEAR YOU. BUT YOU HAVE TO LEAVE NOW. IT'S TOO DANGEROUS...
WHAT DID YOU DO TO ALL THESE PEOPLE?
I DIDN'T DO ANYTHING! IT WAS MY FRIEND! HE STARTED ALL OF THIS!
WHERE IS YOUR FRIEND?
THAT-- THAT'S HIM RIGHT THERE
ON THE FLOOR NEXT TO ME...
HE SUMMONED IT. HE BROUGHT IT HERE
BROUGHT WHAT?
THAT.

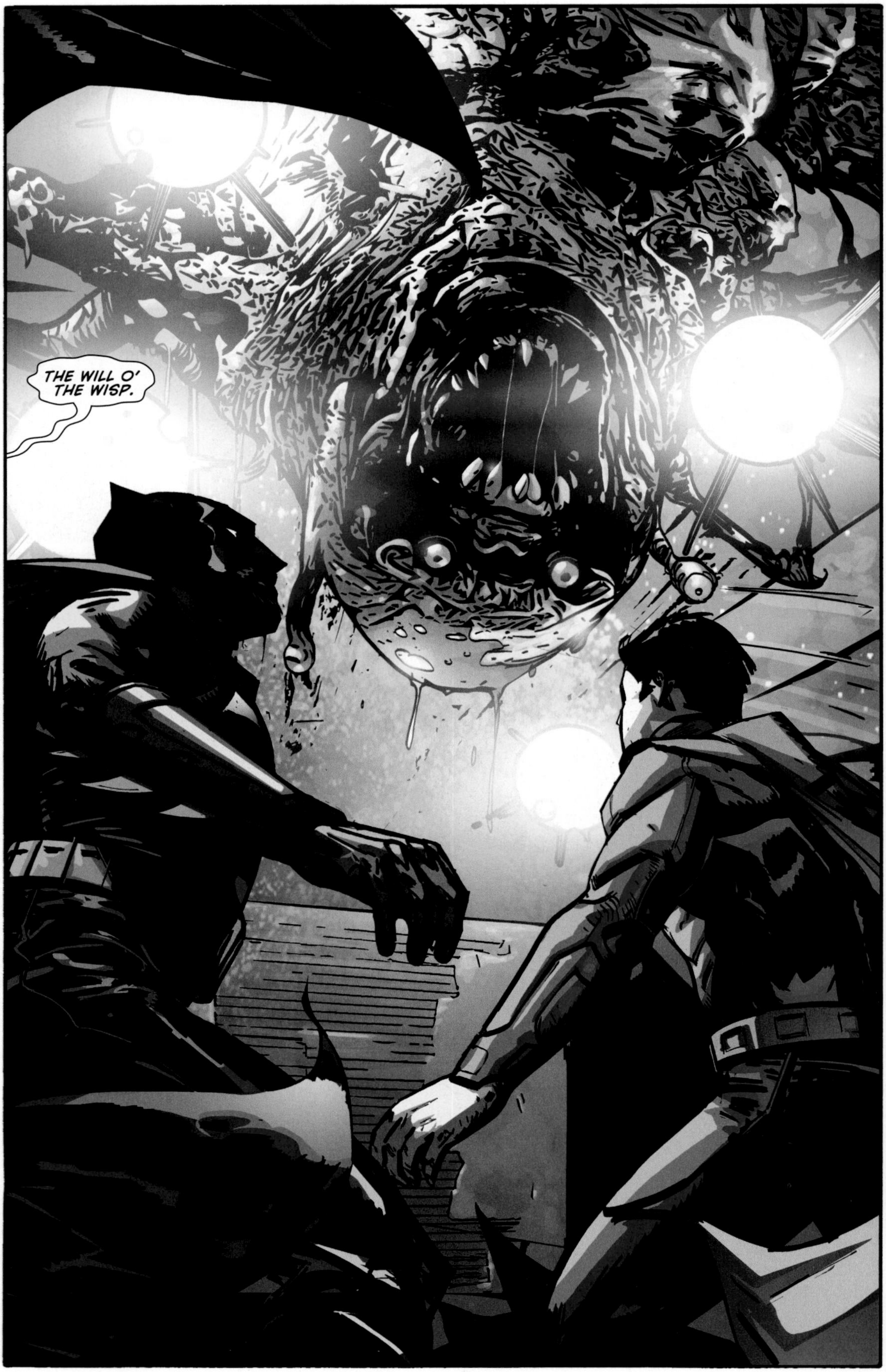
THE WILL O' THE WISP.

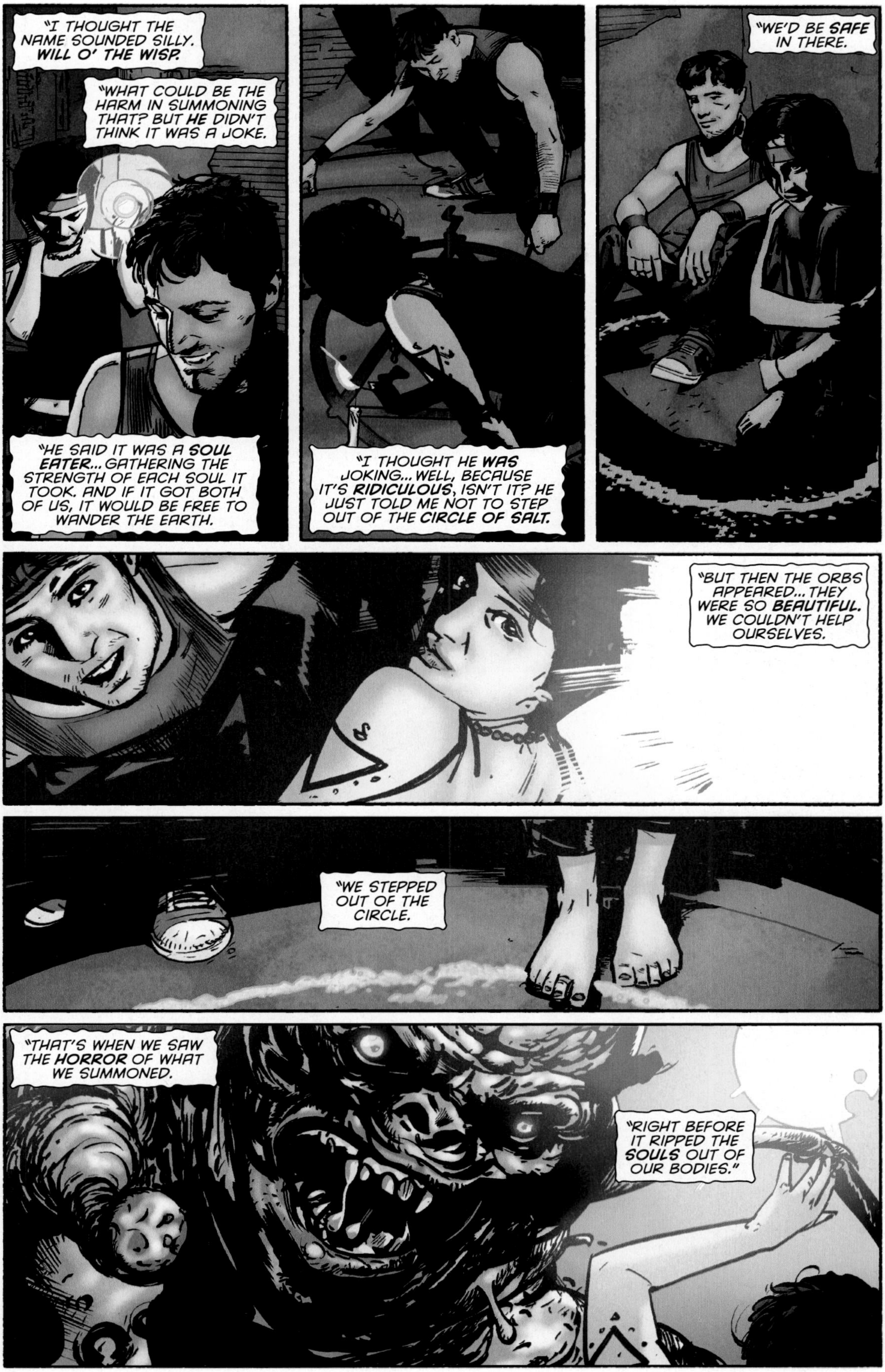
"I THOUGHT THE NAME SOUNDED SILLY. WILL O' THE WISP.
"WHAT COULD BE THE HARM IN SUMMONING THAT? BUT HE DIDN'T THINK IT WAS A JOKE.
"HE SAID IT WAS A SOUL EATER... GATHERING THE STRENGTH OF EACH SOUL IT TOOK. AND IF IT GOT BOTH OF US, IT WOULD BE FREE TO WANDER THE EARTH.
"I THOUGHT HE WAS JOKING... WELL, BECAUSE IT'S RIDICULOUS, ISN'T IT? HE JUST TOLD ME NOT TO STEP OUT OF THE CIRCLE OF SALT.
"WE'D BE SAFE IN THERE.
"BUT THEN THE ORBS APPEARED... THEY WERE SO BEAUTIFUL. WE COULDN'T HELP OURSELVES.
"WE STEPPED OUT OF THE CIRCLE.
"THAT'S WHEN WE SAW THE HORROR OF WHAT WE SUMMONED.
"RIGHT BEFORE IT RIPPED THE SOULS OUT OF OUR BODIES."

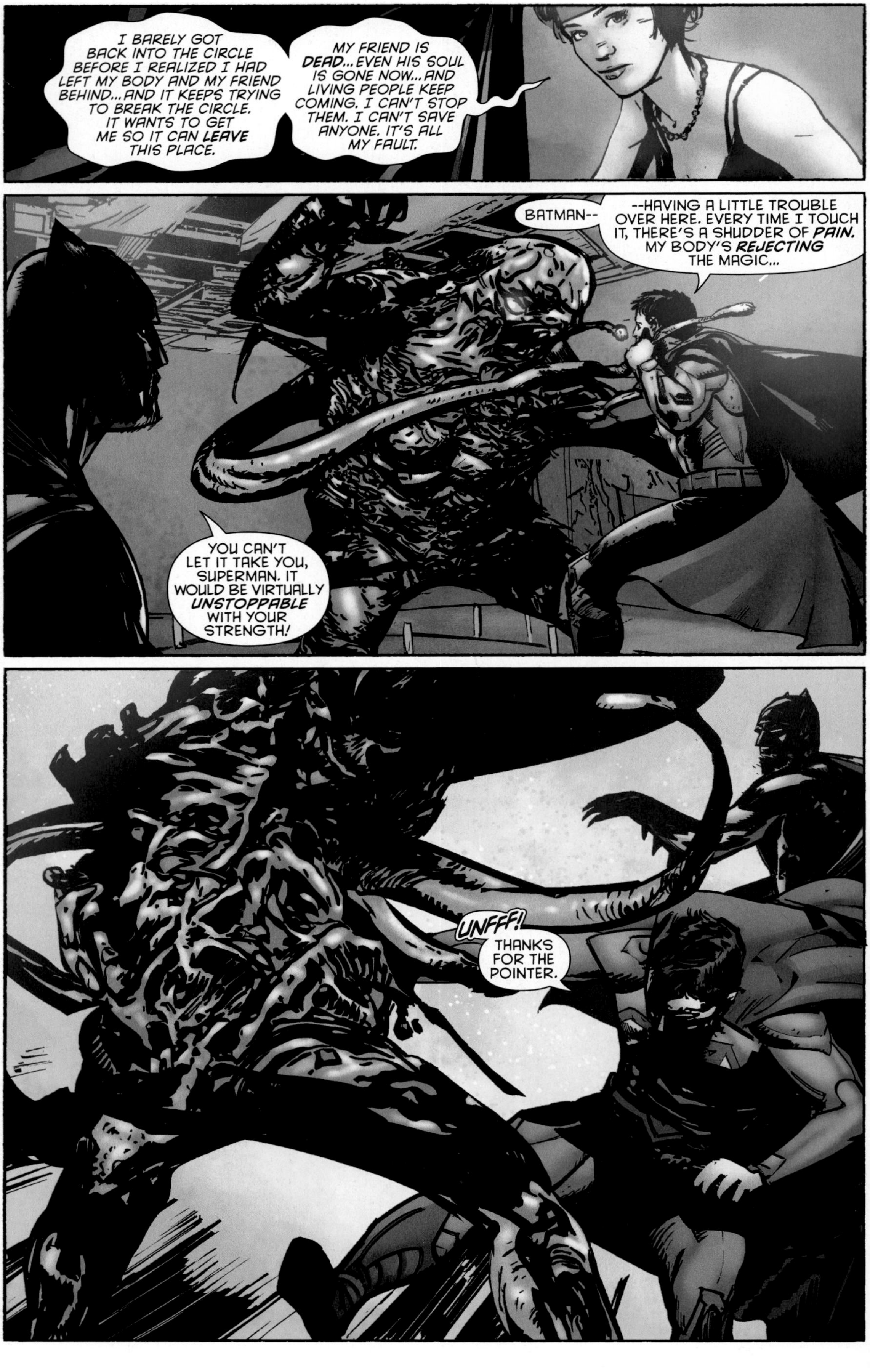
I BARELY GOT BACK INTO THE CIRCLE BEFORE I REALIZED I HAD LEFT MY BODY AND MY FRIEND BEHIND...AND IT KEEPS TRYING TO BREAK THE CIRCLE. IT WANTS TO GET ME SO IT CAN LEAVE THIS PLACE.
MY FRIEND IS DEAD...EVEN HIS SOUL IS GONE NOW...AND LIVING PEOPLE KEEP COMING. I CAN'T STOP THEM. I CAN'T SAVE ANYONE. IT'S ALL MY FAULT.
BATMAN--
--HAVING A LITTLE TROUBLE OVER HERE. EVERY TIME I TOUCH IT, THERE'S A SHUDDER OF PAIN. MY BODY'S REJECTING THE MAGIC...
YOU CAN'T LET IT TAKE YOU, SUPERMAN. IT WOULD BE VIRTUALLY UNSTOPPABLE WITH YOUR STRENGTH!
UNFFF!
THANKS FOR THE POINTER.

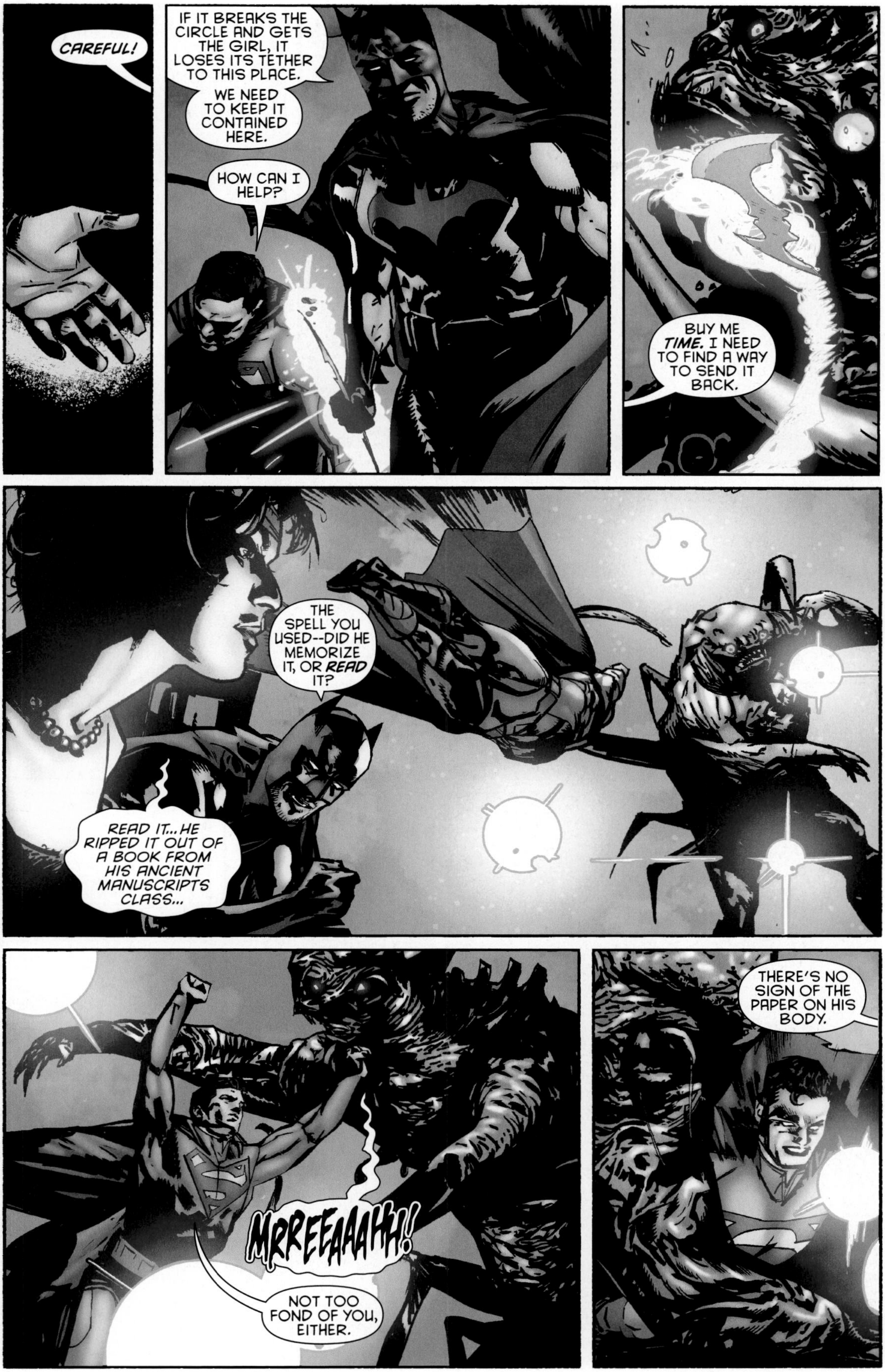
CAREFUL!
IF IT BREAKS THE CIRCLE AND GETS THE GIRL, IT LOSES ITS TETHER TO THIS PLACE.
WE NEED TO KEEP IT CONTAINED HERE.
HOW CAN I HELP?
BUY ME *TIME.* I NEED TO FIND A WAY TO SEND IT BACK.
THE SPELL YOU USED--DID HE MEMORIZE IT, OR *READ* IT?
READ IT... HE RIPPED IT OUT OF A BOOK FROM HIS ANCIENT MANUSCRIPTS CLASS...
MRREEAAAHH!
NOT TOO FOND OF YOU, EITHER.
THERE'S NO SIGN OF THE PAPER ON HIS BODY.

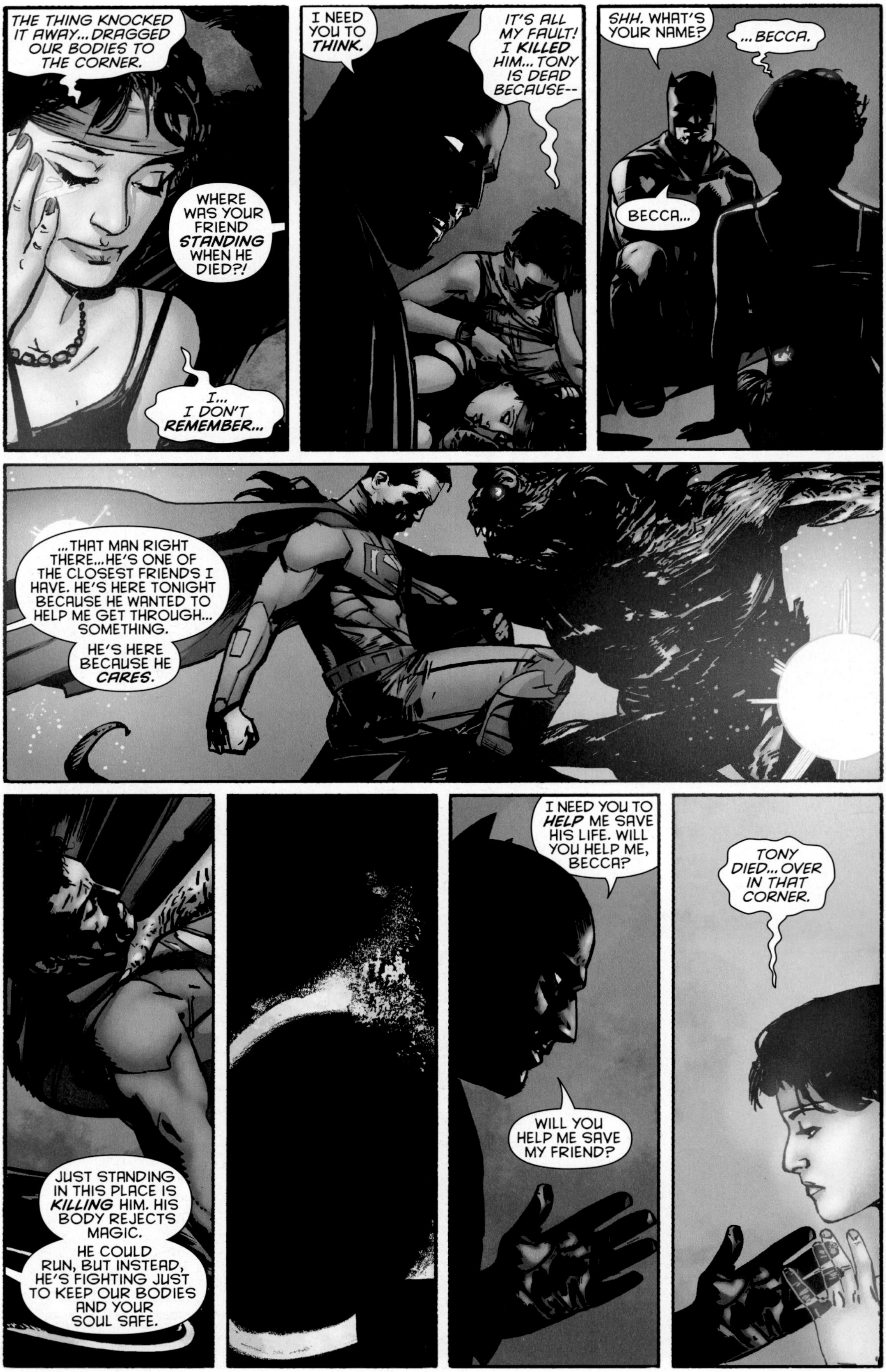

THE THING KNOCKED IT AWAY...DRAGGED OUR BODIES TO THE CORNER.
WHERE WAS YOUR FRIEND STANDING WHEN HE DIED?!
I... I DON'T REMEMBER...
I NEED YOU TO THINK.
IT'S ALL MY FAULT! I KILLED HIM... TONY IS DEAD BECAUSE--
SHH. WHAT'S YOUR NAME?
...BECCA.
BECCA...
...THAT MAN RIGHT THERE...HE'S ONE OF THE CLOSEST FRIENDS I HAVE. HE'S HERE TONIGHT BECAUSE HE WANTED TO HELP ME GET THROUGH... SOMETHING.
HE'S HERE BECAUSE HE CARES.
JUST STANDING IN THIS PLACE IS KILLING HIM. HIS BODY REJECTS MAGIC.
HE COULD RUN, BUT INSTEAD, HE'S FIGHTING JUST TO KEEP OUR BODIES AND YOUR SOUL SAFE.
I NEED YOU TO HELP ME SAVE HIS LIFE. WILL YOU HELP ME, BECCA?
WILL YOU HELP ME SAVE MY FRIEND?
TONY DIED... OVER IN THAT CORNER.

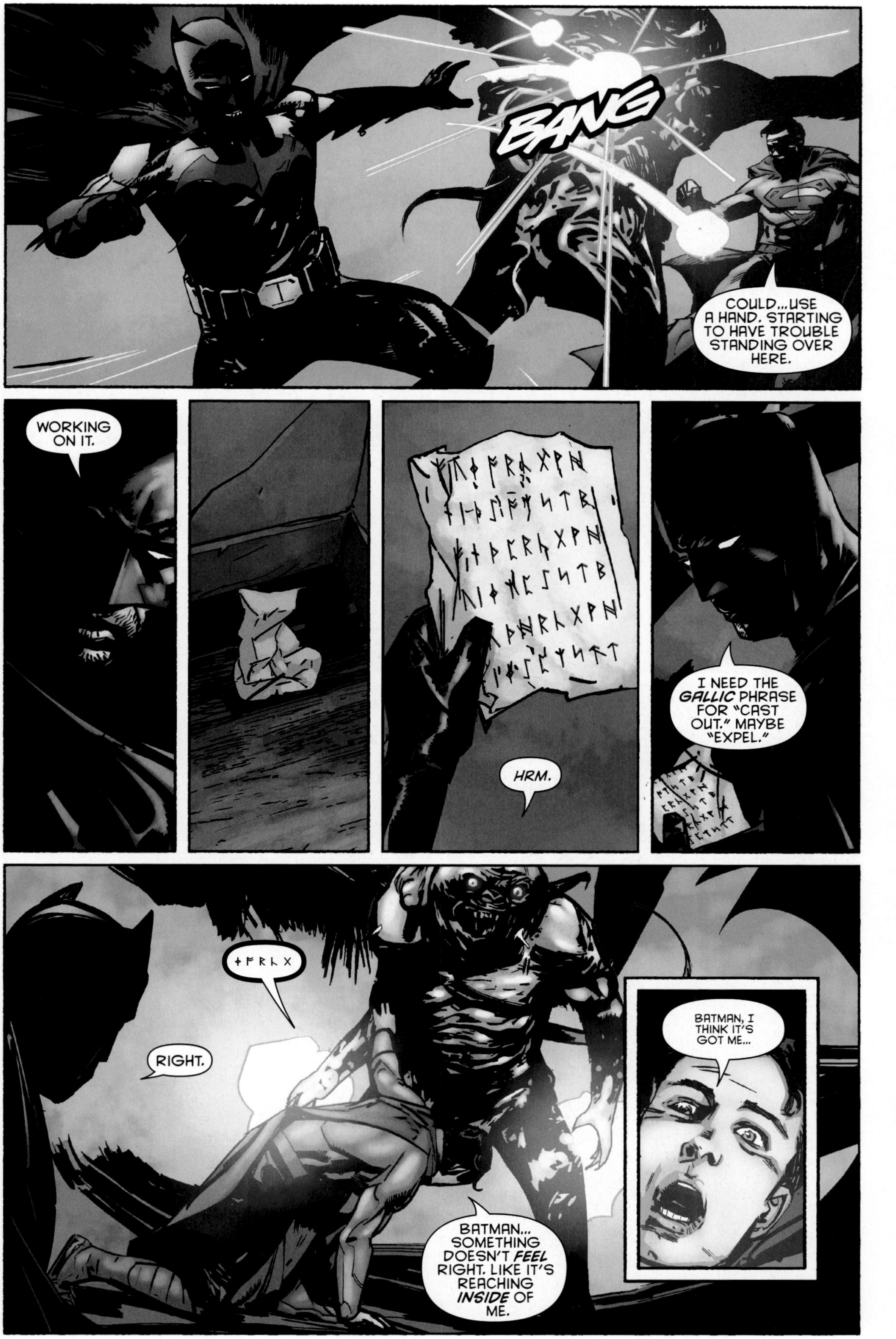
BANG
COULD...USE A HAND. STARTING TO HAVE TROUBLE STANDING OVER HERE.
WORKING ON IT.
HRM.
I NEED THE *GALLIC* PHRASE FOR "CAST OUT." MAYBE "EXPEL."
RIGHT.
BATMAN... SOMETHING DOESN'T *FEEL* RIGHT. LIKE IT'S REACHING *INSIDE* OF ME.
BATMAN, I THINK IT'S GOT ME...

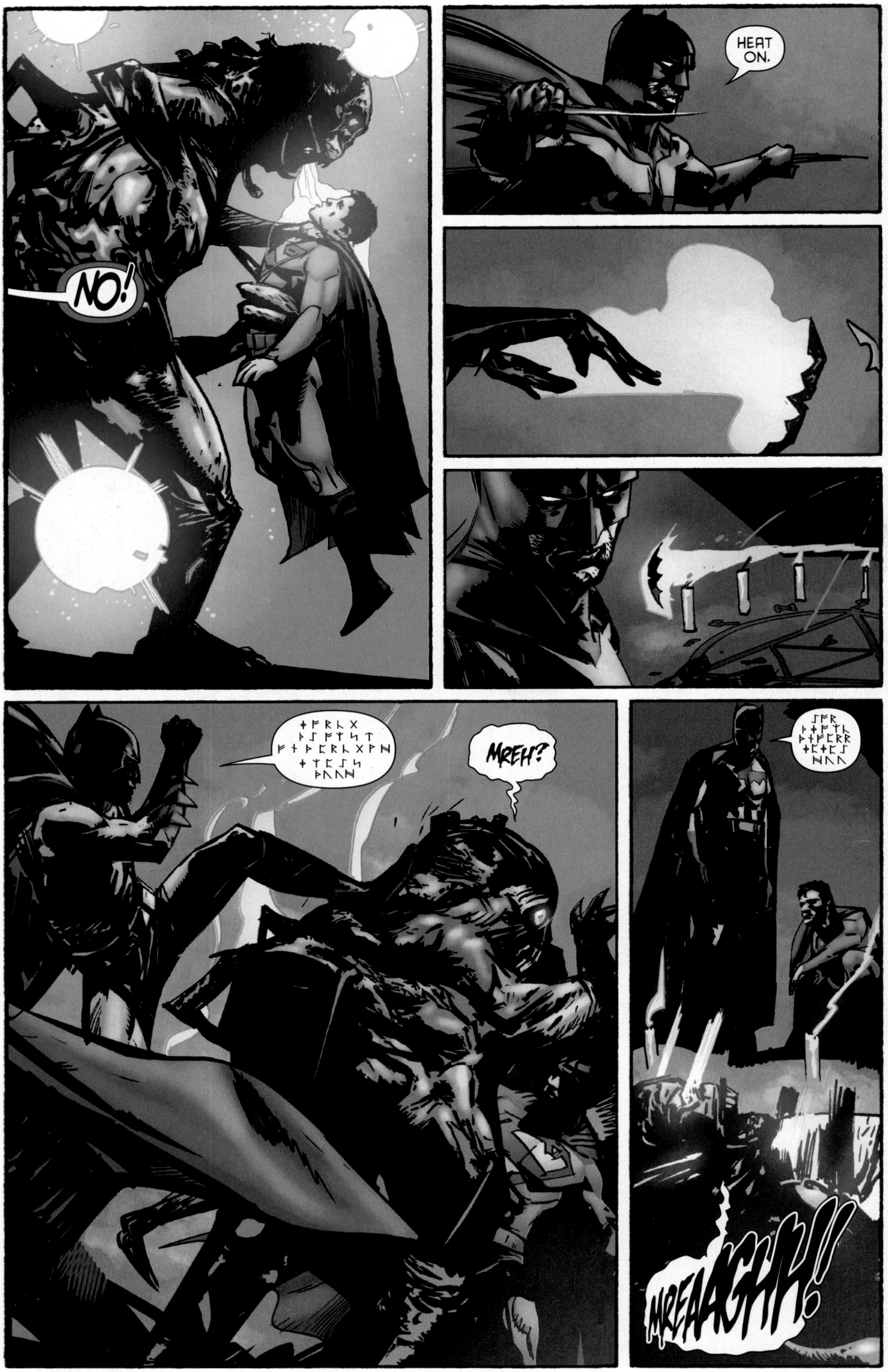

NO!
HEAT ON.
MREH?
MREAAGHH!!

HARUMMMGHP....*

THE MAGIC IN THIS PLACE...IT'S *GONE.*

AND ME NEXT, I'M GUESSING... I CAN FEEL SOMETHING PULLING ME AWAY.

THANK YOU, BECCA.

I'M JUST THE DUMB GIRL WHO GOT US ALL INTO THIS MESS.

YOU HAD NO WAY OF KNOWING WHAT WOULD HAPPEN.

STILL...

HEY, SUPERMAN... TAKE CARE OF THIS ONE, OKAY?

HE MIGHT LOOK SCARY AND ALL, BUT HE'S MUCH SWEETER THAN HE LOOKS.

I'LL TAKE THAT INTO CONSIDERATION.

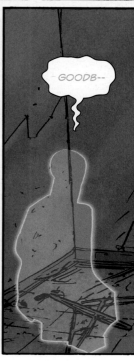

GOODB--

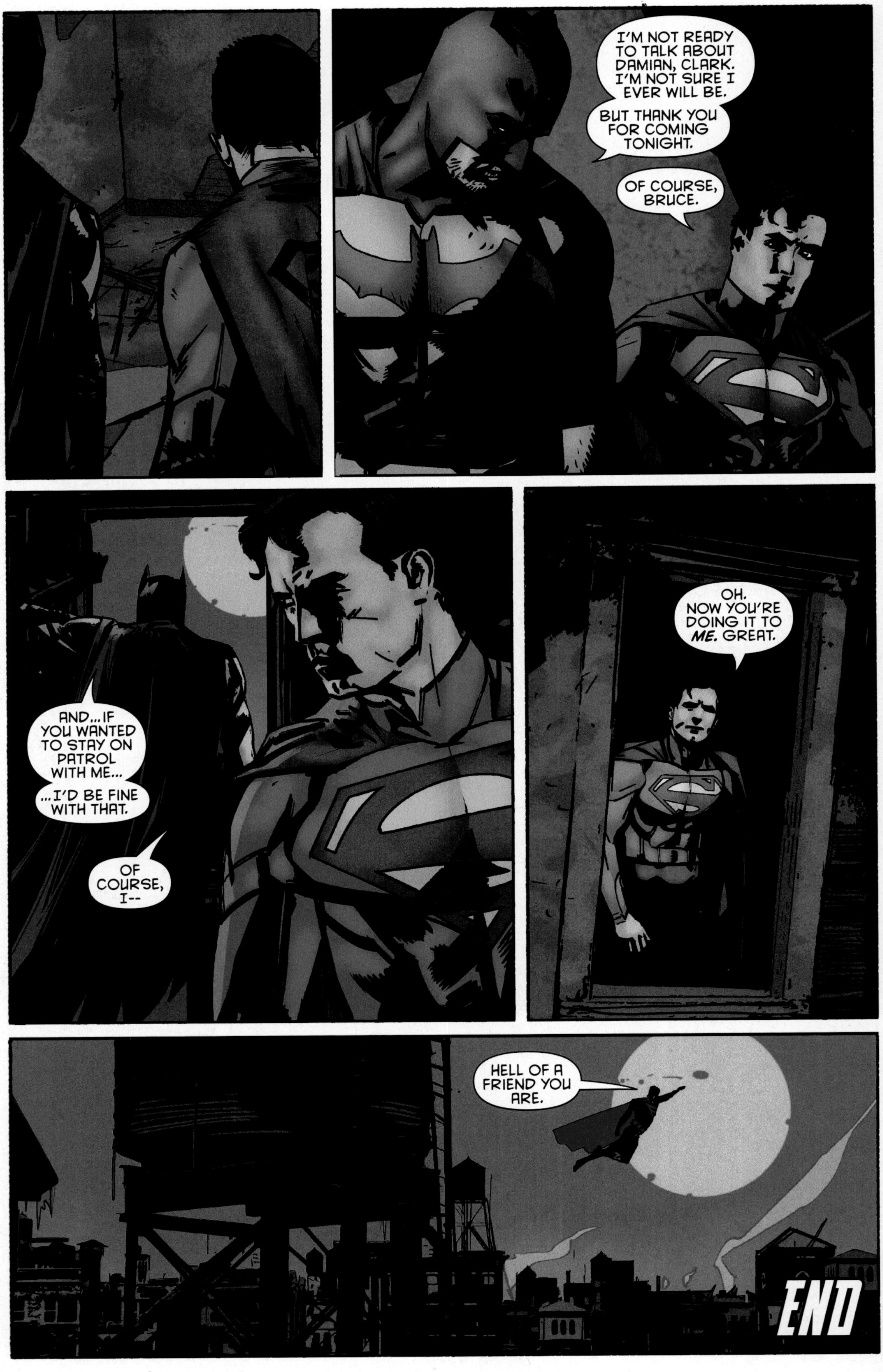
I'M NOT READY TO TALK ABOUT DAMIAN, CLARK. I'M NOT SURE I EVER WILL BE.
BUT THANK YOU FOR COMING TONIGHT.
OF COURSE, BRUCE.
AND... IF YOU WANTED TO STAY ON PATROL WITH ME...
...I'D BE FINE WITH THAT.
OF COURSE, I--
OH. NOW YOU'RE DOING IT TO *ME.* GREAT.
HELL OF A FRIEND YOU ARE.
END

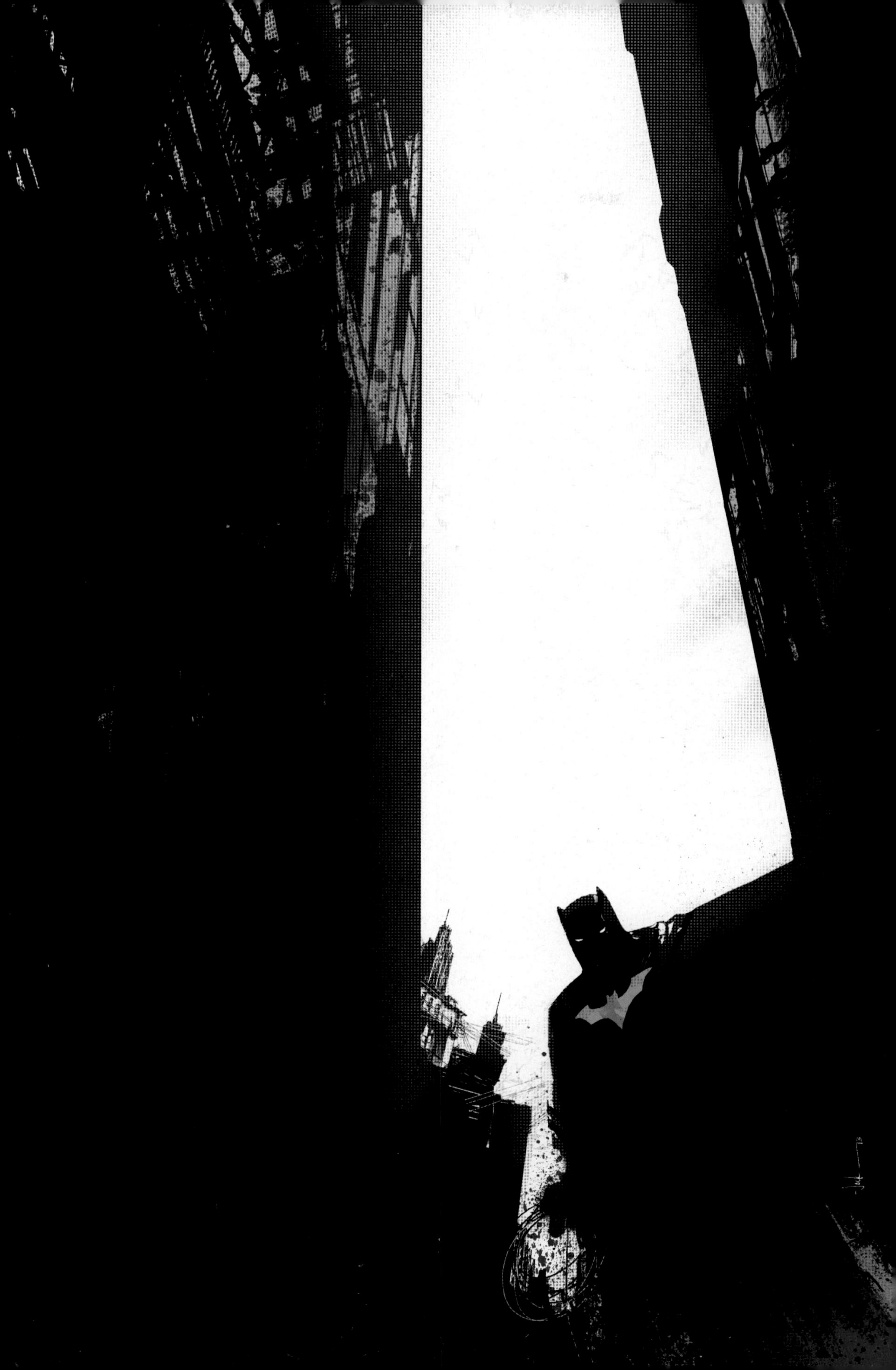

AGES

SCOTT SNYDER MARGUERITE BENNETT plotters MARGUERITE BENNETT writer WES CRAIG penciller CRAIG YEUNG DREW GERACI WES CRAIG JACK PURCELL SANDU FLOREA MARC DEERING inkers IAN HANNIN colorist cover by JOCK

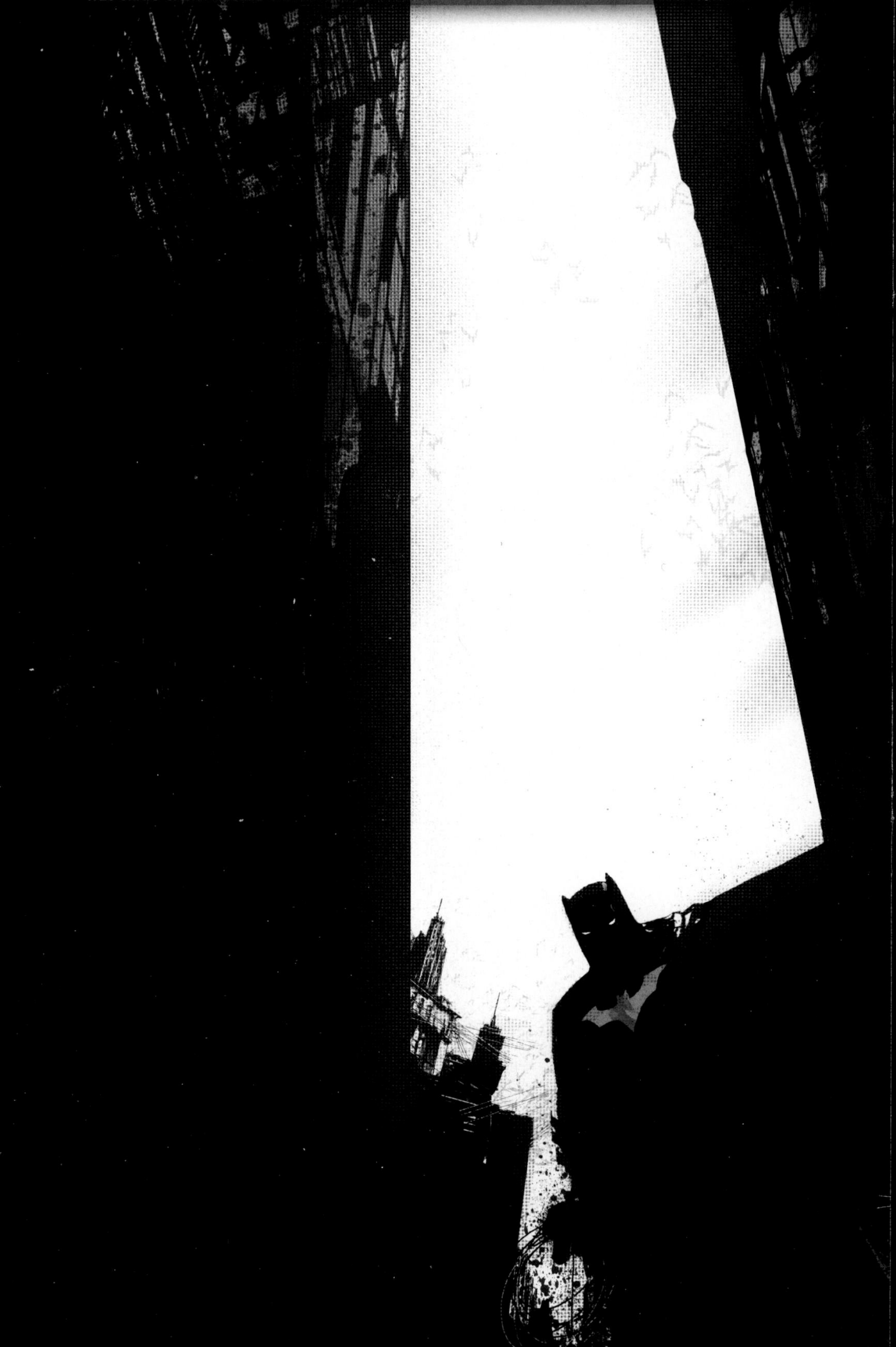

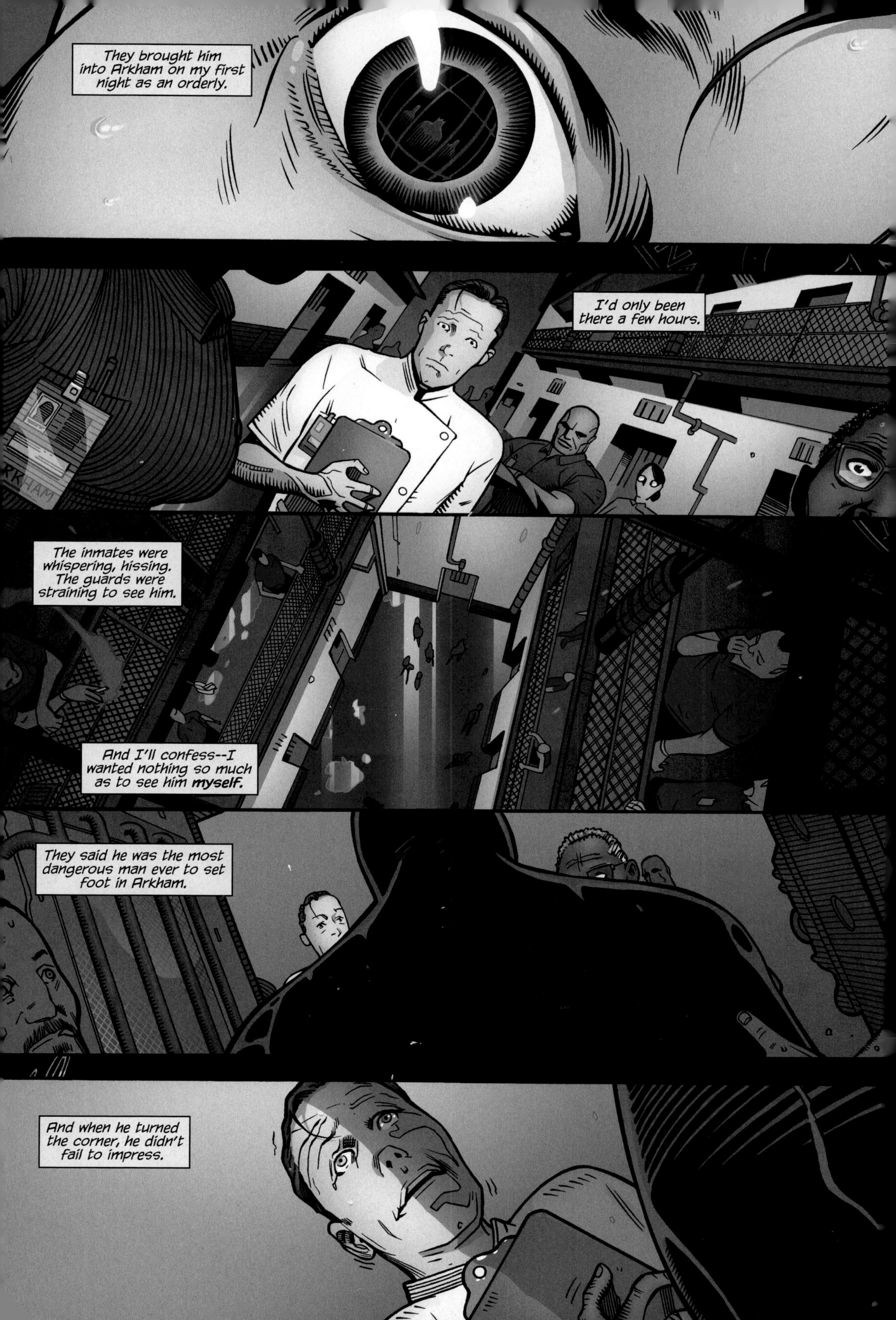
They brought him into Arkham on my first night as an orderly.
I'd only been there a few hours.
ARKHAM
The inmates were whispering, hissing. The guards were straining to see him.
And I'll confess--I wanted nothing so much as to see him **myself**.
They said he was the most dangerous man ever to set foot in Arkham.
And when he turned the corner, he didn't fail to impress.

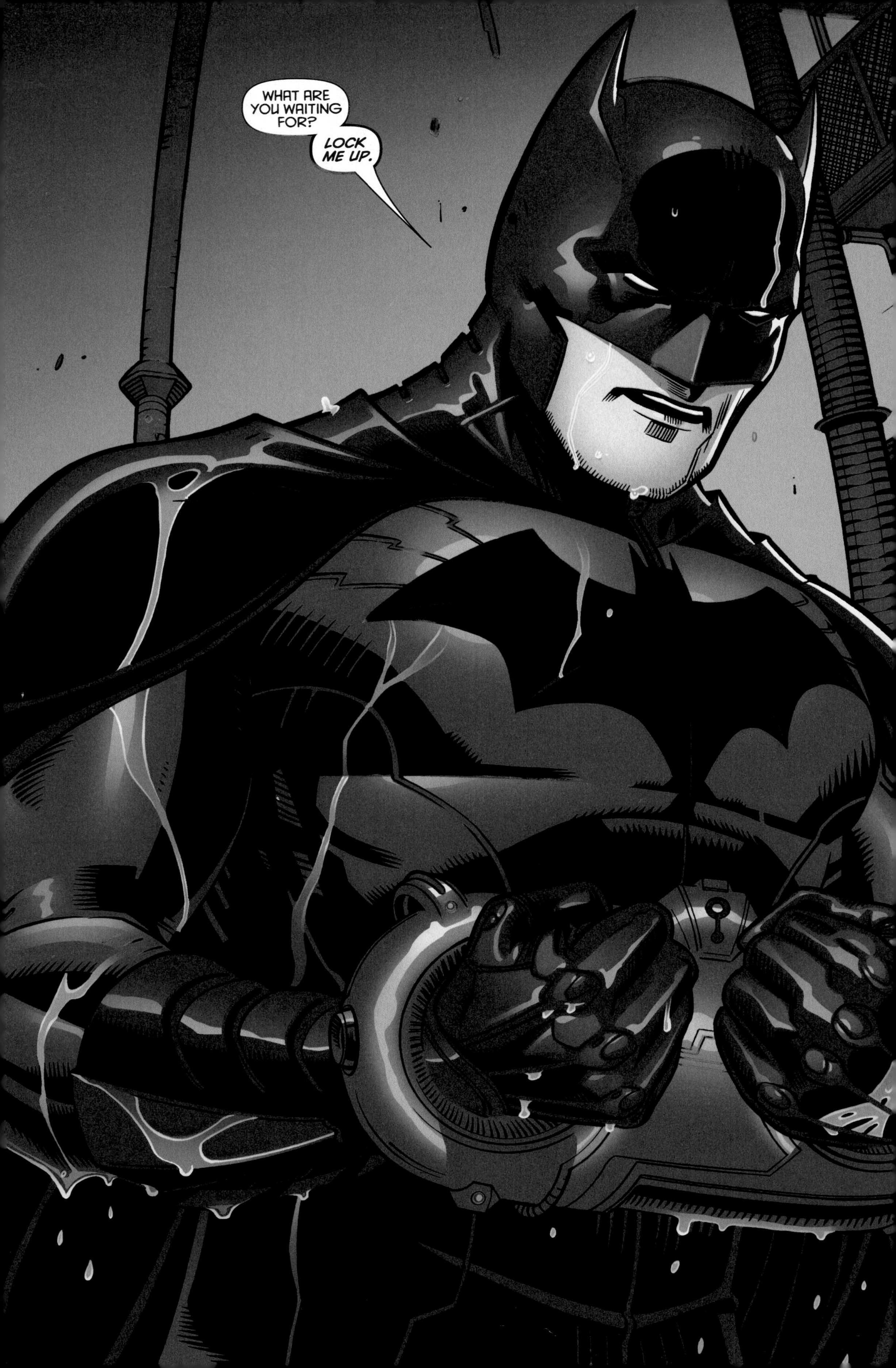
WHAT ARE YOU WAITING FOR?
LOCK ME UP.

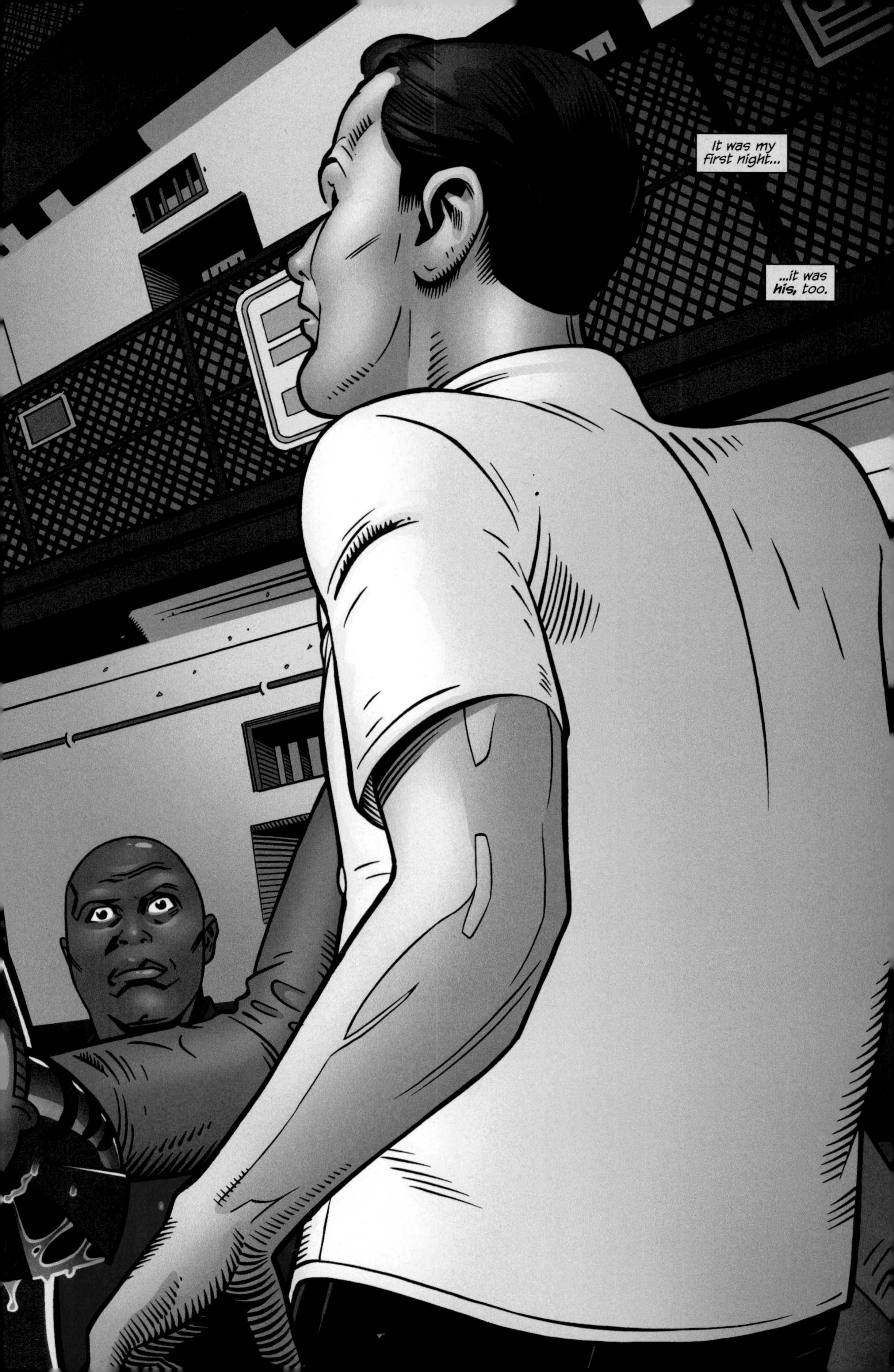
It was my first night...
...it was his, too.

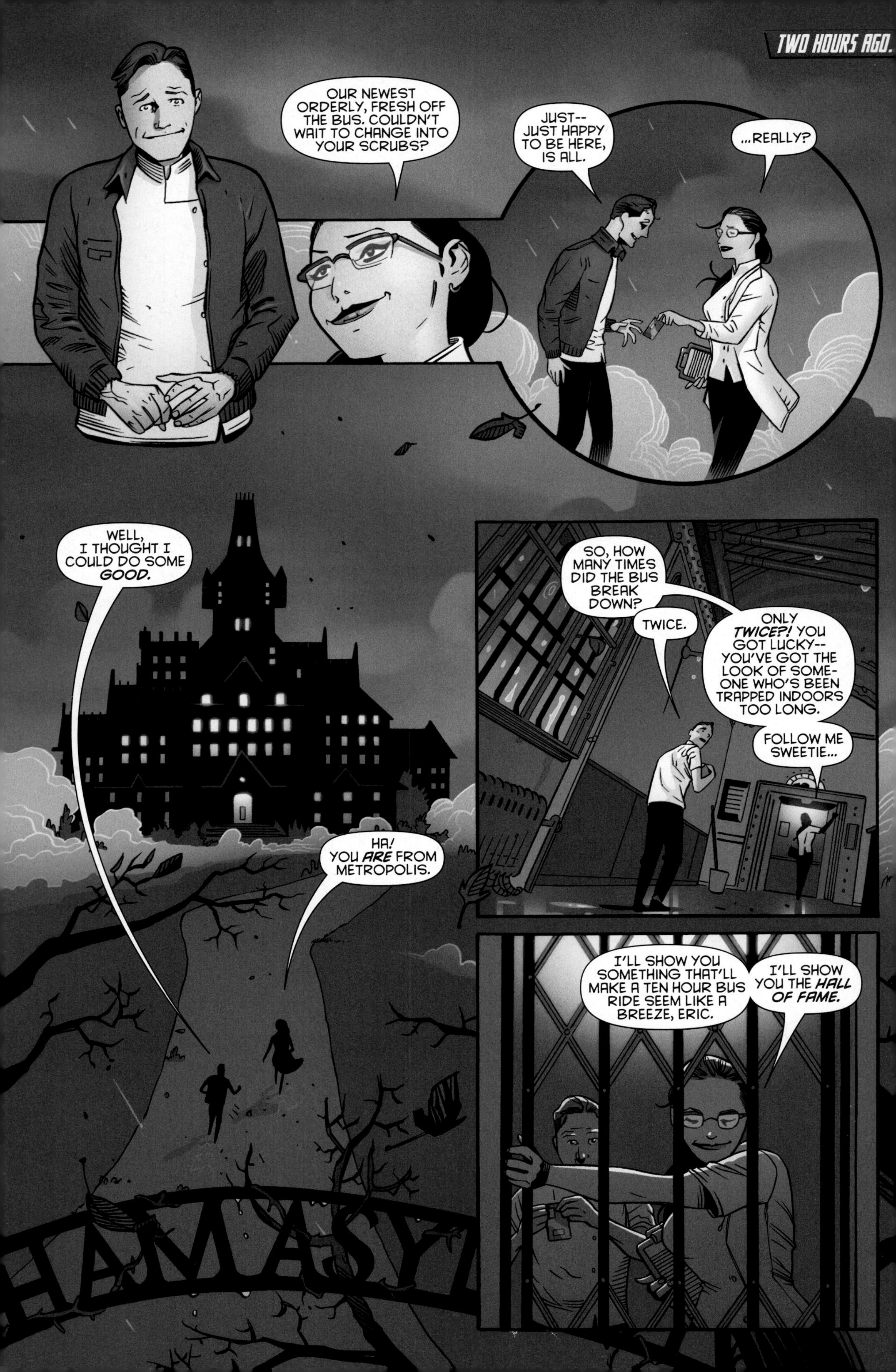

TWO HOURS AGO.
OUR NEWEST ORDERLY, FRESH OFF THE BUS. COULDN'T WAIT TO CHANGE INTO YOUR SCRUBS?
JUST-- JUST HAPPY TO BE HERE, IS ALL.
...REALLY?
WELL, I THOUGHT I COULD DO SOME *GOOD.*
HA! YOU *ARE* FROM METROPOLIS.
SO, HOW MANY TIMES DID THE BUS BREAK DOWN?
TWICE.
ONLY *TWICE?!* YOU GOT LUCKY-- YOU'VE GOT THE LOOK OF SOME-ONE WHO'S BEEN TRAPPED INDOORS TOO LONG.
FOLLOW ME SWEETIE...
I'LL SHOW YOU SOMETHING THAT'LL MAKE A TEN HOUR BUS RIDE SEEM LIKE A BREEZE, ERIC.
I'LL SHOW YOU THE *HALL OF FAME.*
HAM ASY

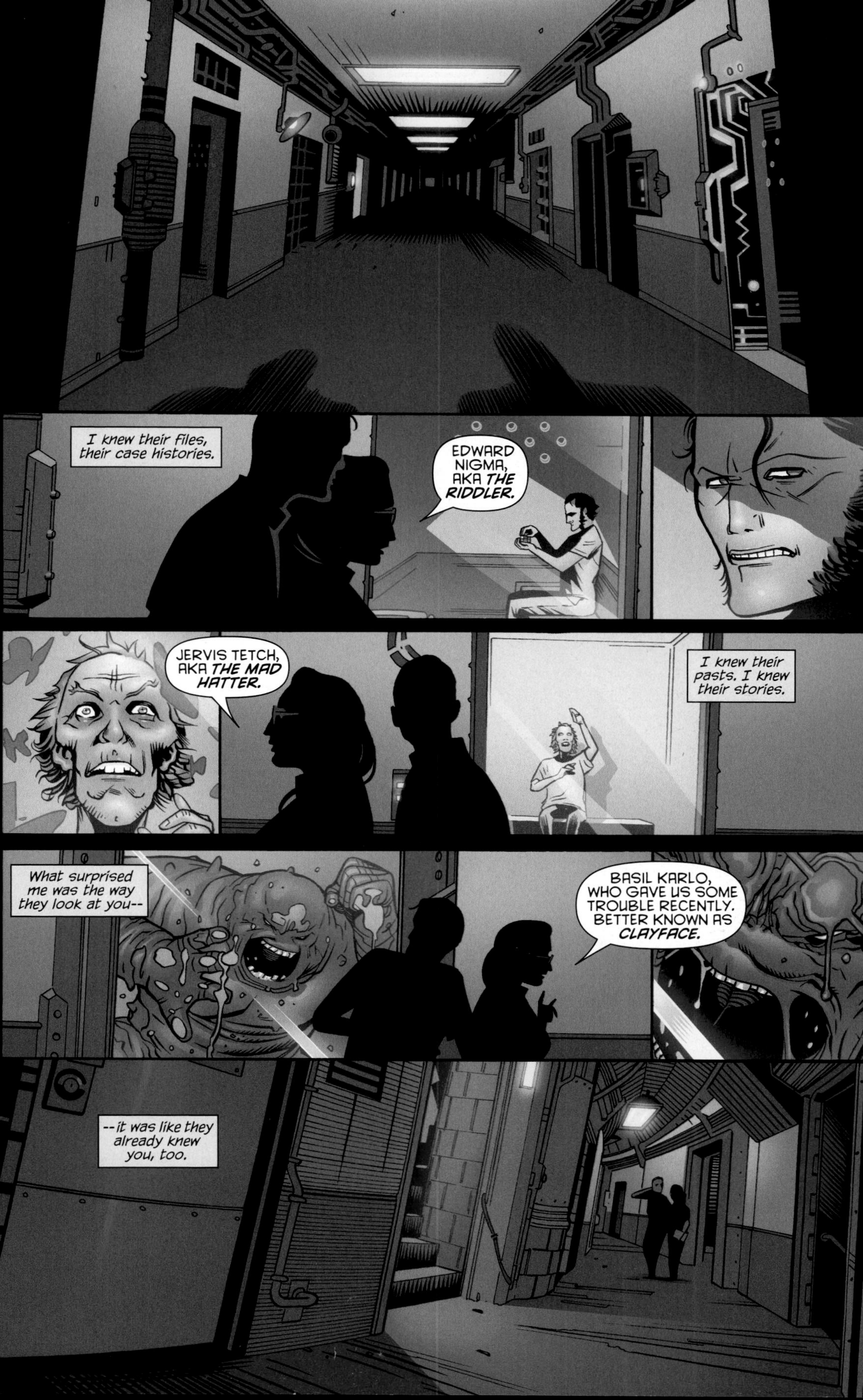
I knew their files, their case histories.
EDWARD NIGMA, AKA THE RIDDLER.
JERVIS TETCH, AKA THE MAD HATTER.
I knew their pasts. I knew their stories.
What surprised me was the way they look at you--
BASIL KARLO, WHO GAVE US SOME TROUBLE RECENTLY. BETTER KNOWN AS CLAYFACE.
--it was like they already knew you, too.

MAHREEN, WHAT'S DOWN THAT WAY?

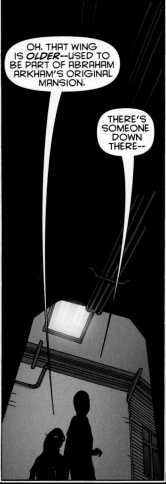

OH. THAT WING IS *OLDER*--USED TO BE PART OF ABRAHAM ARKHAM'S ORIGINAL MANSION.

THERE'S SOMEONE DOWN THERE--

DO NOT TOUCH THE BARS

OUR *FIRST* INMATE. SHE'S BEEN HERE FROM THE BEGINNING. NOT MANY PEOPLE KNOW ABOUT HER. OR...*REMEMBER* HER, I GUESS.

SHE'S CALLED THE *ANCHORESS*.

I'VE HEARD OF HER--

YOU DID YOUR HOMEWORK.

I TRY. SHE'S BEEN HERE THAT LONG?

SOME OF THE INMATES ARE INCURABLE, DR. ARKHAM THINKS.

I DON'T THINK *ANYONE'S* BEYOND HELP, OR SAVING.

AN IDEALIST?

OR AN IDIOT.

TOUCH THE BARS

...PLEASE... COME BACK...

The oldest inmate...

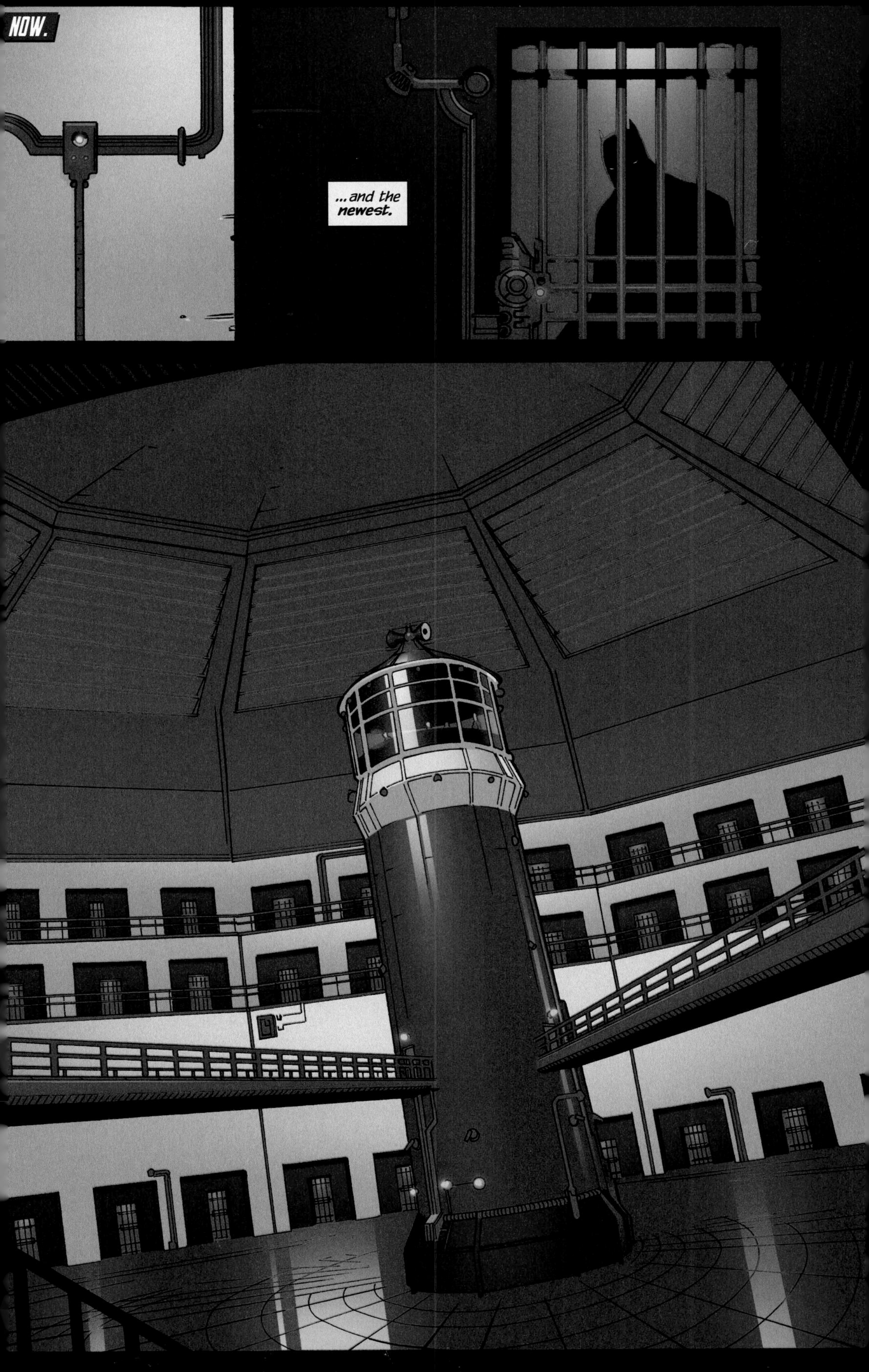
NOW.
...and the newest.

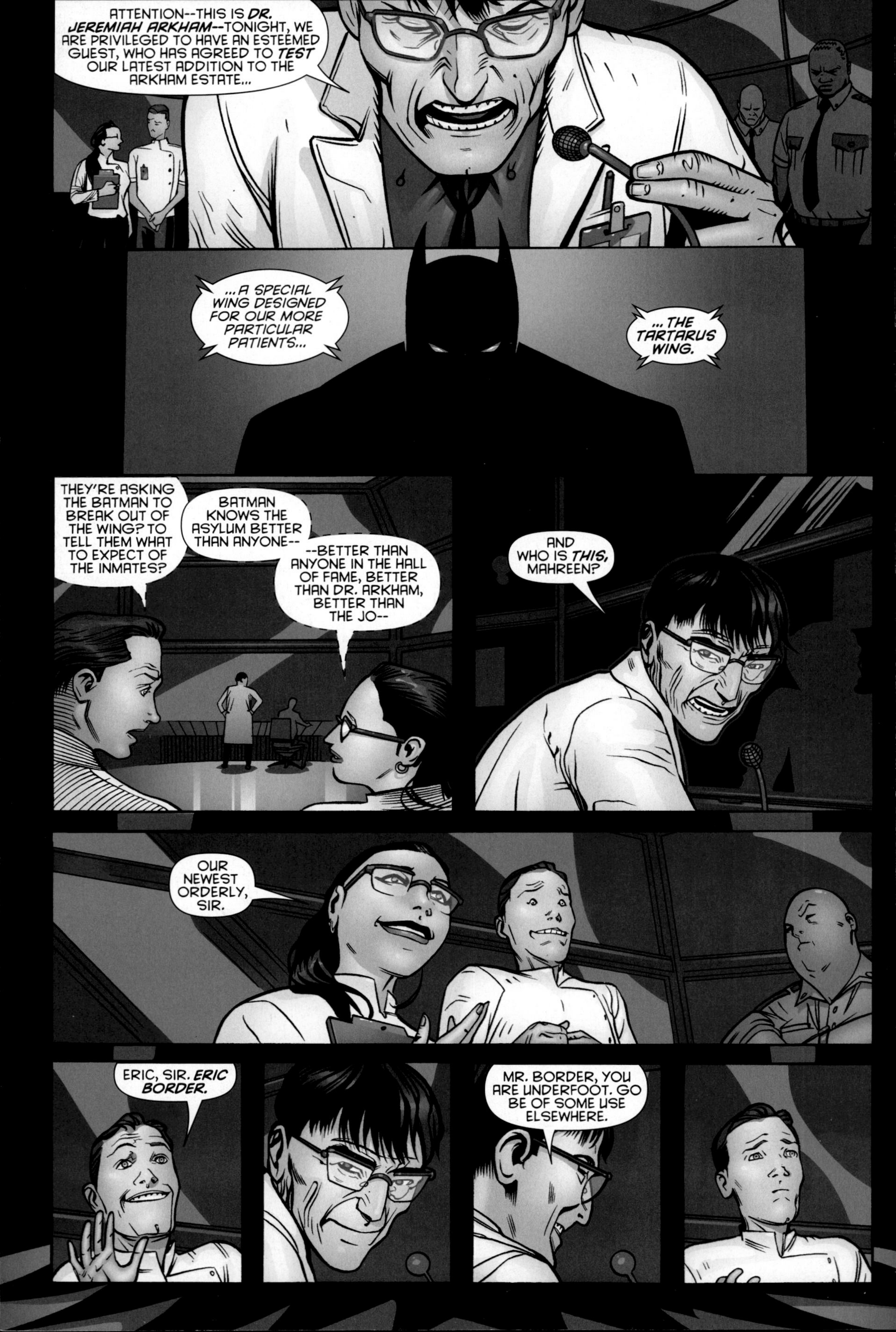
ATTENTION--THIS IS DR. JEREMIAH ARKHAM--TONIGHT, WE ARE PRIVILEGED TO HAVE AN ESTEEMED GUEST, WHO HAS AGREED TO TEST OUR LATEST ADDITION TO THE ARKHAM ESTATE...
...A SPECIAL WING DESIGNED FOR OUR MORE PARTICULAR PATIENTS...
...THE TARTARUS WING.
THEY'RE ASKING THE BATMAN TO BREAK OUT OF THE WING? TO TELL THEM WHAT TO EXPECT OF THE INMATES?
BATMAN KNOWS THE ASYLUM BETTER THAN ANYONE--
--BETTER THAN ANYONE IN THE HALL OF FAME, BETTER THAN DR. ARKHAM, BETTER THAN THE JO--
AND WHO IS THIS, MAHREEN?
OUR NEWEST ORDERLY, SIR.
ERIC, SIR. ERIC BORDER.
MR. BORDER, YOU ARE UNDERFOOT. GO BE OF SOME USE ELSEWHERE.

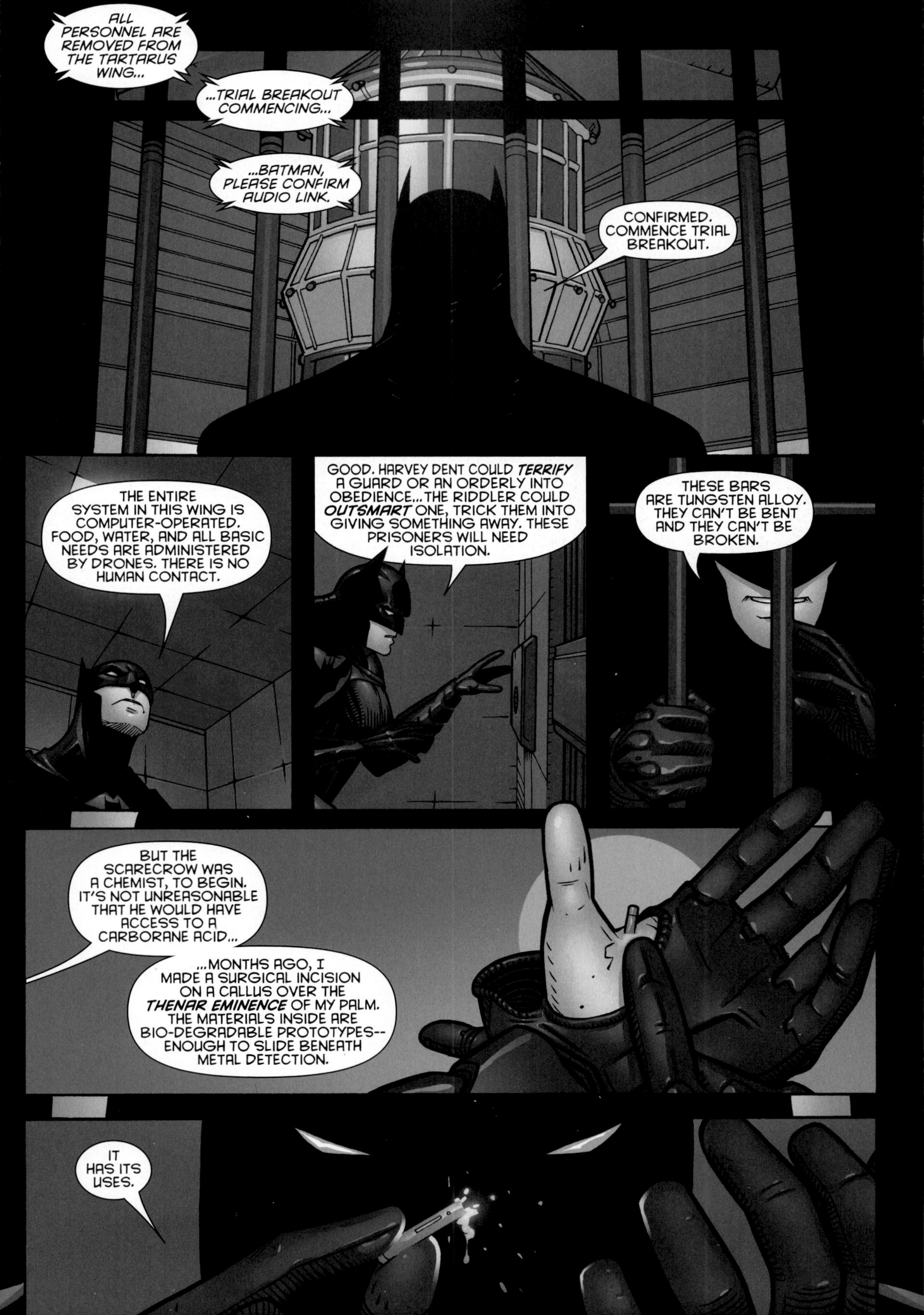
ALL PERSONNEL ARE REMOVED FROM THE TARTARUS WING...
...TRIAL BREAKOUT COMMENCING...
...BATMAN, PLEASE CONFIRM AUDIO LINK.
CONFIRMED. COMMENCE TRIAL BREAKOUT.
THE ENTIRE SYSTEM IN THIS WING IS COMPUTER-OPERATED. FOOD, WATER, AND ALL BASIC NEEDS ARE ADMINISTERED BY DRONES. THERE IS NO HUMAN CONTACT.
GOOD. HARVEY DENT COULD TERRIFY A GUARD OR AN ORDERLY INTO OBEDIENCE...THE RIDDLER COULD OUTSMART ONE, TRICK THEM INTO GIVING SOMETHING AWAY. THESE PRISONERS WILL NEED ISOLATION.
THESE BARS ARE TUNGSTEN ALLOY. THEY CAN'T BE BENT AND THEY CAN'T BE BROKEN.
BUT THE SCARECROW WAS A CHEMIST, TO BEGIN. IT'S NOT UNREASONABLE THAT HE WOULD HAVE ACCESS TO A CARBORANE ACID...
...MONTHS AGO, I MADE A SURGICAL INCISION ON A CALLUS OVER THE THENAR EMINENCE OF MY PALM. THE MATERIALS INSIDE ARE BIO-DEGRADABLE PROTOTYPES-- ENOUGH TO SLIDE BENEATH METAL DETECTION.
IT HAS ITS USES.

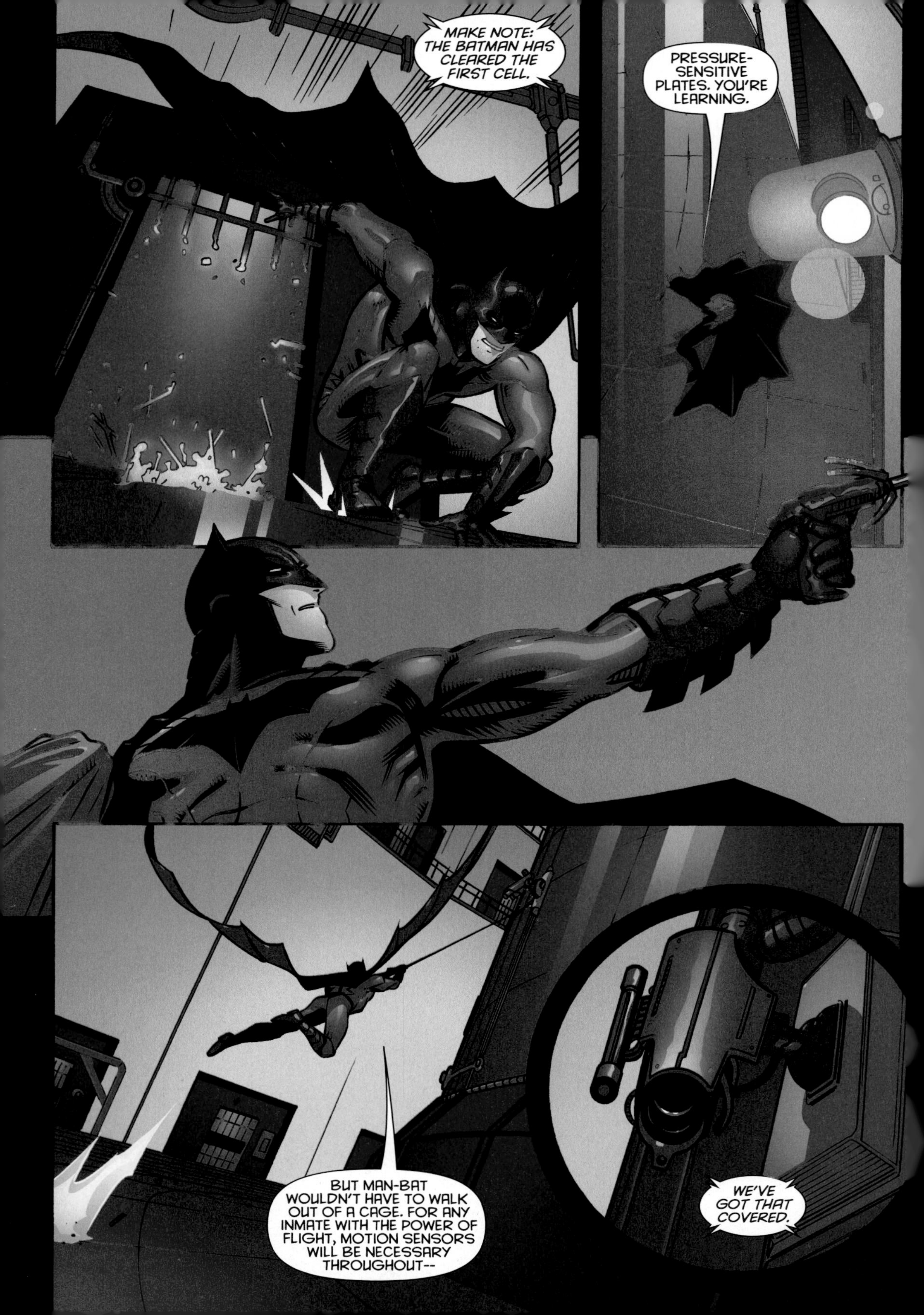
MAKE NOTE: THE BATMAN HAS CLEARED THE FIRST CELL.
PRESSURE-SENSITIVE PLATES. YOU'RE LEARNING.
BUT MAN-BAT WOULDN'T HAVE TO WALK OUT OF A CAGE. FOR ANY INMATE WITH THE POWER OF FLIGHT, MOTION SENSORS WILL BE NECESSARY THROUGHOUT--
WE'VE GOT THAT COVERED.

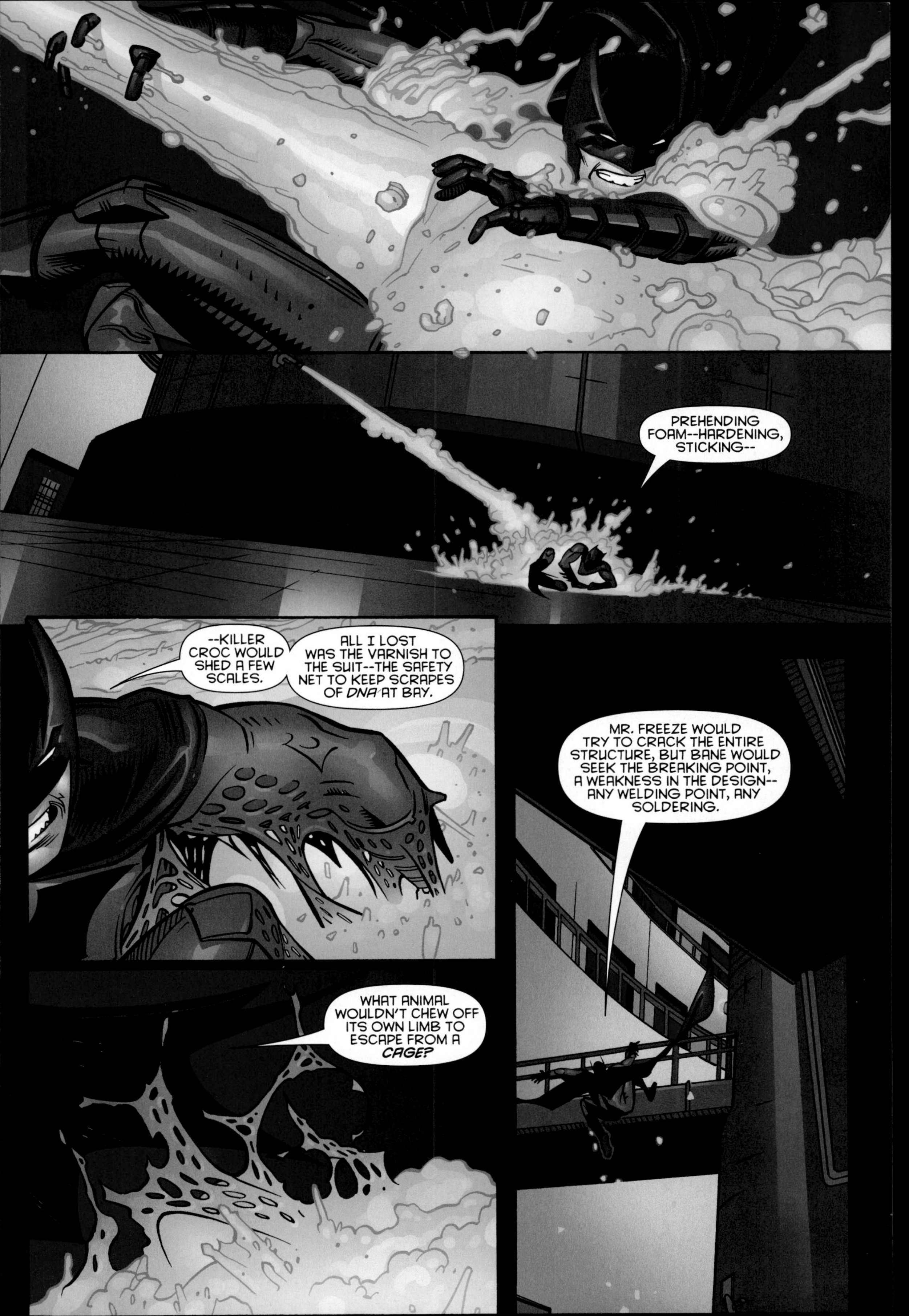
PREHENDING FOAM--HARDENING, STICKING--
--KILLER CROC WOULD SHED A FEW SCALES.
ALL I LOST WAS THE VARNISH TO THE SUIT--THE SAFETY NET TO KEEP SCRAPES OF *DNA* AT BAY.
MR. FREEZE WOULD TRY TO CRACK THE ENTIRE STRUCTURE, BUT BANE WOULD SEEK THE BREAKING POINT, A WEAKNESS IN THE DESIGN--ANY WELDING POINT, ANY SOLDERING.
WHAT ANIMAL WOULDN'T CHEW OFF ITS OWN LIMB TO ESCAPE FROM A ***CAGE?***

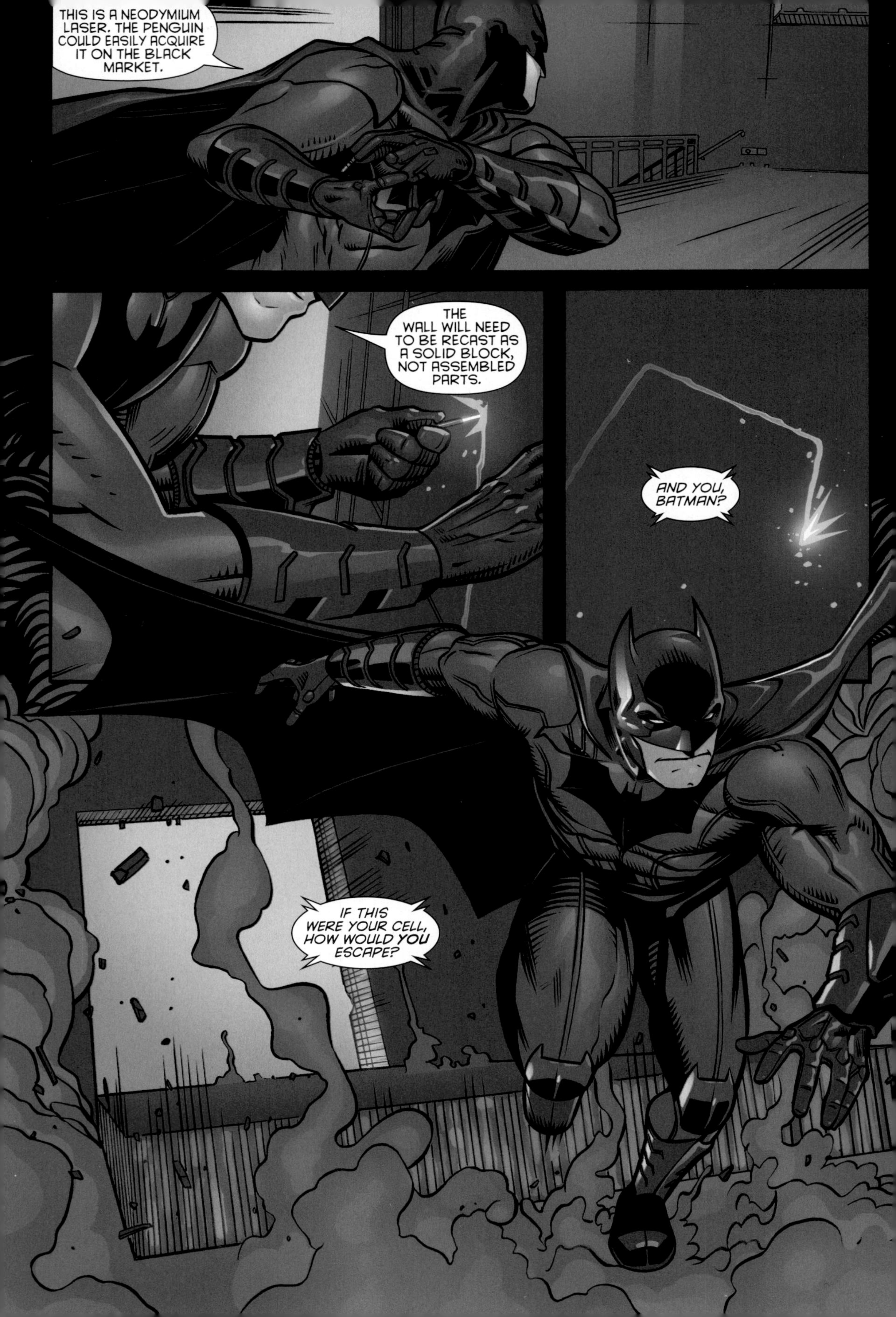
THIS IS A NEODYMIUM LASER. THE PENGUIN COULD EASILY ACQUIRE IT ON THE BLACK MARKET.
THE WALL WILL NEED TO BE RECAST AS A SOLID BLOCK, NOT ASSEMBLED PARTS.
AND YOU, BATMAN?
IF THIS WERE YOUR CELL, HOW WOULD YOU ESCAPE?

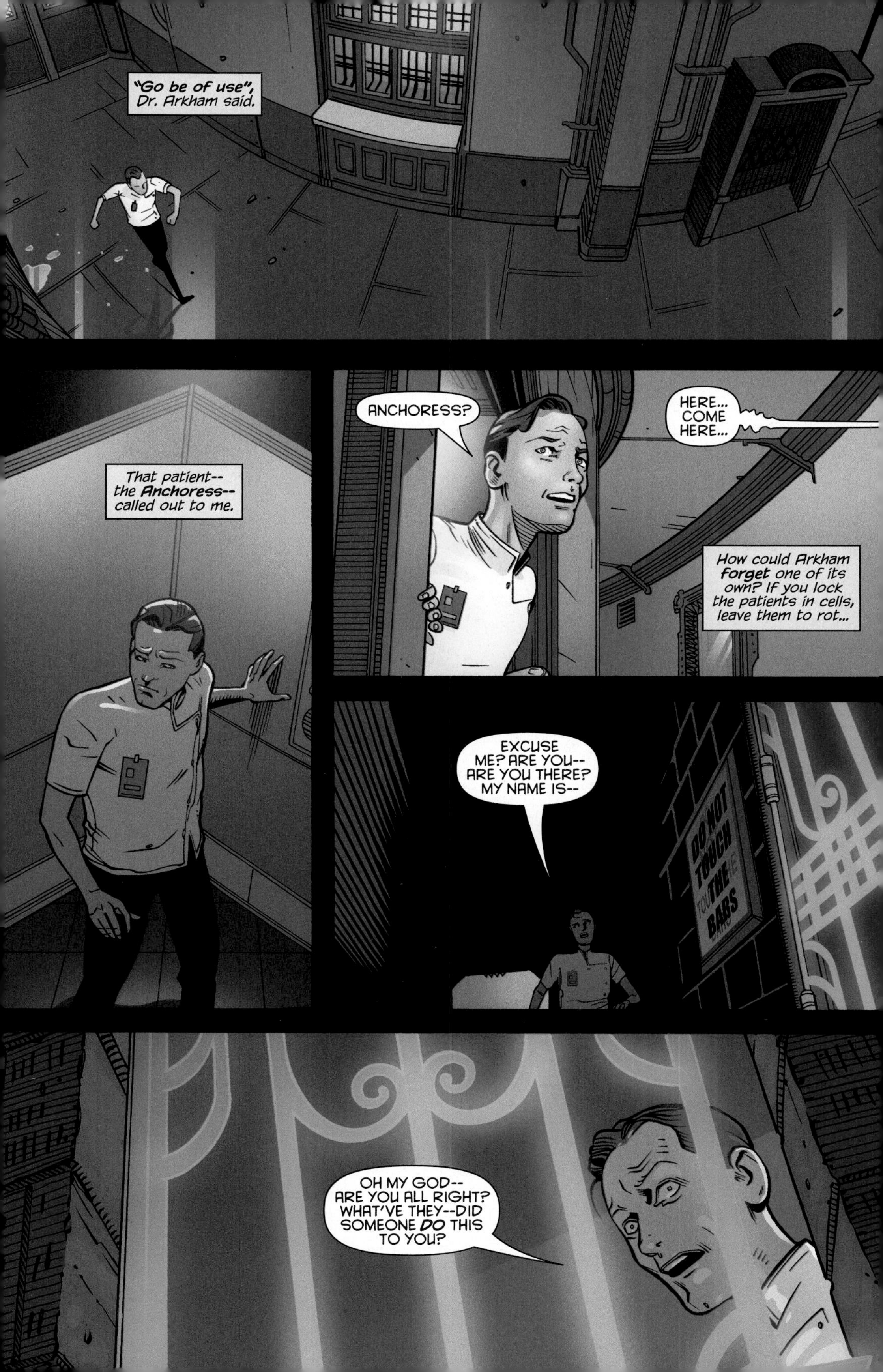
"Go be of use", Dr. Arkham said.
That patient-- the Anchoress-- called out to me.
ANCHORESS?
HERE... COME HERE...
How could Arkham forget one of its own? If you lock the patients in cells, leave them to rot...
EXCUSE ME? ARE YOU-- ARE YOU THERE? MY NAME IS--
DO NOT TOUCH THE BARS
OH MY GOD-- ARE YOU ALL RIGHT? WHAT'VE THEY--DID SOMEONE DO THIS TO YOU?

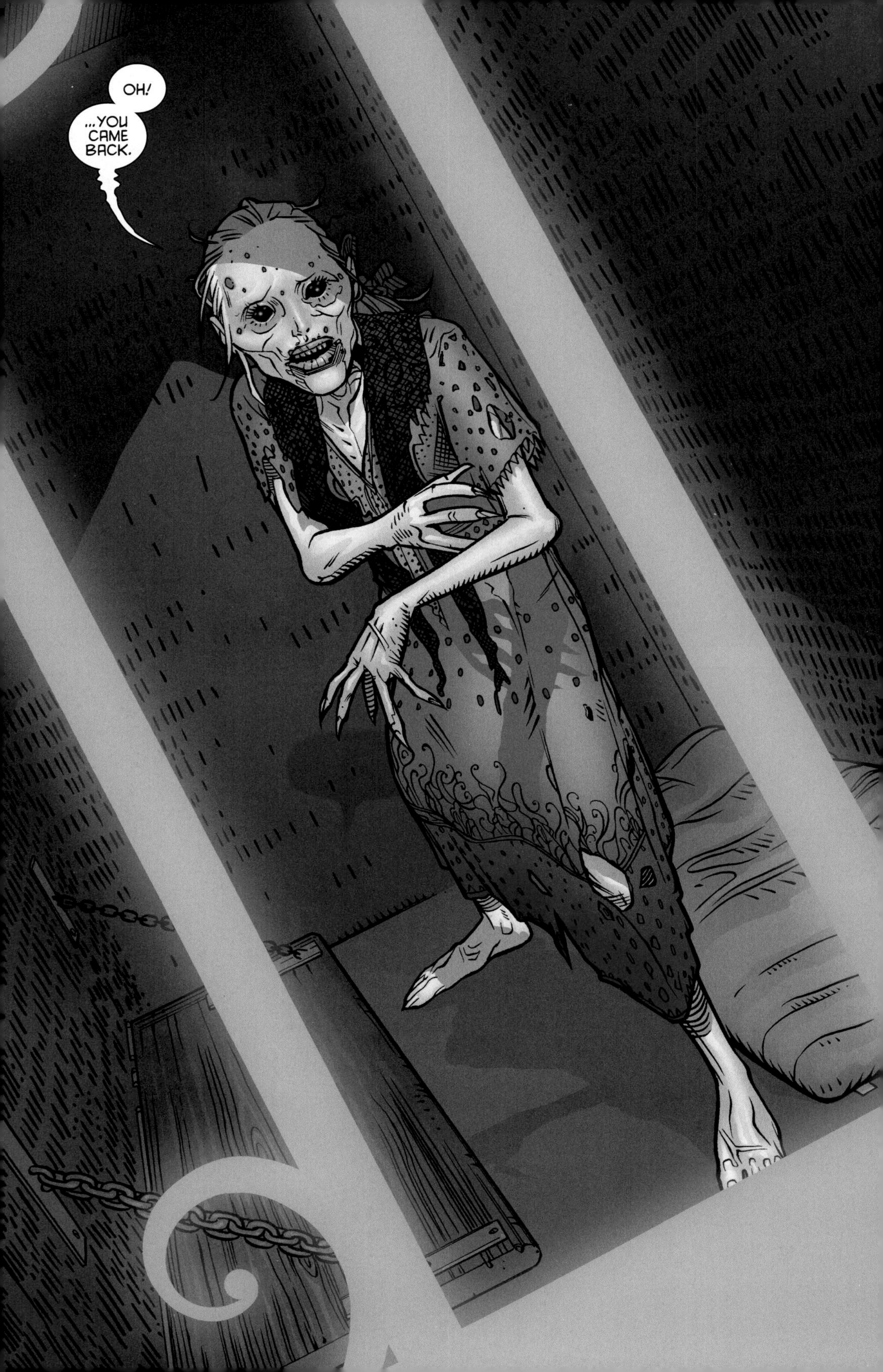
OH!
...YOU CAME BACK.

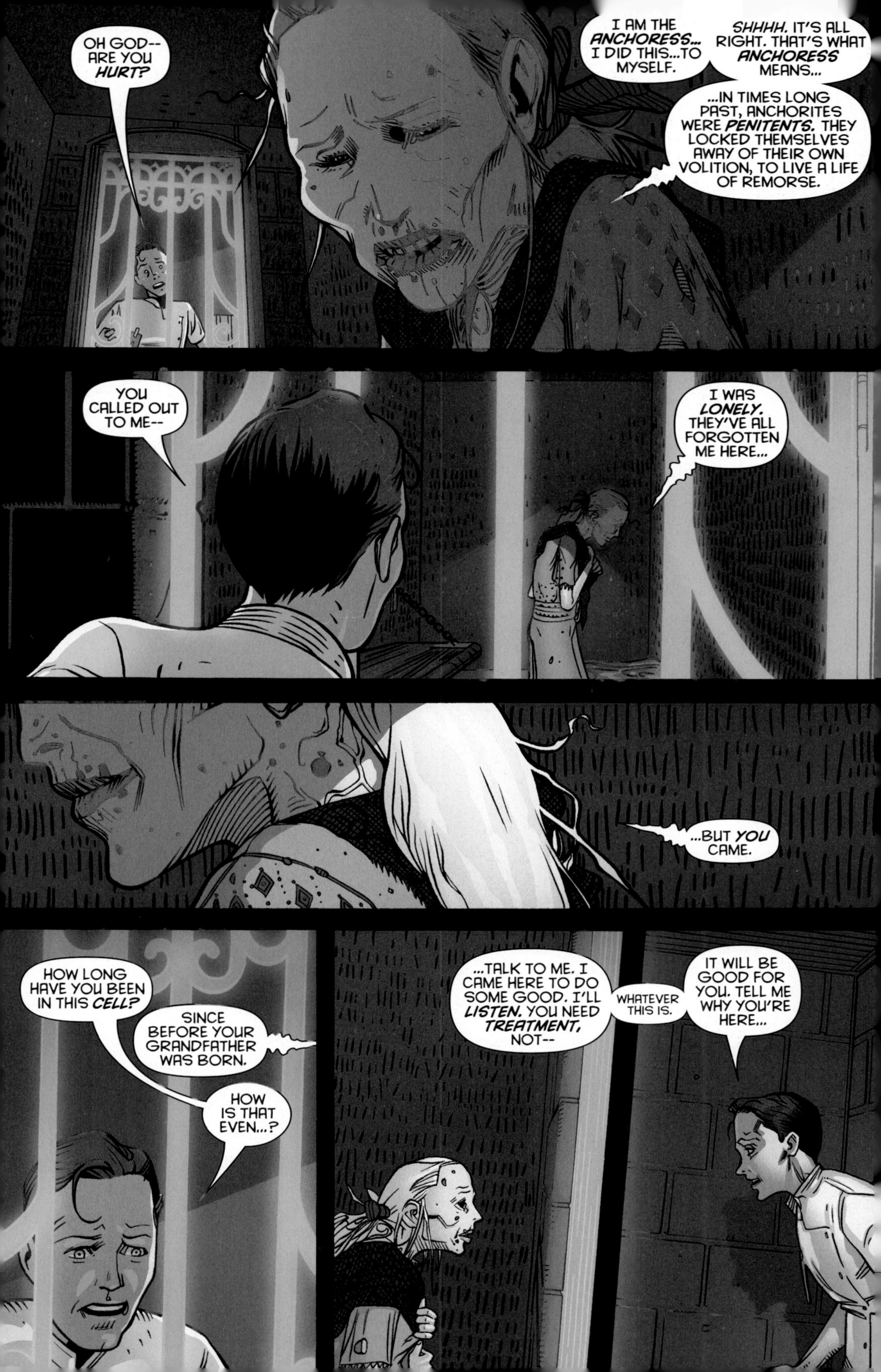
OH GOD-- ARE YOU *HURT?*
I AM THE *ANCHORESS...* I DID THIS...TO MYSELF.
SHHHH. IT'S ALL RIGHT. THAT'S WHAT *ANCHORESS* MEANS...
...IN TIMES LONG PAST, ANCHORITES WERE *PENITENTS.* THEY LOCKED THEMSELVES AWAY OF THEIR OWN VOLITION, TO LIVE A LIFE OF REMORSE.
YOU CALLED OUT TO ME--
I WAS *LONELY.* THEY'VE ALL FORGOTTEN ME HERE...
...BUT *YOU* CAME.
HOW LONG HAVE YOU BEEN IN THIS *CELL?*
SINCE BEFORE YOUR GRANDFATHER WAS BORN.
HOW IS THAT EVEN...?
...TALK TO ME. I CAME HERE TO DO SOME GOOD. I'LL *LISTEN.* YOU NEED *TREATMENT,* NOT--
WHATEVER THIS IS.
IT WILL BE GOOD FOR YOU. TELL ME WHY YOU'RE HERE...

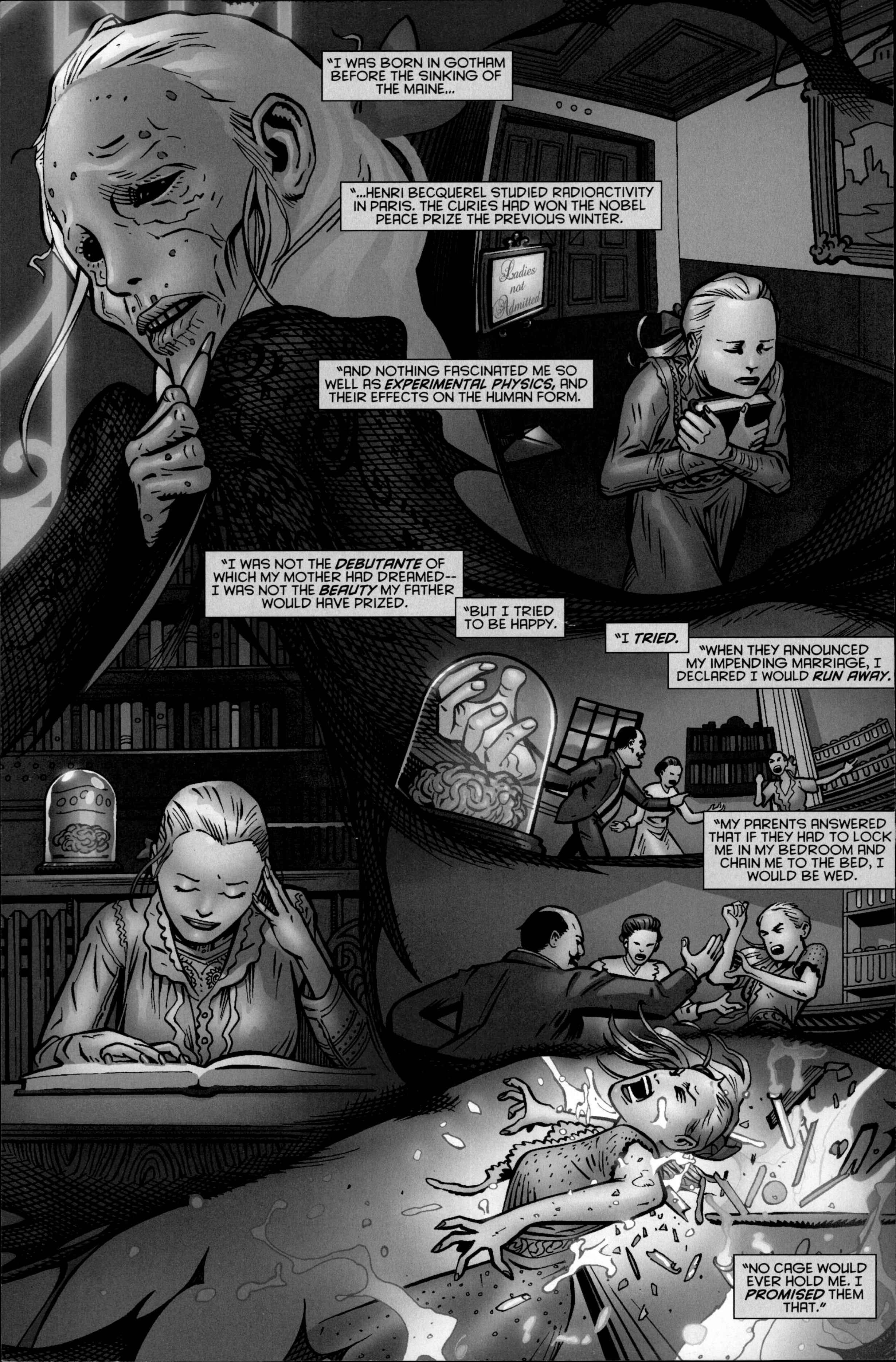
"I WAS BORN IN GOTHAM BEFORE THE SINKING OF THE MAINE...
"...HENRI BECQUEREL STUDIED RADIOACTIVITY IN PARIS. THE CURIES HAD WON THE NOBEL PEACE PRIZE THE PREVIOUS WINTER.
Ladies not Admitted
"AND NOTHING FASCINATED ME SO WELL AS EXPERIMENTAL PHYSICS, AND THEIR EFFECTS ON THE HUMAN FORM.
"I WAS NOT THE DEBUTANTE OF WHICH MY MOTHER HAD DREAMED-- I WAS NOT THE BEAUTY MY FATHER WOULD HAVE PRIZED.
"BUT I TRIED TO BE HAPPY.
"I TRIED.
"WHEN THEY ANNOUNCED MY IMPENDING MARRIAGE, I DECLARED I WOULD RUN AWAY.
"MY PARENTS ANSWERED THAT IF THEY HAD TO LOCK ME IN MY BEDROOM AND CHAIN ME TO THE BED, I WOULD BE WED.
"NO CAGE WOULD EVER HOLD ME. I PROMISED THEM THAT."

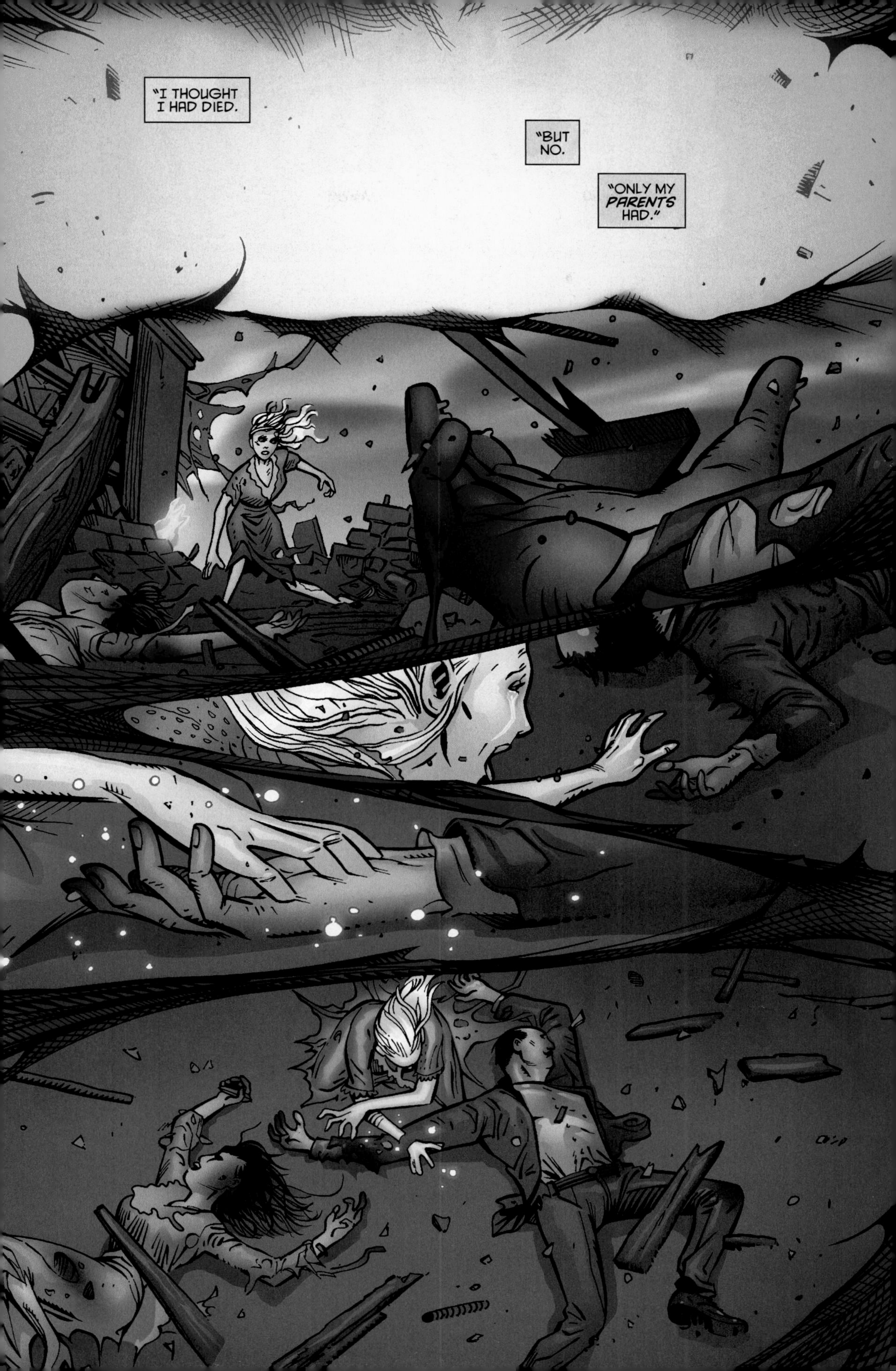
"I THOUGHT I HAD DIED.
"BUT NO.
"ONLY MY PARENTS HAD."

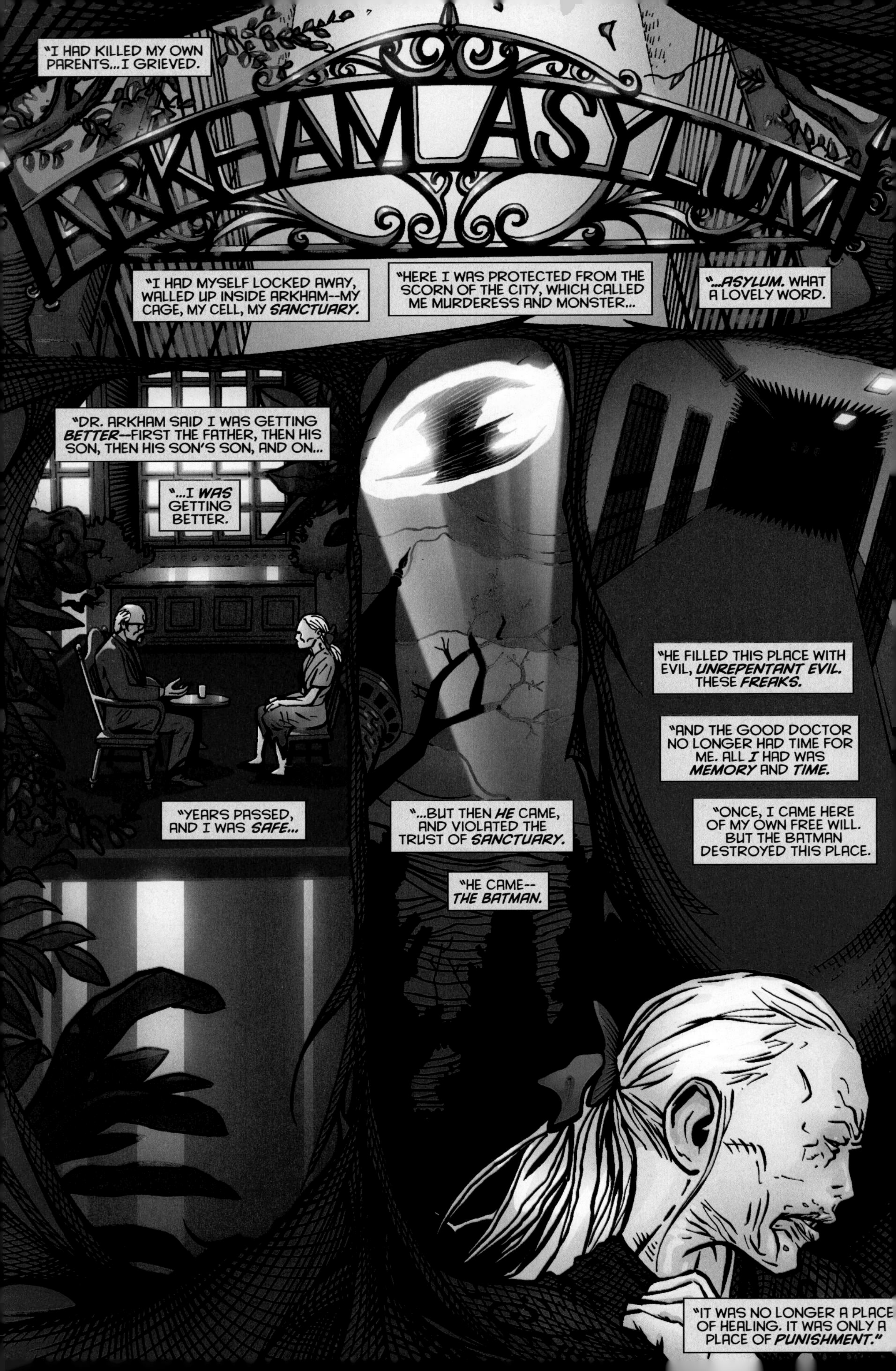
"I HAD KILLED MY OWN PARENTS...I GRIEVED.
ARKHAM ASYLUM
"I HAD MYSELF LOCKED AWAY, WALLED UP INSIDE ARKHAM--MY CAGE, MY CELL, MY SANCTUARY.
"HERE I WAS PROTECTED FROM THE SCORN OF THE CITY, WHICH CALLED ME MURDERESS AND MONSTER...
"...ASYLUM. WHAT A LOVELY WORD.
"DR. ARKHAM SAID I WAS GETTING BETTER--FIRST THE FATHER, THEN HIS SON, THEN HIS SON'S SON, AND ON...
"...I WAS GETTING BETTER.
"YEARS PASSED, AND I WAS SAFE...
"...BUT THEN HE CAME, AND VIOLATED THE TRUST OF SANCTUARY.
"HE CAME-- THE BATMAN.
"HE FILLED THIS PLACE WITH EVIL, UNREPENTANT EVIL. THESE FREAKS.
"AND THE GOOD DOCTOR NO LONGER HAD TIME FOR ME. ALL I HAD WAS MEMORY AND TIME.
"ONCE, I CAME HERE OF MY OWN FREE WILL. BUT THE BATMAN DESTROYED THIS PLACE.
"IT WAS NO LONGER A PLACE OF HEALING. IT WAS ONLY A PLACE OF PUNISHMENT."

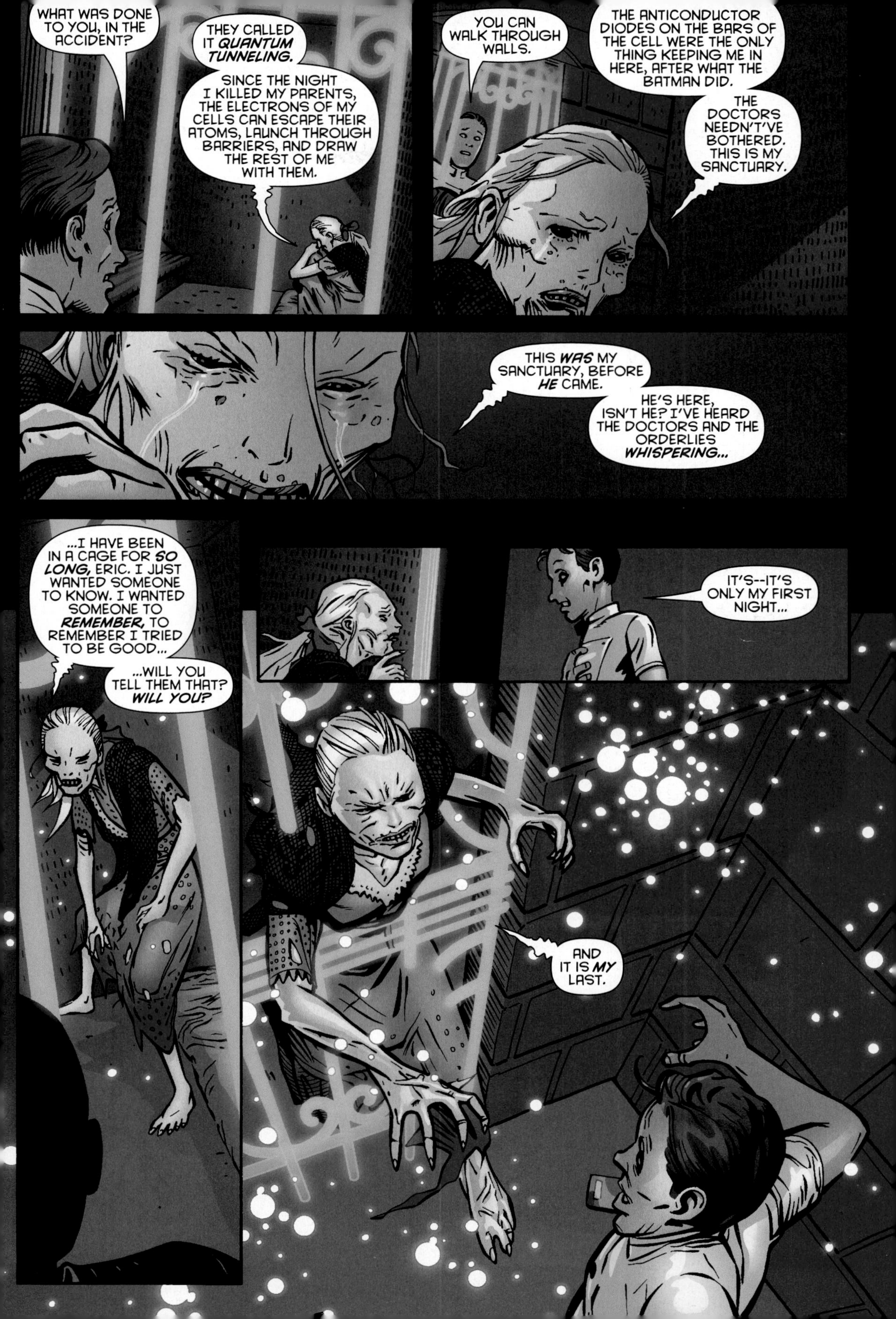
WHAT WAS DONE TO YOU, IN THE ACCIDENT?
THEY CALLED IT QUANTUM TUNNELING.
SINCE THE NIGHT I KILLED MY PARENTS, THE ELECTRONS OF MY CELLS CAN ESCAPE THEIR ATOMS, LAUNCH THROUGH BARRIERS, AND DRAW THE REST OF ME WITH THEM.
YOU CAN WALK THROUGH WALLS.
THE ANTICONDUCTOR DIODES ON THE BARS OF THE CELL WERE THE ONLY THING KEEPING ME IN HERE, AFTER WHAT THE BATMAN DID.
THE DOCTORS NEEDN'T'VE BOTHERED. THIS IS MY SANCTUARY.
THIS WAS MY SANCTUARY, BEFORE HE CAME.
HE'S HERE, ISN'T HE? I'VE HEARD THE DOCTORS AND THE ORDERLIES WHISPERING...
...I HAVE BEEN IN A CAGE FOR SO LONG, ERIC. I JUST WANTED SOMEONE TO KNOW. I WANTED SOMEONE TO REMEMBER, TO REMEMBER I TRIED TO BE GOOD...
...WILL YOU TELL THEM THAT? WILL YOU?
IT'S--IT'S ONLY MY FIRST NIGHT...
AND IT IS MY LAST.

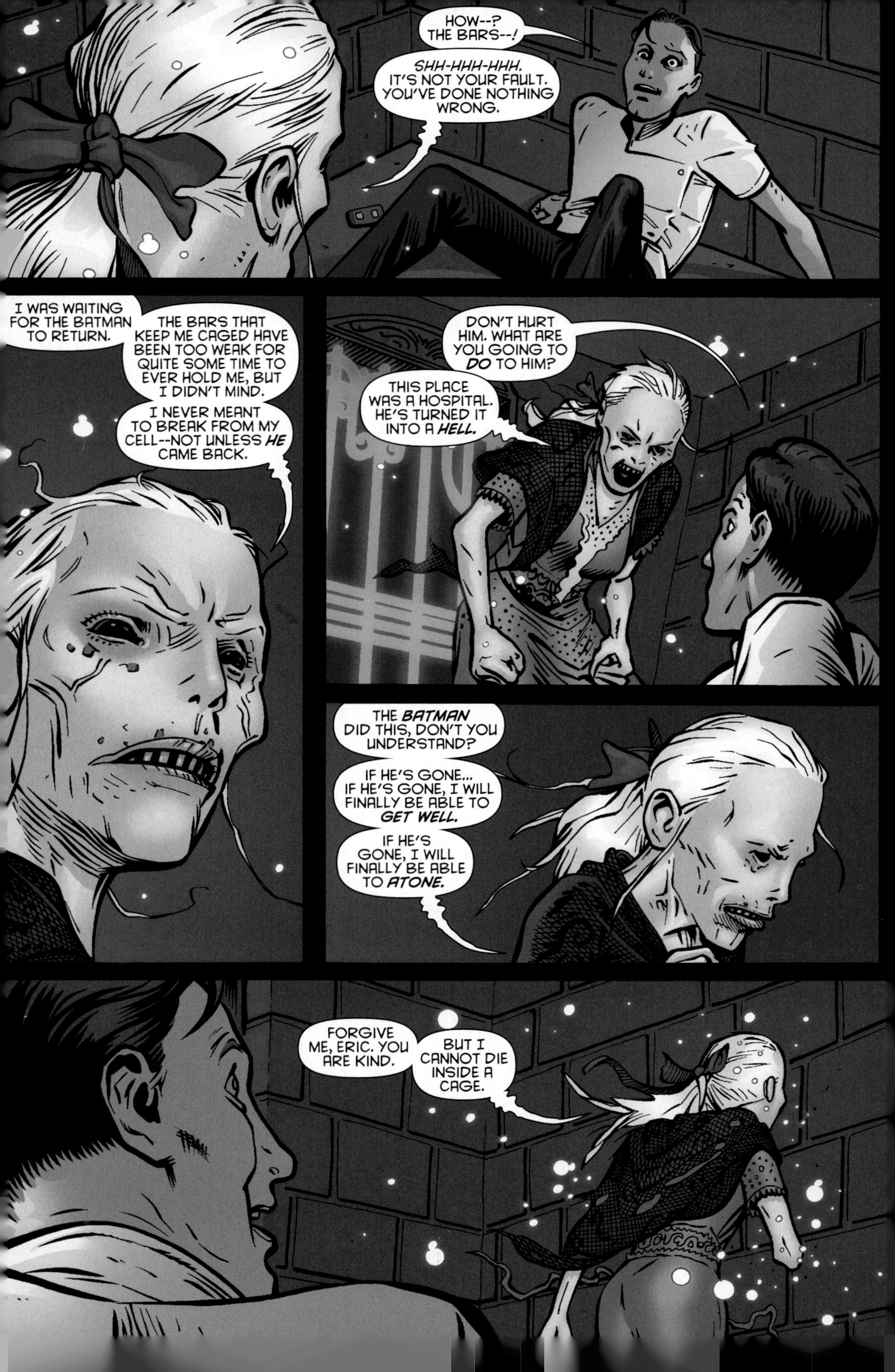
HOW--? THE BARS--!
SHH-HHH-HHH. IT'S NOT YOUR FAULT. YOU'VE DONE NOTHING WRONG.
I WAS WAITING FOR THE BATMAN TO RETURN.
THE BARS THAT KEEP ME CAGED HAVE BEEN TOO WEAK FOR QUITE SOME TIME TO EVER HOLD ME, BUT I DIDN'T MIND.
I NEVER MEANT TO BREAK FROM MY CELL--NOT UNLESS HE CAME BACK.
DON'T HURT HIM. WHAT ARE YOU GOING TO DO TO HIM?
THIS PLACE WAS A HOSPITAL. HE'S TURNED IT INTO A HELL.
THE BATMAN DID THIS, DON'T YOU UNDERSTAND?
IF HE'S GONE... IF HE'S GONE, I WILL FINALLY BE ABLE TO GET WELL.
IF HE'S GONE, I WILL FINALLY BE ABLE TO ATONE.
FORGIVE ME, ERIC. YOU ARE KIND.
BUT I CANNOT DIE INSIDE A CAGE.

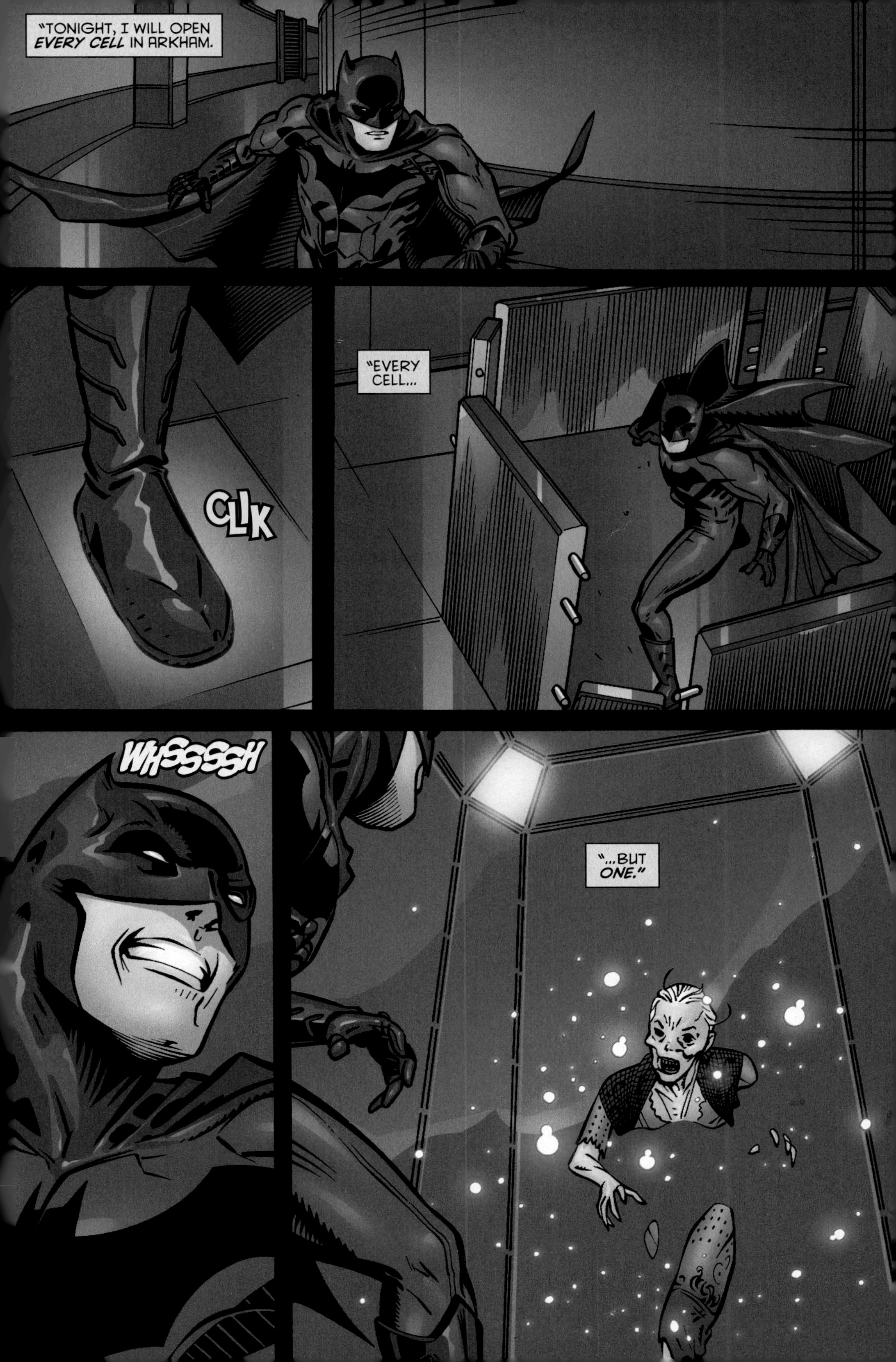
"TONIGHT, I WILL OPEN *EVERY CELL* IN ARKHAM.
CLIK
"EVERY CELL...
WHSSSSH
"...BUT *ONE.*"

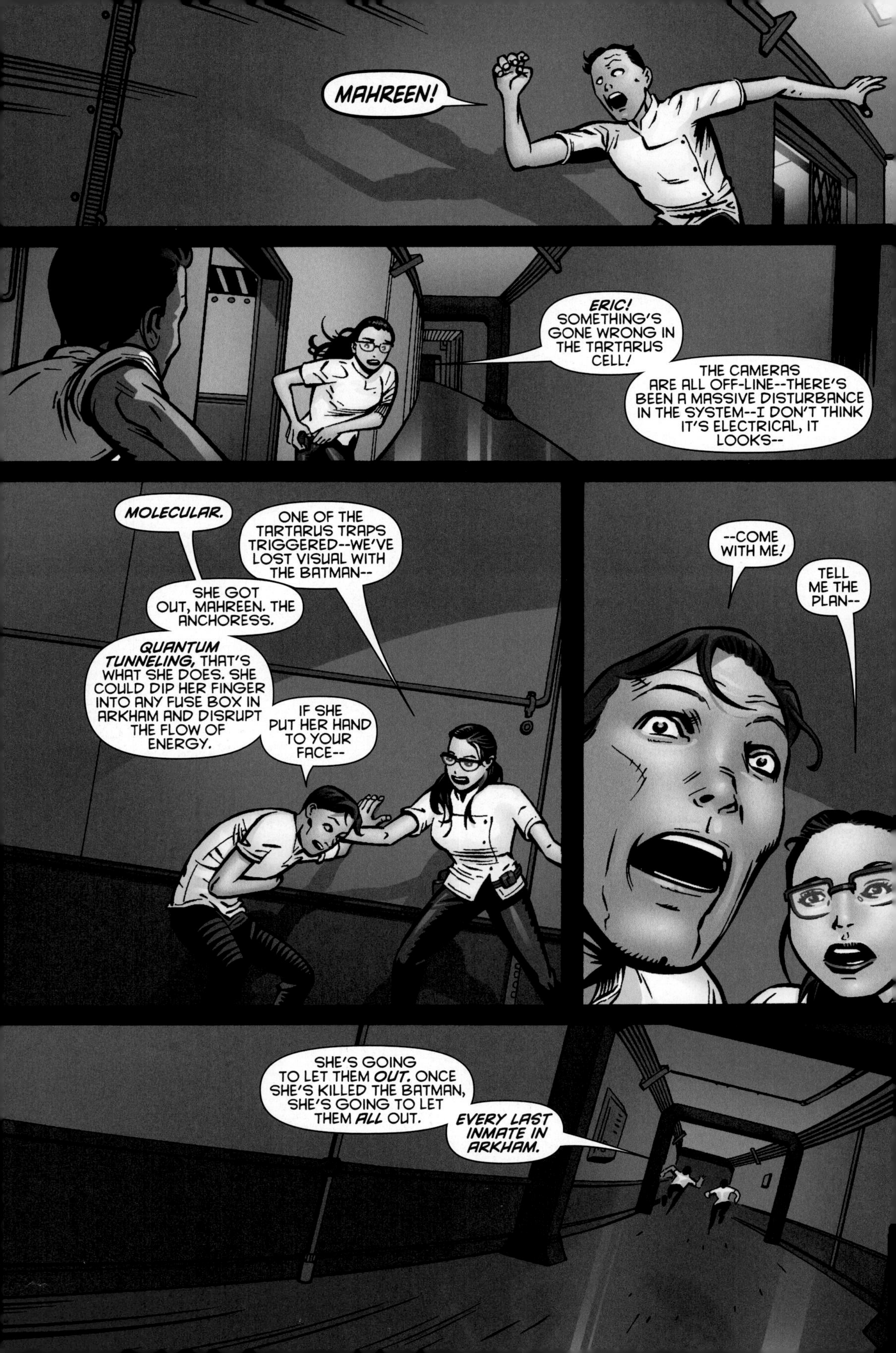
MAHREEN!
ERIC! SOMETHING'S GONE WRONG IN THE TARTARUS CELL!
THE CAMERAS ARE ALL OFF-LINE--THERE'S BEEN A MASSIVE DISTURBANCE IN THE SYSTEM--I DON'T THINK IT'S ELECTRICAL, IT LOOKS--
MOLECULAR.
ONE OF THE TARTARUS TRAPS TRIGGERED--WE'VE LOST VISUAL WITH THE BATMAN--
SHE GOT OUT, MAHREEN. THE ANCHORESS.
QUANTUM TUNNELING, THAT'S WHAT SHE DOES. SHE COULD DIP HER FINGER INTO ANY FUSE BOX IN ARKHAM AND DISRUPT THE FLOW OF ENERGY.
IF SHE PUT HER HAND TO YOUR FACE--
--COME WITH ME!
TELL ME THE PLAN--
SHE'S GOING TO LET THEM OUT. ONCE SHE'S KILLED THE BATMAN, SHE'S GOING TO LET THEM ALL OUT.
EVERY LAST INMATE IN ARKHAM.

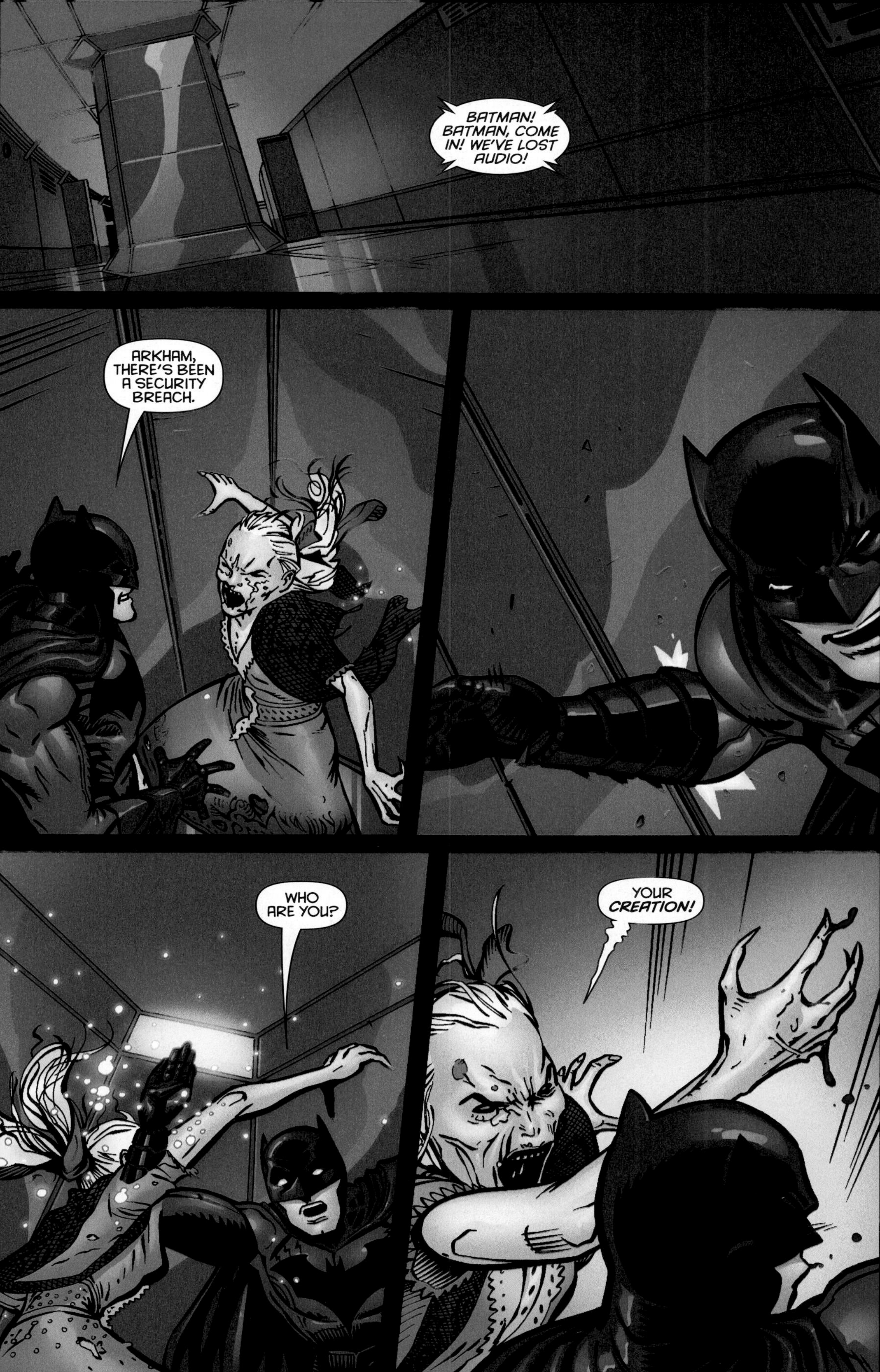
BATMAN! BATMAN, COME IN! WE'VE LOST AUDIO!
ARKHAM, THERE'S BEEN A SECURITY BREACH.
WHO ARE YOU?
YOUR CREATION!

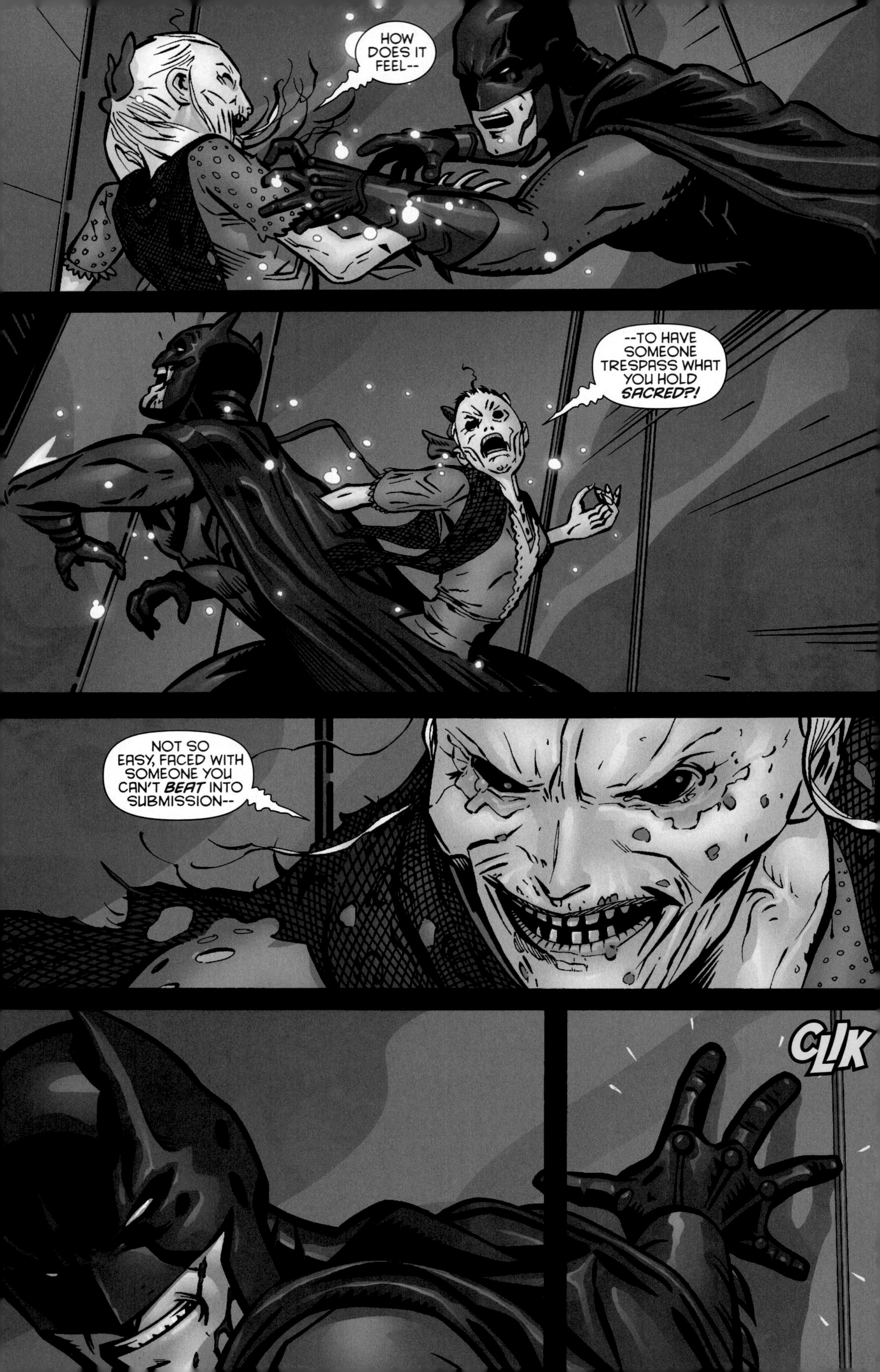
HOW DOES IT FEEL--
--TO HAVE SOMEONE TRESPASS WHAT YOU HOLD SACRED?!
NOT SO EASY, FACED WITH SOMEONE YOU CAN'T BEAT INTO SUBMISSION--
CLIK

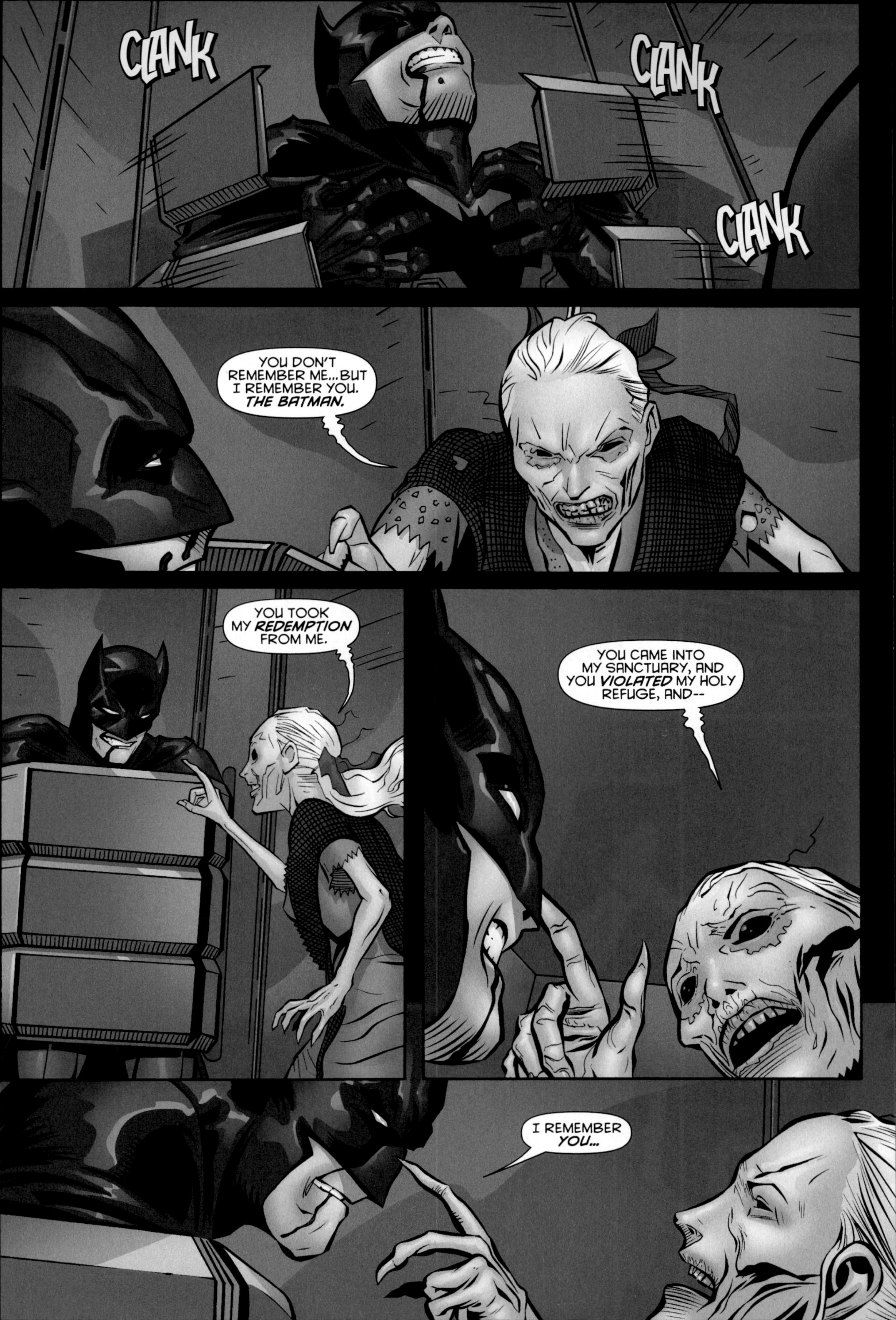
CLANK
CLANK
CLANK
YOU DON'T REMEMBER ME...BUT I REMEMBER YOU. *THE BATMAN.*
YOU TOOK MY *REDEMPTION* FROM ME.
YOU CAME INTO MY SANCTUARY, AND YOU *VIOLATED* MY HOLY REFUGE, AND--
I REMEMBER *YOU...*

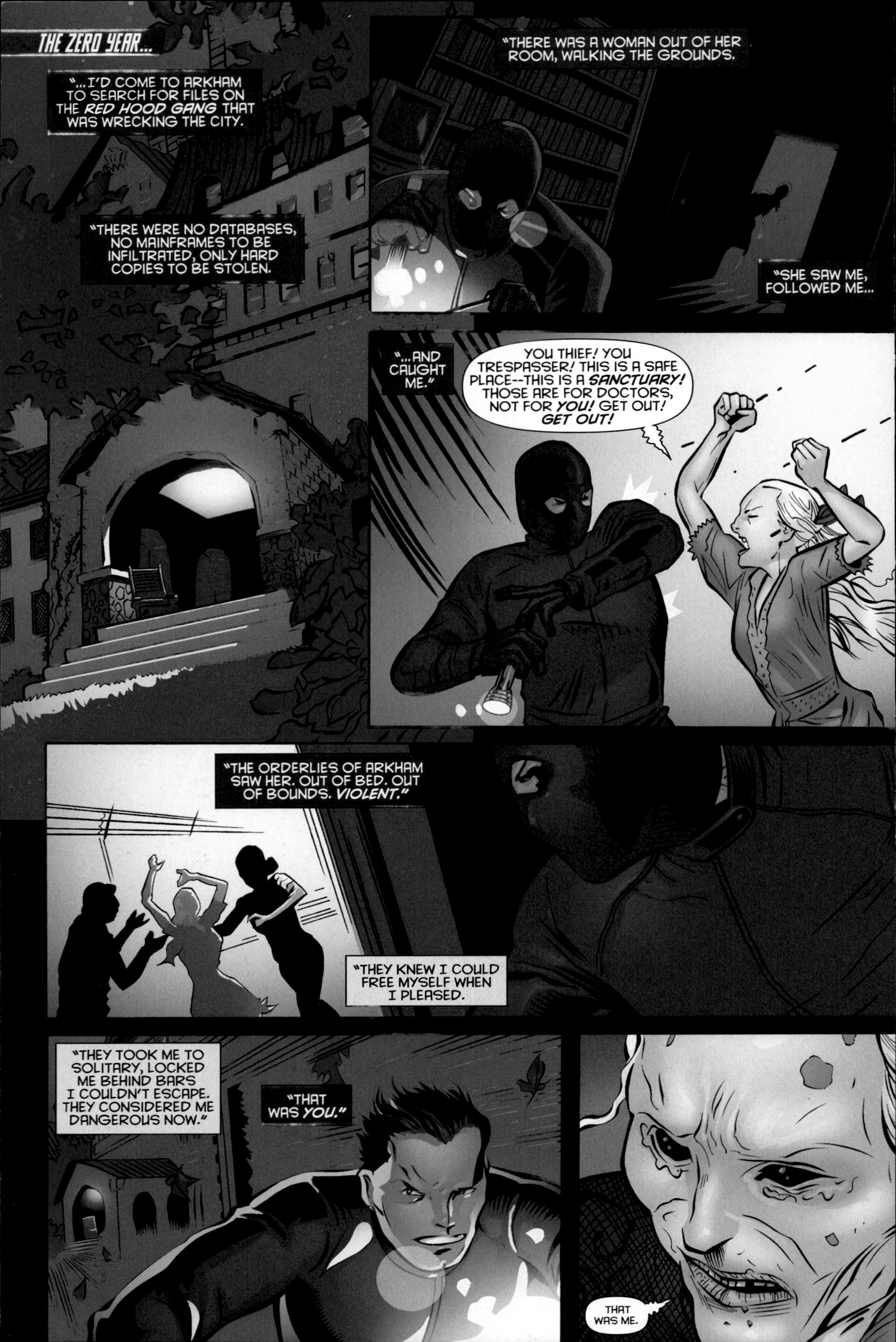
THE ZERO YEAR...
"...I'D COME TO ARKHAM TO SEARCH FOR FILES ON THE RED HOOD GANG THAT WAS WRECKING THE CITY.
"THERE WERE NO DATABASES, NO MAINFRAMES TO BE INFILTRATED, ONLY HARD COPIES TO BE STOLEN.
"THERE WAS A WOMAN OUT OF HER ROOM, WALKING THE GROUNDS.
"SHE SAW ME, FOLLOWED ME...
"...AND CAUGHT ME."
YOU THIEF! YOU TRESPASSER! THIS IS A SAFE PLACE--THIS IS A SANCTUARY! THOSE ARE FOR DOCTORS, NOT FOR YOU! GET OUT! GET OUT!
"THE ORDERLIES OF ARKHAM SAW HER. OUT OF BED. OUT OF BOUNDS. VIOLENT."
"THEY KNEW I COULD FREE MYSELF WHEN I PLEASED.
"THEY TOOK ME TO SOLITARY, LOCKED ME BEHIND BARS I COULDN'T ESCAPE. THEY CONSIDERED ME DANGEROUS NOW."
"THAT WAS YOU."
THAT WAS ME.

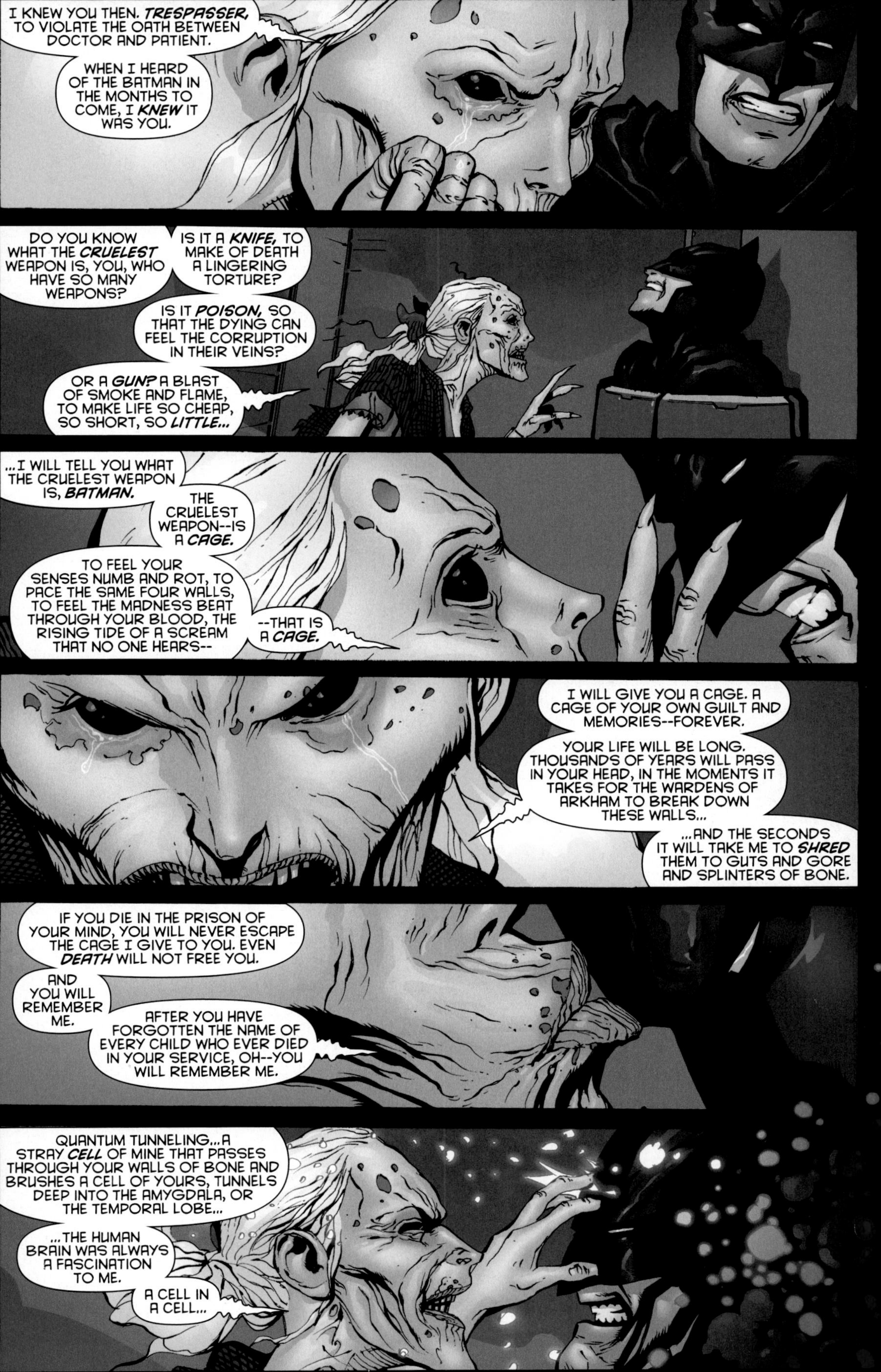
I KNEW YOU THEN. TRESPASSER, TO VIOLATE THE OATH BETWEEN DOCTOR AND PATIENT.
WHEN I HEARD OF THE BATMAN IN THE MONTHS TO COME, I KNEW IT WAS YOU.
DO YOU KNOW WHAT THE CRUELEST WEAPON IS, YOU, WHO HAVE SO MANY WEAPONS?
IS IT A KNIFE, TO MAKE OF DEATH A LINGERING TORTURE?
IS IT POISON, SO THAT THE DYING CAN FEEL THE CORRUPTION IN THEIR VEINS?
OR A GUN? A BLAST OF SMOKE AND FLAME, TO MAKE LIFE SO CHEAP, SO SHORT, SO LITTLE...
...I WILL TELL YOU WHAT THE CRUELEST WEAPON IS, BATMAN.
THE CRUELEST WEAPON--IS A CAGE.
TO FEEL YOUR SENSES NUMB AND ROT, TO PACE THE SAME FOUR WALLS, TO FEEL THE MADNESS BEAT THROUGH YOUR BLOOD, THE RISING TIDE OF A SCREAM THAT NO ONE HEARS--
--THAT IS A CAGE.
I WILL GIVE YOU A CAGE. A CAGE OF YOUR OWN GUILT AND MEMORIES--FOREVER.
YOUR LIFE WILL BE LONG. THOUSANDS OF YEARS WILL PASS IN YOUR HEAD, IN THE MOMENTS IT TAKES FOR THE WARDENS OF ARKHAM TO BREAK DOWN THESE WALLS...
...AND THE SECONDS IT WILL TAKE ME TO SHRED THEM TO GUTS AND GORE AND SPLINTERS OF BONE.
IF YOU DIE IN THE PRISON OF YOUR MIND, YOU WILL NEVER ESCAPE THE CAGE I GIVE TO YOU. EVEN DEATH WILL NOT FREE YOU.
AND YOU WILL REMEMBER ME.
AFTER YOU HAVE FORGOTTEN THE NAME OF EVERY CHILD WHO EVER DIED IN YOUR SERVICE, OH--YOU WILL REMEMBER ME.
QUANTUM TUNNELING...A STRAY CELL OF MINE THAT PASSES THROUGH YOUR WALLS OF BONE AND BRUSHES A CELL OF YOURS, TUNNELS DEEP INTO THE AMYGDALA, OR THE TEMPORAL LOBE...
...THE HUMAN BRAIN WAS ALWAYS A FASCINATION TO ME.
A CELL IN A CELL...

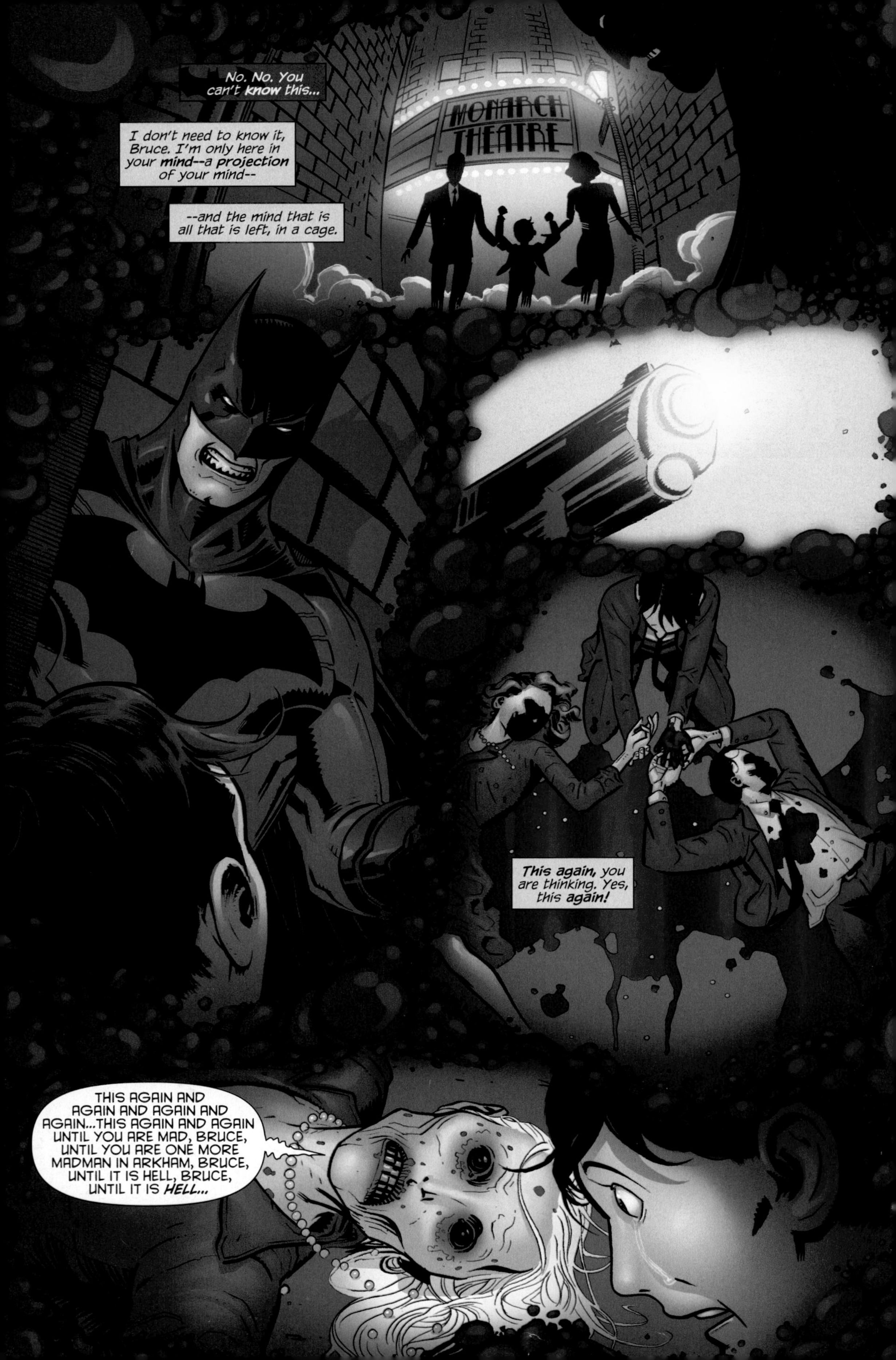
No. No. You can't **know** this...
I don't need to know it, Bruce. I'm only here in your **mind**--a **projection** of your mind--
--and the mind that is all that is left, in a cage.
MONARCH THEATRE
This again, you are thinking. Yes, this **again!**
THIS AGAIN AND AGAIN AND AGAIN AND AGAIN...THIS AGAIN AND AGAIN UNTIL YOU ARE MAD, BRUCE, UNTIL YOU ARE ONE MORE MADMAN IN ARKHAM, BRUCE, UNTIL IT IS HELL, BRUCE, UNTIL IT IS **HELL**...

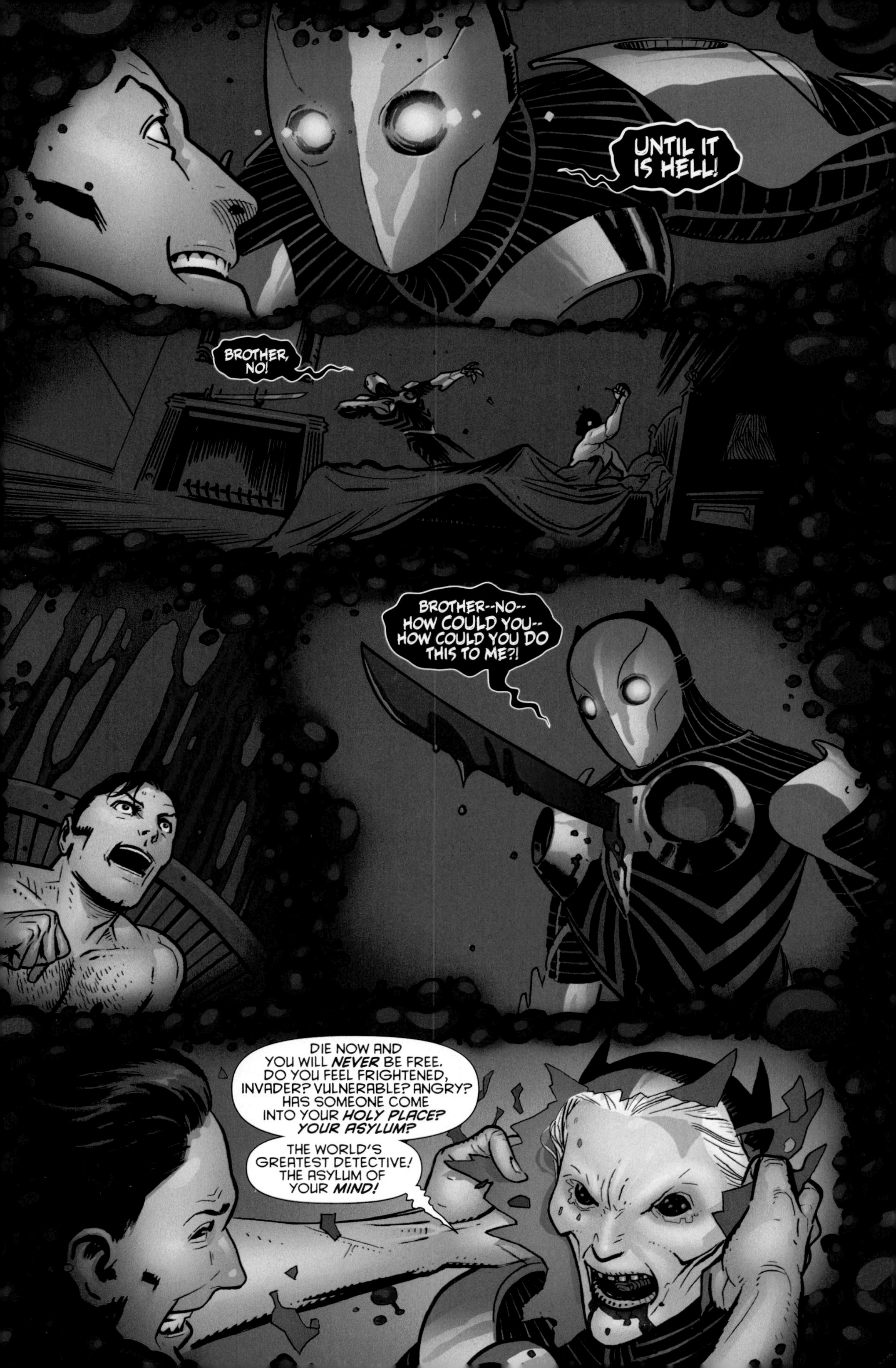
UNTIL IT IS HELL!
BROTHER, NO!
BROTHER--NO-- HOW COULD YOU-- HOW COULD YOU DO THIS TO ME?!
DIE NOW AND YOU WILL NEVER BE FREE. DO YOU FEEL FRIGHTENED, INVADER? VULNERABLE? ANGRY? HAS SOMEONE COME INTO YOUR HOLY PLACE? YOUR ASYLUM?
THE WORLD'S GREATEST DETECTIVE! THE ASYLUM OF YOUR MIND!

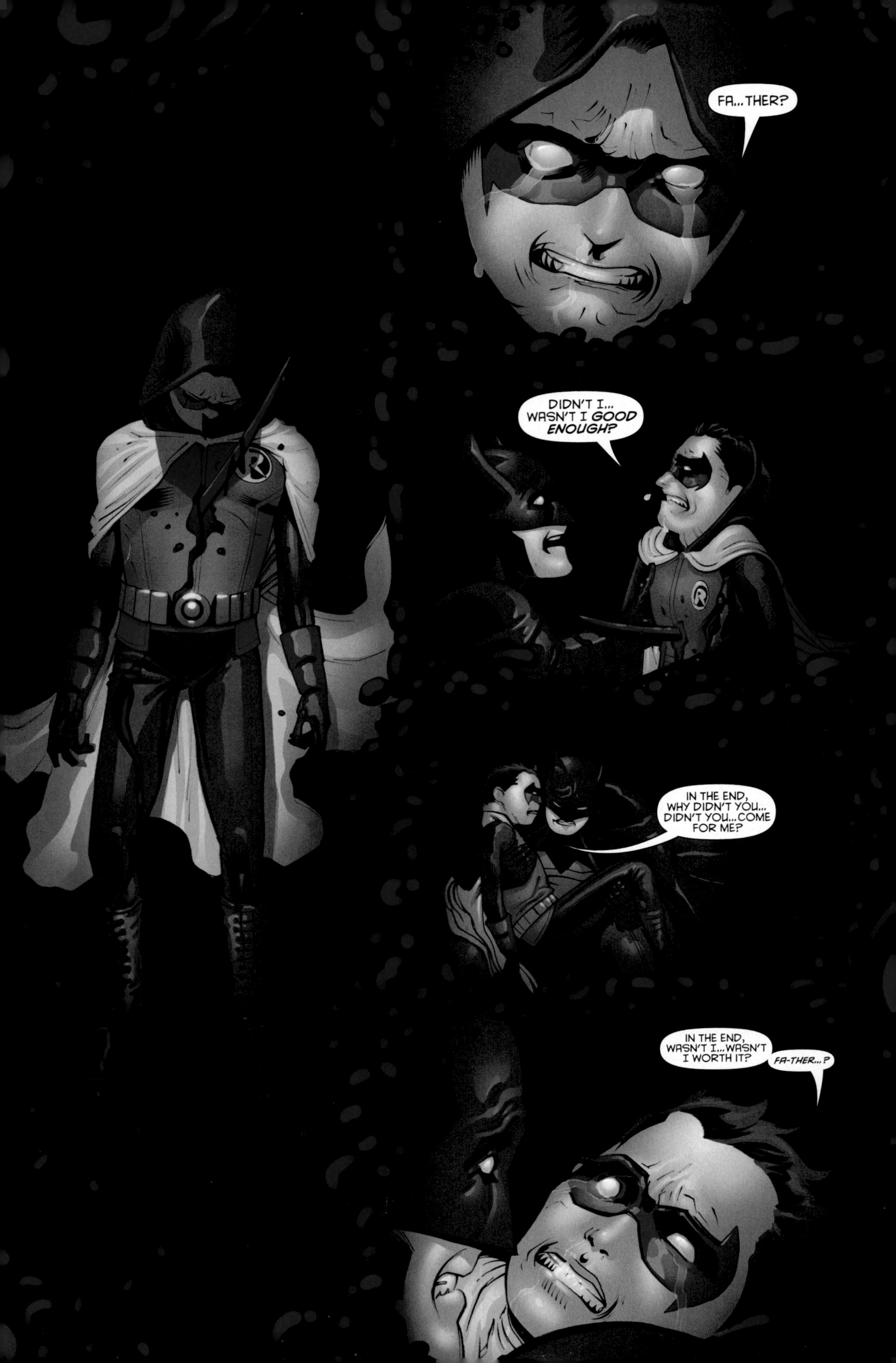
FA...THER?
DIDN'T I... WASN'T I *GOOD ENOUGH?*
IN THE END, WHY DIDN'T YOU... DIDN'T YOU...COME FOR ME?
IN THE END, WASN'T I...WASN'T I WORTH IT?
FA-THER...?

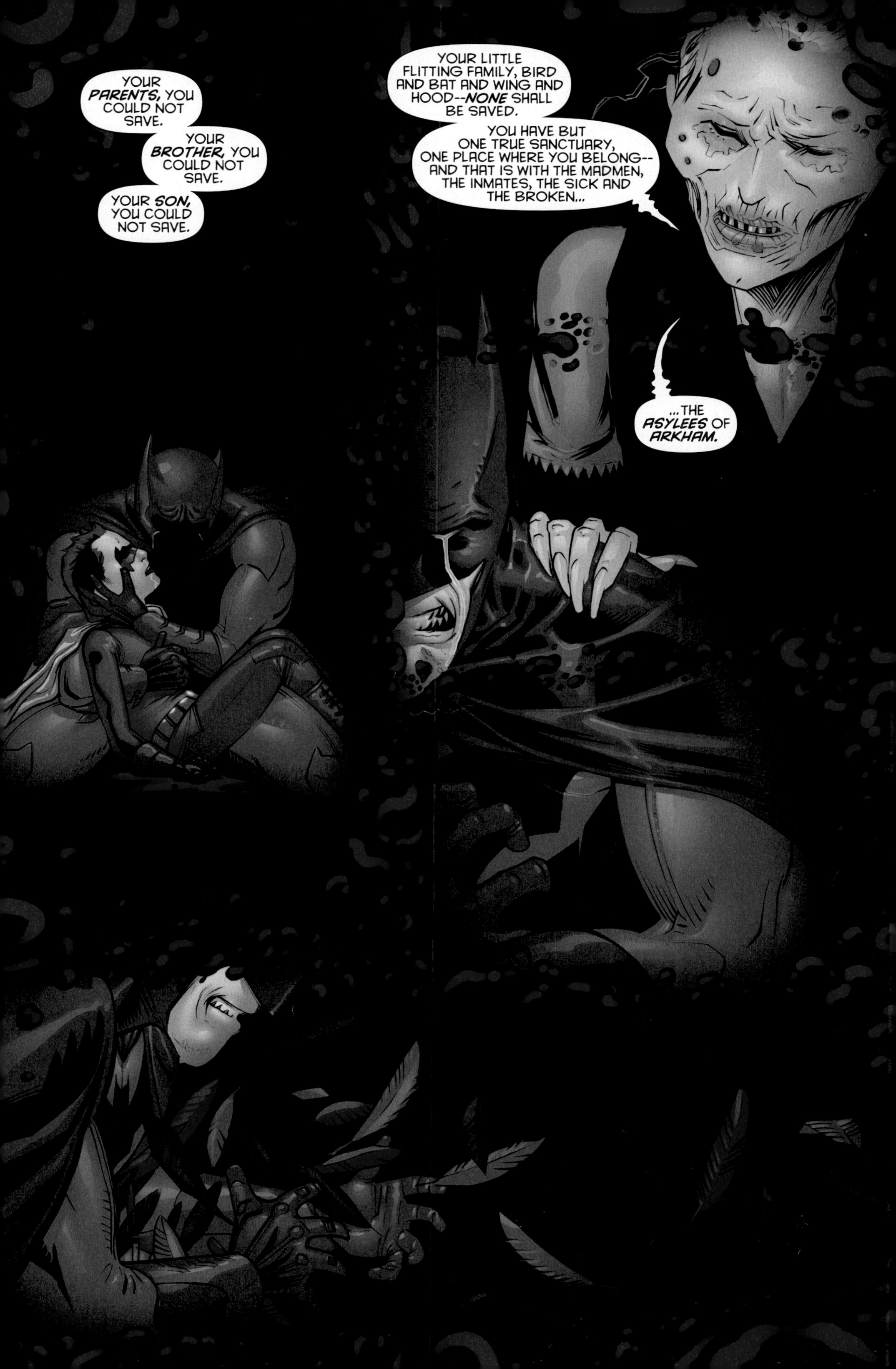
YOUR PARENTS, YOU COULD NOT SAVE.
YOUR BROTHER, YOU COULD NOT SAVE.
YOUR SON, YOU COULD NOT SAVE.
YOUR LITTLE FLITTING FAMILY, BIRD AND BAT AND WING AND HOOD--NONE SHALL BE SAVED.
YOU HAVE BUT ONE TRUE SANCTUARY, ONE PLACE WHERE YOU BELONG-- AND THAT IS WITH THE MADMEN, THE INMATES, THE SICK AND THE BROKEN...
...THE ASYLEES OF ARKHAM.

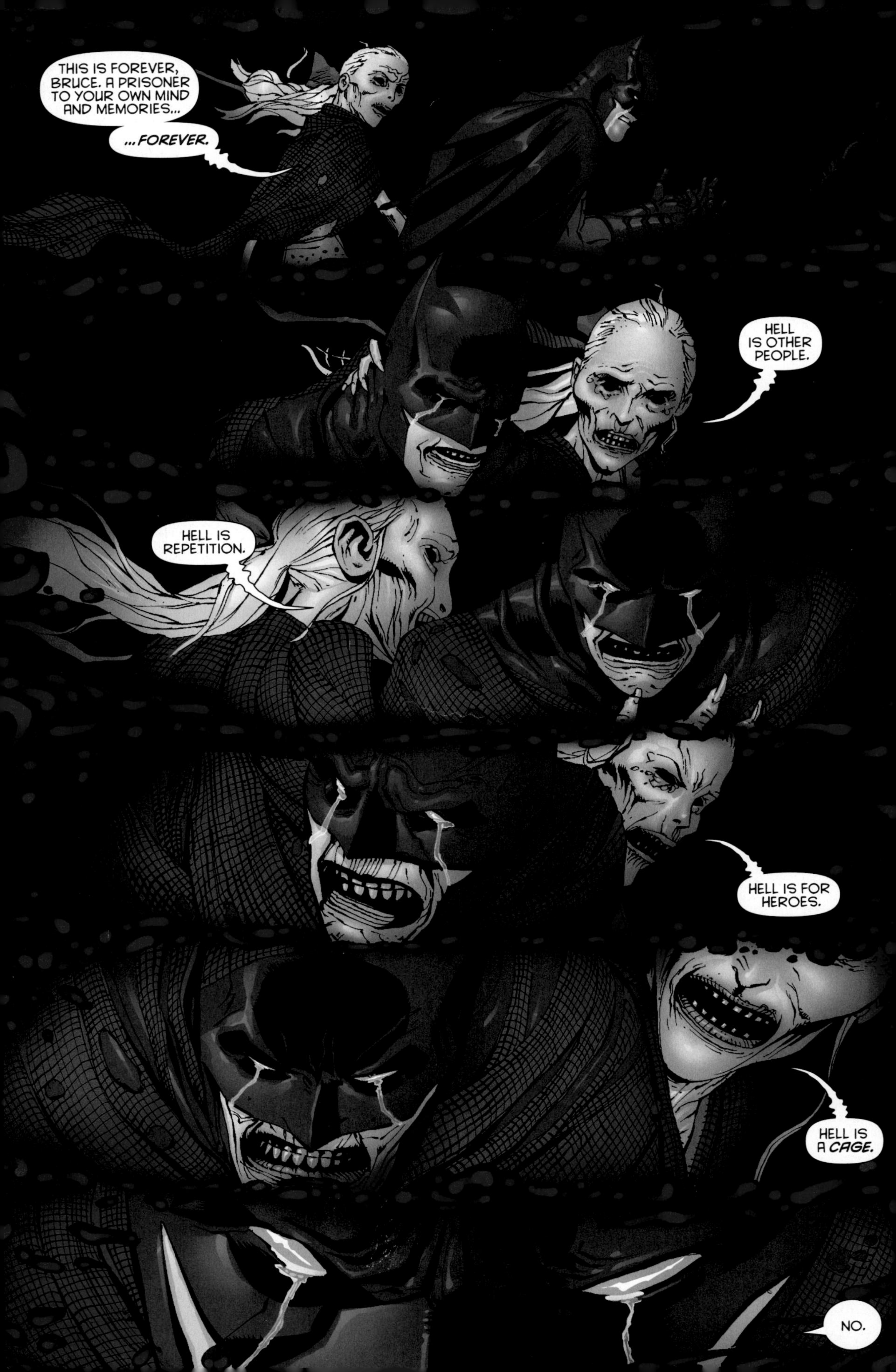
THIS IS FOREVER, BRUCE. A PRISONER TO YOUR OWN MIND AND MEMORIES...
...FOREVER.
HELL IS OTHER PEOPLE.
HELL IS REPETITION.
HELL IS FOR HEROES.
HELL IS A CAGE.
NO.

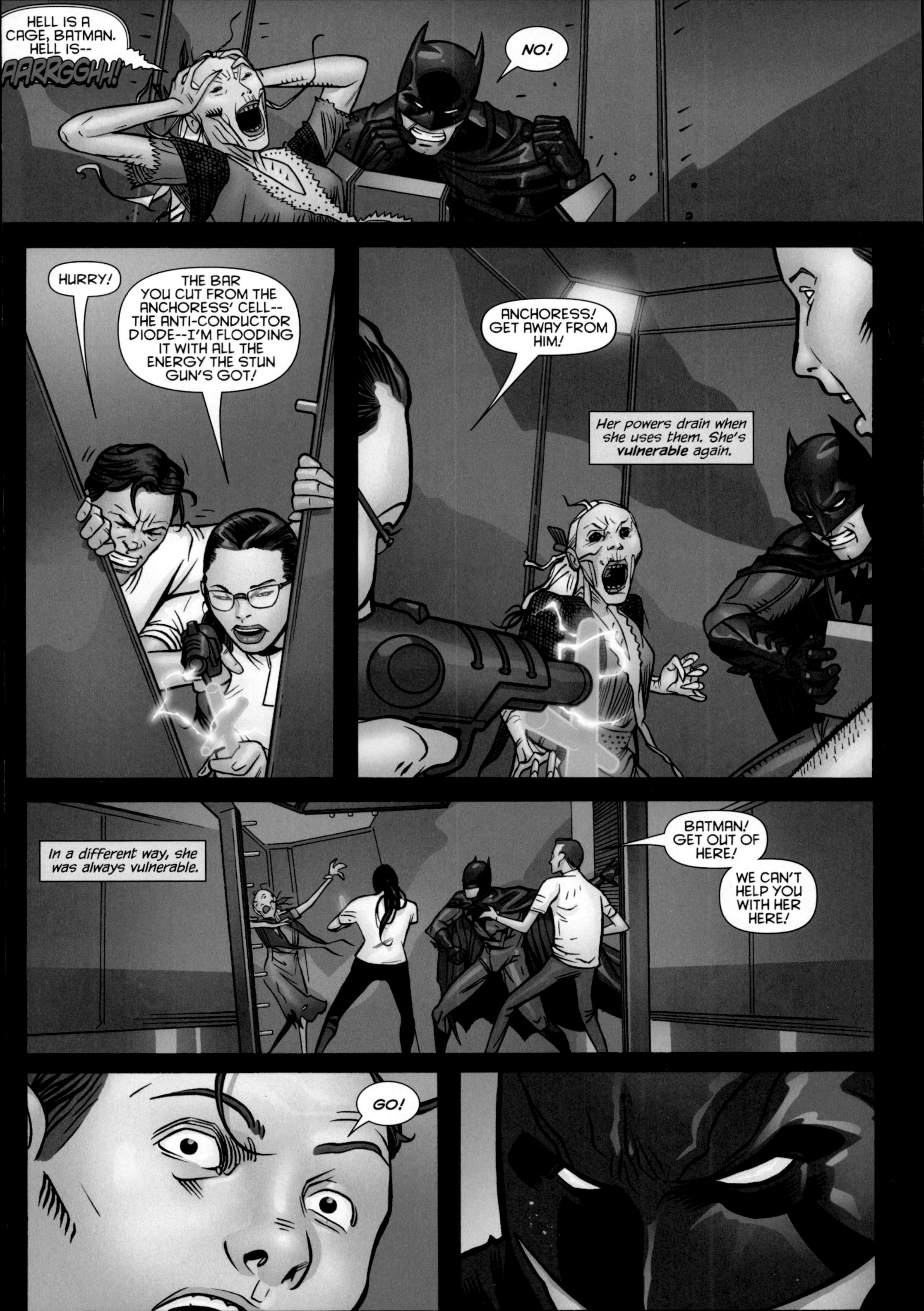
HELL IS A CAGE, BATMAN. HELL IS--
AARRGGHH!
NO!
HURRY!
THE BAR YOU CUT FROM THE ANCHORESS' CELL-- THE ANTI-CONDUCTOR DIODE--I'M FLOODING IT WITH ALL THE ENERGY THE STUN GUN'S GOT!
ANCHORESS! GET AWAY FROM HIM!
Her powers drain when she uses them. She's vulnerable again.
In a different way, she was always vulnerable.
BATMAN! GET OUT OF HERE!
WE CAN'T HELP YOU WITH HER HERE!
GO!

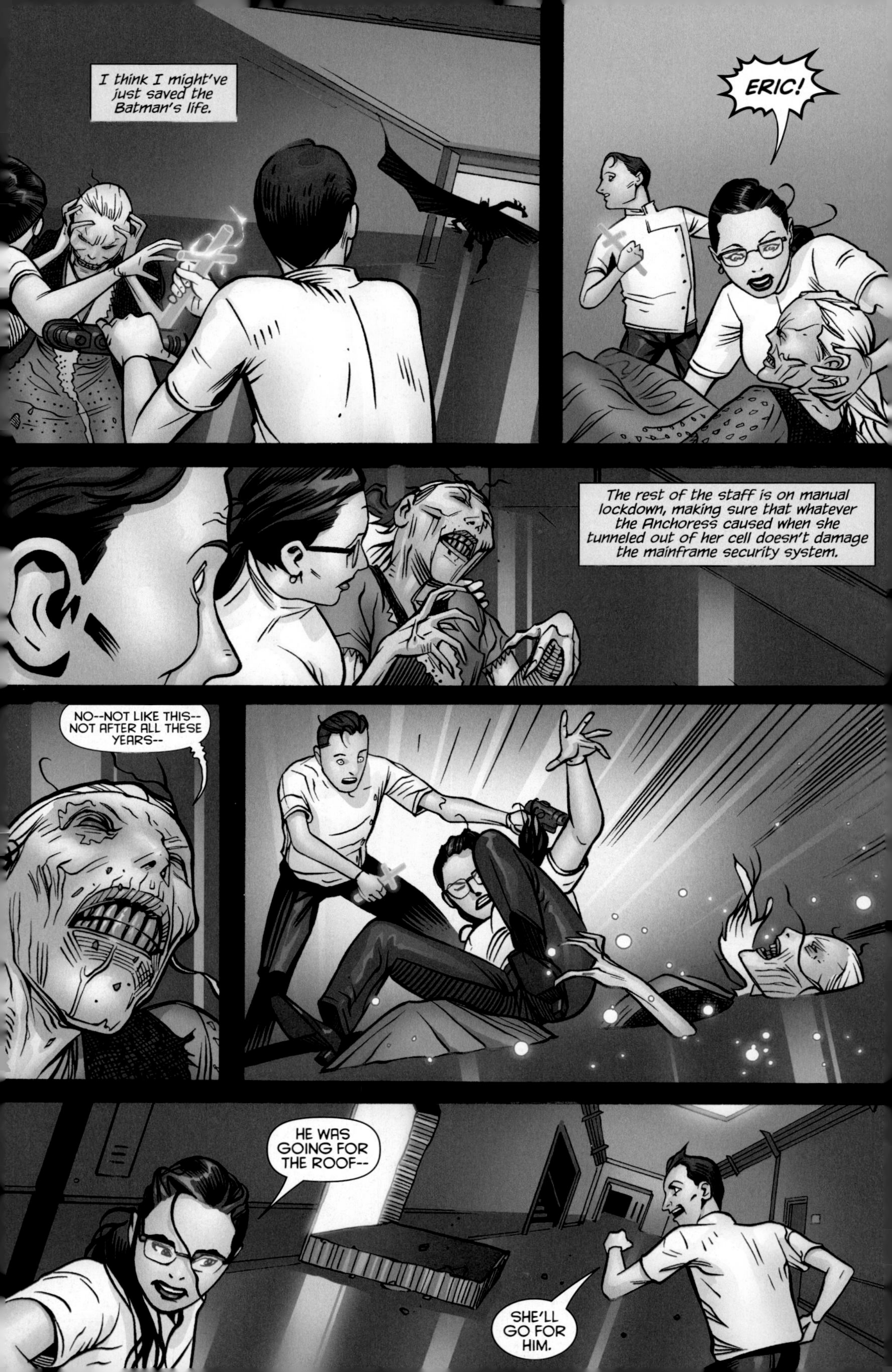
I think I might've just saved the Batman's life.
ERIC!
The rest of the staff is on manual lockdown, making sure that whatever the Anchoress caused when she tunneled out of her cell doesn't damage the mainframe security system.
NO--NOT LIKE THIS--NOT AFTER ALL THESE YEARS--
HE WAS GOING FOR THE ROOF--
SHE'LL GO FOR HIM.

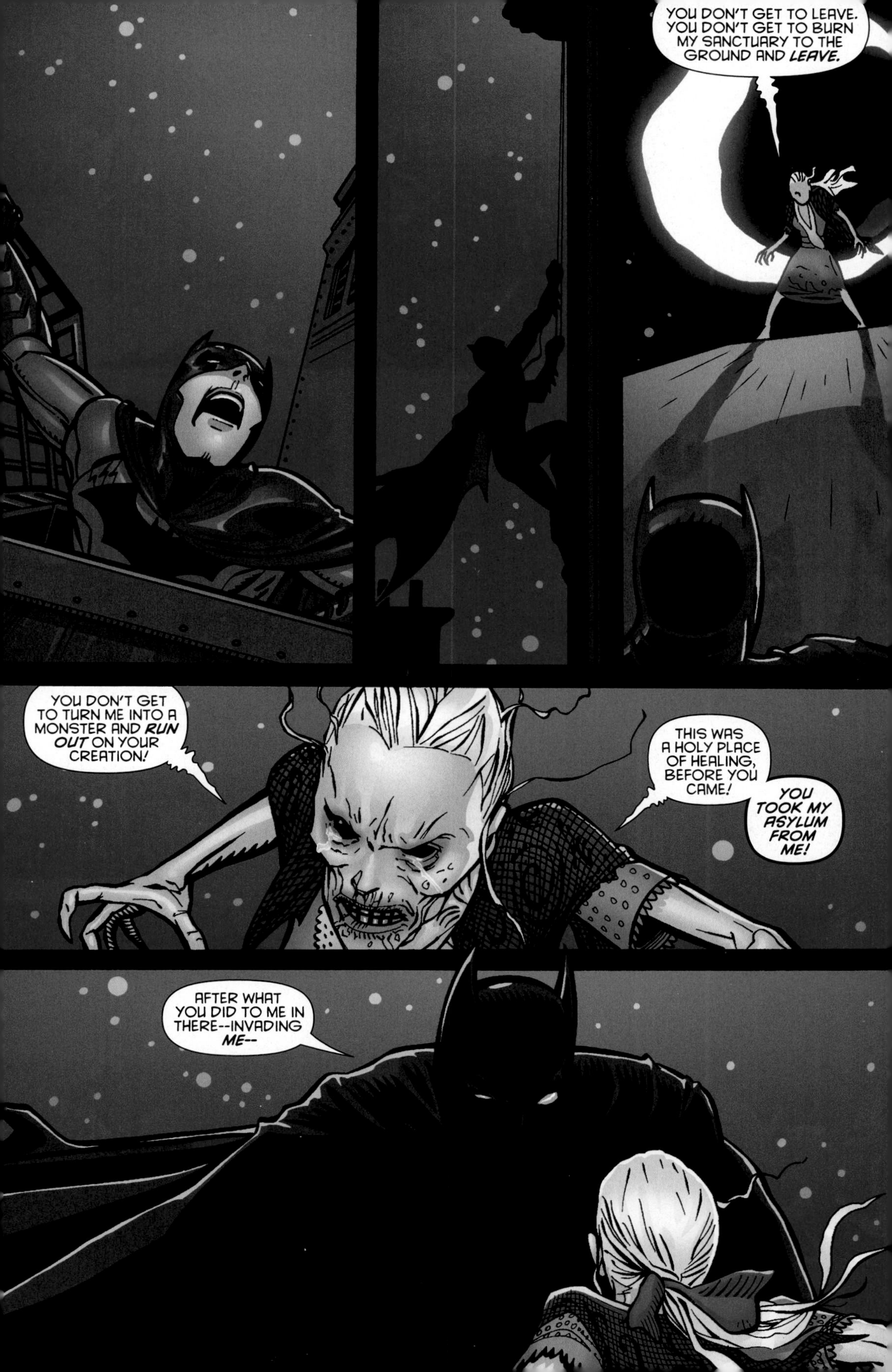
YOU DON'T GET TO LEAVE. YOU DON'T GET TO BURN MY SANCTUARY TO THE GROUND AND *LEAVE.*
YOU DON'T GET TO TURN ME INTO A MONSTER AND *RUN OUT* ON YOUR CREATION!
THIS WAS A HOLY PLACE OF HEALING, BEFORE YOU CAME!
YOU TOOK MY ASYLUM FROM ME!
AFTER WHAT YOU DID TO ME IN THERE--INVADING *ME--*

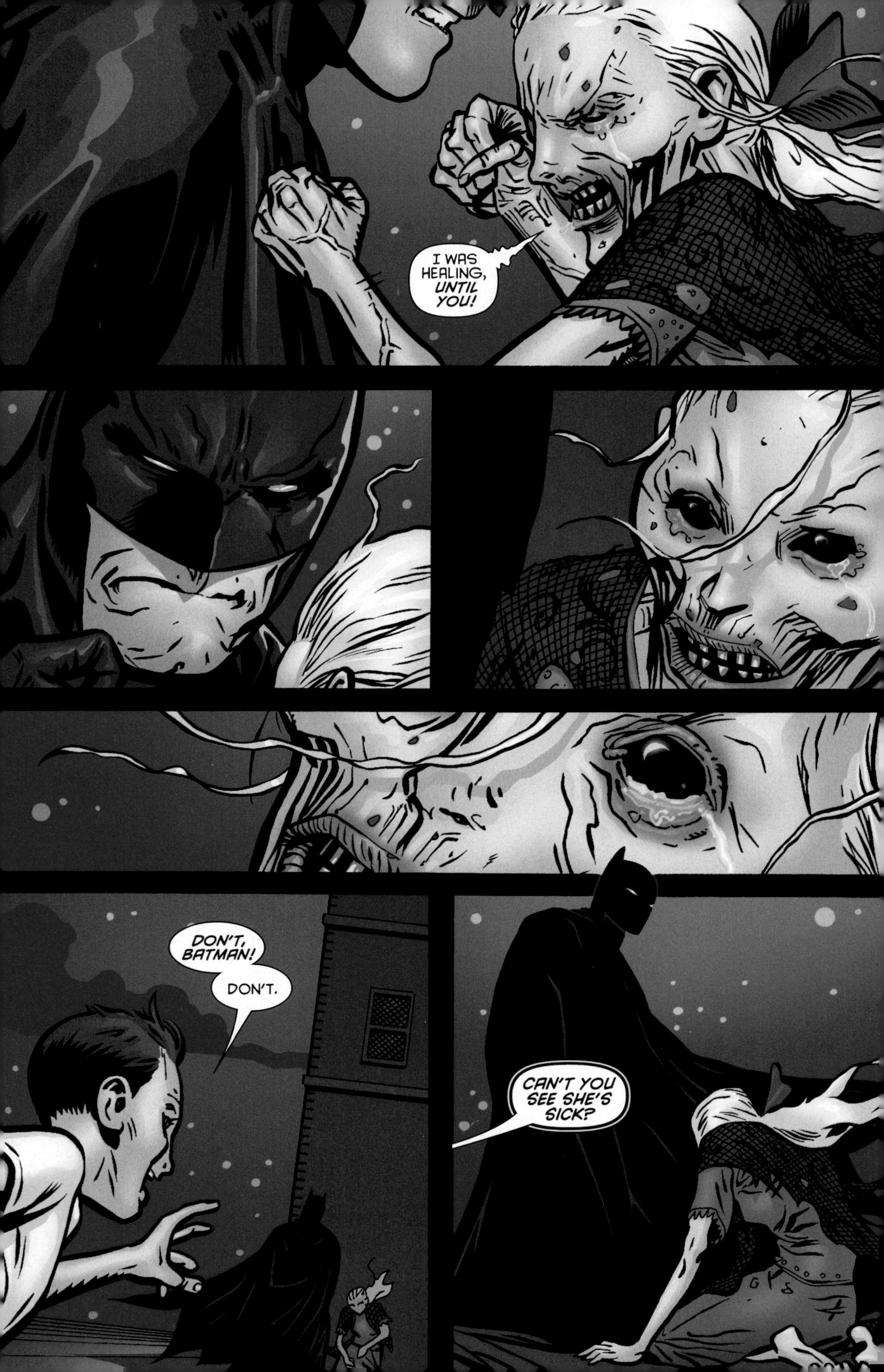
I WAS HEALING, UNTIL YOU!
DON'T, BATMAN!
DON'T.
CAN'T YOU SEE SHE'S SICK?

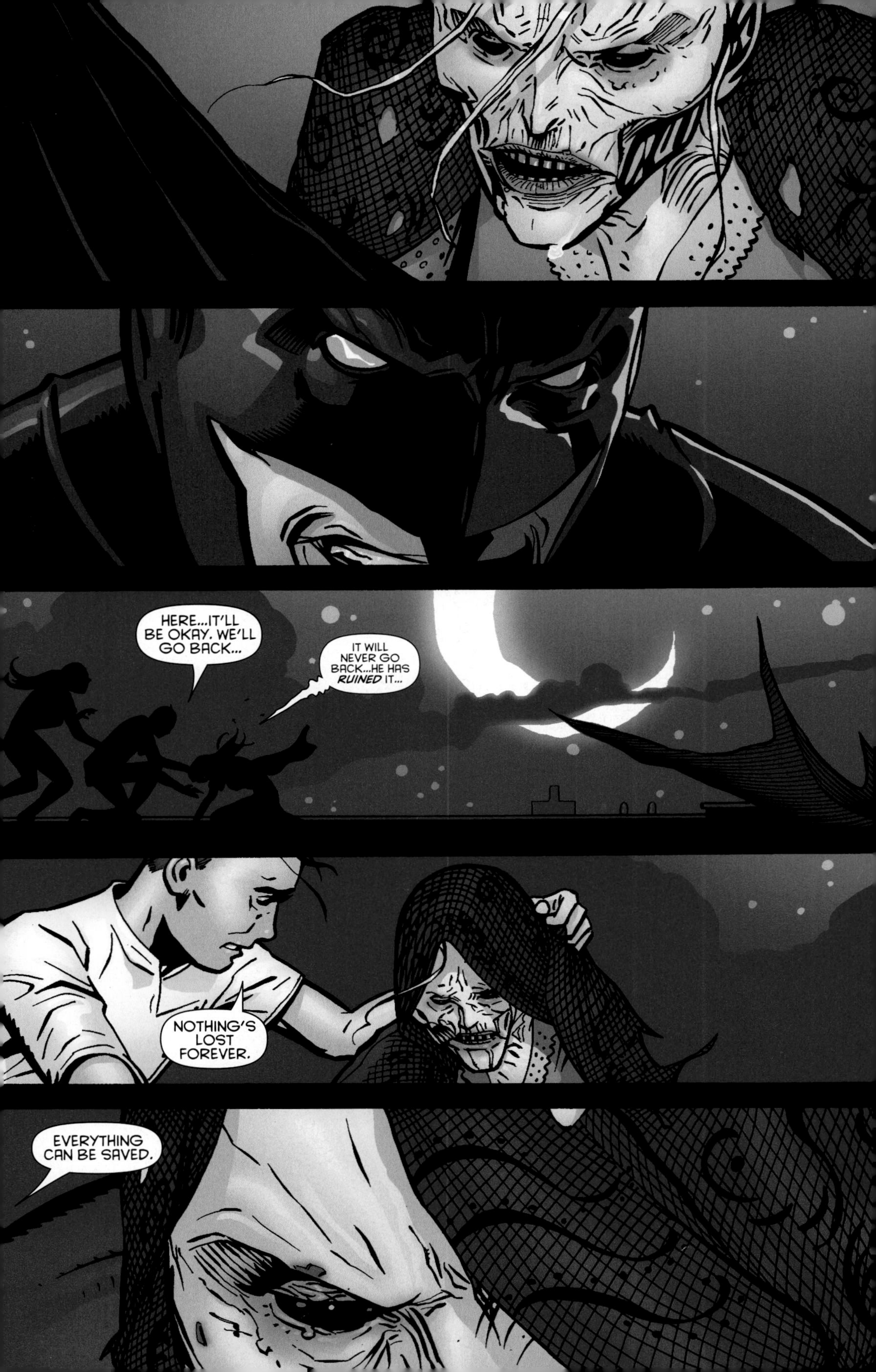
HERE...IT'LL BE OKAY. WE'LL GO BACK...
IT WILL NEVER GO BACK...HE HAS RUINED IT...
NOTHING'S LOST FOREVER.
EVERYTHING CAN BE SAVED.

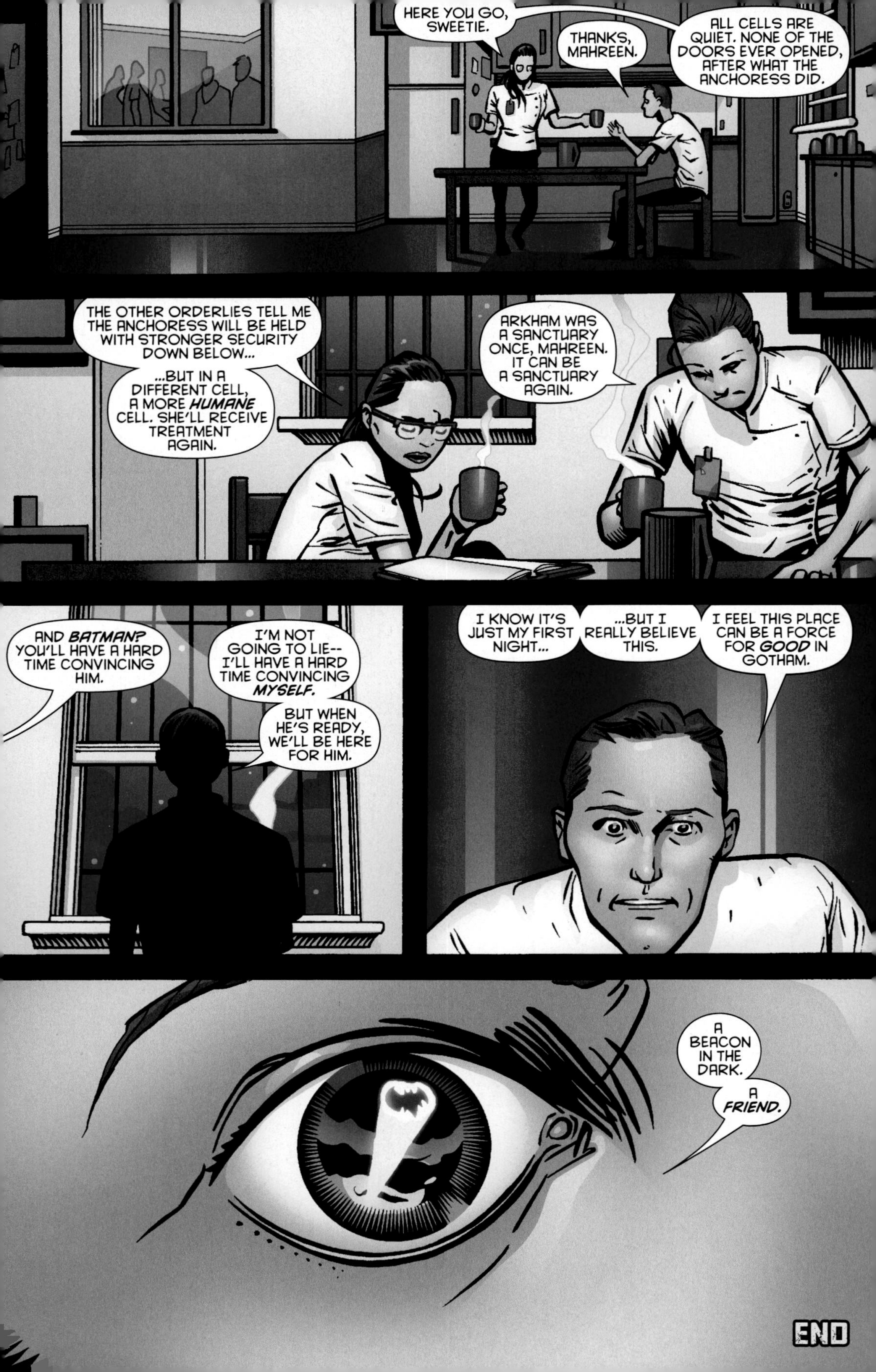

HERE YOU GO, SWEETIE.
THANKS, MAHREEN.
ALL CELLS ARE QUIET. NONE OF THE DOORS EVER OPENED, AFTER WHAT THE ANCHORESS DID.
THE OTHER ORDERLIES TELL ME THE ANCHORESS WILL BE HELD WITH STRONGER SECURITY DOWN BELOW...
...BUT IN A DIFFERENT CELL, A MORE HUMANE CELL. SHE'LL RECEIVE TREATMENT AGAIN.
ARKHAM WAS A SANCTUARY ONCE, MAHREEN. IT CAN BE A SANCTUARY AGAIN.
AND BATMAN? YOU'LL HAVE A HARD TIME CONVINCING HIM.
I'M NOT GOING TO LIE-- I'LL HAVE A HARD TIME CONVINCING MYSELF.
BUT WHEN HE'S READY, WE'LL BE HERE FOR HIM.
I KNOW IT'S JUST MY FIRST NIGHT...
...BUT I REALLY BELIEVE THIS.
I FEEL THIS PLACE CAN BE A FORCE FOR GOOD IN GOTHAM.
A BEACON IN THE DARK.
A FRIEND.
END

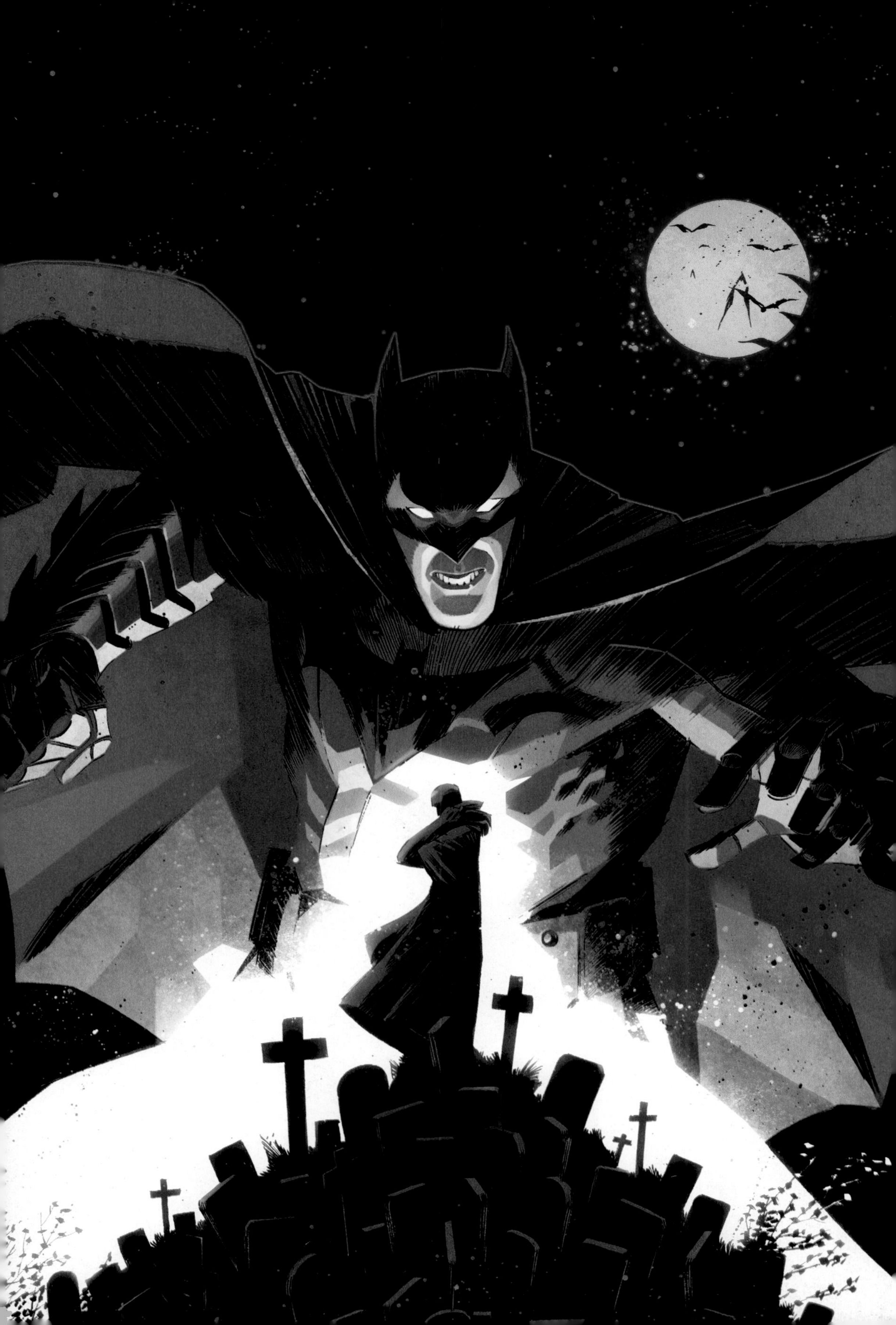

THE MEEK

SCOTT SNYDER GERRY DUGGAN plotters **GERRY DUGGAN** writer **MATTEO SCALERA** artist **LEE LOUGHRIDGE** colorist
cover by **MATTEO SCALERA** and **MORENO DINISIO**

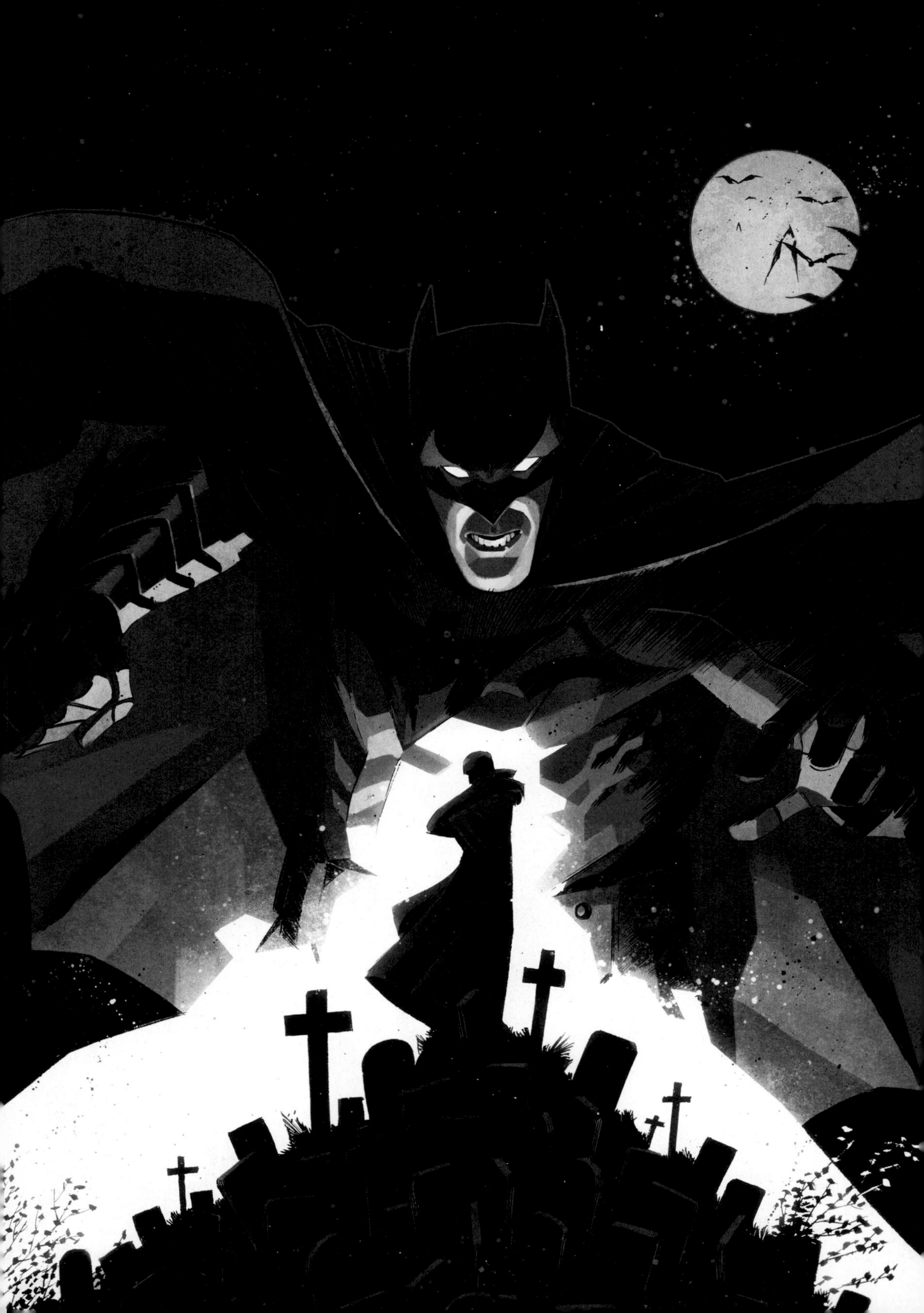

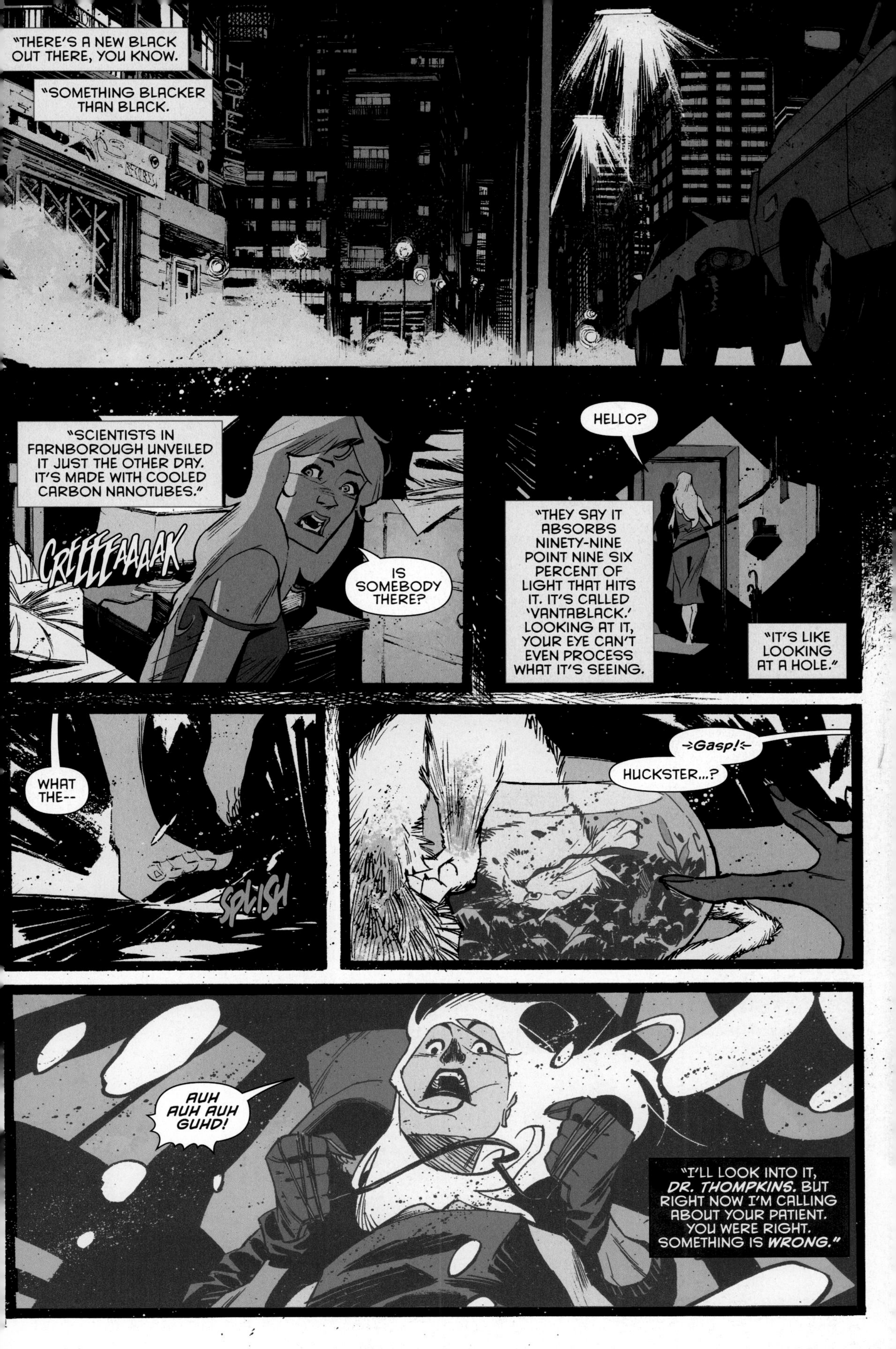

"THERE'S A NEW BLACK OUT THERE, YOU KNOW.
"SOMETHING BLACKER THAN BLACK.
HOTEL
"SCIENTISTS IN FARNBOROUGH UNVEILED IT JUST THE OTHER DAY. IT'S MADE WITH COOLED CARBON NANOTUBES."
CREEEEAAAAK
IS SOMEBODY THERE?
HELLO?
"THEY SAY IT ABSORBS NINETY-NINE POINT NINE SIX PERCENT OF LIGHT THAT HITS IT. IT'S CALLED 'VANTABLACK.' LOOKING AT IT, YOUR EYE CAN'T EVEN PROCESS WHAT IT'S SEEING.
"IT'S LIKE LOOKING AT A HOLE."
WHAT THE--
SPLISH
Gasp!
HUCKSTER...?
AUH AUH AUH GUHD!
"I'LL LOOK INTO IT, *DR. THOMPKINS.* BUT RIGHT NOW I'M CALLING ABOUT YOUR PATIENT. YOU WERE RIGHT. SOMETHING IS *WRONG.*"

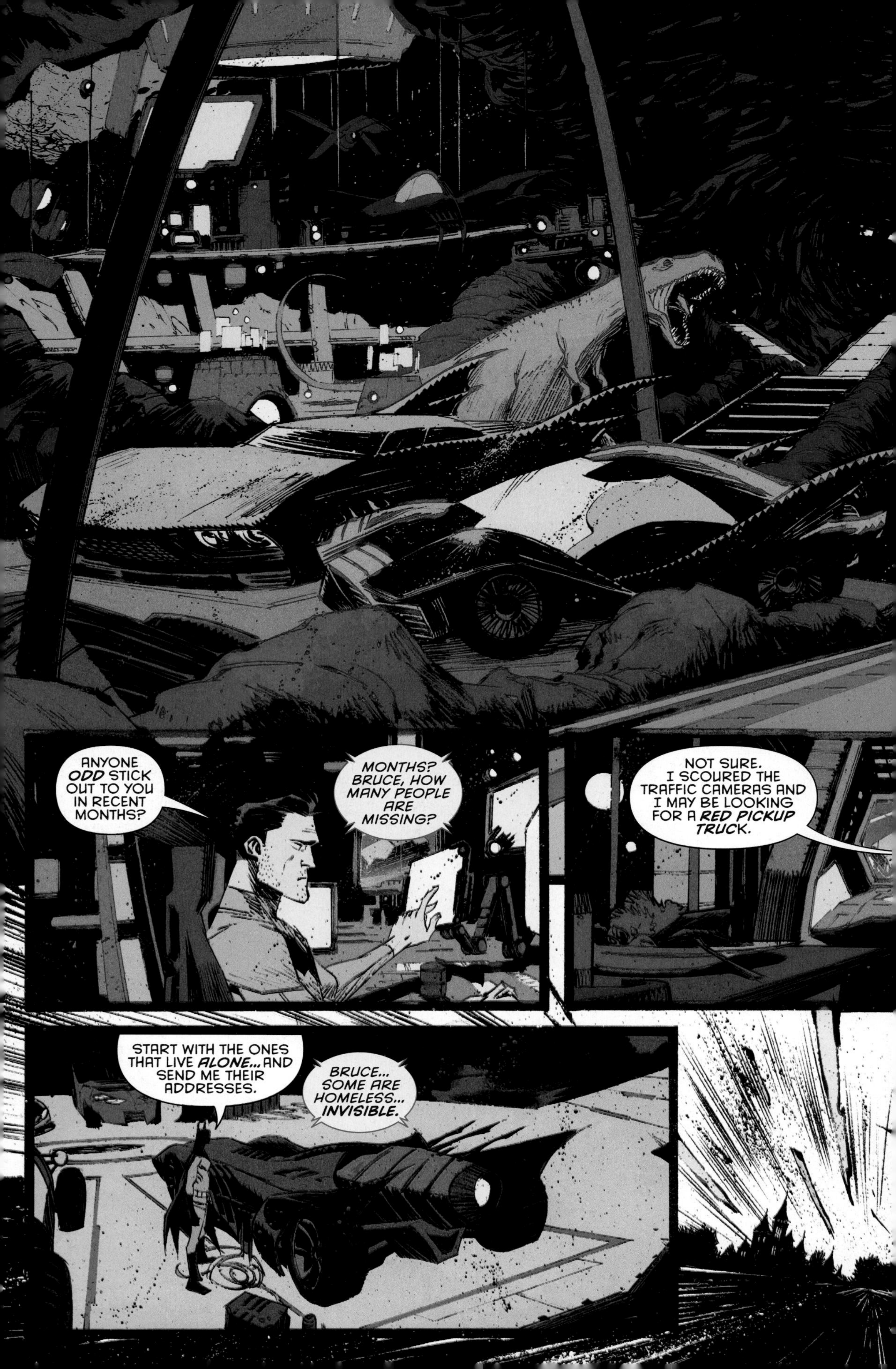
ANYONE *ODD* STICK OUT TO YOU IN RECENT MONTHS?
MONTHS? BRUCE, HOW MANY PEOPLE ARE MISSING?
NOT SURE. I SCOURED THE TRAFFIC CAMERAS AND I MAY BE LOOKING FOR A ***RED PICKUP TRUCK.***
START WITH THE ONES THAT LIVE ***ALONE...*** AND SEND ME THEIR ADDRESSES.
BRUCE... SOME ARE HOMELESS... ***INVISIBLE.***

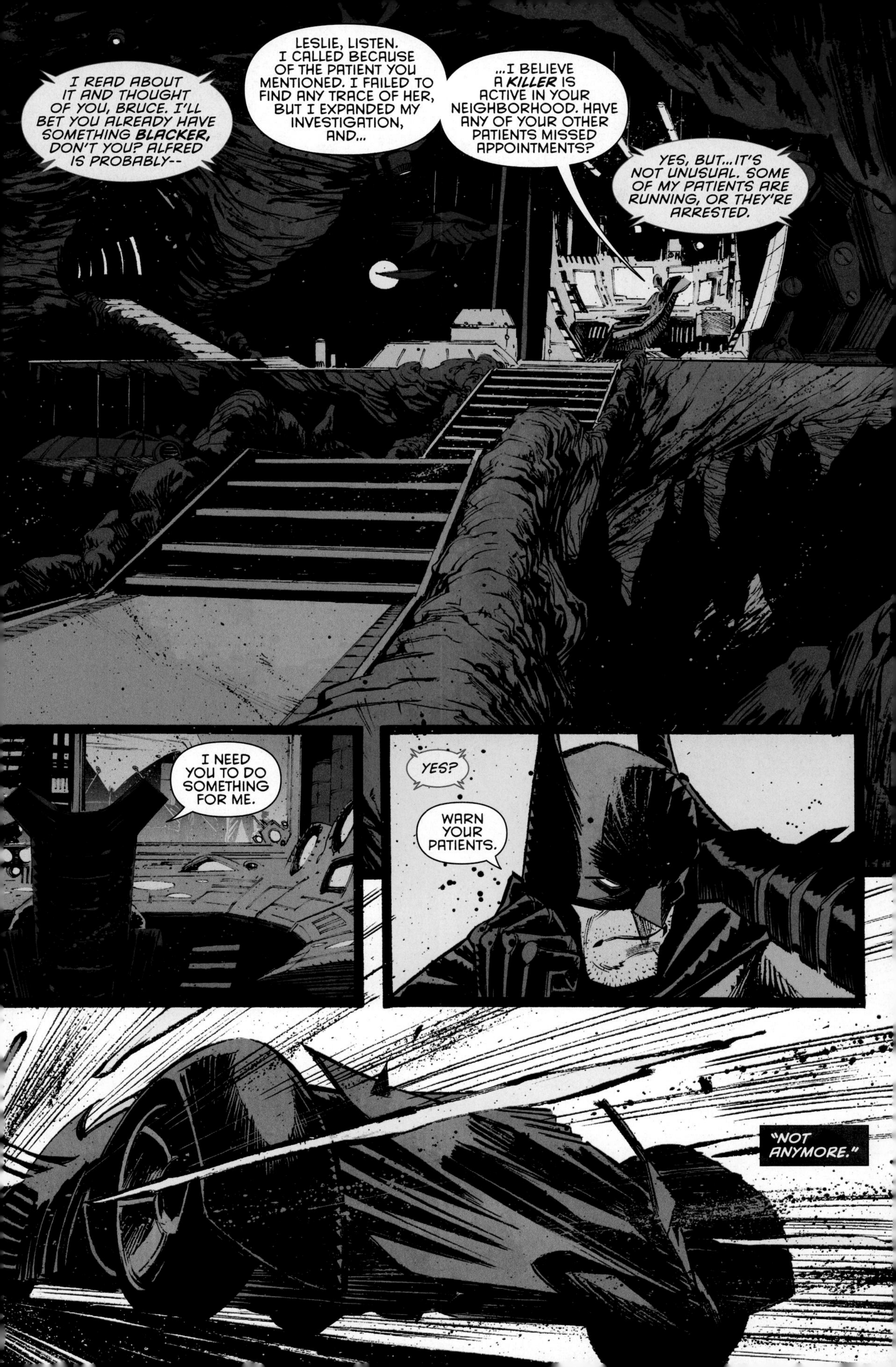
I READ ABOUT IT AND THOUGHT OF YOU, BRUCE. I'LL BET YOU ALREADY HAVE SOMETHING BLACKER, DON'T YOU? ALFRED IS PROBABLY--
LESLIE, LISTEN. I CALLED BECAUSE OF THE PATIENT YOU MENTIONED. I FAILED TO FIND ANY TRACE OF HER, BUT I EXPANDED MY INVESTIGATION, AND...
...I BELIEVE A KILLER IS ACTIVE IN YOUR NEIGHBORHOOD. HAVE ANY OF YOUR OTHER PATIENTS MISSED APPOINTMENTS?
YES, BUT...IT'S NOT UNUSUAL. SOME OF MY PATIENTS ARE RUNNING, OR THEY'RE ARRESTED.
I NEED YOU TO DO SOMETHING FOR ME.
YES?
WARN YOUR PATIENTS.
"NOT ANYMORE."

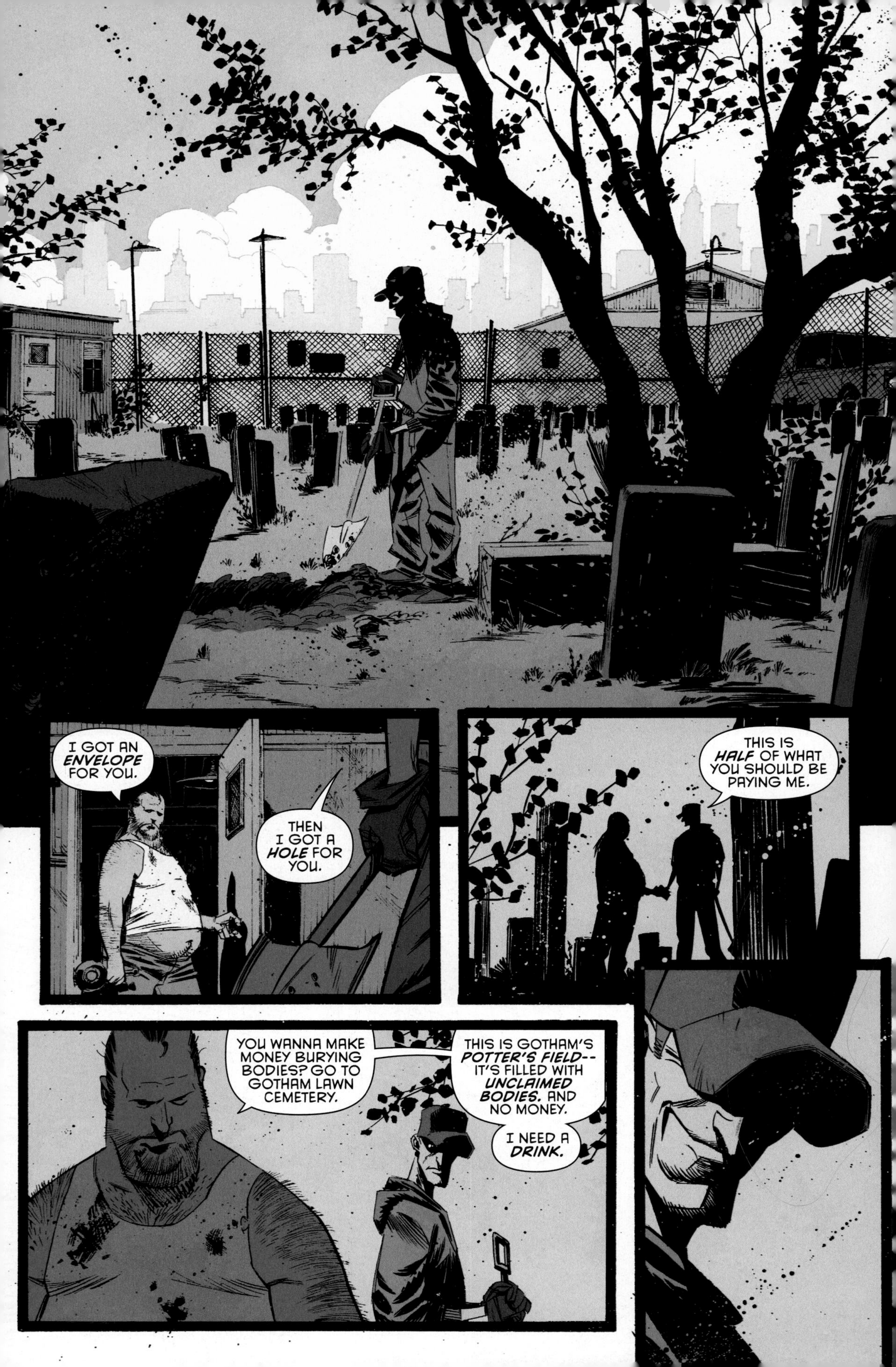
I GOT AN *ENVELOPE* FOR YOU.
THEN I GOT A *HOLE* FOR YOU.
THIS IS *HALF* OF WHAT YOU SHOULD BE PAYING ME.
YOU WANNA MAKE MONEY BURYING BODIES? GO TO GOTHAM LAWN CEMETERY.
THIS IS GOTHAM'S *POTTER'S FIELD*-- IT'S FILLED WITH *UNCLAIMED BODIES.* AND NO MONEY.
I NEED A *DRINK.*

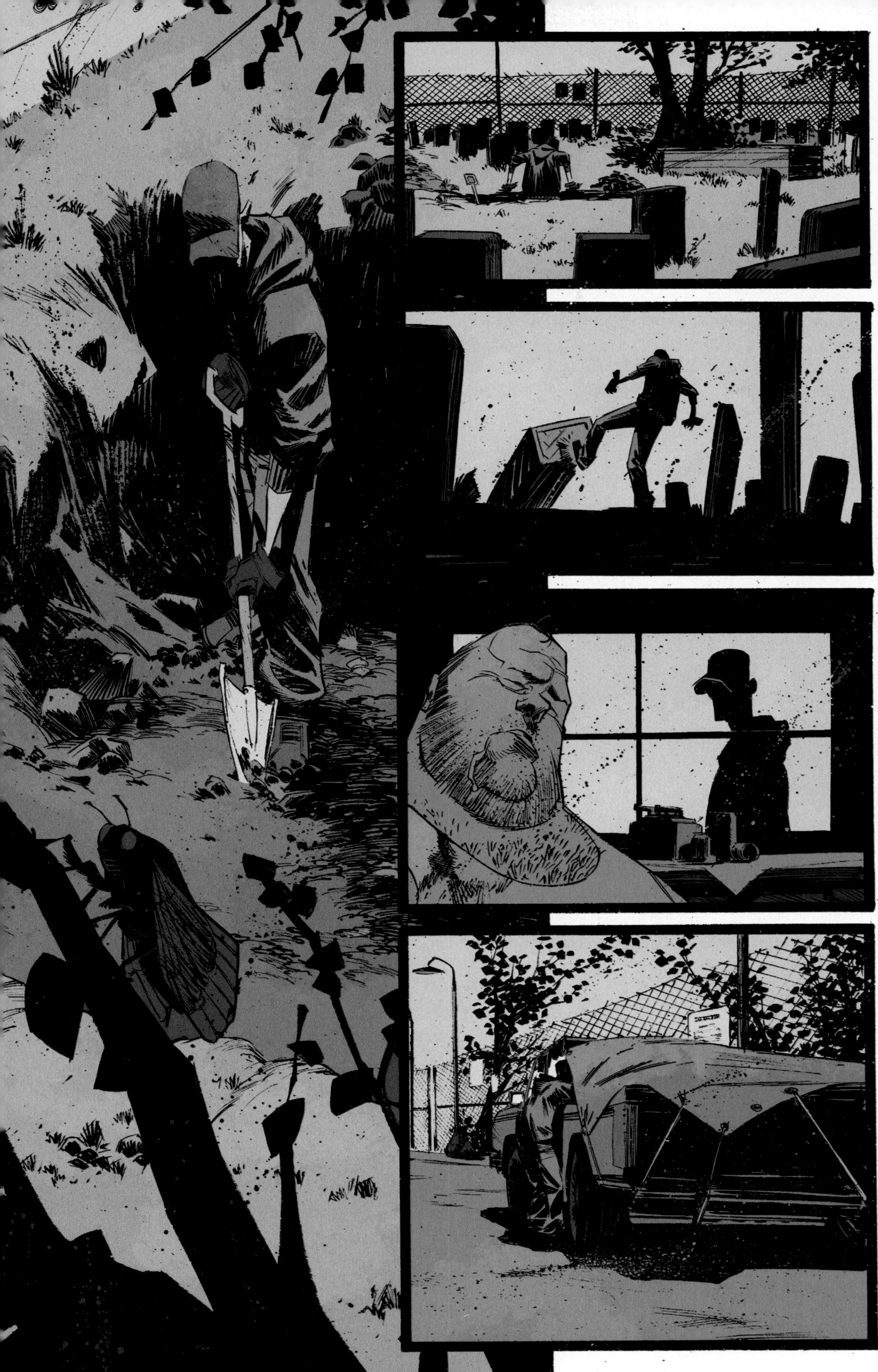

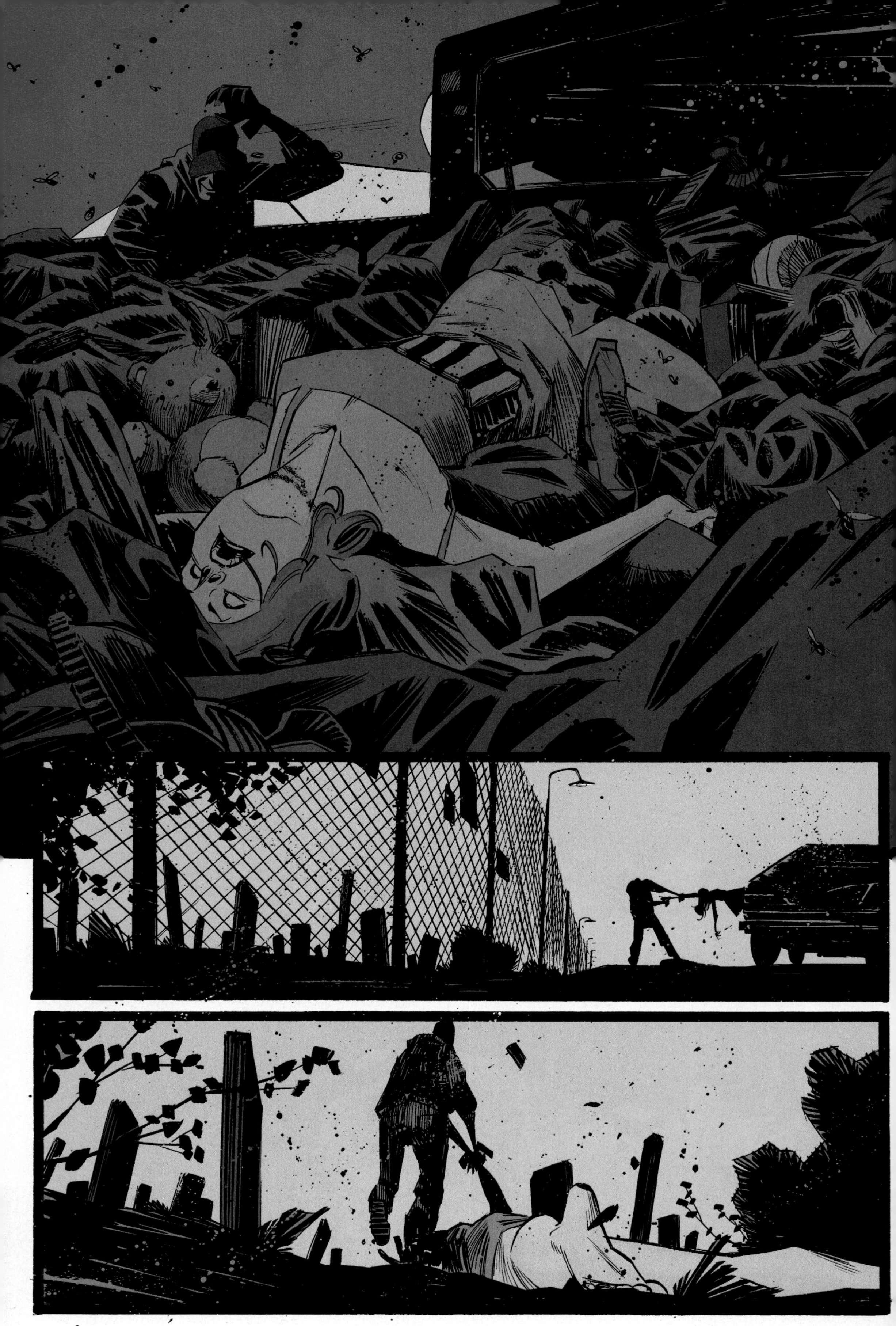

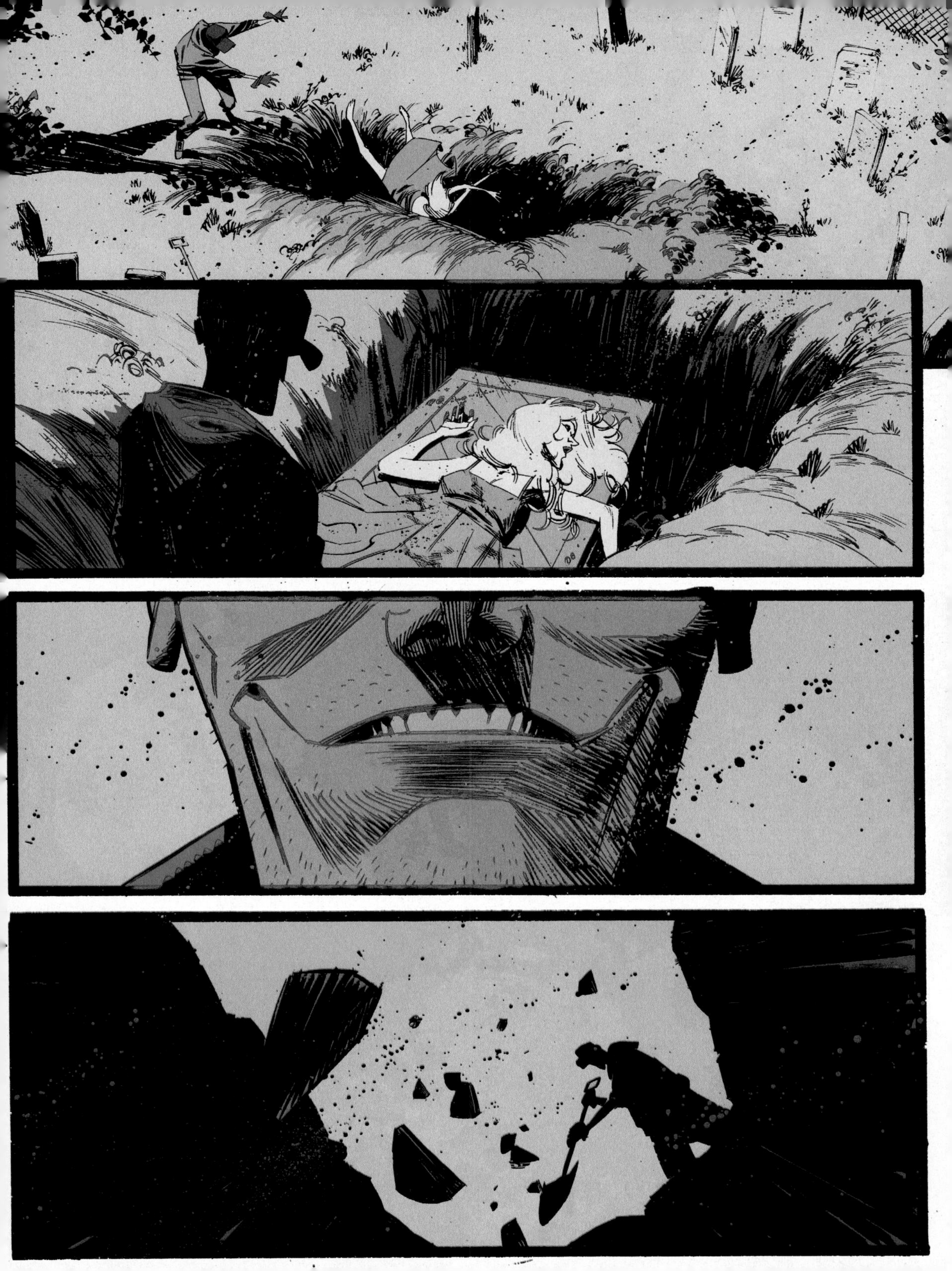

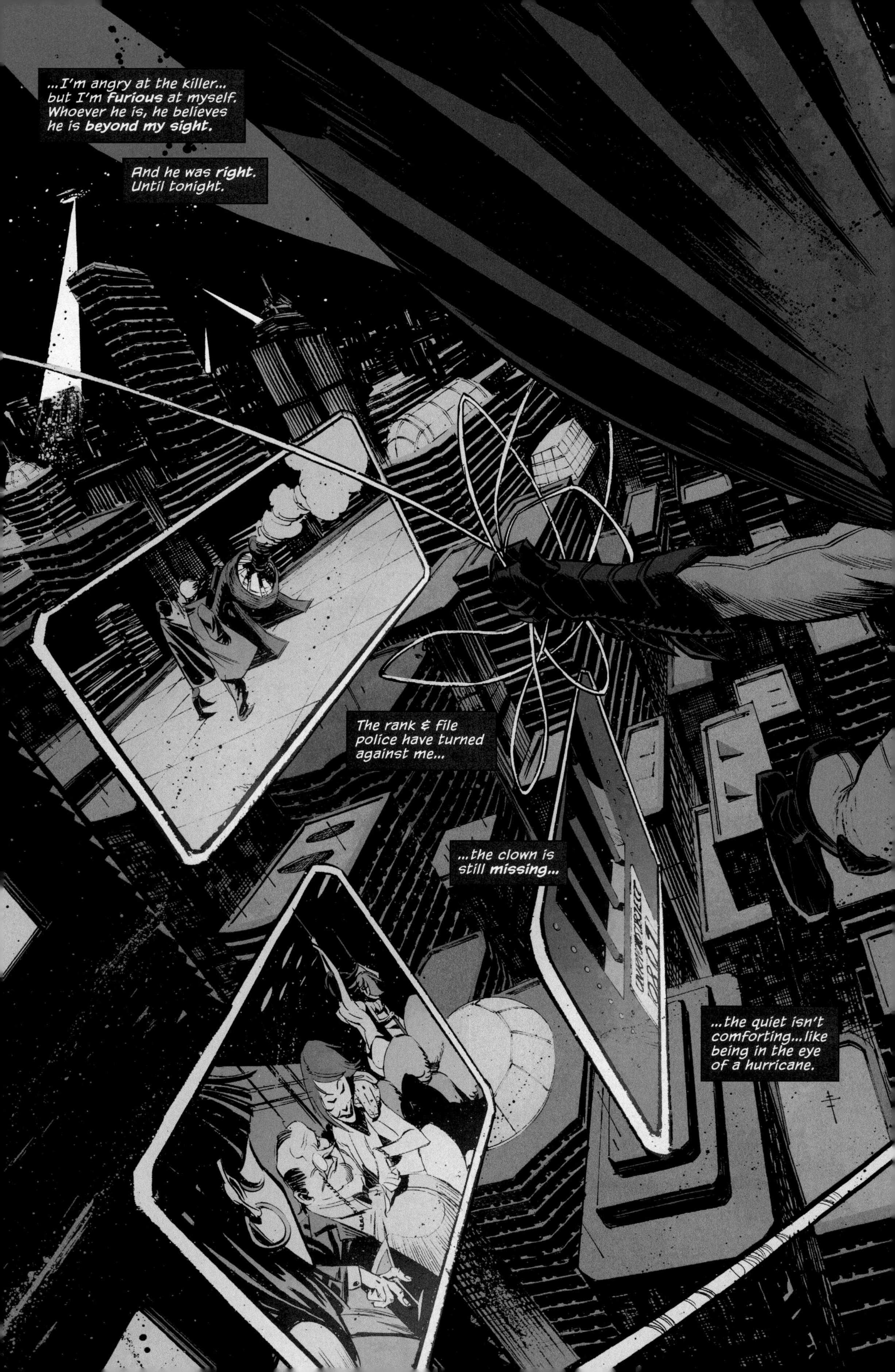
...I'm angry at the killer... but I'm furious at myself. Whoever he is, he believes he is beyond my sight.
And he was right. Until tonight.
The rank & file police have turned against me...
...the clown is still missing...
...the quiet isn't comforting... like being in the eye of a hurricane.

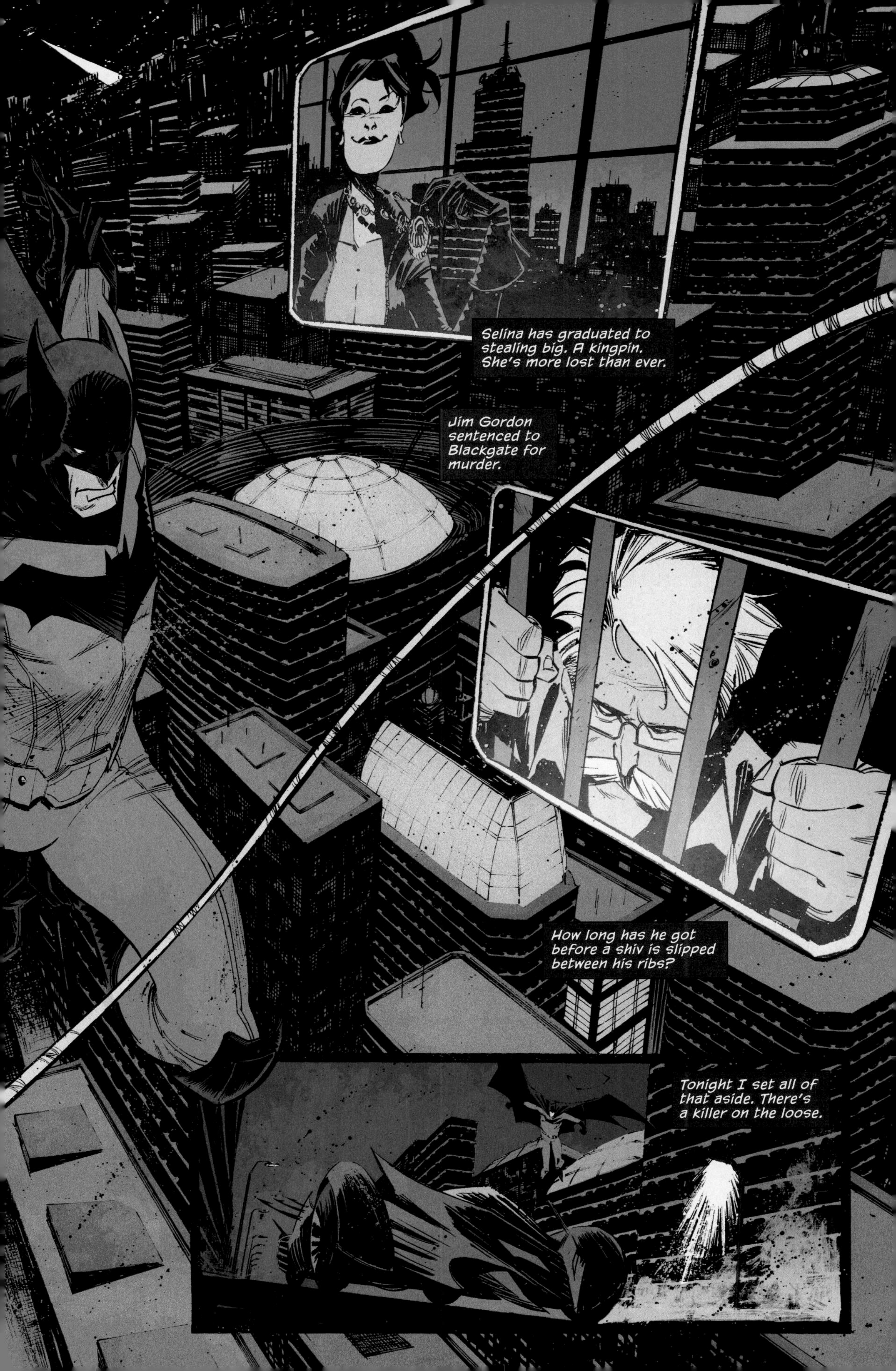

Selina has graduated to stealing big. A kingpin. She's more lost than ever.
Jim Gordon sentenced to Blackgate for murder.
How long has he got before a shiv is slipped between his ribs?
Tonight I set all of that aside. There's a killer on the loose.

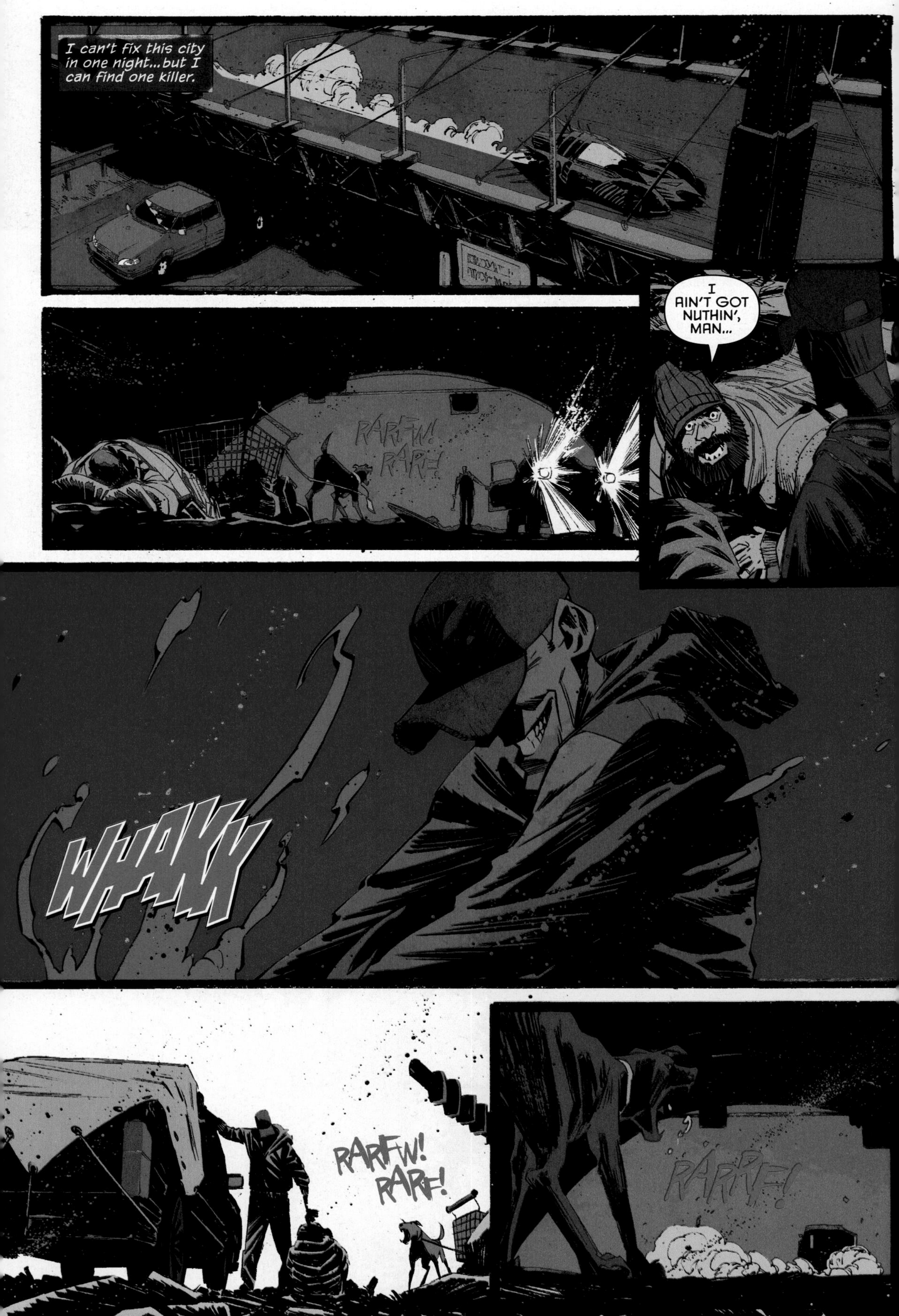
I can't fix this city in one night...but I can find one killer.
RARFW! RARF!
I AIN'T GOT NUTHIN', MAN...
WHAKK
RARFW! RARF!
RARRF!

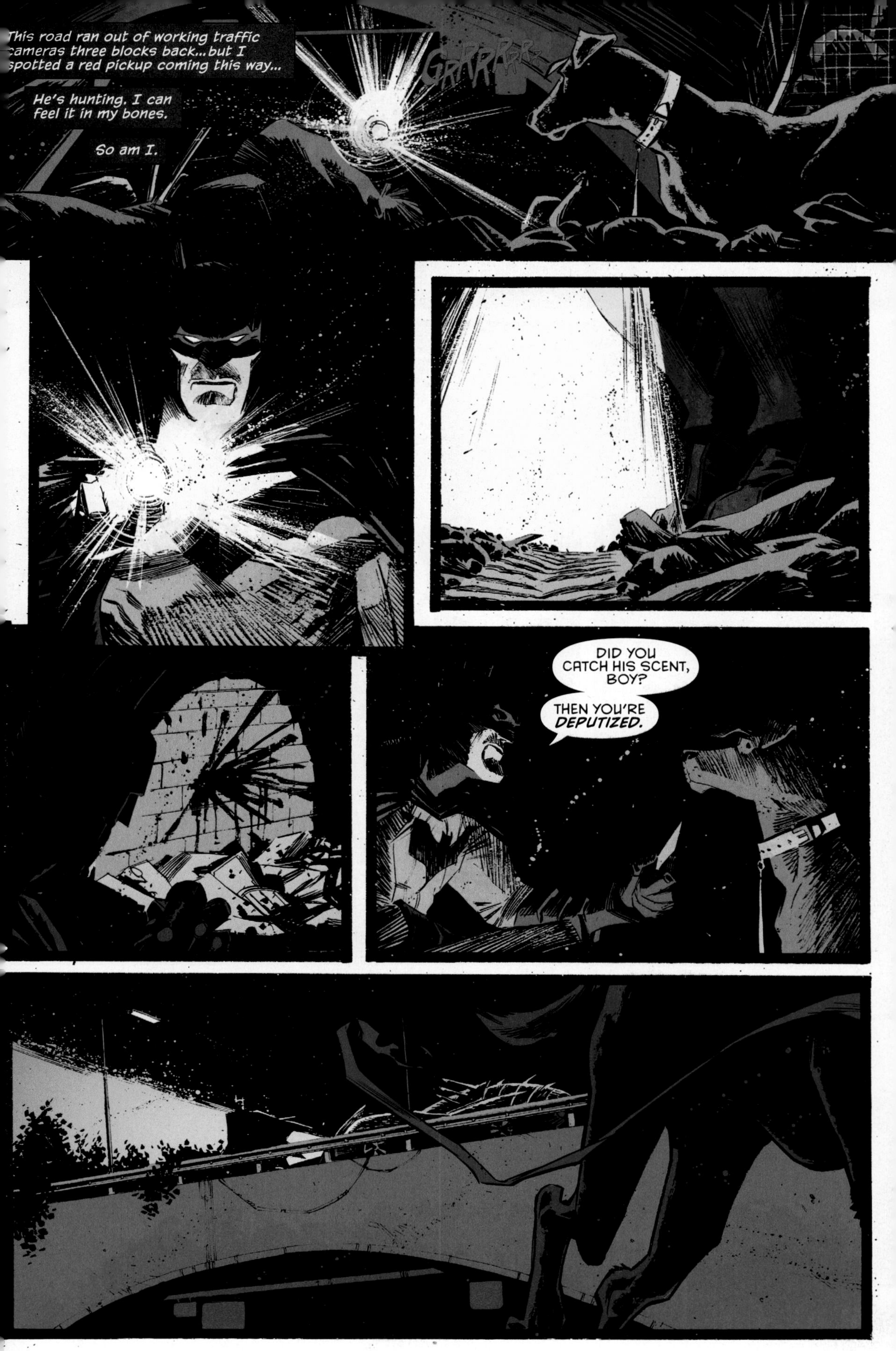
This road ran out of working traffic cameras three blocks back...but I spotted a red pickup coming this way...
GRRRRRRR
He's hunting. I can feel it in my bones.
So am I.
DID YOU CATCH HIS SCENT, BOY?
THEN YOU'RE DEPUTIZED.

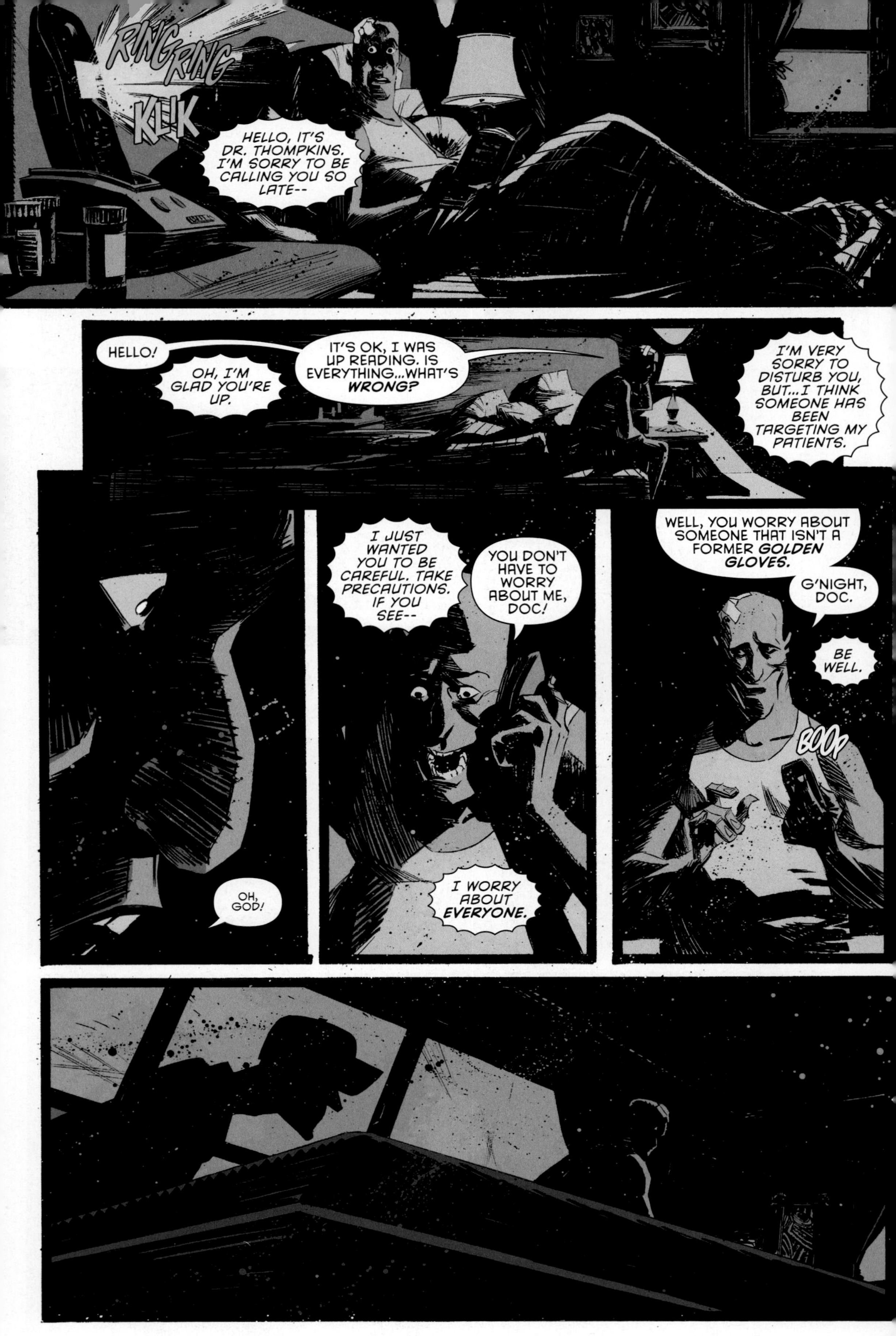
RINGRING
KLIK
HELLO, IT'S DR. THOMPKINS. I'M SORRY TO BE CALLING YOU SO LATE--
HELLO!
OH, I'M GLAD YOU'RE UP.
IT'S OK, I WAS UP READING. IS EVERYTHING...WHAT'S WRONG?
I'M VERY SORRY TO DISTURB YOU, BUT...I THINK SOMEONE HAS BEEN TARGETING MY PATIENTS.
OH, GOD!
I JUST WANTED YOU TO BE CAREFUL. TAKE PRECAUTIONS. IF YOU SEE--
YOU DON'T HAVE TO WORRY ABOUT ME, DOC!
I WORRY ABOUT EVERYONE.
WELL, YOU WORRY ABOUT SOMEONE THAT ISN'T A FORMER GOLDEN GLOVES.
G'NIGHT, DOC.
BE WELL.
BOOP

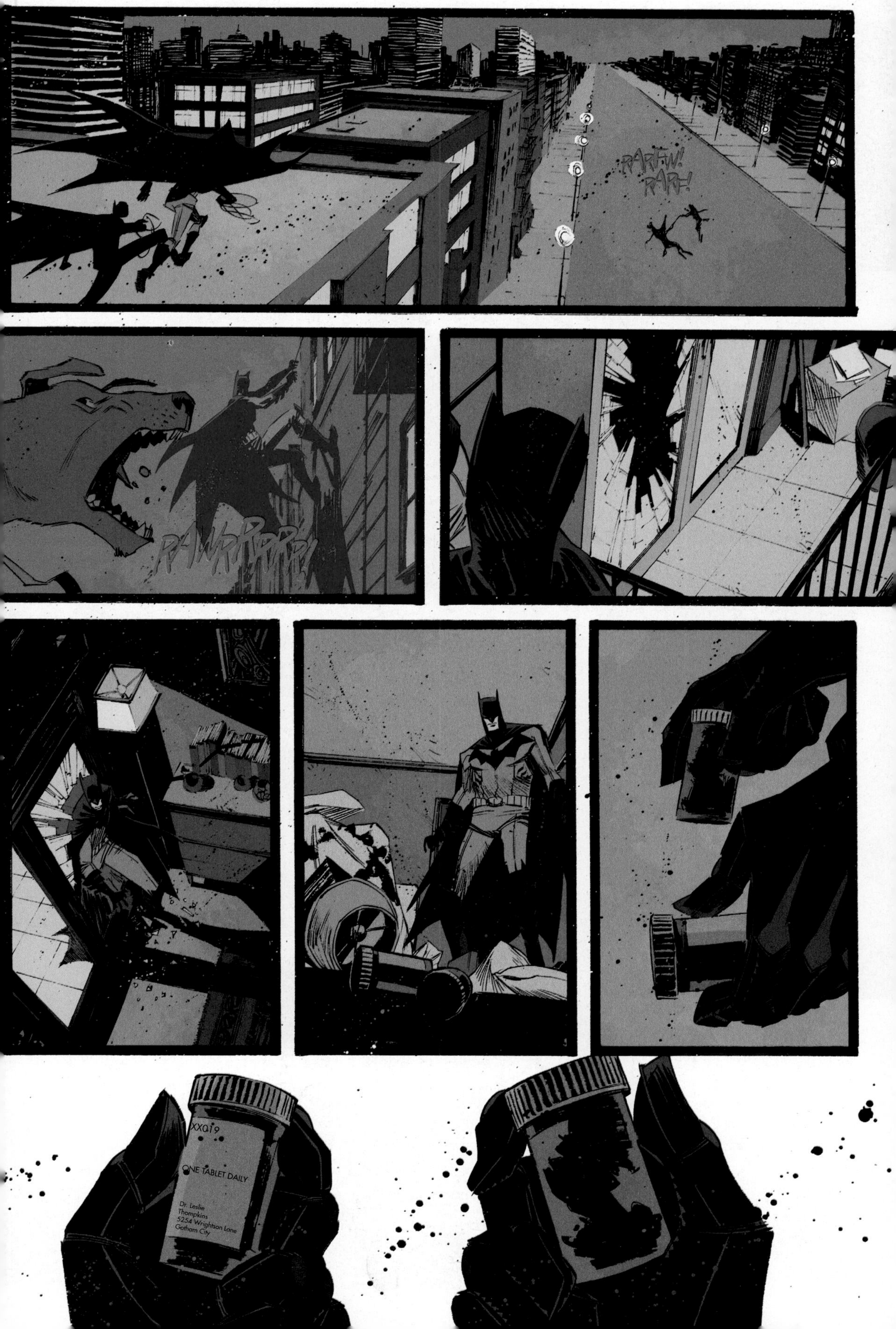
RARFW! RARF!
RAWRRRRR!
XX019
ONE TABLET DAILY
Dr. Leslie
Thompkins
5254 Wrightson Lane
Gotham City

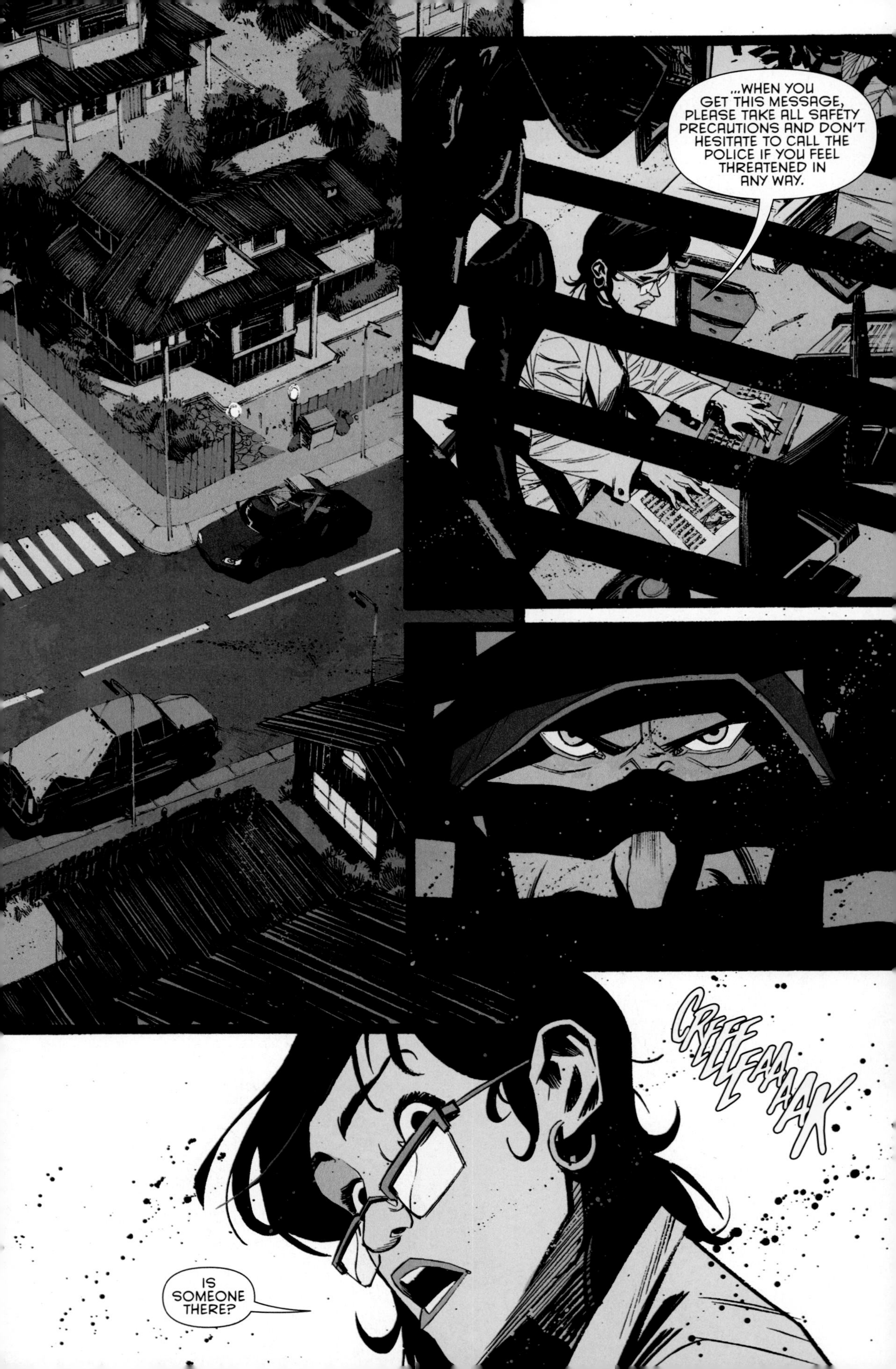
...WHEN YOU GET THIS MESSAGE, PLEASE TAKE ALL SAFETY PRECAUTIONS AND DON'T HESITATE TO CALL THE POLICE IF YOU FEEL THREATENED IN ANY WAY.
CREEEAAAAK
IS SOMEONE THERE?

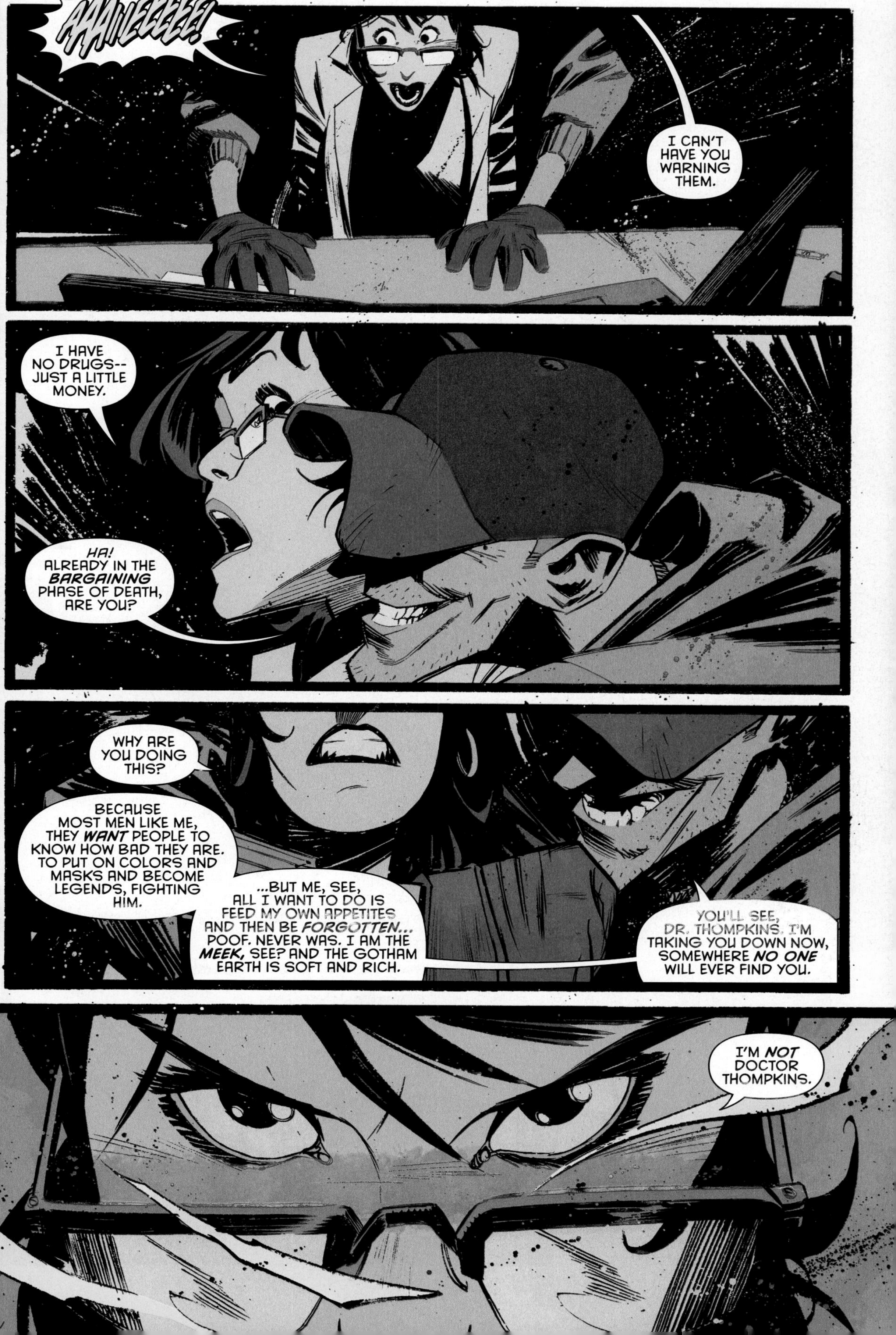
AAAIIEEEEE!
I CAN'T HAVE YOU WARNING THEM.
I HAVE NO DRUGS-- JUST A LITTLE MONEY.
HA! ALREADY IN THE BARGAINING PHASE OF DEATH, ARE YOU?
WHY ARE YOU DOING THIS?
BECAUSE MOST MEN LIKE ME, THEY WANT PEOPLE TO KNOW HOW BAD THEY ARE. TO PUT ON COLORS AND MASKS AND BECOME LEGENDS, FIGHTING HIM.
...BUT ME, SEE, ALL I WANT TO DO IS FEED MY OWN APPETITES AND THEN BE FORGOTTEN... POOF. NEVER WAS. I AM THE MEEK, SEE? AND THE GOTHAM EARTH IS SOFT AND RICH.
YOU'LL SEE, DR. THOMPKINS. I'M TAKING YOU DOWN NOW, SOMEWHERE NO ONE WILL EVER FIND YOU.
I'M NOT DOCTOR THOMPKINS.

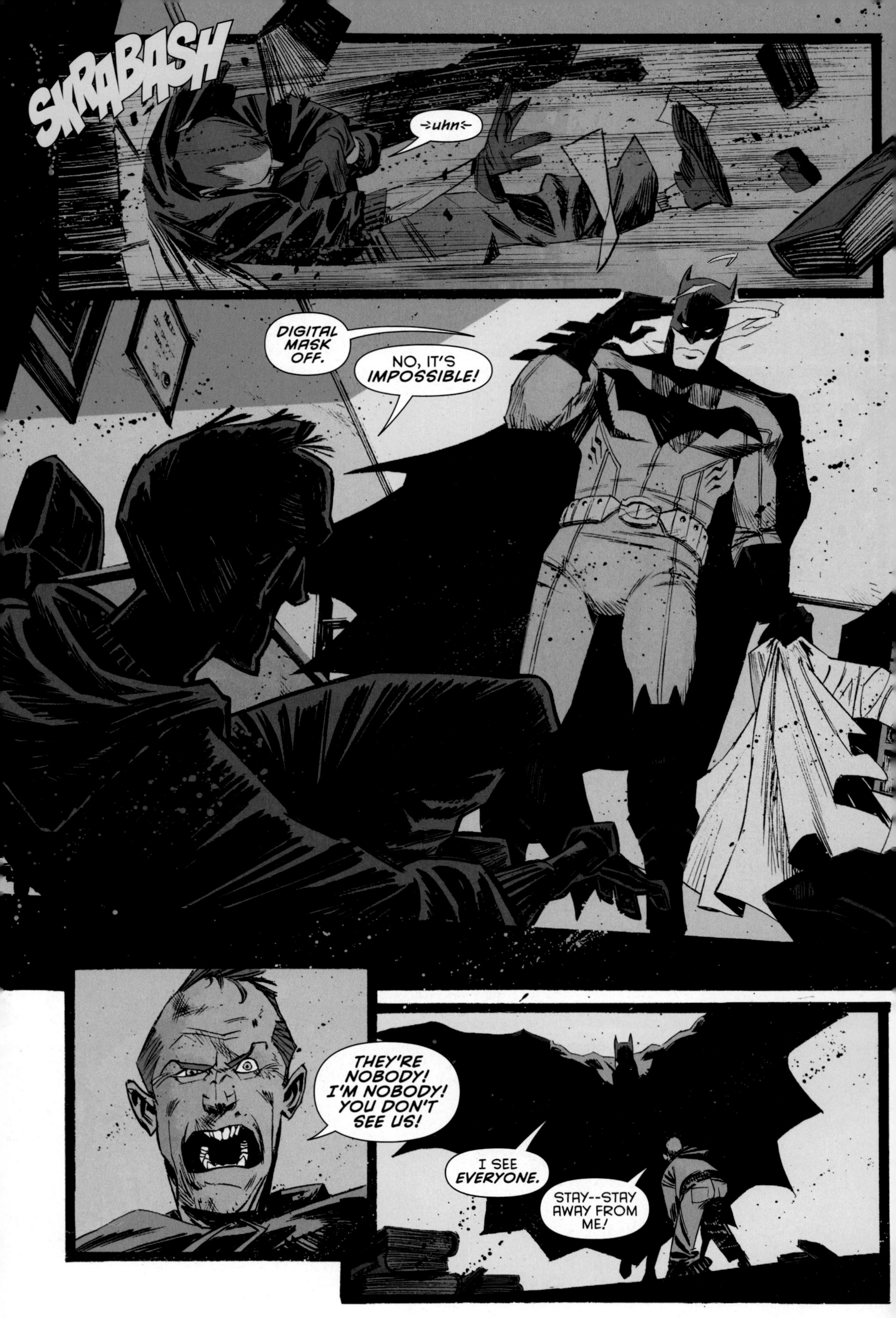
SKRABASH
uhn
DIGITAL MASK OFF.
NO, IT'S IMPOSSIBLE!
THEY'RE NOBODY! I'M NOBODY! YOU DON'T SEE US!
I SEE EVERYONE.
STAY--STAY AWAY FROM ME!

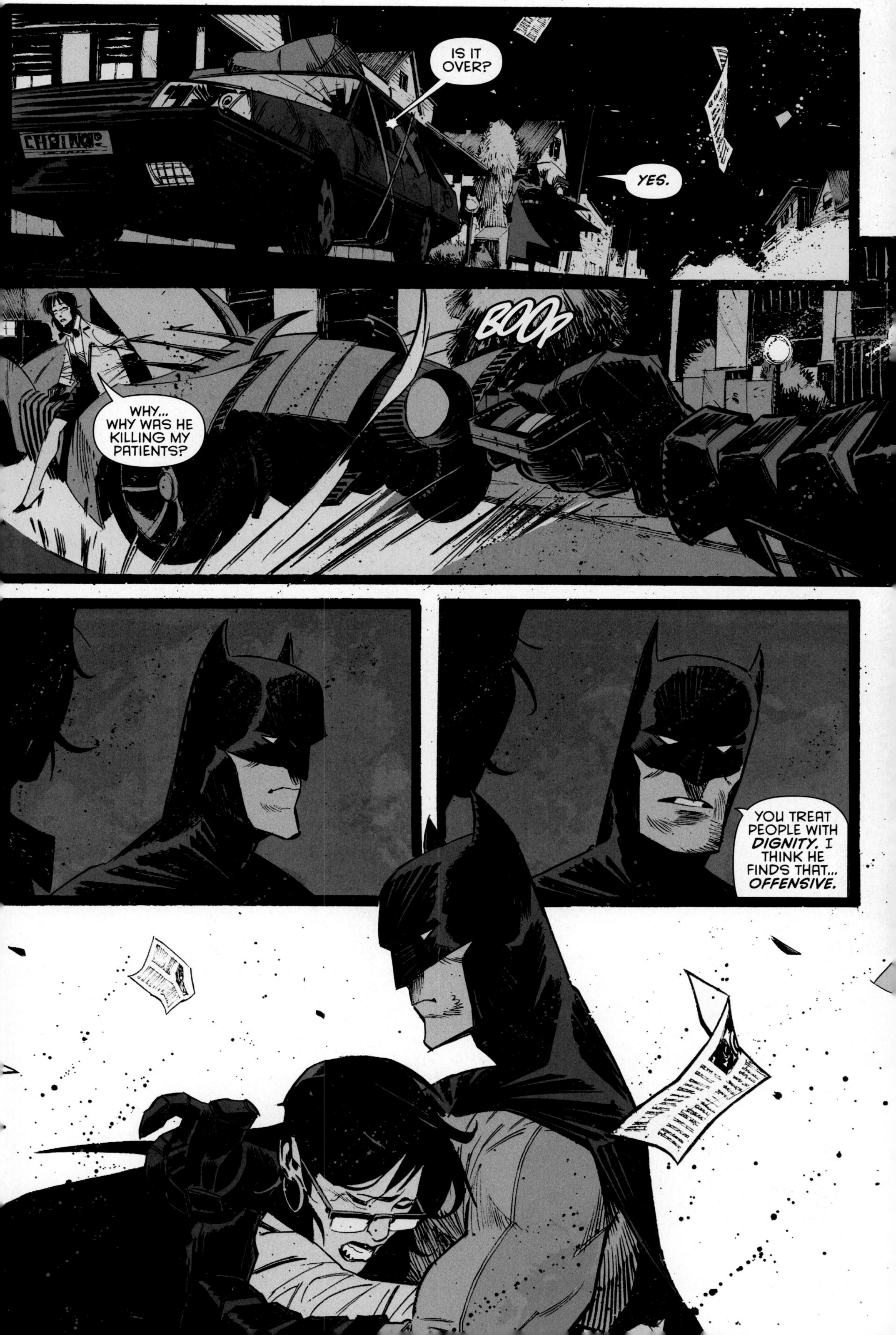

IS IT OVER?
YES.
BOOM
WHY... WHY WAS HE KILLING MY PATIENTS?
YOU TREAT PEOPLE WITH *DIGNITY.* I THINK HE FINDS THAT... *OFFENSIVE.*

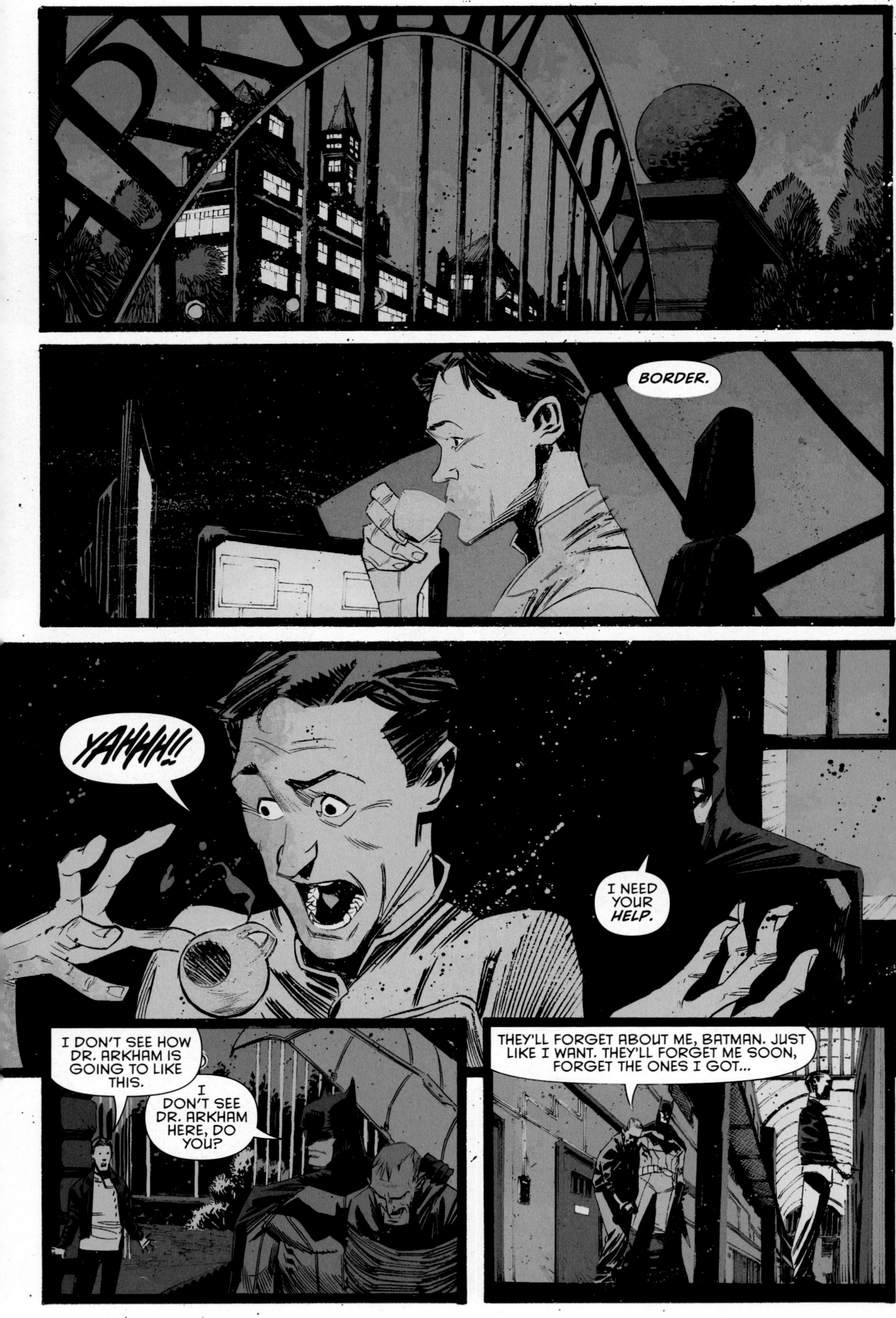
BORDER.
YAHHH!!
I NEED YOUR HELP.
I DON'T SEE HOW DR. ARKHAM IS GOING TO LIKE THIS.
I DON'T SEE DR. ARKHAM HERE, DO YOU?
THEY'LL FORGET ABOUT ME, BATMAN. JUST LIKE I WANT. THEY'LL FORGET ME SOON, FORGET THE ONES I GOT...

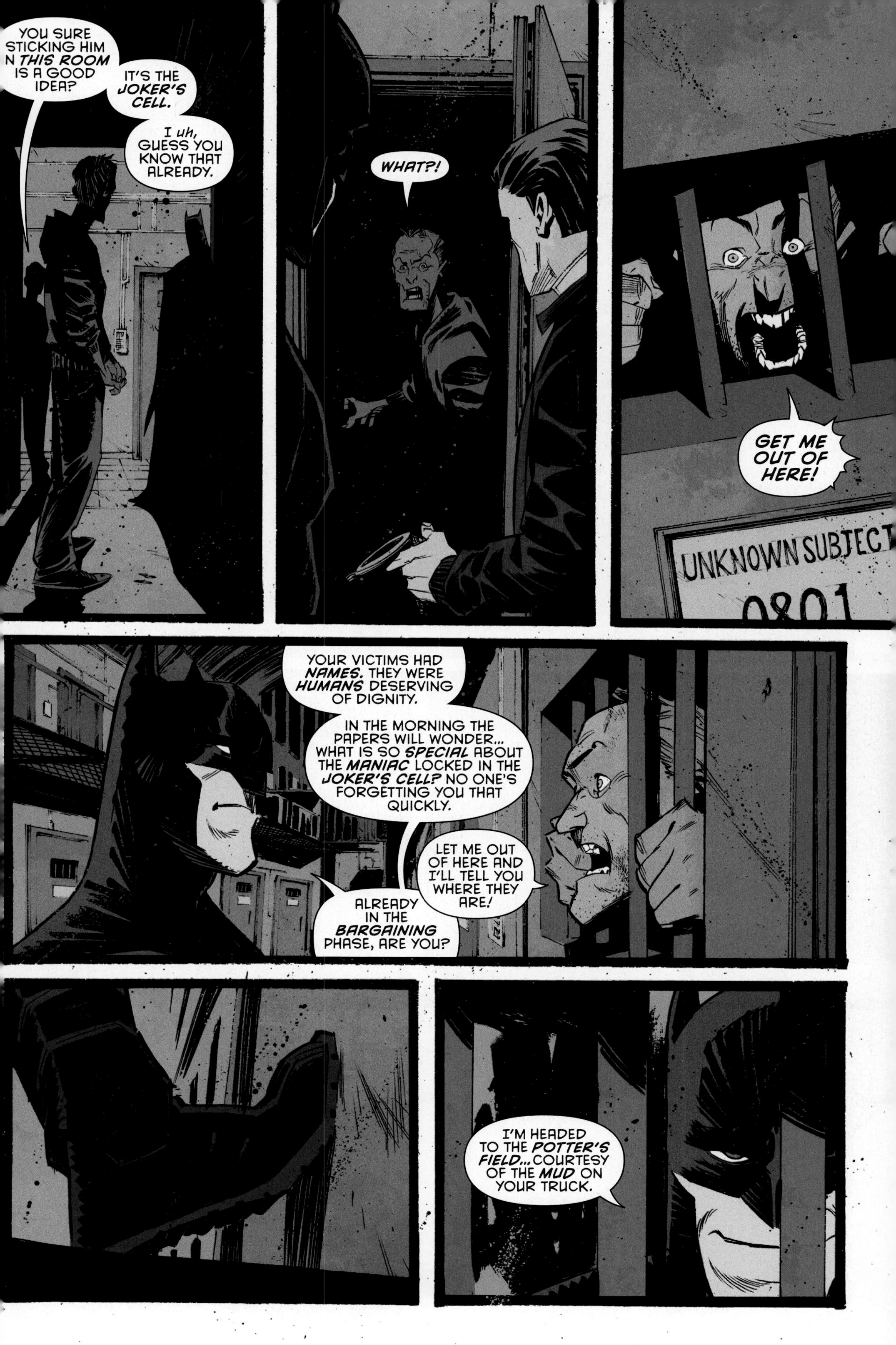
YOU SURE STICKING HIM N THIS ROOM IS A GOOD IDEA?
IT'S THE JOKER'S CELL.
I uh, GUESS YOU KNOW THAT ALREADY.
WHAT?!
GET ME OUT OF HERE!
UNKNOWN SUBJECT
0801
YOUR VICTIMS HAD NAMES. THEY WERE HUMANS DESERVING OF DIGNITY.
IN THE MORNING THE PAPERS WILL WONDER... WHAT IS SO SPECIAL ABOUT THE MANIAC LOCKED IN THE JOKER'S CELL? NO ONE'S FORGETTING YOU THAT QUICKLY.
LET ME OUT OF HERE AND I'LL TELL YOU WHERE THEY ARE!
ALREADY IN THE BARGAINING PHASE, ARE YOU?
I'M HEADED TO THE POTTER'S FIELD... COURTESY OF THE MUD ON YOUR TRUCK.

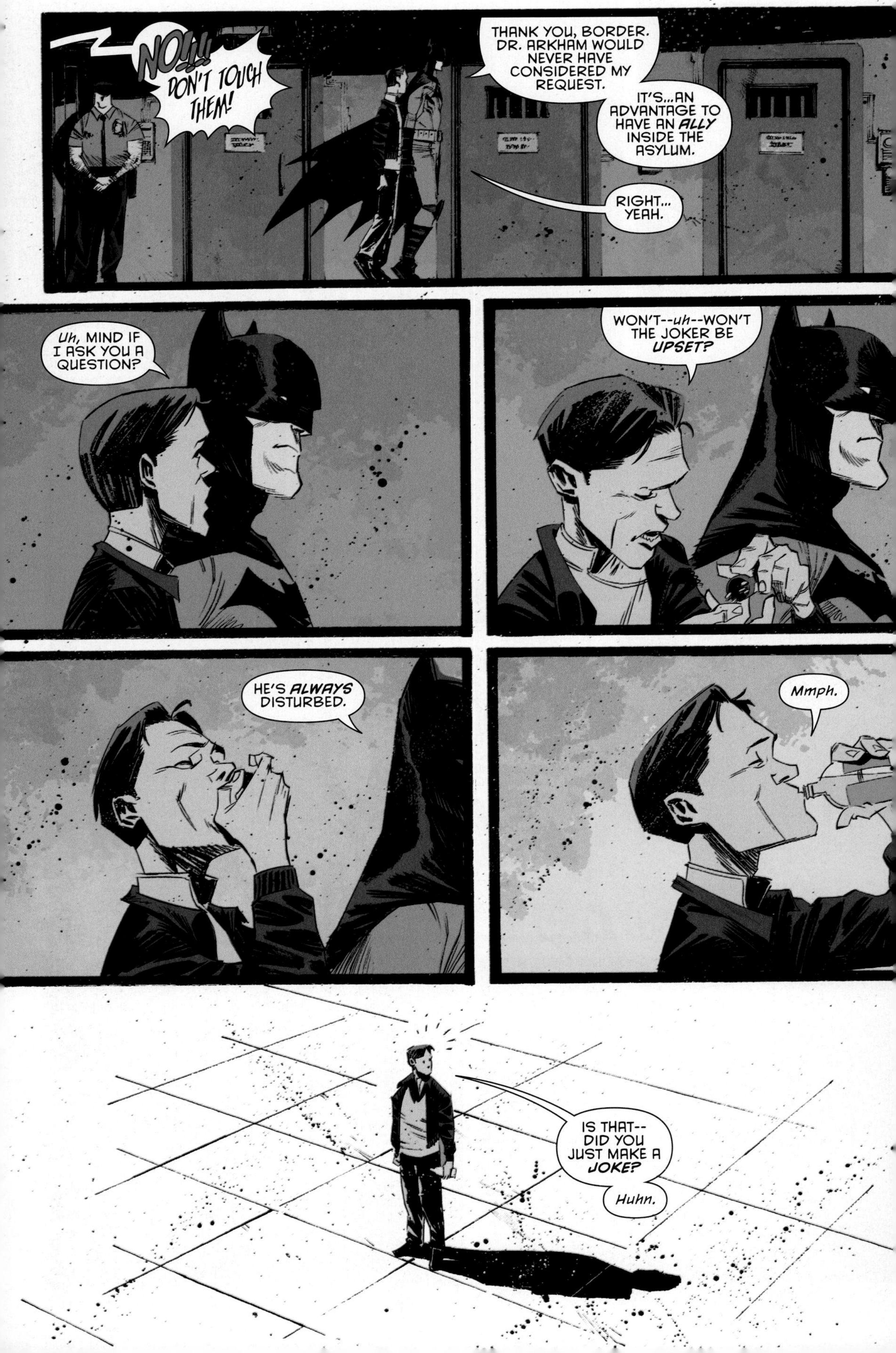
NO!!!! DON'T TOUCH THEM!
THANK YOU, BORDER. DR. ARKHAM WOULD NEVER HAVE CONSIDERED MY REQUEST.
IT'S...AN ADVANTAGE TO HAVE AN *ALLY* INSIDE THE ASYLUM.
RIGHT... YEAH.
Uh, MIND IF I ASK YOU A QUESTION?
WON'T--*uh*--WON'T THE JOKER BE *UPSET?*
HE'S *ALWAYS* DISTURBED.
Mmph.
IS THAT-- DID YOU JUST MAKE A *JOKE?*
Huhn.

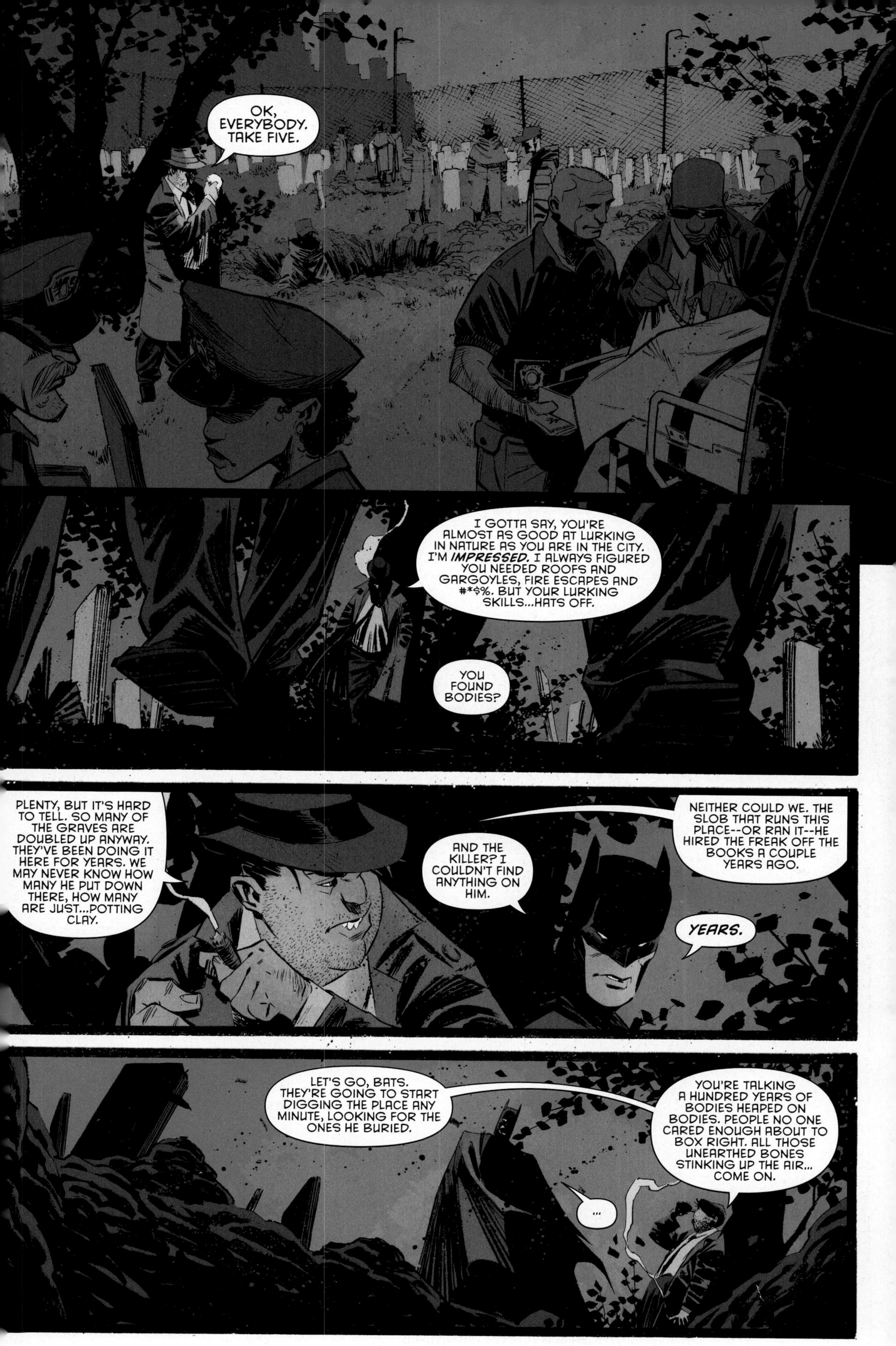
OK, EVERYBODY. TAKE FIVE.
I GOTTA SAY, YOU'RE ALMOST AS GOOD AT LURKING IN NATURE AS YOU ARE IN THE CITY. I'M *IMPRESSED.* I ALWAYS FIGURED YOU NEEDED ROOFS AND GARGOYLES, FIRE ESCAPES AND #*$%. BUT YOUR LURKING SKILLS...HATS OFF.
YOU FOUND BODIES?
PLENTY, BUT IT'S HARD TO TELL. SO MANY OF THE GRAVES ARE DOUBLED UP ANYWAY. THEY'VE BEEN DOING IT HERE FOR YEARS. WE MAY NEVER KNOW HOW MANY HE PUT DOWN THERE, HOW MANY ARE JUST...POTTING CLAY.
AND THE KILLER? I COULDN'T FIND ANYTHING ON HIM.
NEITHER COULD WE. THE SLOB THAT RUNS THIS PLACE--OR RAN IT--HE HIRED THE FREAK OFF THE BOOKS A COUPLE YEARS AGO.
YEARS.
LET'S GO, BATS. THEY'RE GOING TO START DIGGING THE PLACE ANY MINUTE, LOOKING FOR THE ONES HE BURIED.
YOU'RE TALKING A HUNDRED YEARS OF BODIES HEAPED ON BODIES. PEOPLE NO ONE CARED ENOUGH ABOUT TO BOX RIGHT. ALL THOSE UNEARTHED BONES STINKING UP THE AIR... COME ON.
...

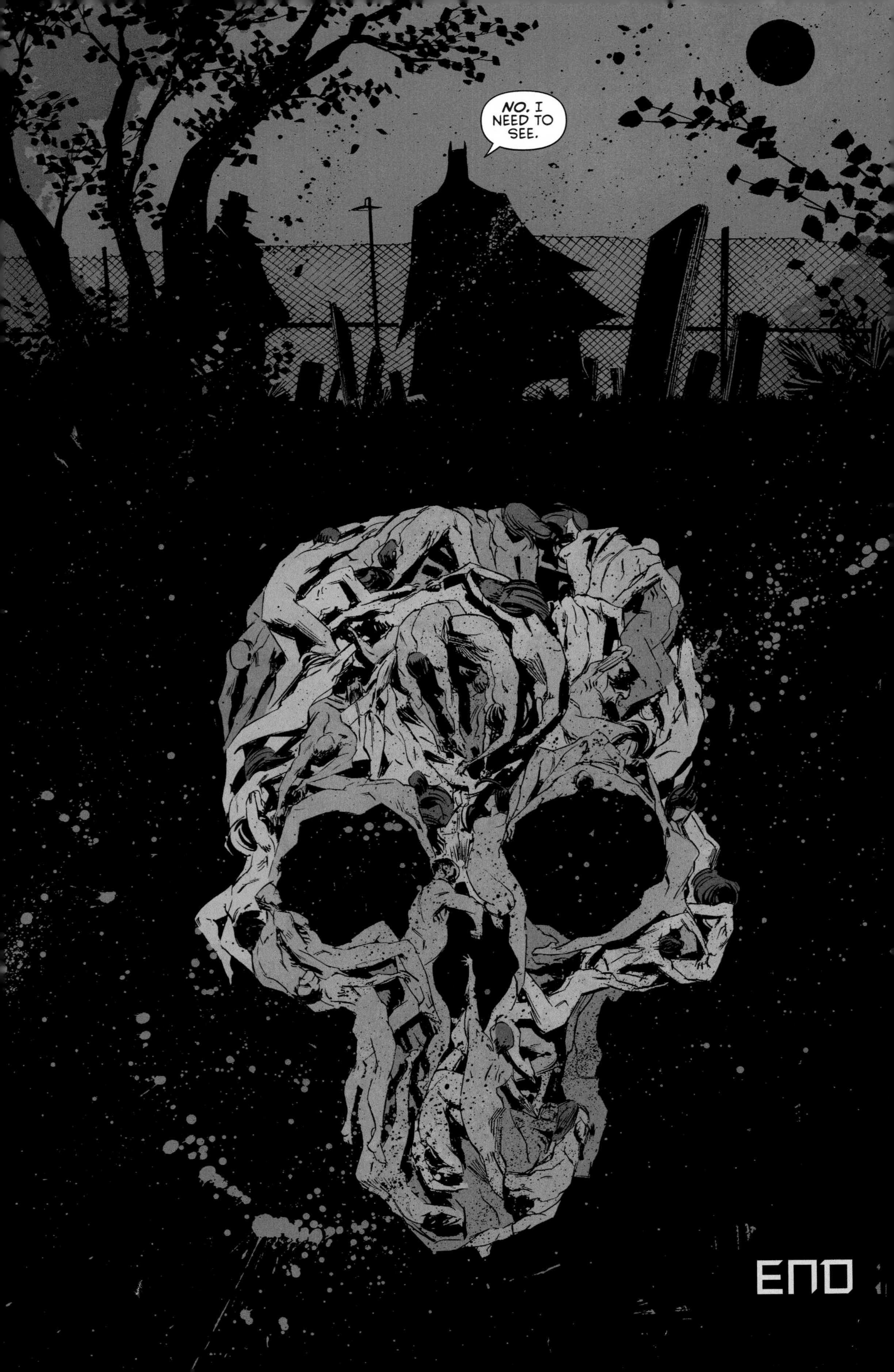
NO. I NEED TO SEE.
END

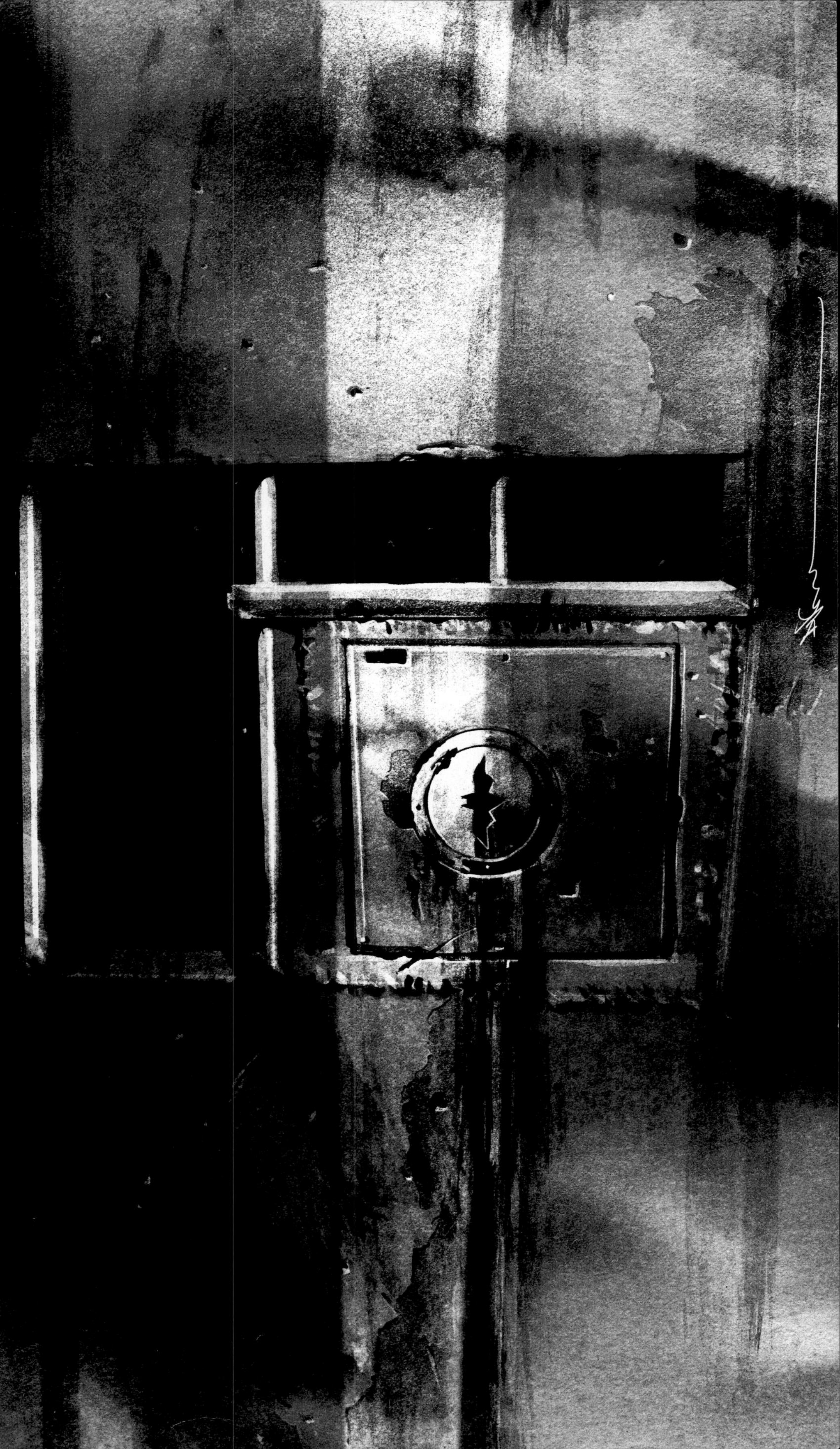

GOTHAM ETERNAL

SCOTT SNYDER JAMES TYNION IV writers DUSTIN NGUYEN penciller DEREK FRIDOLFS inker JOHN KALISZ colorist cover by DUSTIN NGUYEN

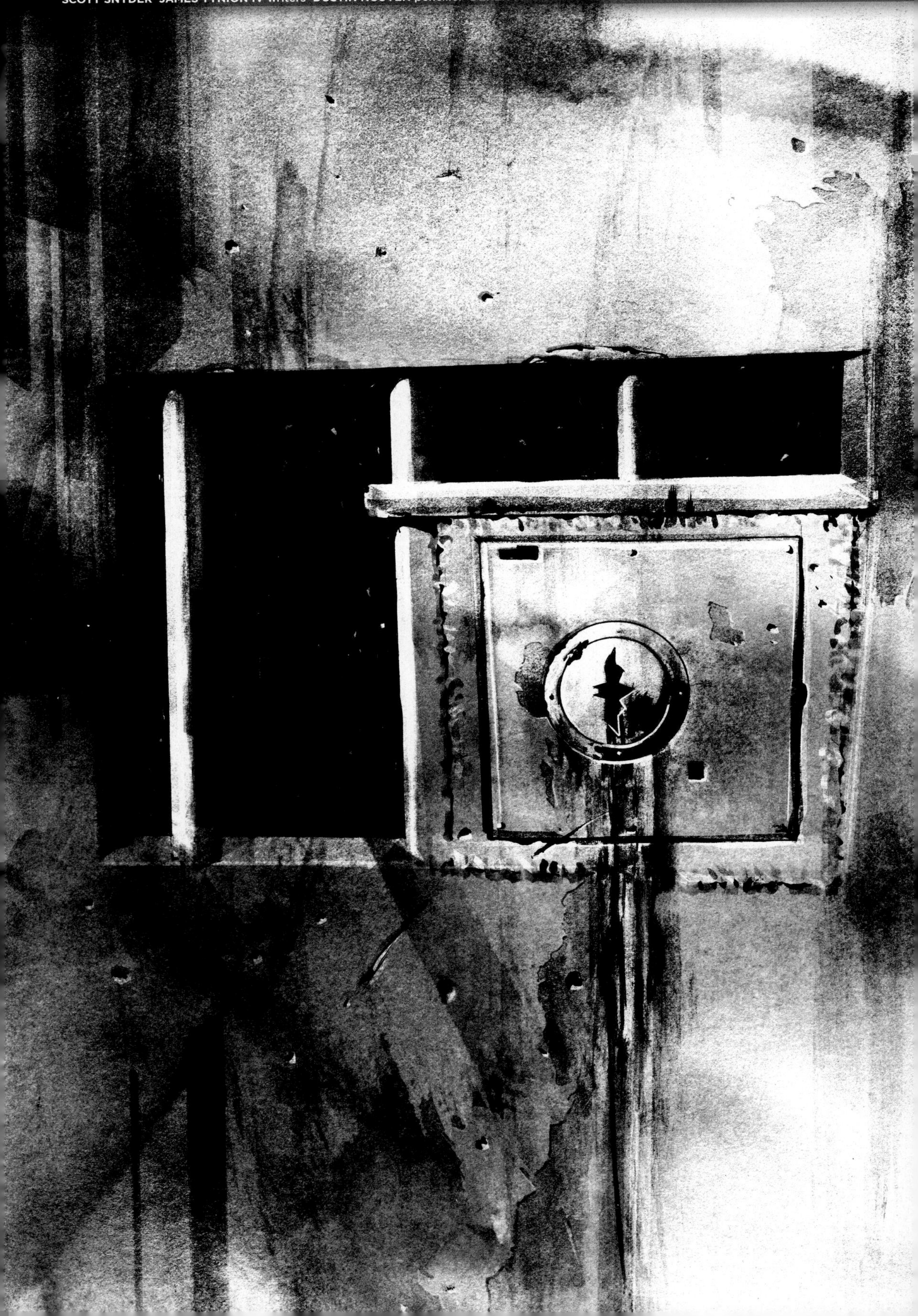

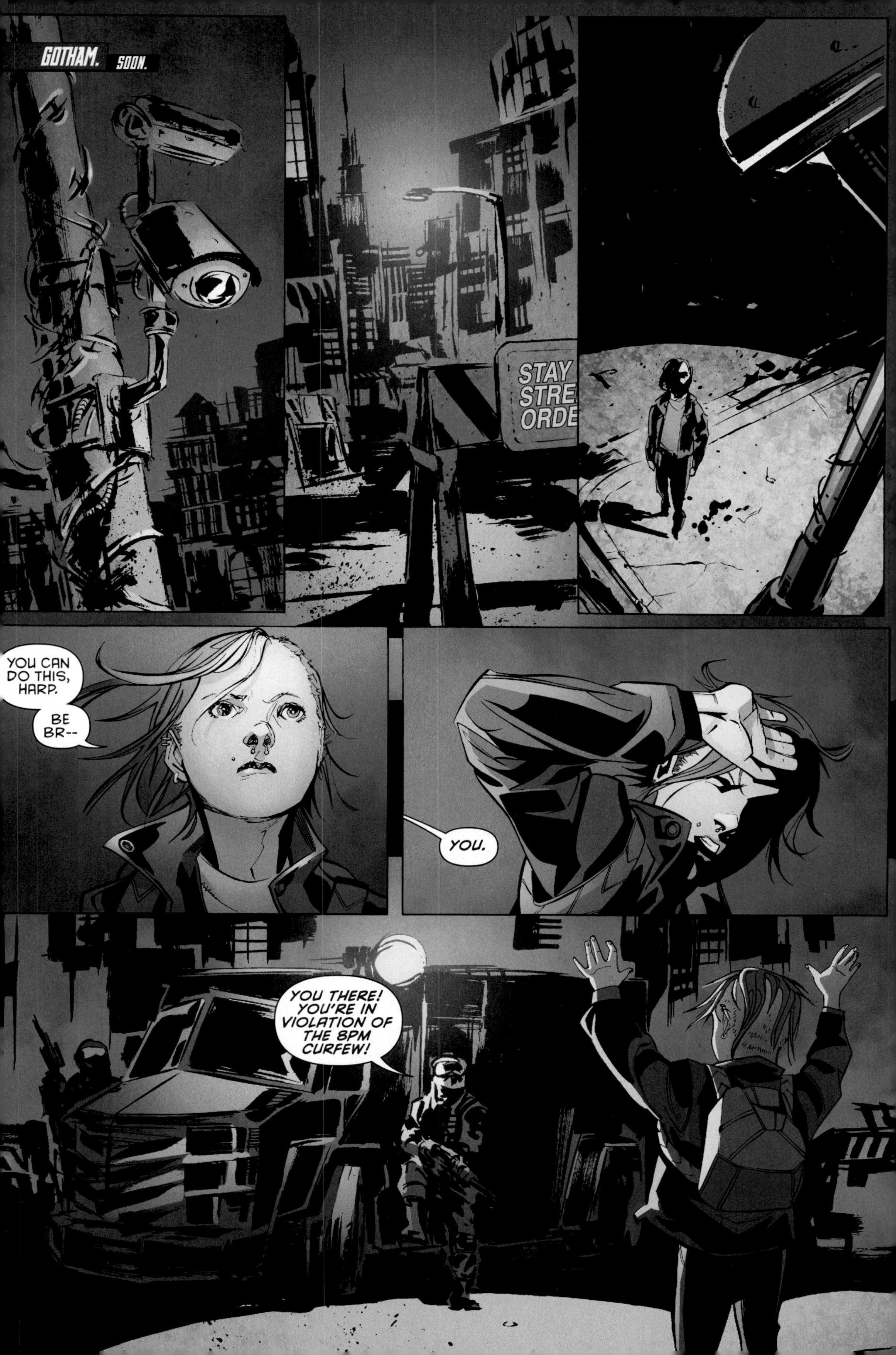
GOTHAM. SOON.
STAY
STRE
ORDE
YOU CAN DO THIS, HARP.
BE BR--
YOU.
YOU THERE! YOU'RE IN VIOLATION OF THE 8PM CURFEW!

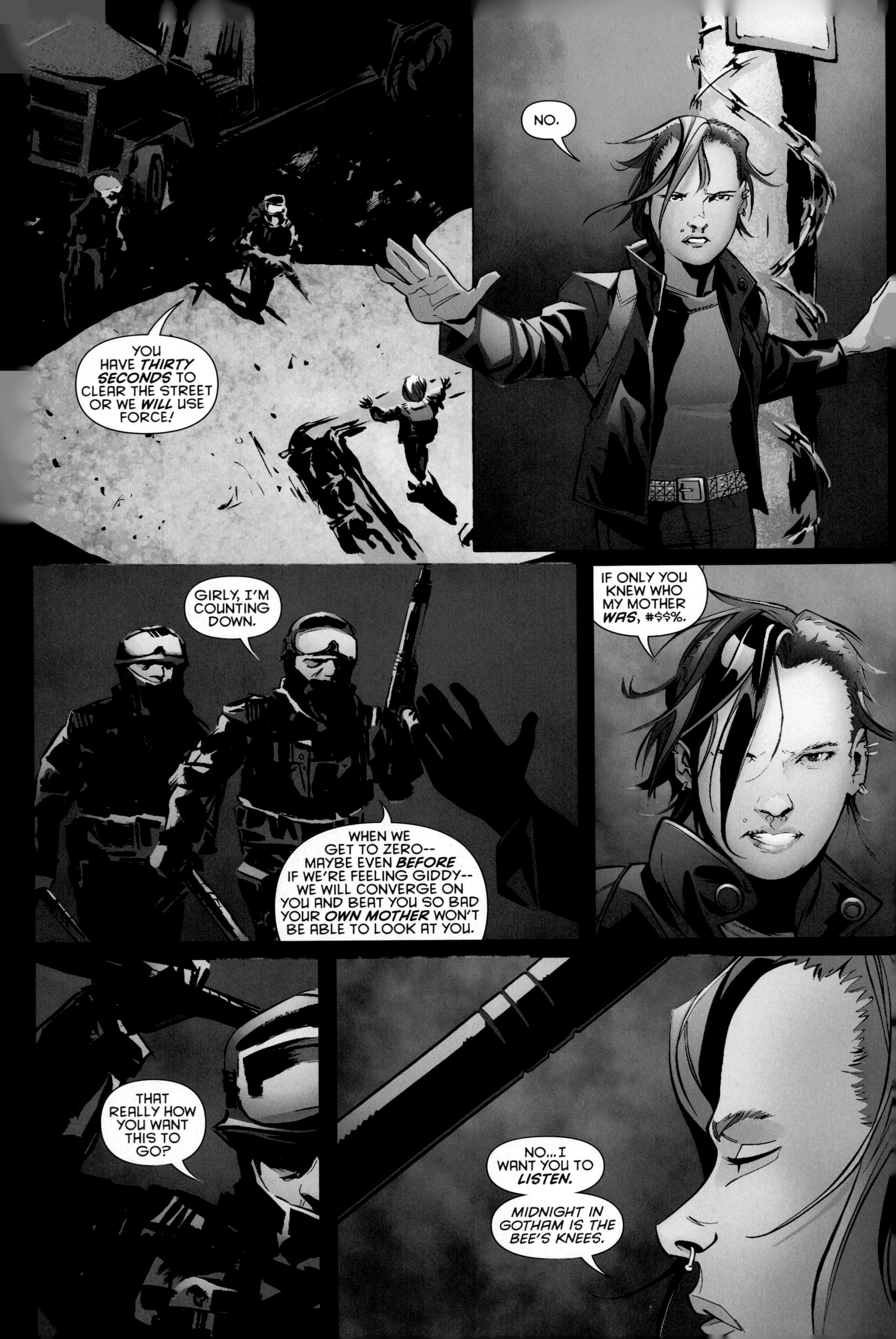
NO.
YOU HAVE THIRTY SECONDS TO CLEAR THE STREET OR WE WILL USE FORCE!
GIRLY, I'M COUNTING DOWN.
WHEN WE GET TO ZERO-- MAYBE EVEN BEFORE IF WE'RE FEELING GIDDY-- WE WILL CONVERGE ON YOU AND BEAT YOU SO BAD YOUR OWN MOTHER WON'T BE ABLE TO LOOK AT YOU.
IF ONLY YOU KNEW WHO MY MOTHER WAS, #$$%.
THAT REALLY HOW YOU WANT THIS TO GO?
NO... I WANT YOU TO LISTEN.
MIDNIGHT IN GOTHAM IS THE BEE'S KNEES.

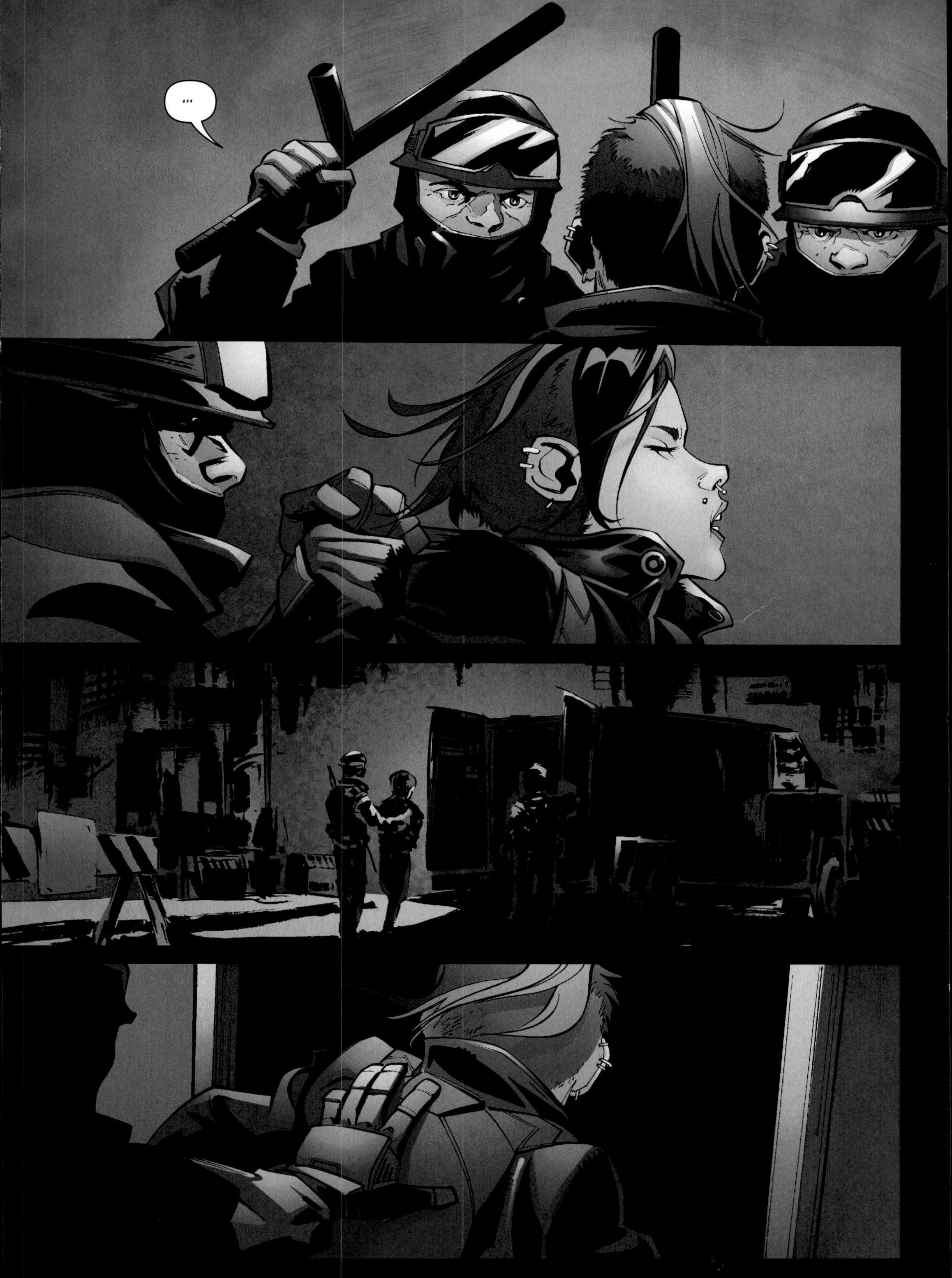
...

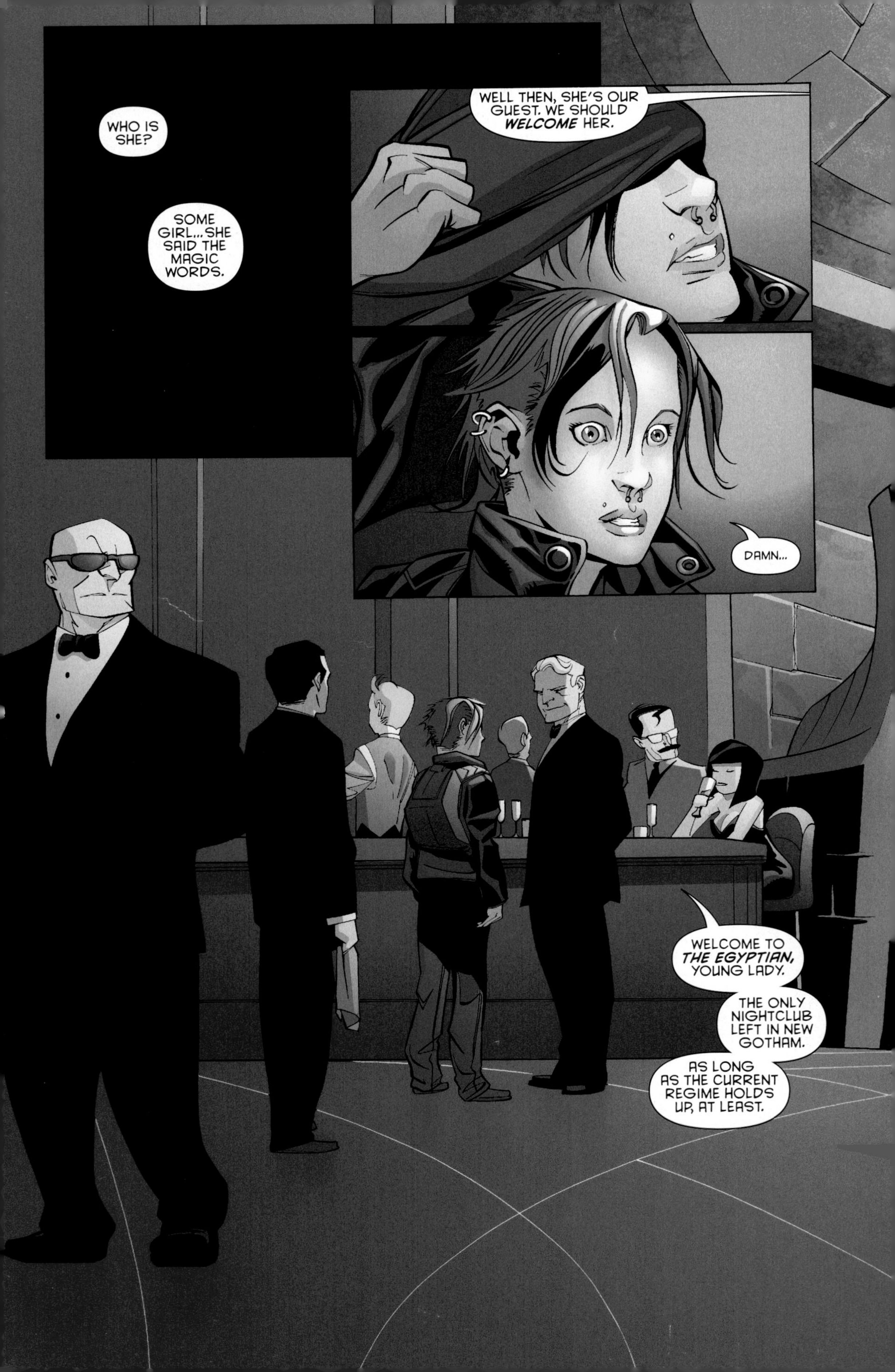
WHO IS SHE?
SOME GIRL... SHE SAID THE MAGIC WORDS.
WELL THEN, SHE'S OUR GUEST. WE SHOULD *WELCOME* HER.
DAMN...
WELCOME TO *THE EGYPTIAN,* YOUNG LADY.
THE ONLY NIGHTCLUB LEFT IN NEW GOTHAM.
AS LONG AS THE CURRENT REGIME HOLDS UP, AT LEAST.

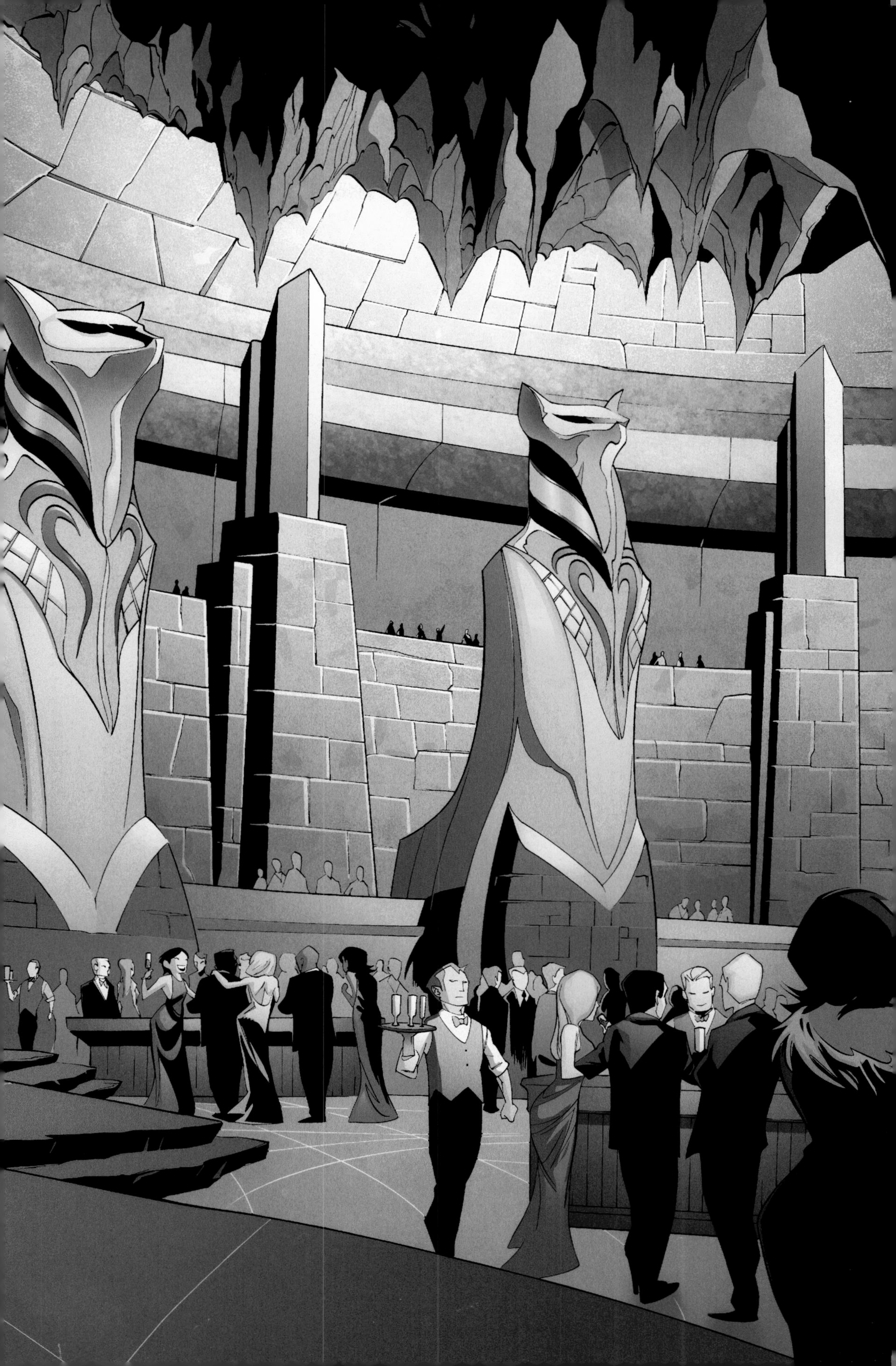

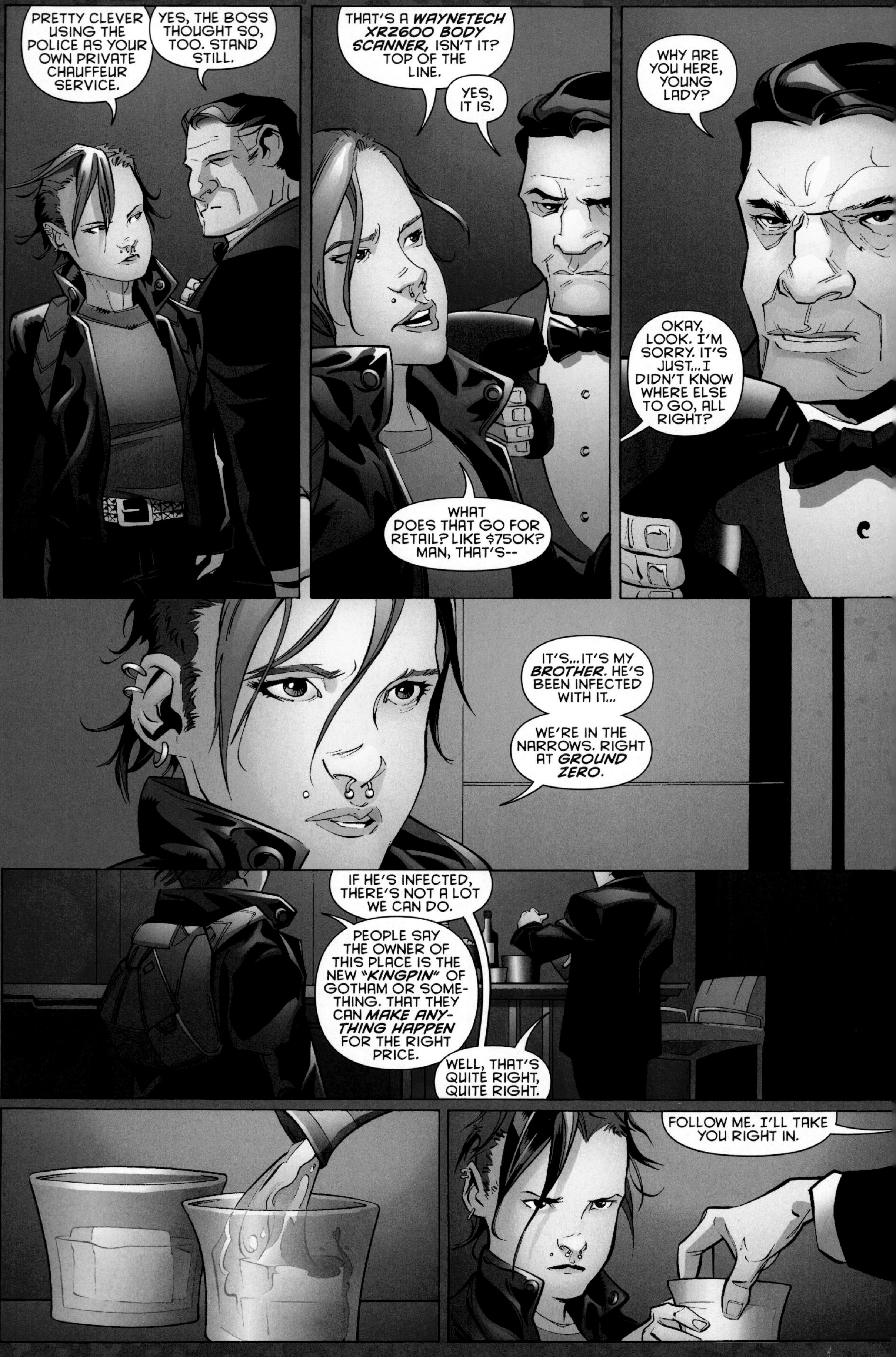
PRETTY CLEVER USING THE POLICE AS YOUR OWN PRIVATE CHAUFFEUR SERVICE.
YES, THE BOSS THOUGHT SO, TOO. STAND STILL.
THAT'S A WAYNETECH XR2600 BODY SCANNER, ISN'T IT? TOP OF THE LINE.
YES, IT IS.
WHAT DOES THAT GO FOR RETAIL? LIKE $750K? MAN, THAT'S--
WHY ARE YOU HERE, YOUNG LADY?
OKAY, LOOK. I'M SORRY. IT'S JUST... I DIDN'T KNOW WHERE ELSE TO GO, ALL RIGHT?
IT'S... IT'S MY BROTHER. HE'S BEEN INFECTED WITH IT...
WE'RE IN THE NARROWS. RIGHT AT GROUND ZERO.
IF HE'S INFECTED, THERE'S NOT A LOT WE CAN DO.
PEOPLE SAY THE OWNER OF THIS PLACE IS THE NEW "KINGPIN" OF GOTHAM OR SOMETHING. THAT THEY CAN MAKE ANYTHING HAPPEN FOR THE RIGHT PRICE.
WELL, THAT'S QUITE RIGHT, QUITE RIGHT.
FOLLOW ME. I'LL TAKE YOU RIGHT IN.

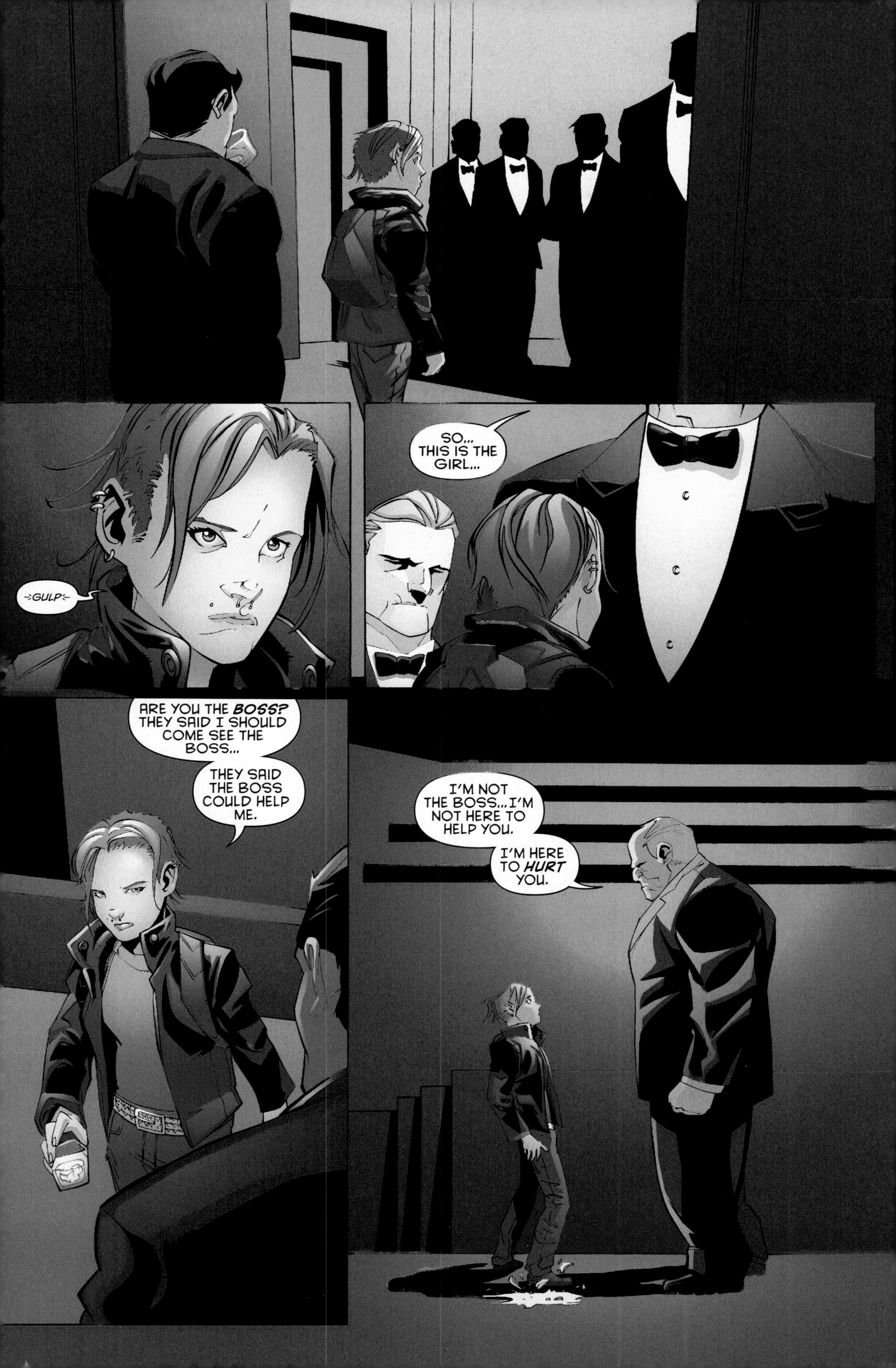
=GULP=
SO... THIS IS THE GIRL...
ARE YOU THE BOSS? THEY SAID I SHOULD COME SEE THE BOSS...
THEY SAID THE BOSS COULD HELP ME.
I'M NOT THE BOSS...I'M NOT HERE TO HELP YOU.
I'M HERE TO HURT YOU.

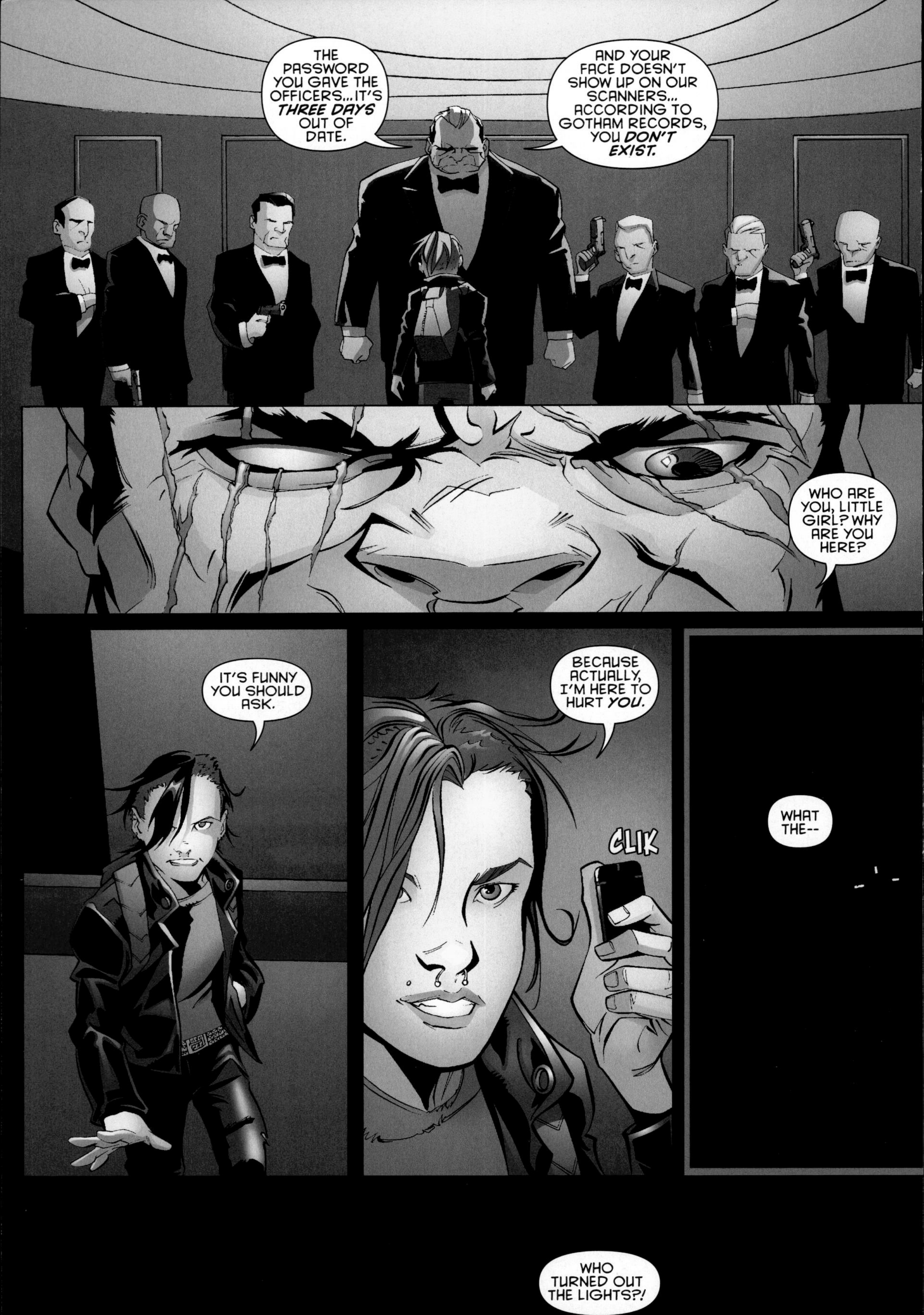
THE PASSWORD YOU GAVE THE OFFICERS...IT'S *THREE DAYS* OUT OF DATE.
AND YOUR FACE DOESN'T SHOW UP ON OUR SCANNERS... ACCORDING TO GOTHAM RECORDS, YOU *DON'T EXIST.*
WHO ARE YOU, LITTLE GIRL? WHY ARE YOU HERE?
IT'S FUNNY YOU SHOULD ASK.
BECAUSE ACTUALLY, I'M HERE TO HURT *YOU*.
CLIK
WHAT THE--
WHO TURNED OUT THE LIGHTS?!

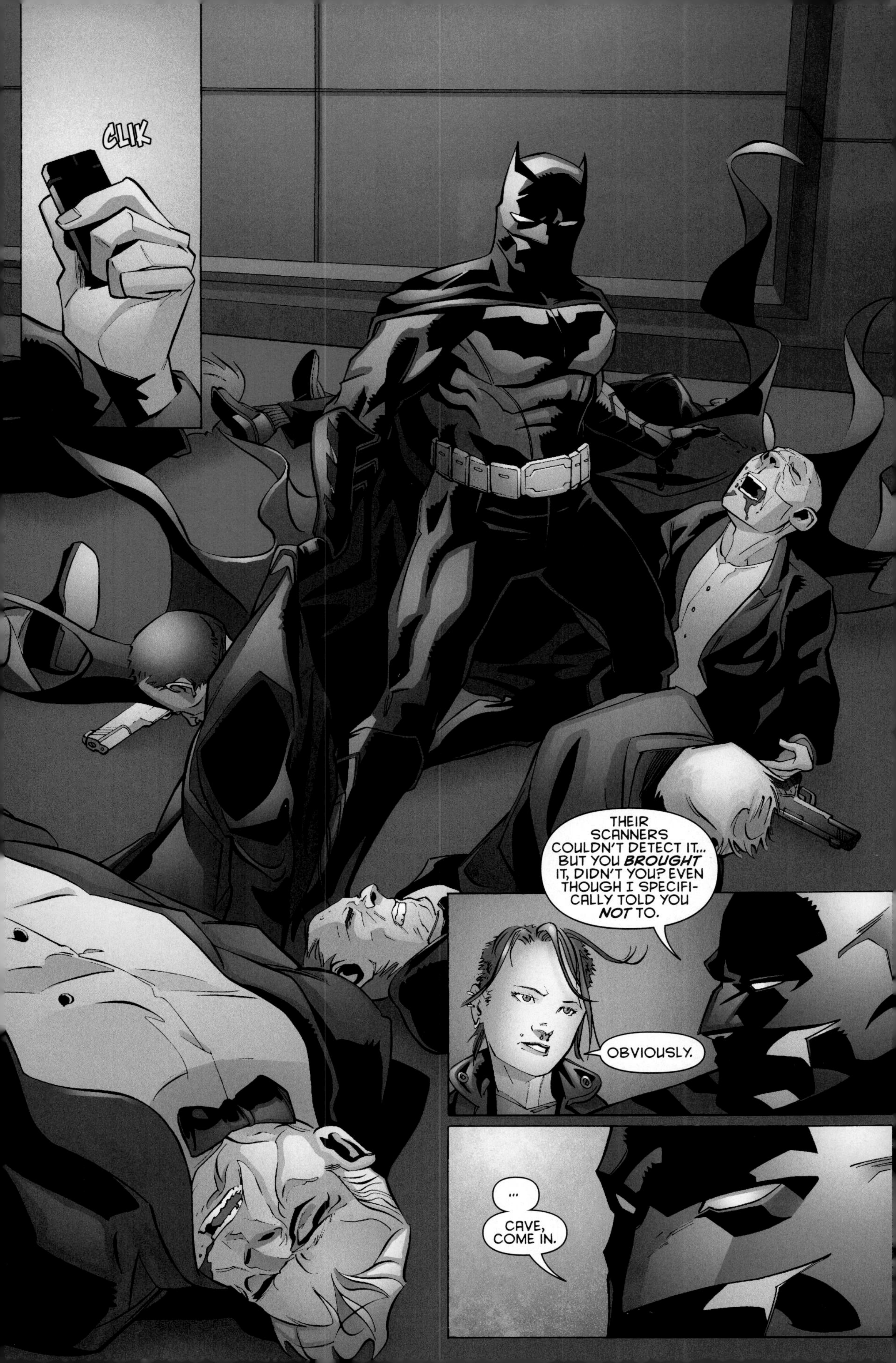
CLIK
THEIR SCANNERS COULDN'T DETECT IT... BUT YOU BROUGHT IT, DIDN'T YOU? EVEN THOUGH I SPECIFI-CALLY TOLD YOU NOT TO.
OBVIOUSLY.
...
CAVE, COME IN.

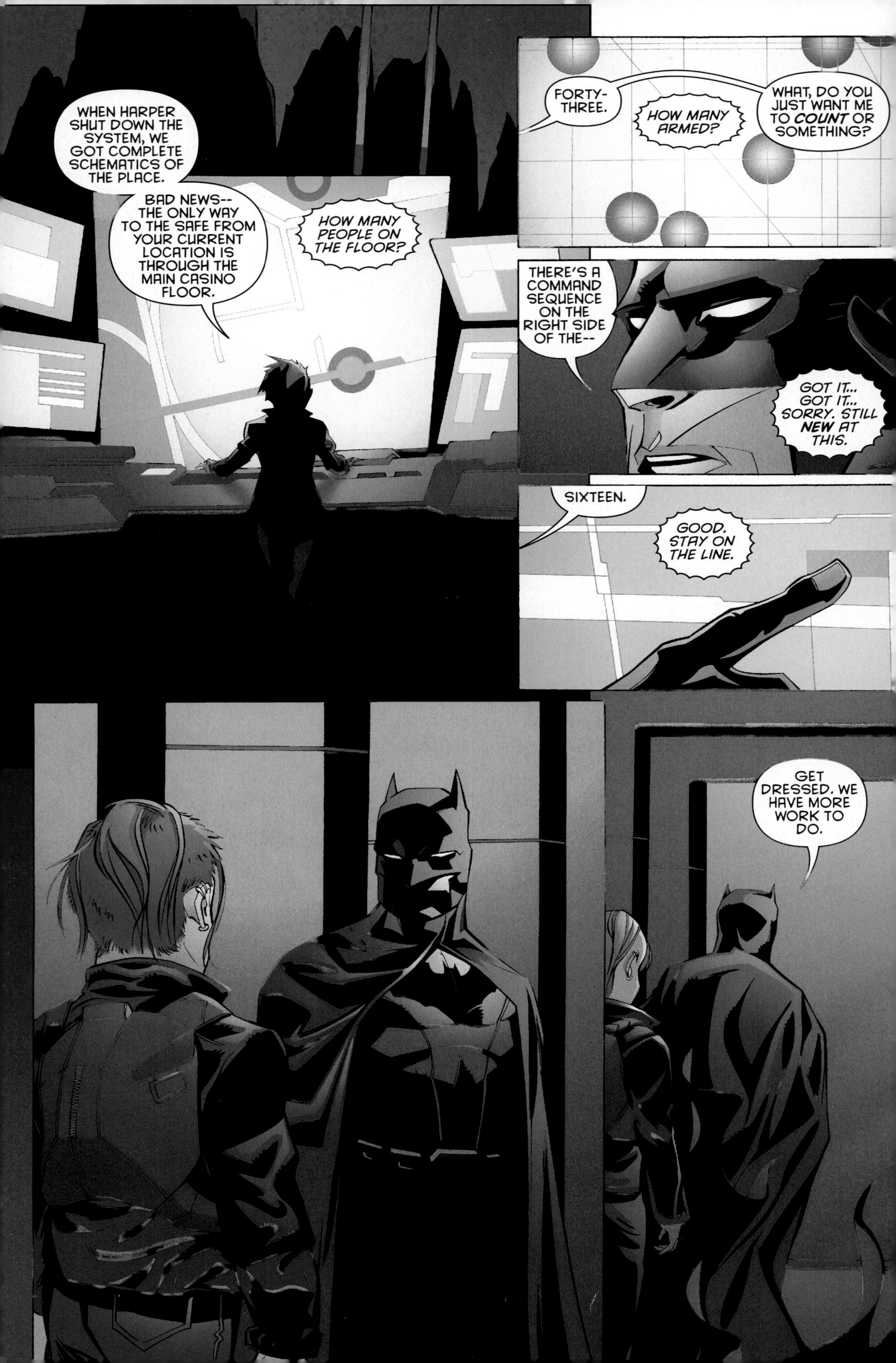
WHEN HARPER SHUT DOWN THE SYSTEM, WE GOT COMPLETE SCHEMATICS OF THE PLACE.
BAD NEWS-- THE ONLY WAY TO THE SAFE FROM YOUR CURRENT LOCATION IS THROUGH THE MAIN CASINO FLOOR.
HOW MANY PEOPLE ON THE FLOOR?
FORTY-THREE.
HOW MANY ARMED?
WHAT, DO YOU JUST WANT ME TO COUNT OR SOMETHING?
THERE'S A COMMAND SEQUENCE ON THE RIGHT SIDE OF THE--
GOT IT... GOT IT... SORRY. STILL NEW AT THIS.
SIXTEEN.
GOOD. STAY ON THE LINE.
GET DRESSED. WE HAVE MORE WORK TO DO.

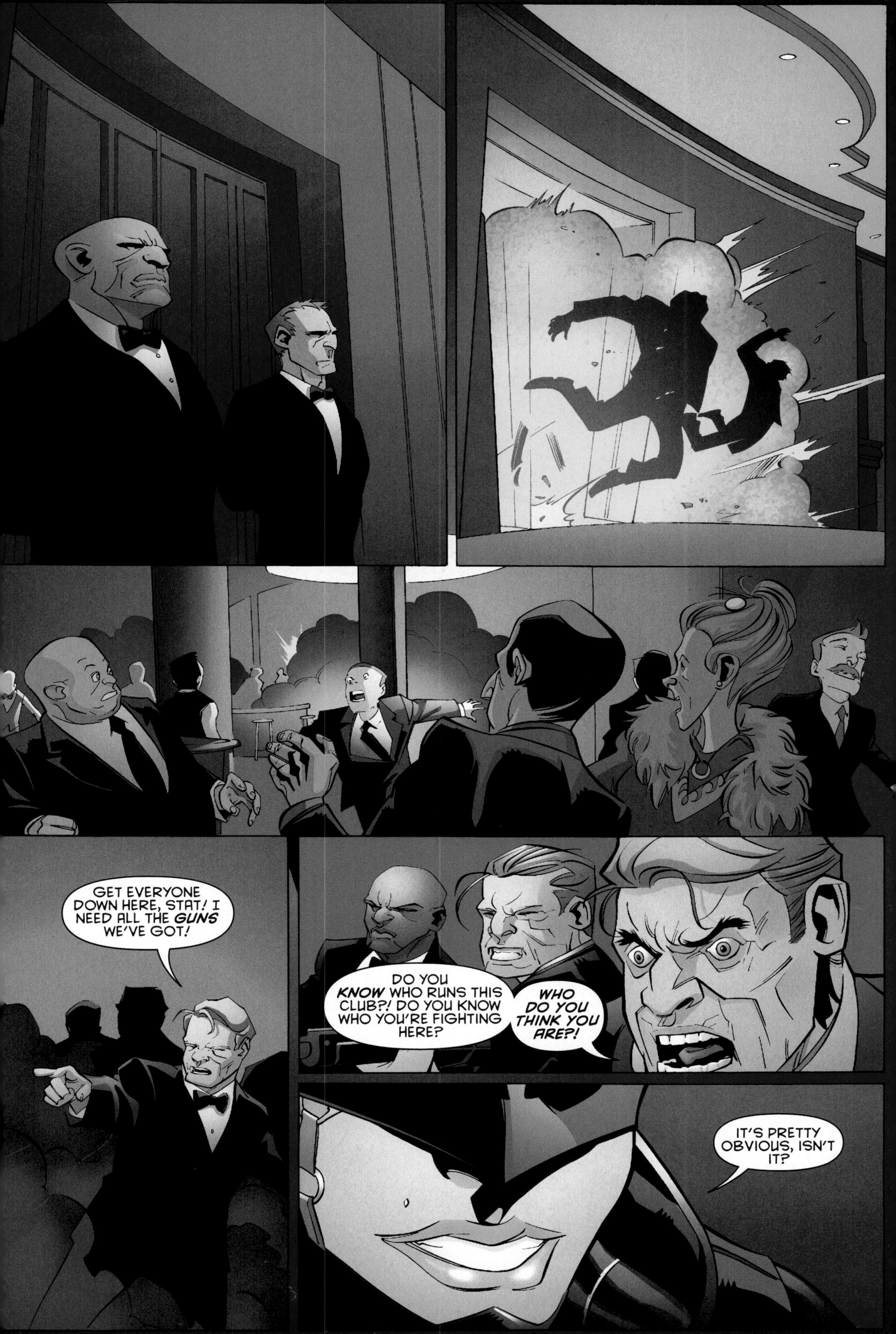
GET EVERYONE DOWN HERE, STAT! I NEED ALL THE GUNS WE'VE GOT!
DO YOU KNOW WHO RUNS THIS CLUB?! DO YOU KNOW WHO YOU'RE FIGHTING HERE?
WHO DO YOU THINK YOU ARE?!
IT'S PRETTY OBVIOUS, ISN'T IT?

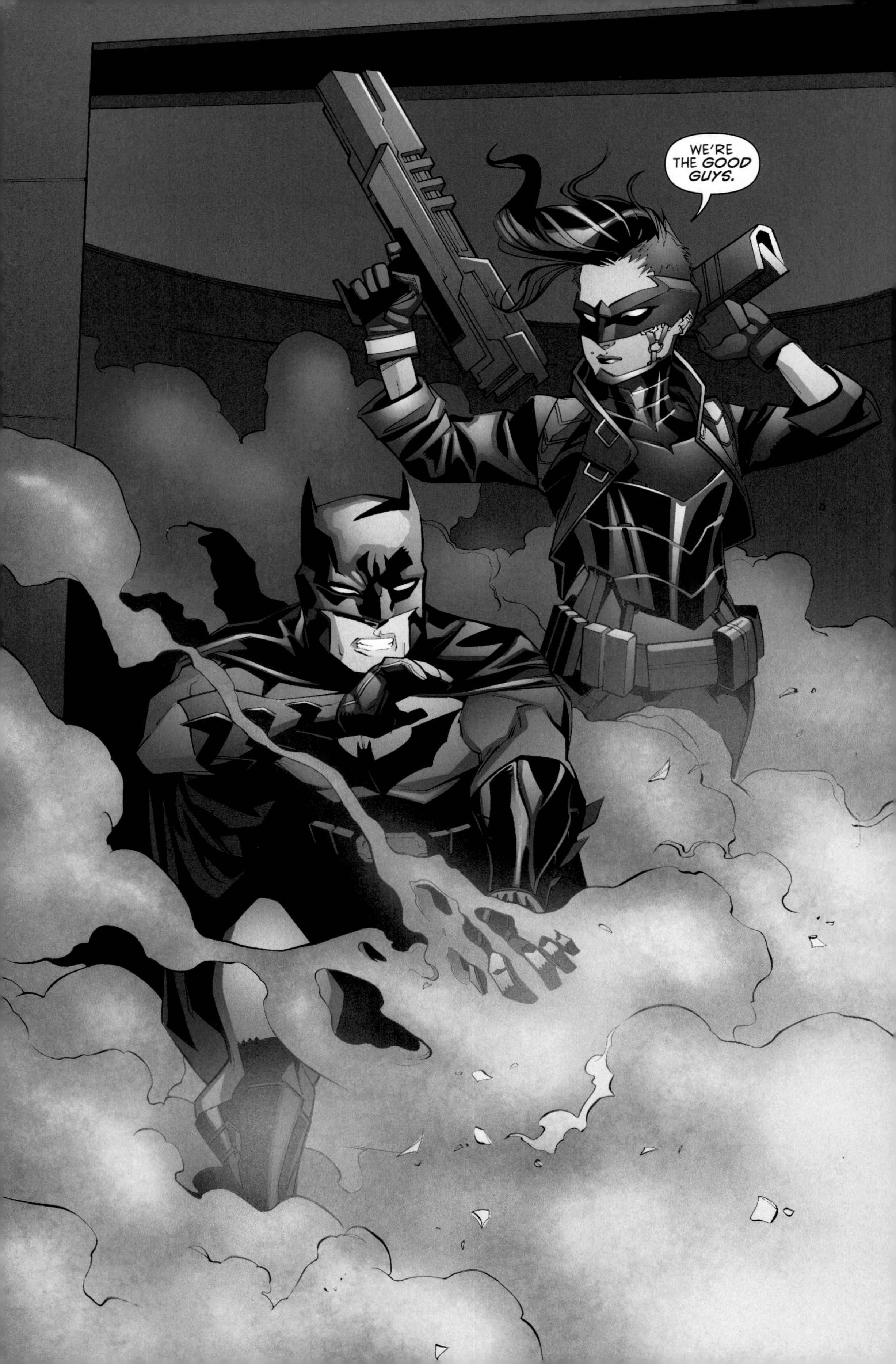
WE'RE THE GOOD GUYS.

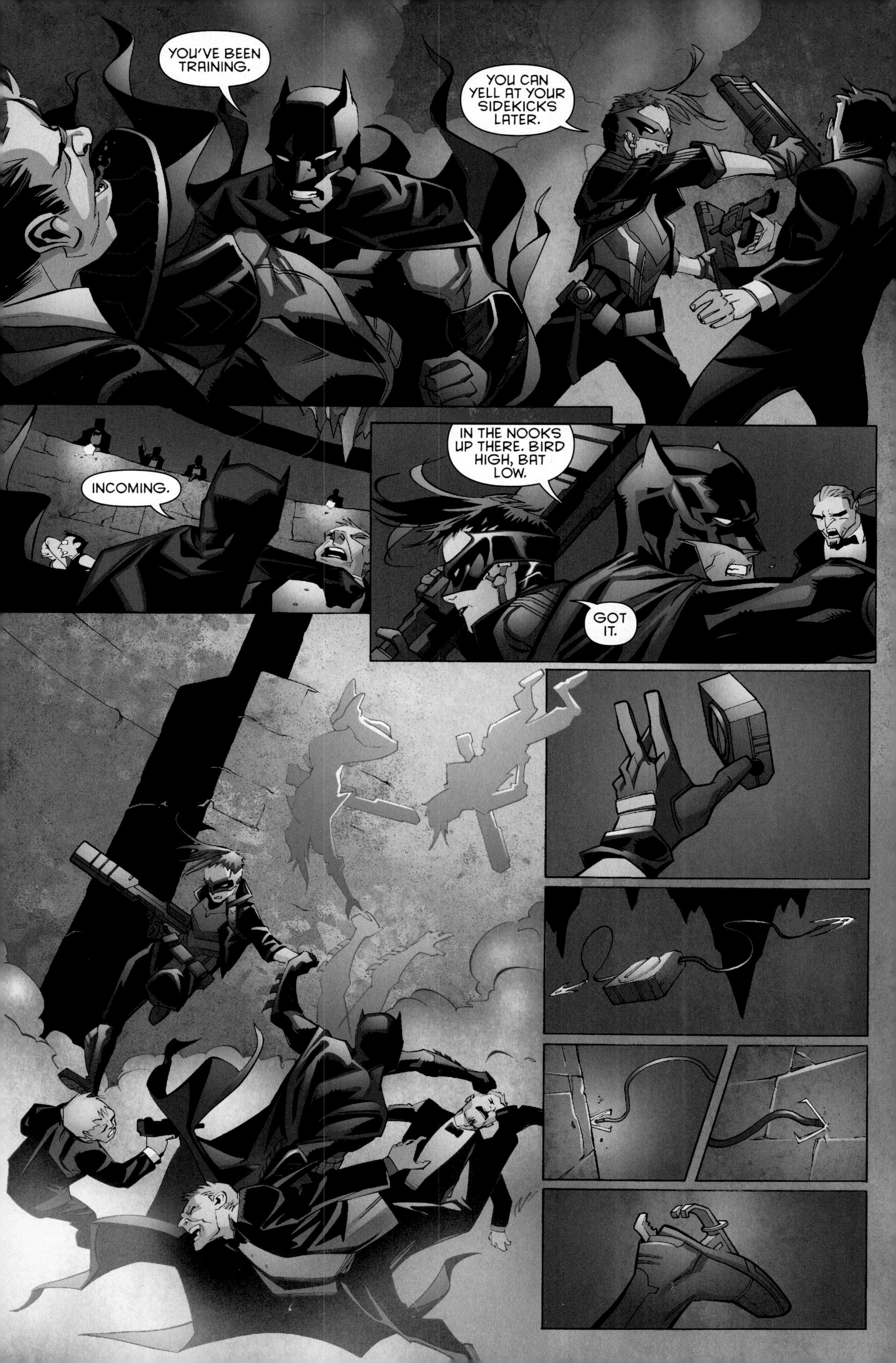
YOU'VE BEEN TRAINING.
YOU CAN YELL AT YOUR SIDEKICKS LATER.
INCOMING.
IN THE NOOKS UP THERE. BIRD HIGH, BAT LOW.
GOT IT.

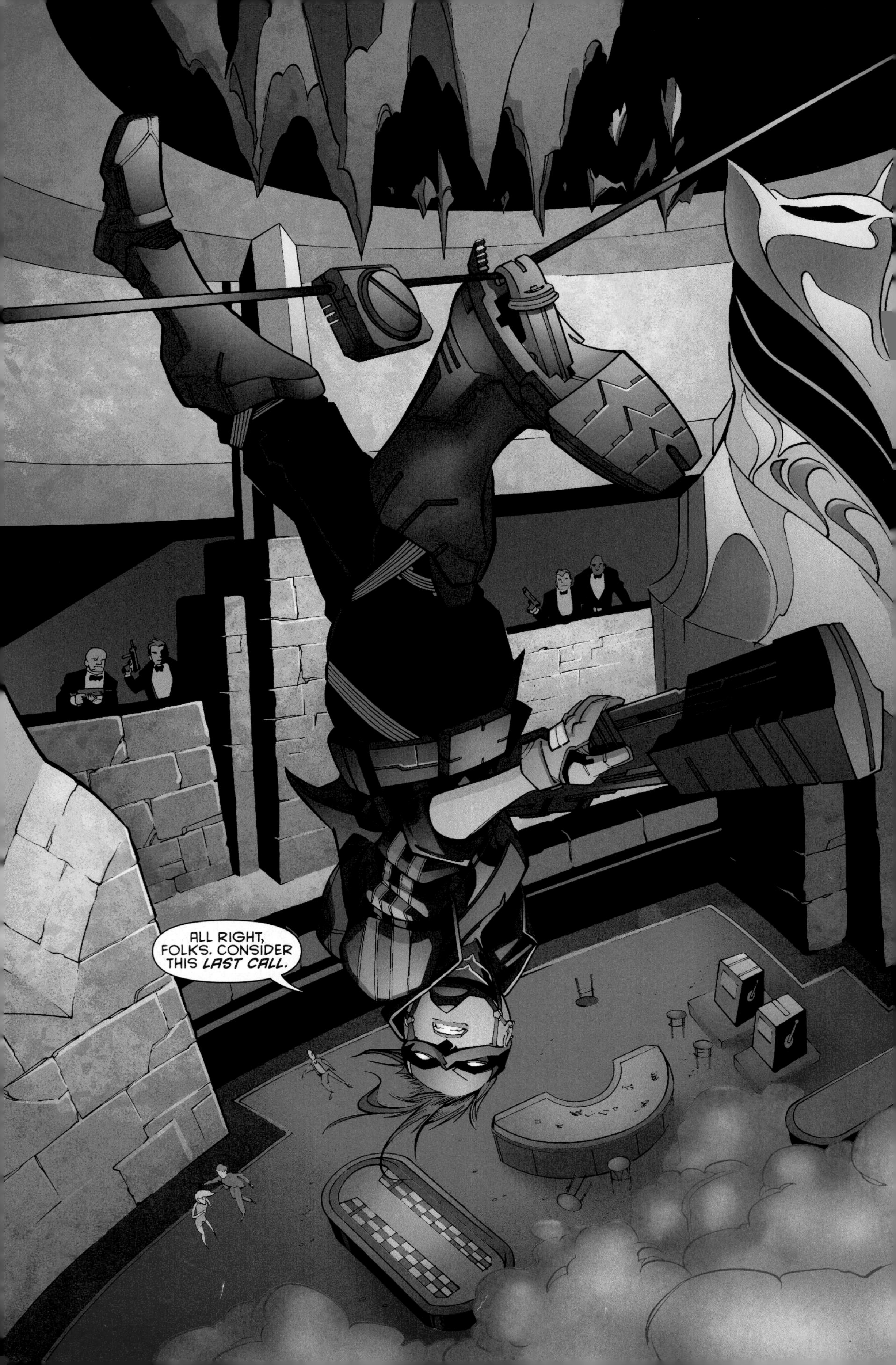
ALL RIGHT, FOLKS. CONSIDER THIS LAST CALL.

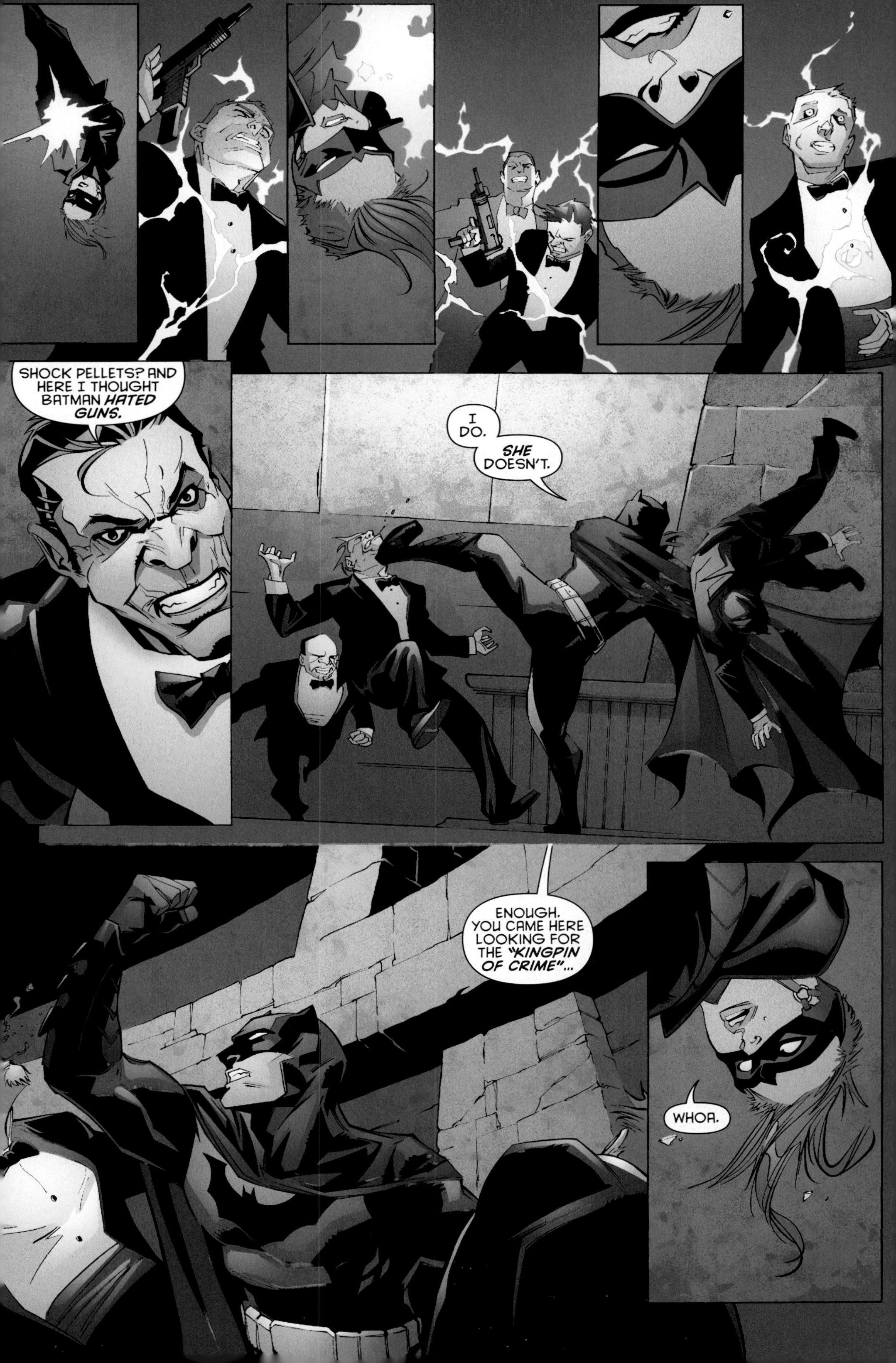
SHOCK PELLETS? AND HERE I THOUGHT BATMAN *HATED GUNS.*
I DO. *SHE* DOESN'T.
ENOUGH. YOU CAME HERE LOOKING FOR THE *"KINGPIN OF CRIME"*...
WHOA.

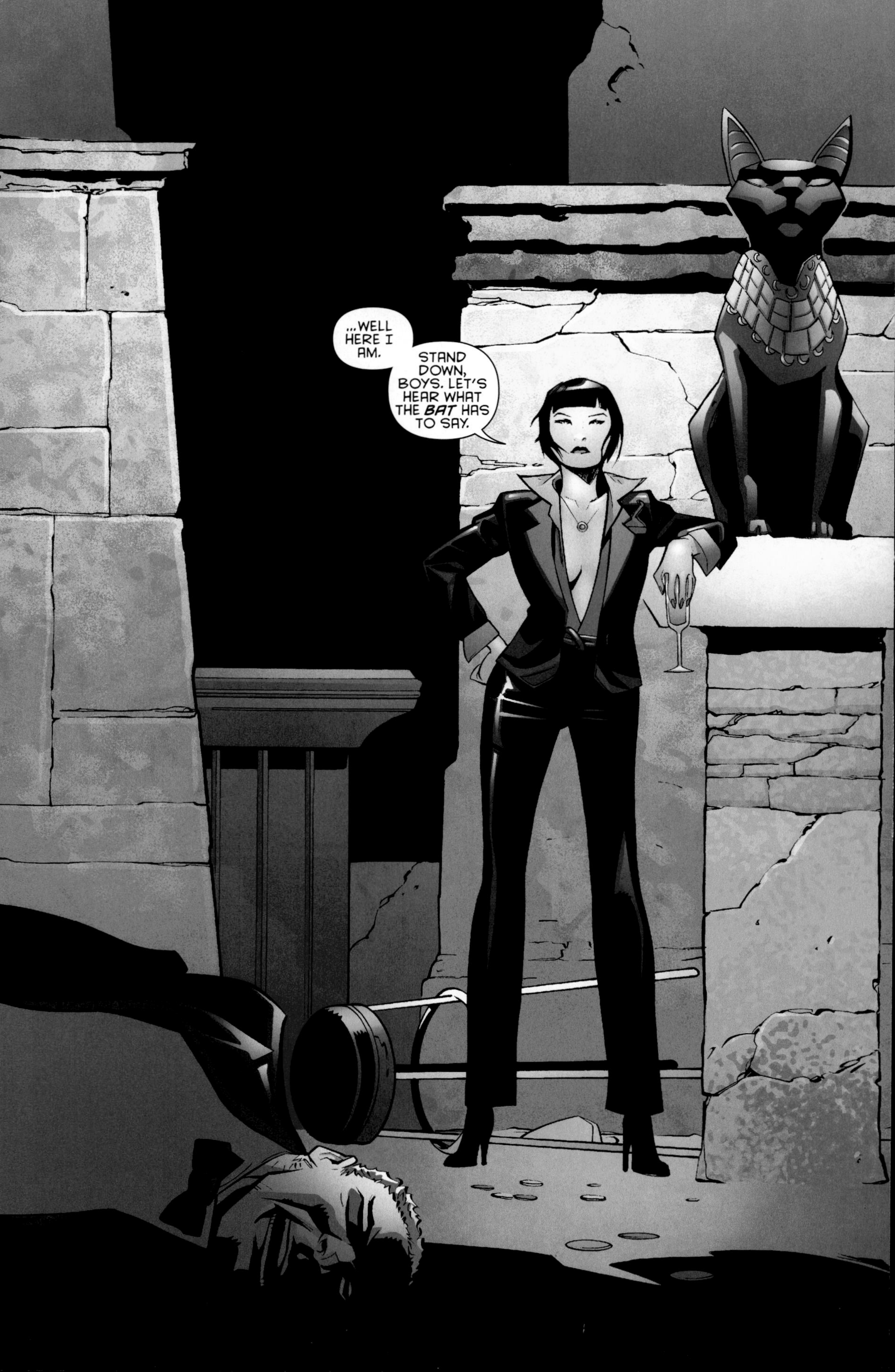
...WELL HERE I AM.
STAND DOWN, BOYS. LET'S HEAR WHAT THE BAT HAS TO SAY.

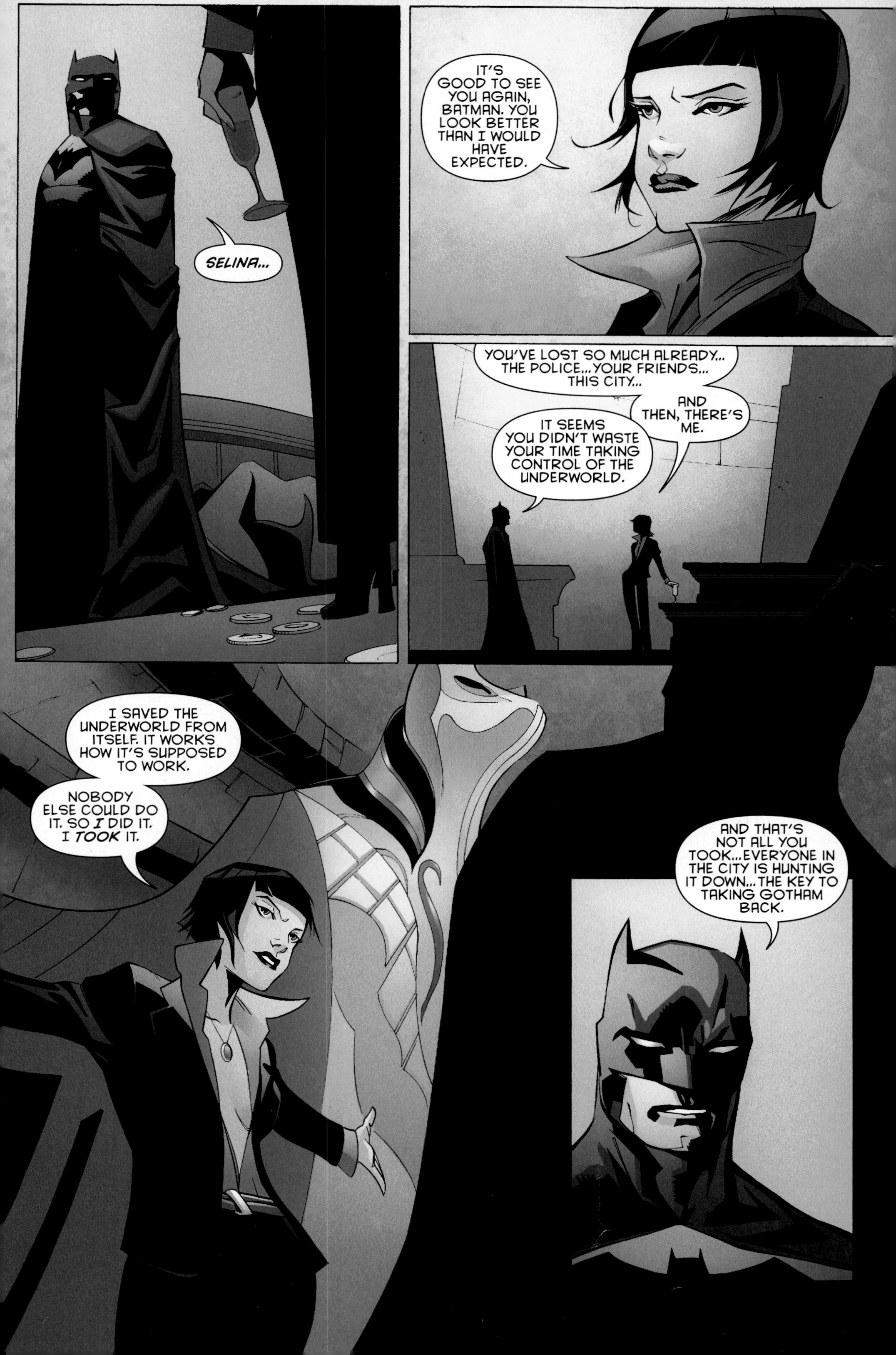
SELINA...
IT'S GOOD TO SEE YOU AGAIN, BATMAN. YOU LOOK BETTER THAN I WOULD HAVE EXPECTED.
YOU'VE LOST SO MUCH ALREADY... THE POLICE...YOUR FRIENDS... THIS CITY...
AND THEN, THERE'S ME.
IT SEEMS YOU DIDN'T WASTE YOUR TIME TAKING CONTROL OF THE UNDERWORLD.
I SAVED THE UNDERWORLD FROM ITSELF. IT WORKS HOW IT'S SUPPOSED TO WORK.
NOBODY ELSE COULD DO IT. SO *I* DID IT. I *TOOK* IT.
AND THAT'S NOT ALL YOU TOOK...EVERYONE IN THE CITY IS HUNTING IT DOWN...THE KEY TO TAKING GOTHAM BACK.

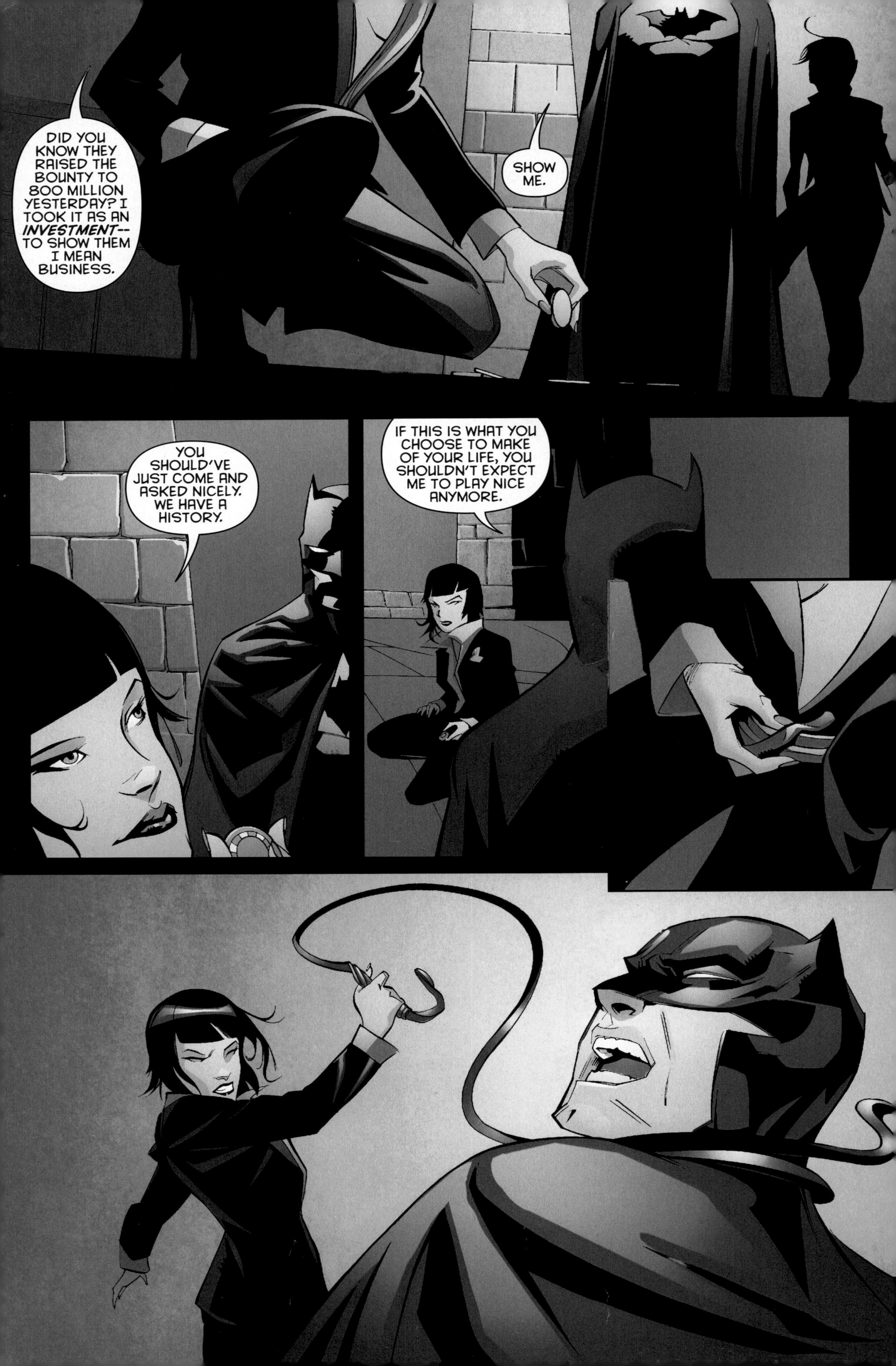
DID YOU KNOW THEY RAISED THE BOUNTY TO 800 MILLION YESTERDAY? I TOOK IT AS AN *INVESTMENT*-- TO SHOW THEM I MEAN BUSINESS.
SHOW ME.
YOU SHOULD'VE JUST COME AND ASKED NICELY. WE HAVE A HISTORY.
IF THIS IS WHAT YOU CHOOSE TO MAKE OF YOUR LIFE, YOU SHOULDN'T EXPECT ME TO PLAY NICE ANYMORE.

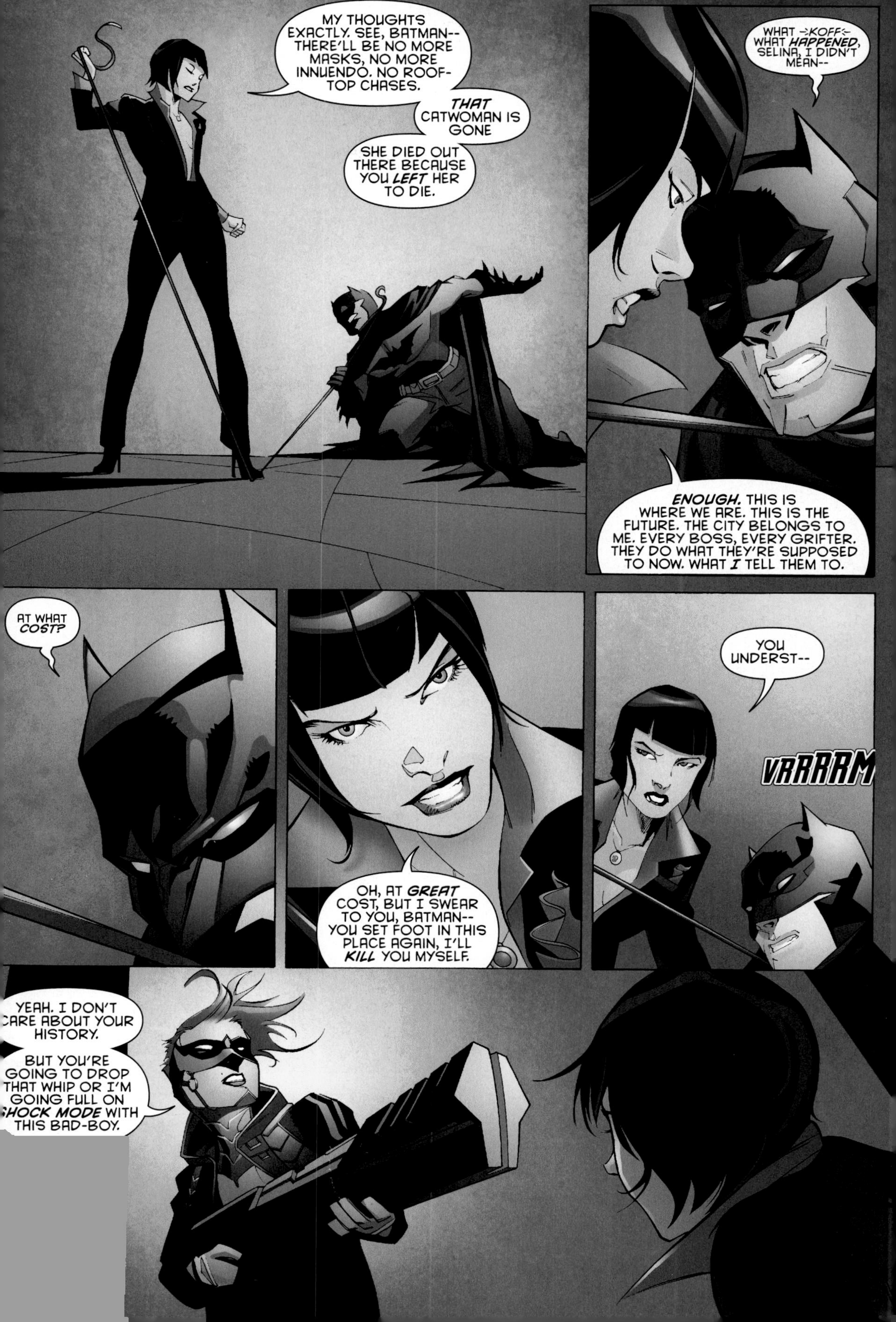
MY THOUGHTS EXACTLY. SEE, BATMAN-- THERE'LL BE NO MORE MASKS, NO MORE INNUENDO. NO ROOF-TOP CHASES.
THAT CATWOMAN IS GONE
SHE DIED OUT THERE BECAUSE YOU LEFT HER TO DIE.
WHAT -KOFF- WHAT HAPPENED, SELINA, I DIDN'T MEAN--
ENOUGH. THIS IS WHERE WE ARE. THIS IS THE FUTURE. THE CITY BELONGS TO ME. EVERY BOSS, EVERY GRIFTER. THEY DO WHAT THEY'RE SUPPOSED TO NOW. WHAT I TELL THEM TO.
AT WHAT COST?
OH, AT GREAT COST, BUT I SWEAR TO YOU, BATMAN-- YOU SET FOOT IN THIS PLACE AGAIN, I'LL KILL YOU MYSELF.
YOU UNDERST--
VRRRRM
YEAH. I DON'T CARE ABOUT YOUR HISTORY.
BUT YOU'RE GOING TO DROP THAT WHIP OR I'M GOING FULL ON SHOCK MODE WITH THIS BAD-BOY.

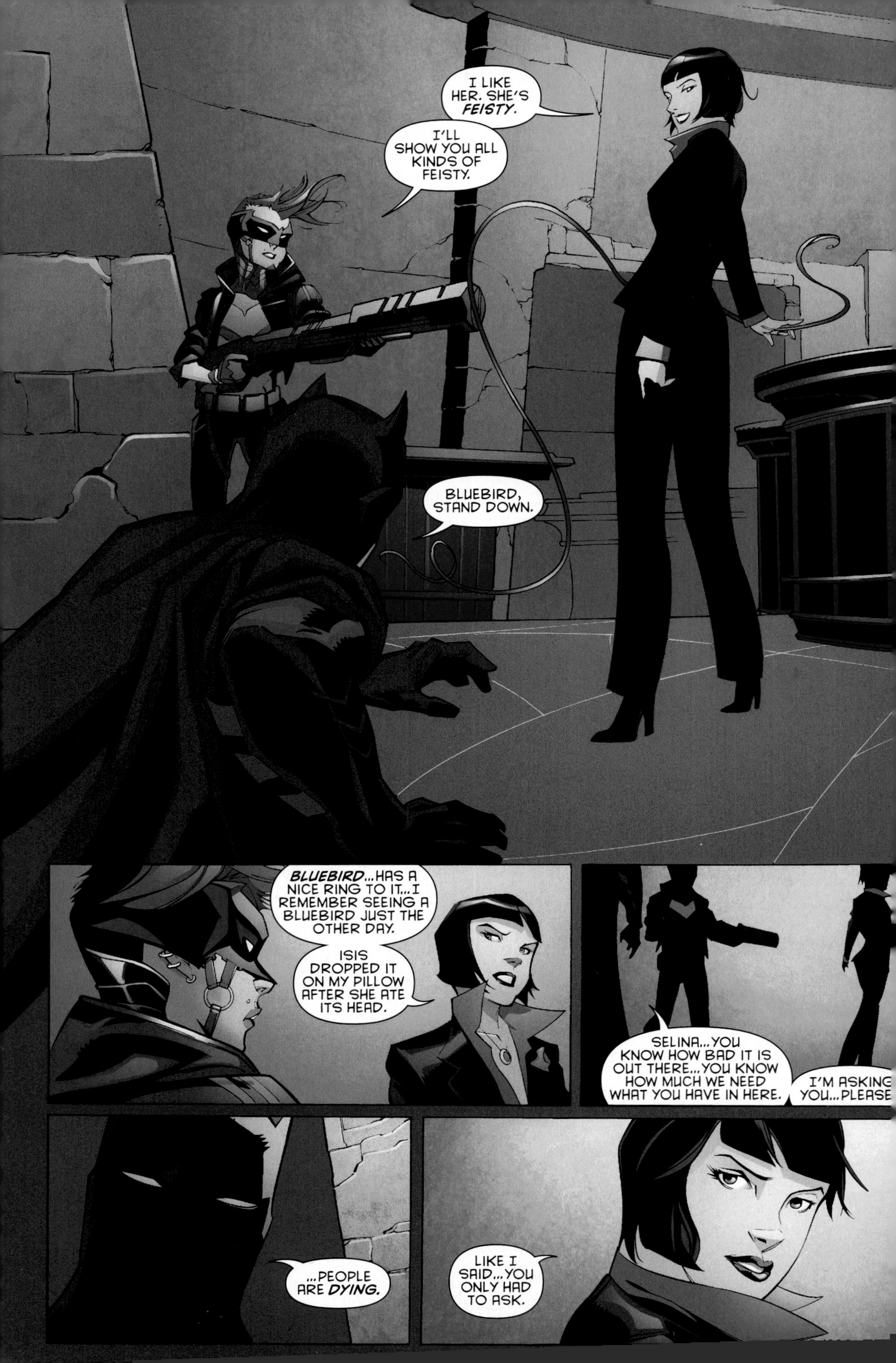
I LIKE HER. SHE'S *FEISTY*.
I'LL SHOW YOU ALL KINDS OF FEISTY.
BLUEBIRD, STAND DOWN.
BLUEBIRD... HAS A NICE RING TO IT... I REMEMBER SEEING A BLUEBIRD JUST THE OTHER DAY.
ISIS DROPPED IT ON MY PILLOW AFTER SHE ATE ITS HEAD.
SELINA... YOU KNOW HOW BAD IT IS OUT THERE... YOU KNOW HOW MUCH WE NEED WHAT YOU HAVE IN HERE.
I'M ASKING YOU... PLEASE
...PEOPLE ARE *DYING*.
LIKE I SAID... YOU ONLY HAD TO ASK.

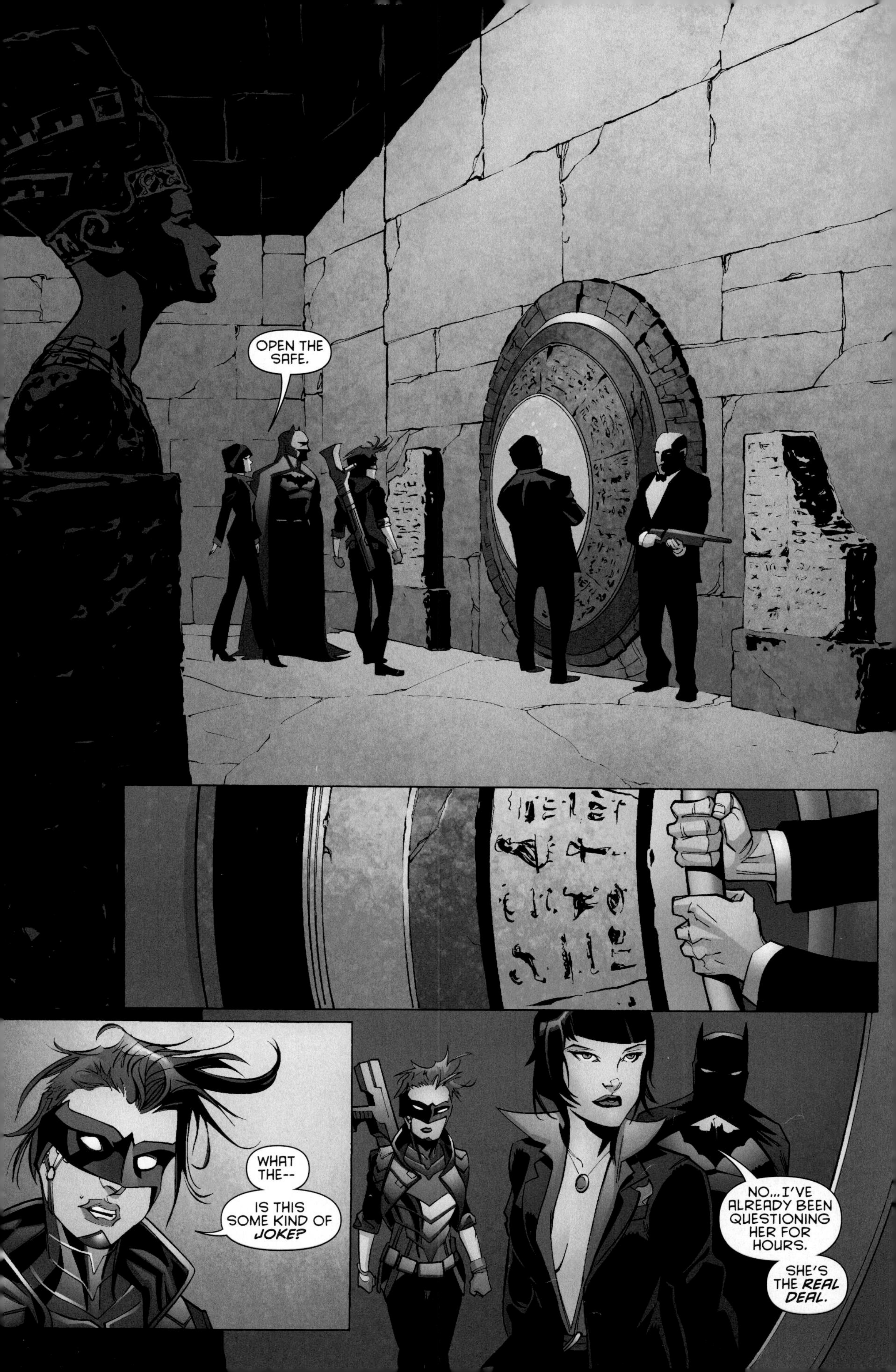
OPEN THE SAFE.
WHAT THE--
IS THIS SOME KIND OF *JOKE?*
NO...I'VE ALREADY BEEN QUESTIONING HER FOR HOURS.
SHE'S THE *REAL DEAL.*

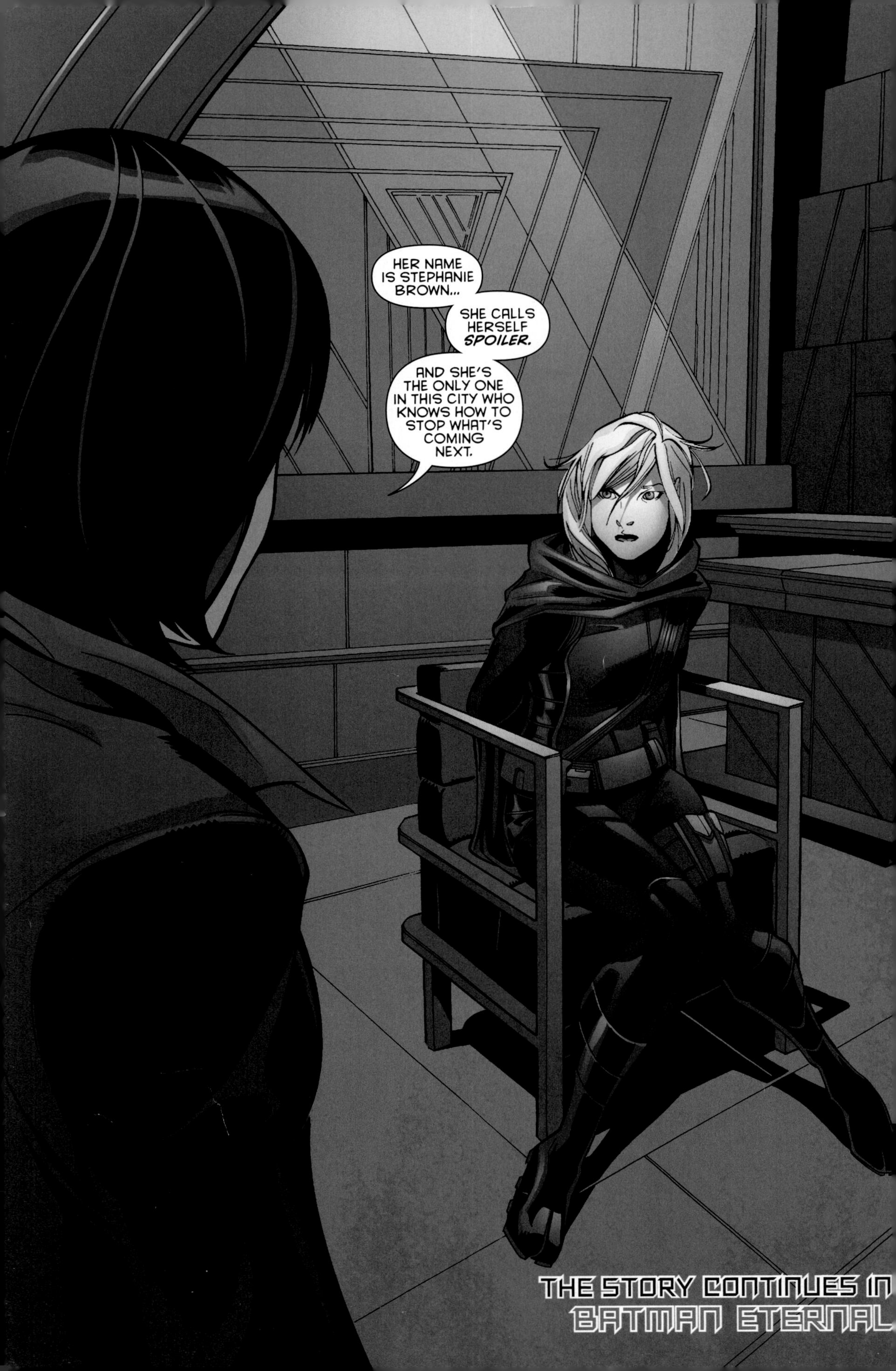
HER NAME IS STEPHANIE BROWN...
SHE CALLS HERSELF *SPOILER.*
AND SHE'S THE ONLY ONE IN THIS CITY WHO KNOWS HOW TO STOP WHAT'S COMING NEXT.
THE STORY CONTINUES IN
BATMAN ETERNAL

BATMAN 18
Variant cover by Andy Kubert & Brad Anderson

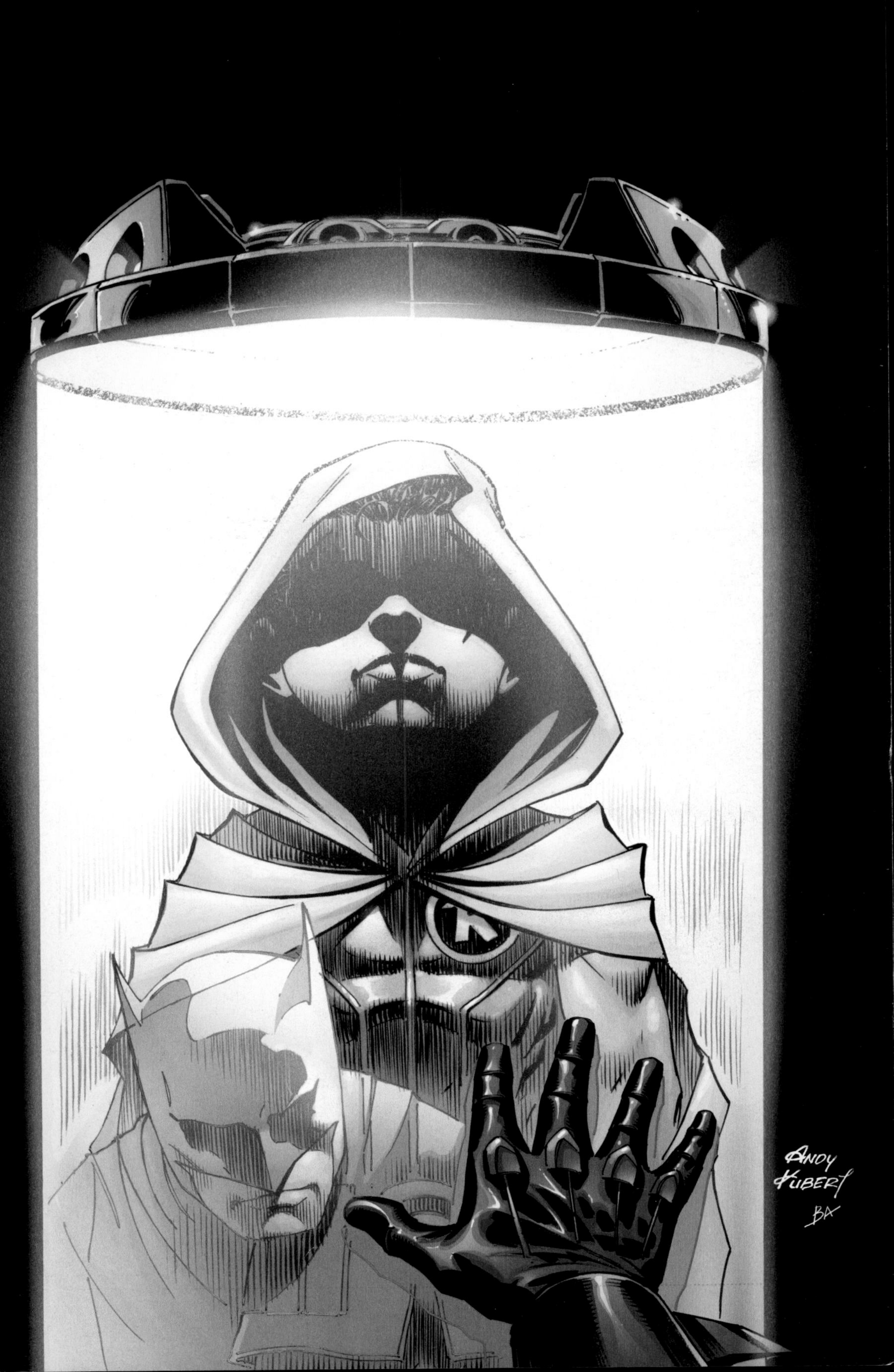
ANDY KUBERT
BA

BATMAN 19
MAD Magazine variant cover by Al Jaffee

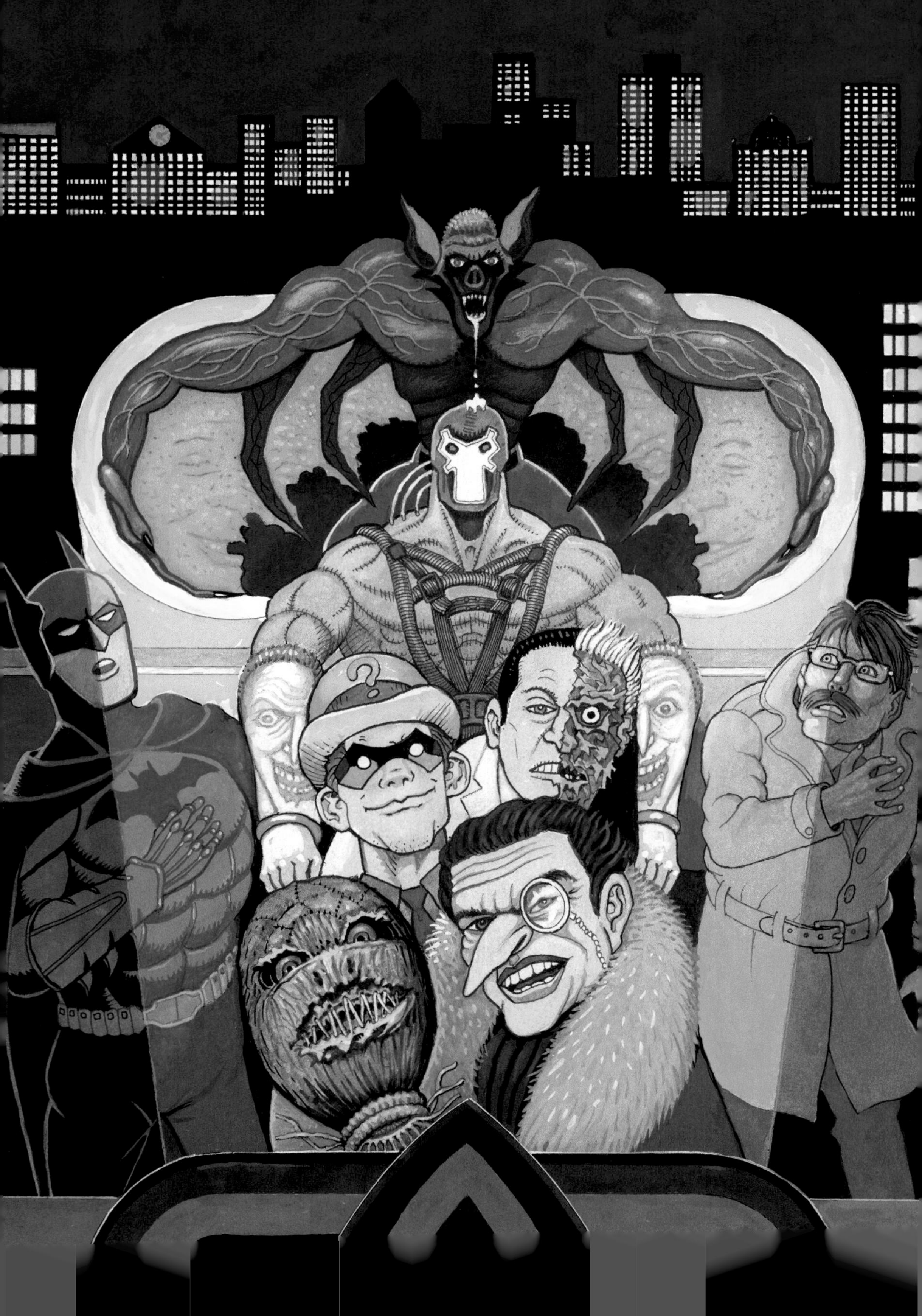

BATMAN 20
Cover by Greg Capullo & FCO Plascencia

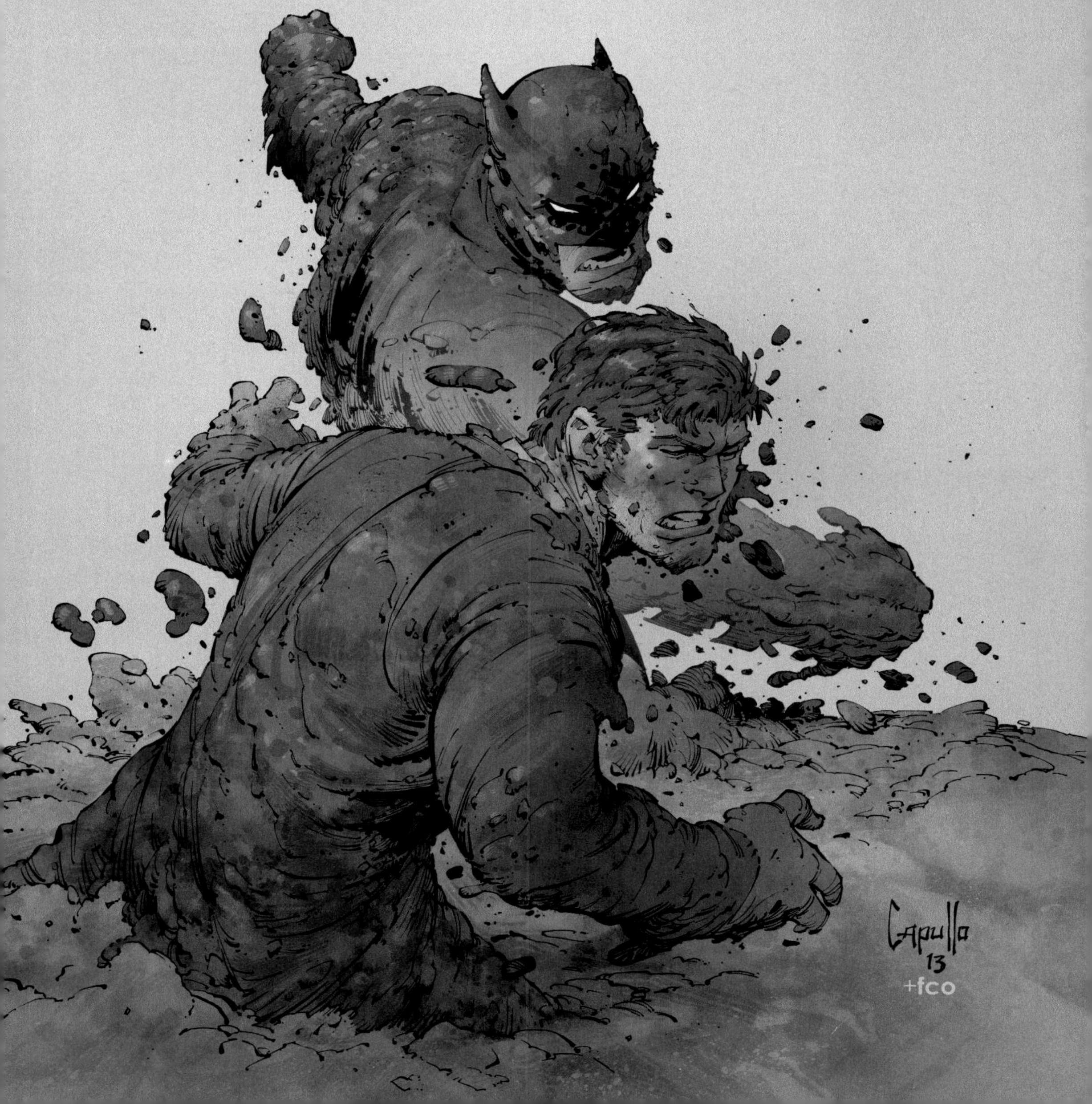
CAPULLO
13
+fco

BATMAN 34
Variant cover by Rafael Albuquerque

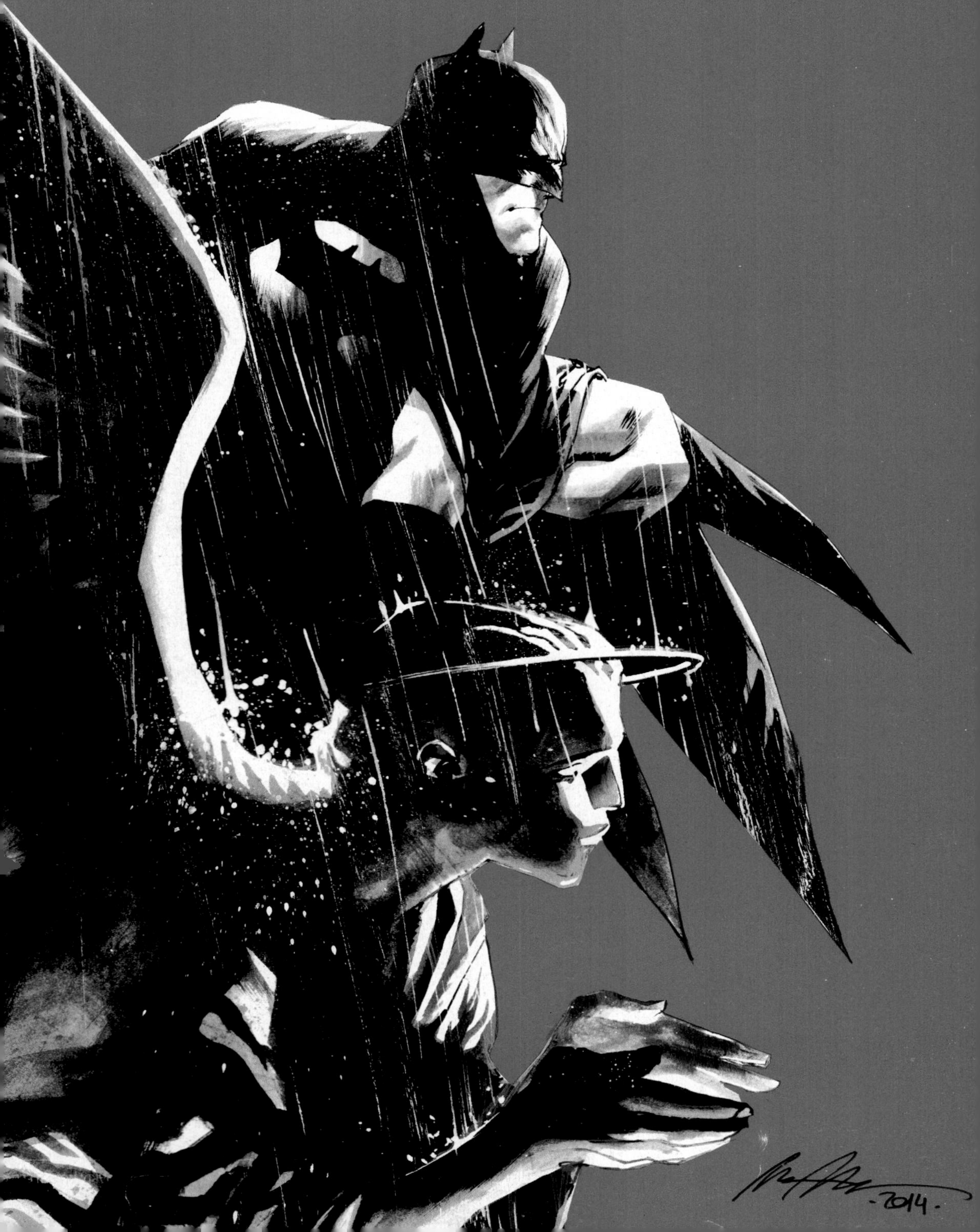
-2014-

BATMAN 34
Selfie variant cover by Ryan Sook

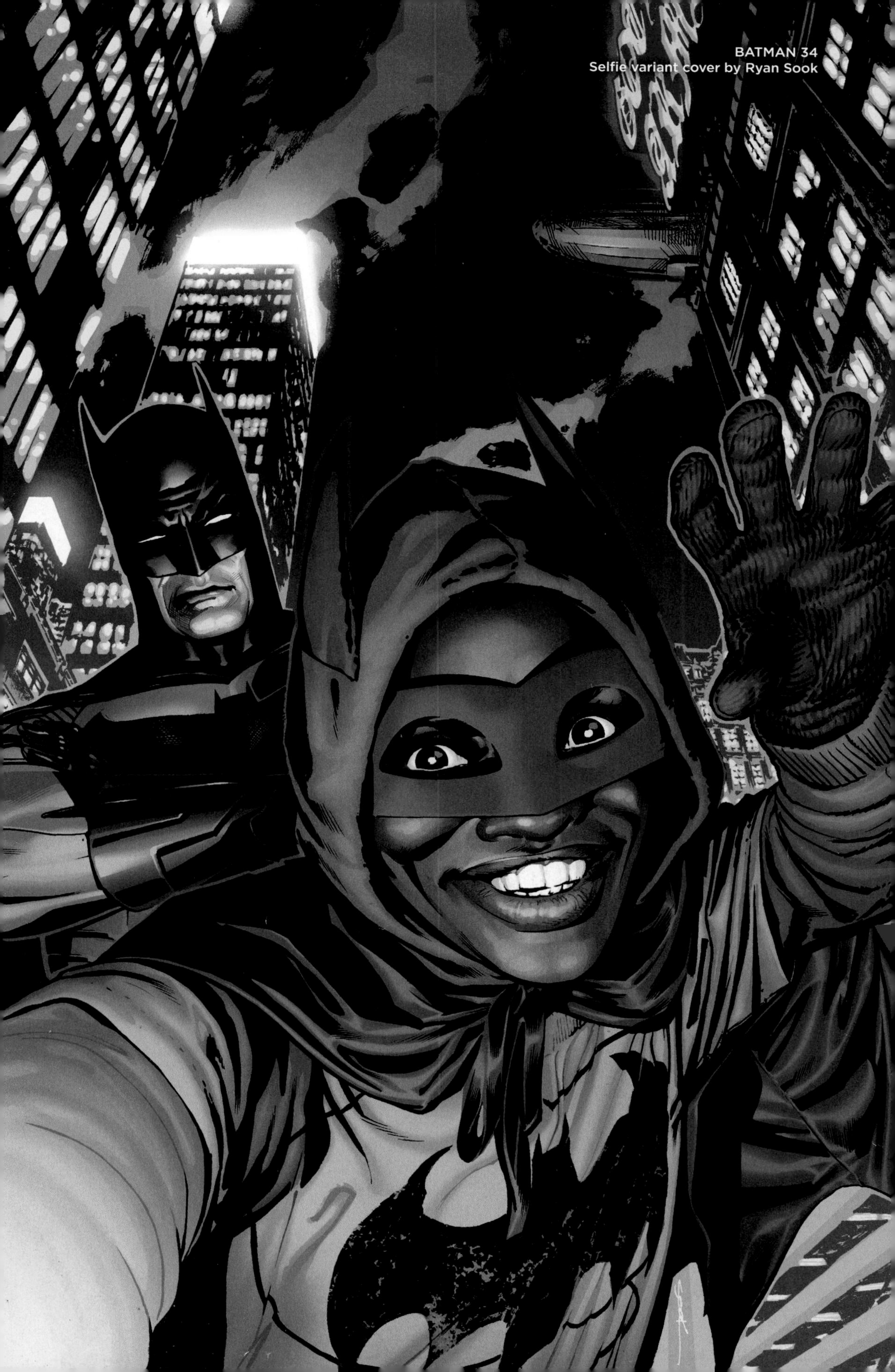

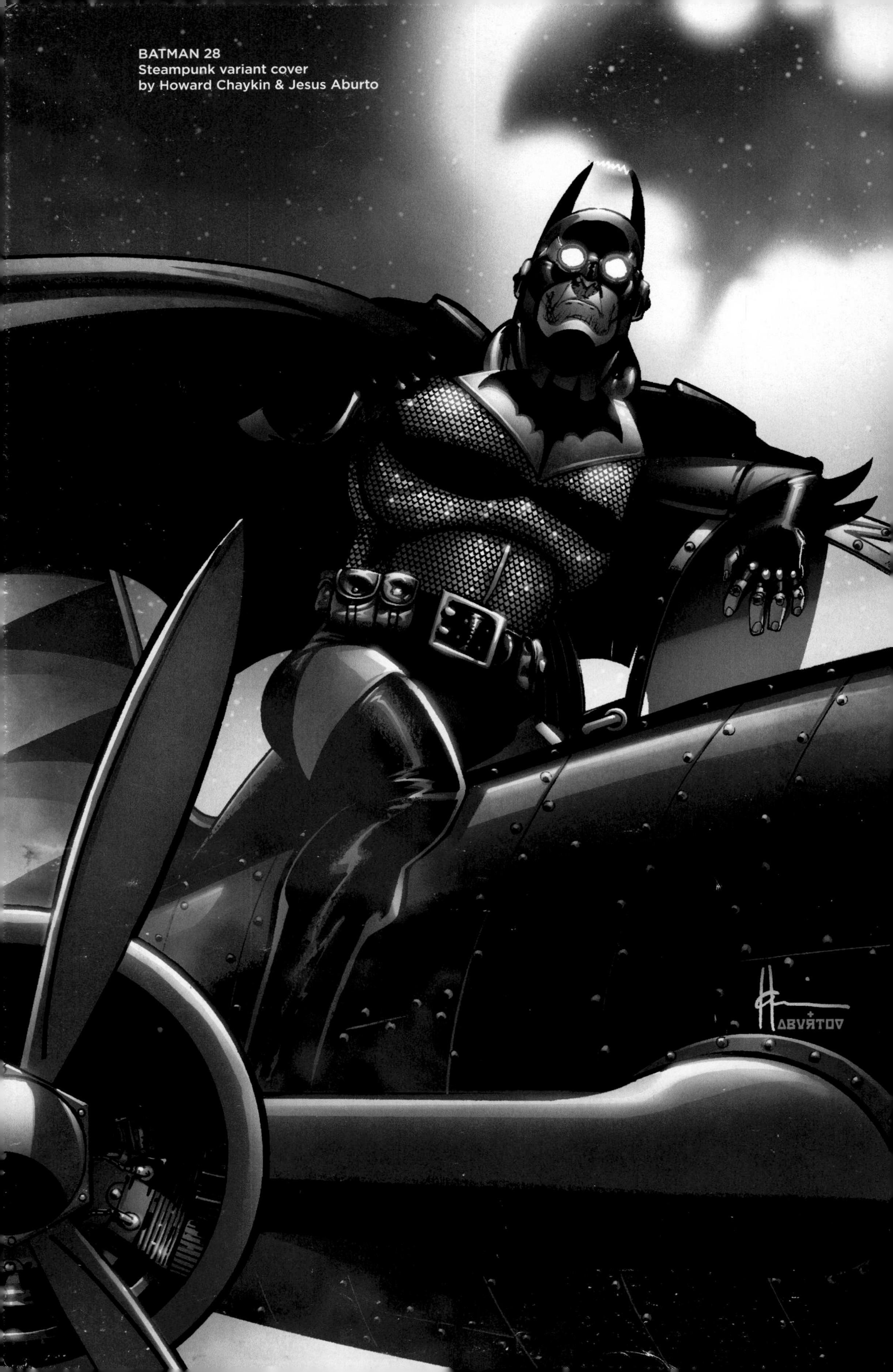

BATMAN 28
Steampunk variant cover
by Howard Chaykin & Jesus Aburto